Atlantic
Quarterly
Summer/Fall 1998
Volume 97
Number 3/4

The *South Atlantic Quarterly* (ISSN 0038-2876) is published quarterly, at $92.00 for libraries and institutions and $30.00 for individuals, by Duke University Press, 905 W. Main St., 18-B, Durham, NC 27701. Periodicals postage paid at Durham, NC. POSTMASTER: Send address changes to *South Atlantic Quarterly*, Box 90660, Duke University, Durham, NC 27708-0660.

Library exchanges and orders for them should be sent to Duke University Library, Gift and Exchange Department, Durham, NC 27708.

The *South Atlantic Quarterly* is indexed in *Abstracts of English Studies, Academic Abstracts, Academic Index, America: History and Life, American Bibliography of Slavic & East European Studies, American Humanities Index, Arts & Humanities Citation Index, Book Review Index, CERDIC, Children's Book Review Index (1965–), Current Contents, Historical Abstracts, Humanities Index, Index to Book Reviews in the Humanities, LCR, Middle East: Abstract & Index, MLA Bibliography, PAIS,* and *Social Science Source.* This journal is a member of the Council of Editors of Learned Journals.

ISSN 0038-2876

ISBN for this issue: 0-8223-6461-1

Bakhtin/"Bakhtin": Studies in the Archive and Beyond

SPECIAL ISSUE EDITOR: PETER HITCHCOCK

The South Atlantic Quarterly
Summer/Fall 1998
Volume 97
Number 3/4

Peter Hitchcock

Introduction: *Bakhtin/"Bakhtin"*

Mikhail Bakhtin was, without doubt, a preeminent thinker of the twentieth century. How to characterize his oeuvre and its philosophical underpinnings remains a matter of intense dispute nonetheless. Is he to be viewed primarily as a theorist of the novel, a cultural critic of carnival, a neo-Kantian philosopher of act and responsibility, a philologist of Great Time and its disparate coordinates, a radical conservative of Western classicism, or the materialist extraordinaire of the word's relationship to ideology? It would be relatively easy to show how Bakhtin, having made significant contributions to all these areas, became one of Russia's most prominent modern polymaths. But the lure entailed by this judgment would be to treat these efforts as part of an internally consistent project, a *grand récit* if you will, that could define and order the parameters of each contribution. For several reasons I find this approach entirely unsatisfactory, and it is in large part against this tendency that *Bakhtin/"Bakhtin"* is offered. Before elaborating the conceptual space between the titular Bakhtin and "Bakhtin," let me enumerate some of the principal objections to such an integral or comprehensive Bakhtin.

The *South Atlantic Quarterly* 97:3/4, Summer/Fall 1998.

First, a unified theory negates the special logic that each mode of Bakhtin's analysis requires. As Michael F. Bernard-Donals has noted, the "umbrella" approach often has to explain away the contradictions of Bakhtin's thinking even as it highlights what are clearly methodological themes, or recurring tropes, from one work to the next.[1] For instance, however broadly one wants to define "author," the author in Bakhtin's critique of Dostoevsky does not bear the same agential coordinates as the author who "acts" (i.e., authors an action) in Bakhtin's early philosophical manuscripts. Indeed, even if we let authorship slide into a general theory of the subject, the literary mode of praxis is not ultimately reconcilable with, or representative of, subject action *tout court.* (For philosophy as well as law, the idea that an ethics can proceed from a theory of literary authorship is absurd—it can inform it, but it cannot model it.) And, as Bakhtin was well aware, the notion of a collective authorship obviates the role of an organizing individual consciousness in the words that form upon the page. The one can be a mask for the other, but not its essence.

Second, a more comprehensive approach to Bakhtin's thought contradicts his penchant for marking his concepts with the "eventness" or unique situation that provides their genesis. (As we will see, the more one specifies such eventness, the more complex and controversial Bakhtin becomes.) This is not just a point about his concrete lived experience (though it remains vital to understanding the logic of contradiction in Bakhtinian thinking), but also a statement about the function of disjunction—or fragmentary thinking, as Anthony Wall usefully suggests—in modern philosophy. The eventness of Being that Bakhtin elucidates (which is more about the *process* of Being, or *becoming*, than about Being itself) is not particularly original (most readers of Kant or mainstream Romantic philosophy will recognize key elements of the discourse), but when it is read back into the shifting registers of Bakhtin's "reaccentuation," a vibrant and conflictual image of philosophical intervention offers its own "event" in twentieth-century thought.

Third, the emergence of a Bakhtin industry in academic publishing (a fact that, of course, cancels through the eventness of this text) provides an alternative logic of totality in which the summary statement, the unifying urge, must answer the singularity of the "Bakhtin" that appears in an individual work's title. I am fascinated by this will to mythology by anthology, not least because it makes any "Bakhtinian" book a persistent exercise in irony (as several recent anthologies have affirmed). Of course, I do not recommend that we answer fire with fire rather than water, that we assemble a modernist montage of different-colored notebooks, for instance, as Bakhtin himself did under the guise of an extraordinary and incomplete "architectonics." The demands of the industry—the desire for *a Bakhtin* between two covers—need not undermine a sense of the diversity of his thinking as long as that sense is not itself presented as somehow completing (or "consummating," as Bakhtin implies) the given author. Those readers who have pondered the formula of answerability (as variously found in *Toward a Philosophy of the Act* and *Art and Answerability*) may wonder whether the critic can perform the "transgredient completion" that the author cannot. According to this view, the critic provides an excess of seeing that the author, for subjective as well as objective/historical criteria, fails to forward in his own terms. Critics are thus true to Bakhtinian thinking to an extent that Bakhtin cannot be, as he himself perceives. This interpretation of "exotopy" (to which I will return) squares the circle rather than breaks it where the Bakhtin industry is concerned. In short, the logic of academia and academic publishing is also in excess of the specific intervention that a volume of this kind might enact. And what may seem like an endless regression draws further attention to the novelty of Bakhtin's approach to questions of authorship.

The fourth problem with a comprehensive reading of Bakhtin is the rather basic difficulty of the state of the archive. On the one hand, the Bakhtin material available for research, in Russian and in translation, represents only part of Bakhtin's writing (a representation that can be completed even when the author cannot). This is simultaneously a reflection of the custodial rights over the archive—its fragmentary nature—and a sign of the complex decision-making processes involved in translation. The multivolume Collected Works currently being assembled in Russia may correct this shortfall to a certain extent, but the editing process employed will again have a profound impact on the Bakhtin who emerges from that major archival undertaking. On the other hand, even with more of the archive available (including the tapes and transcripts of a series of interviews, portions of which were played at the Seventh International Bakhtin Conference in Moscow in 1995), some of the mysteries of Bakhtin will remain just that. What theory literally went up in smoke, if any? How much of what Bakhtin wrote was lost to mice or misplacement? More importantly, how much remains to be discovered about the extent to which Bakhtin rifled other people's work and presented it as his own? Should we continue to publish material that Bakhtin never intended for circulation without at least framing its possible interpretation within the implications of that caveat? How much of the archive is archive enough for proponents of an integral Bakhtin? Or is the nature of the archive itself perhaps a lesson in authorship and answerability?

The fifth difficulty, linked to all the others, concerns the time/space of Bakhtinian studies—or the chronotopic Bakhtin, to borrow from his interpretation of the term. It is clear that most Western scholarship, including the wealth of Slavicist scholarship now available, bears little relation to the ongoing Russian debates about Bakhtin since his death in 1975. As Caryl Emerson has pointed out, "In Russia, Bakhtin is being read in quite a different key."[2] Many of those interpretations are driven not just by greater familiarity with the Russian texts (by a better sense of Bakhtin's bent for shifting neologisms in Russian), but also by the concrete contexts of Russian scholarship in general, which means *both* taking into account the *longue durée* of Russian schools of thought *and* recognizing the immediate influences peculiar to Russia's recent history. The waning of the Cold War and the emergence of the "market" (which for most Russians remains a Western phantasm) have reinforced the different Bakhtinian perspectives and profiles of his Russian interpreters and of those beyond. I have commented elsewhere about the emergence of the ethical and religious Bakhtin in Russia, especially since the collapse of the Soviet Union, and there are simple and complex explanations for this phenomenon.[3] The latter include coming to terms with the trajectories of modern Russian philosophical thinking, particularly from the Revolution of 1917 on, when repressed theological issues get rearticulated in innovative ways. A more basic issue is economics. To Western critics with the mobility to go places (like Russia) or the means to purchase the latest theoretic tomes, the spiritual leanings of many Russian Bakhtinians may appear curiously abstract. Yet considering that, economically, Russian academics are among the poorest on earth, their extolling the spirituality and ethics of Bakhtin is not an inexplicable way to address the time/space predicaments of Russia's present. However free we may feel to unravel Bakhtin's trenchant allegories of state repression (*Rabelais and His World* being the most over-cited example), the differences between Russian and Western Bakhtinian scholarship exemplify the glaring inequities of the world system and the travesties of its market where ideas are concerned. It seems to me that to offer a unified Bakhtin under these circumstances is to play out the nefarious "integrity" of a colonizing, if not colonial, epistemology. And again, while I personally marvel at the Russian scholarship on offer here and elsewhere, no trendy inclusiveness will right the wrongs that a geopolitical reading of Bakhtin might now bring to the fore.

So what Bakhtin is in evidence in these pages who does not merely confirm that, after all, the more contributors one has the more/different readings will be produced? Together, if not individually, the essays here are a measure of the incommensurate Bakhtin and "Bakhtin." What might appear to be a harmless indication of the real and the reanimated actually goes to the heart of the politics of knowledge, to which Bakhtin's work is not immune and indeed makes an enduring contribution. This not only counters the will to unify the fragmentary in Bakhtin's thinking, but also addresses the normative modes of representing the individual intellect in general. With Bakhtin, the usual approaches have been to segment or periodize his work, to follow a progressivist or developmental model which emphasizes the emergence of particular themes over time, or to posit a philosophical archetype of sorts to which Bakhtin returns again and again. Obviously, such approaches have provided significant insights into the nature of Bakhtin's thought as well as into the key disputes that continue to galvanize different schools of Bakhtinian thought (the stark methodological contrasts between Katerina Clark and Michael Holquist's *Mikhail Bakhtin* and Gary Saul Morson and Caryl Emerson's *Mikhail Bakhtin* being important touchstones). While readings such as those two represent the most sustained examples of anglophone Bakhtinian scholarship to date, the idiosyncrasies of Bakhtin's key concepts themselves (*exotopy, the carnivalesque, dialogism, eventness, the chronotope, novelization, answerability*, etc.) of necessity demand alternative modes of appreciation and understanding. Again, it has to be said that none of the readings included here offers a "party line" (despite the fervent convictions of the editor!), but their constellation does provide a glimpse of an architectonics that must remain open in order to come to terms with the eventness of Bakhtin's Being—a Being that cannot cohere in the space between Bakhtin and "Bakhtin." It is to the difficulties of this philosophical position that I now turn.

I have argued that much is at stake in any comprehensive attempt to characterize Bakhtin's oeuvre, especially because of his emerging centrality in the thinking of our time. The task, however, comes with its own liar's paradox, for to be "true" to Bakhtin's theorization means that one must decenter Bakhtin as an author, yet there is simply no way, politically or philosophically, to do so without acknowledging the incommensurability of Bakhtin with "Bakhtin." The first denominates a historically, empirically verifiable human being, a man who wrote exquisitely tortuous prose for much of this century; the second, however, designates the product of what is implied in his thinking (in the *Author and Hero* essay, for instance, or the Marxist critique of language), an author who is so exceeded by what defines his possibility (the hero, the other, the addressee, the reader, the event, the unfinalizable, etc.) that to "authorize" him would be to negate the very author who spurred such interest. While this *differend* might keep presses publishing and résumés expanding, all Bakhtinians worth their salt must begin their investigations not with the presumptuous *who's Bakhtin?*, but with the more reflexively discursive *whose Bakhtin?* The answer to that question will not solve the paradox of Bakhtin (which is not the point of this volume), but it can provide an integer of where in the current critical landscape Bakhtin fits according to the key terms of his theoretic approaches.

The "fix" of fixing Bakhtin, then, is not about the pious invocation of dialogism against monologism (which is already to misread the centrifugal and centripetal forces of language as a basic philosophical binary); it is, however, connected to the intrinsic logic of dialogism. As numerous critics have noted, there is an epistemological and categorical danger in limiting dialogism to the realm of dialogue (Platonic or otherwise). Simply put, dialogism describes the converging and conflicting relations between and around subject positions at any one moment, including, but not limited to, the language of putative addressers and addressees. The watchword for Bakhtin was "context"—the conditions which make any extant speech or conversation possible in the first place. In this light, the notion of a transcendent Bakhtin (as an interlocutor) is not negated, but it is certainly called into question. The ambivalence of the dialogic is symptomatic of that perennial paroxysm of Bakhtinian scholarship, the author question, in which the identity of an author ("Bakhtin") and a theory of authoring seem inextricably and irresolvably entwined. Again, the identity fix of a *particular* author seems to militate against the logic of identity espoused by that author—a logic that challenges the regulatory or normative practices of adjudicating what counts as a subject, as an identity, as an author.

The problem of the author and the authoring of Bakhtin (including the debate about the Vološinov/Medvedev texts) was compounded by the translation and 1990 publication of *Author and Hero in Aesthetic Activity*, the centerpiece of the *Art and Answerability* collection.[4] Symptomatic of the difference (or perhaps more properly *differance*) of Bakhtin/"Bakhtin,"[5] the controversy of this early essay arose from the perception that it might unlock the mystery of the disputed texts and settle, once and for all, what *the author is Bakhtin* signifies. Fortunately, at least for the Bakhtin industry, what it opened was a Pandora's box as unlikely to authenticate authorship as dialogism is to secure dialogue. Interestingly, critics who have linked Bakhtin to either the theoretic move characterized by Barthes's "death of the author" or the lineage announced in Benjamin's "author as producer" are likely to be equally flummoxed by Bakhtin's "author" essay—the weight of its idiosyncrasy seeming to betray most, if not all, positions with any currency in contemporary cultural theory, including, surprisingly, Bakhtin's. As Michael Holquist notes in his introduction to *Art and Answerability*, "These essays are . . . important because, with their appearance, any opinion of Bakhtin formed on the basis of his previously published work must now be modified or discarded." Holquist points out that for fifty years Bakhtin kept some yellowing school notebooks within which *Author and Hero* was contained—a fact that validates its importance as a reference while underlining its fragmentary nature, its incompleteness. The text of the essay itself is "unconsummated [*nezavershën*]" (or incomplete), allowing Holquist to add, somewhat cryptically, that "Bakhtin is already 'Bakhtin' here, but it is in the nature of his own complex views on biography-as-task that not *all* of Bakhtin should be here yet."[6] Cunningly, Holquist suggests that a complete Bakhtin will indeed arrive—but at whose behest and to what end? The use of "consummation" for "completion" in the making moment of architectonics, itself a nod in the direction of Bakhtin's religious discourse (as is Holquist's averring that Bakhtin was a "very complicated sort of Christian"), has a crucial bearing on the "author question," for there is nothing intrinsically innovative in the hybridization of author and god in aesthetic practice, just as the fetish of the hero has long been a staple of masculinist aesthetics. Here one should note that, like a god, the author is in the business of making, but (in what is, perhaps, an uncomplicated sort of Marxism) the author does not make *alone*. Answerability entails a "co-authoring": a process achieved with and by the "other." In this, Holquist notes, Bakhtin has found a role for aesthetics as "work—the struggle to effect a whole out of the potential chaos of parts . . . precisely what, in fact, architectonics theorizes."[7]

Of course, we now live in an age when the most we can expect from architectonics is the organization of the "chaos of parts" itself, not the teleological goal of the whole, which, in the immediate aftermath of the Russian Revolution, looked desirable to Bakhtin. One reason why Fredric Jameson, for instance, is no paramour of the philosophers of the fragment is his continuing to suggest that the conditions of political transformation necessitate a totalizing critique. In Bakhtin's terms, architectonics bears this instinct, even if its very possibility is overdetermined by the first principle of the centrifugal fragment (recalling that centrifugal force within the sign which Bakhtin develops as dialogism). Thus the work of making is constantly in collision with the work of communicative relations, but this does not mean that architectonics is synonymous with the centripetal will of monologism (precisely because the latter excludes the principle of co-authoring).

Architectonics is therefore aesthetics as *activity*, but this also leads to an assertion about subjectivity because the "I" needs the "other" in order to constitute itself. We are thus given the intriguing formula that architectonics is to aesthetics what "event" (as the process of co-authoring) is to being. Aesthetics, then, entails work, for the work of art is finished off (consummated) in the act of apprehending it. This knowledge, of course, confirms not the completeness of the "I" but its dependence on the axiological character of the "other." We are authored through others, not ourselves—a flexible and provocative form of authority. Thus do we, in Holquist's words, "interlocate each other": the dialogic self is the "interlocative" self. The activity of perception itself is seen as the structure of authoring: I read author/hero as self/other—an architectonic activity for which I am answerable, and so on. From this it follows that "we must *do* what these essays are *about*."[8]

Written during Bakhtin's twenties, *Author and Hero in Aesthetic Activity* bears all the exuberance and idealism that youth and a recent revolution could muster: it is both a *tour de force* and a *tour de pensée*. The essay is in part an extended rumination on conceiving "subjectivity" and "aesthetics," theoretical problems that define "Bakhtinian," yet those familiar with Bakhtin's work on Dostoevsky's authoring immediately perceive a stumbling block: where that work emphasizes a crucial unfinalizability in the aesthetic act, an openness in both form and content that profoundly challenges authoritarian structures of authorship, *Author and Hero* begins with assertions about "completion" (or "consummation"). Thus an aesthetic reaction (or answer) in a work is defined precisely by its wholeness in relation to its "hero," who is "consummated" by such a reaction/relation.[9] This necessary principle links author to hero as it does subject to object, and without such a principle, Bakhtin suggests, objects become cognitively indeterminate (i.e., they disintegrate). The author's attempt to stabilize an image of the hero is described as a struggle with himself, but this is not just creeping narcissism, for, as Bakhtin notes, "the process of creation is altogether *in* the product created." Indeed, in a riposte to avatars of authorial intention, Bakhtin articulates authoring as activity, and although the hero is worked, there is no assumed correspondence between the author's and hero's worldviews. The aesthetic act is thus the "incarnation of meaning" rather than a demonstration of truth.[10]

Yet if these remarks rightly challenge some of the founding myths of the author, Bakhtin also reconstitutes them as though "creation" and "answerability" were synonyms for the same act (of god). This divine author(ity) is surely undermined as the essay progresses even as consummation is privileged at its most crucial junctures. But, of course, Bakhtin could just as well be describing the activity of some kinds of *criticism*, particularly those with a tendency, if not an explicit aim, to universalize or reify the author/hero nexus (thus the occasion and the need for this elaboration). Here, suffice to say that Bakhtin's polemic proceeds as a series of tentative proposals that advance an argument only to fold back on it. Of course, that Bakhtin kept the notebooks of this essay with him for fifty years is not surprising, for pushing the envelope of the author question is what took him to metalinguistics, or "translinguistics," another one of his major contributions to twentieth-century thought.

Quickly then, in *Author and Hero* the author as god (no doubt quietly paring his fingernails) is decentered, for there can be no monotheism where aesthetics is concerned. Why? Bakhtin claims that "if there is only one unitary and unique participant, there can be no *aesthetic* event."[11] Thus the aesthetic means *more than one*, and certain trajectories of the aesthetic, from the Romantics through the modernists, are put into question. The author does remain above and beyond his hero, but this outsideness (*exotopy*) is a condition of his dependence: wholeness or consummation is achieved only by the author's remaining fundamentally outside the hero with respect to space and time, value and meaning. Again, however, once Bakhtin has established this condition of outsideness, the logic of such authoring almost immediately becomes convoluted. If he destabilizes the individual certitude of the Romantic ego, Bakhtin nevertheless recuperates Romantic organicism when he attempts to spatialize the hero. This spatiality, which depends on an excess of seeing between the author and hero (with the aesthetic event depending on the incommensurability of the positions from which they see), is rendered thus: "The excess of my seeing is the bud in which slumbers form, and whence form unfolds like a blossom."[12] The problem here is not only the imagery but the excess itself, which completes the hero by spilling over from the surplus of the author's seeing, knowing, desiring, and feeling. This is obviously an aesthetic and political weakness: ideologically, the project of Orientalism, for instance, has been to provide or facilitate precisely this act of completing from a position of dominance. (Patriarchy is similarly nothing but the authoring of a dominant gender, with all the oppressive hero worship that such authority confers.) From the author as god to the aesthetic as the creation of more than one, from the aesthetic as event to the blossoming of authorial intent, Bakhtin continually attempts to see which possibility precludes another. The spatial metaphor is therefore challenged by the metaphor of the body in order to prove that the key issue is not the authorial transcendence of Kantianism, but rather the authorial *transgredience* (stepping over) of outsideness. In exploring the body's relationship to itself, Bakhtin notes that the body can only image itself through the other and for the other, which is the root of ethical and aesthetic objectification. The awkward but imperative neologism "I-for-myself" describes an act, a process that never actually coincides with "myself" (just as the Bakhtin here cannot ultimately merge with the "Bakhtin"). These are not moments of cognition (in the Kantian mode) but of "concrete lived experience." By starting with the body, Bakhtin shows how human situatedness articulates author/hero relations in the aesthetic sphere (a body-politicking that would subsequently be developed in his Rabelais book).

Interestingly, to show that the body can constitute value Bakhtin uses the example of the mother/child relationship, in which lips can provide initial determinations: indeed, the necessity of touching and love from outside is a determinate proof of existence. For Bakhtin, this is the importance or "value of the human body in history" because, clearly, "I myself cannot be the author of my own value, just as I cannot lift myself by my own hair"[13]—which, again, invokes the responsibility or answerability of the other. But, as Judith Butler has noted in discussing Lacanian and Kristevan theories, how symbolic value is constituted discursively from a "prediscursive libidinal economy," a range of sensorial information, remains highly problematic with or without foundational principles like the drive or the Law of the Father.[14] Even such an admirable bridging concept as dialogics fails to pinpoint adequately the intricacies of touch in human development. (Ironically, this should be seen as an advantage in an age when master tropes are in fear of falling.)

Bakhtin's strategic deployment of the aesthetics of "body value" includes using it both as a critique of "expressive" aesthetics (because it has no adequate theory of form, i.e., form does not consummate content but merely expresses it) and as a prolegomenon to "impressive" aesthetics. Briefly, if the aesthetic moment is always already more than one, then questions of form and content must be based on what Bakhtin calls "sympathetic co-experiencing." Thus "aesthetic form is pronounced and justified by an aesthetically productive sympathy or love that *comes to meet* the co-experienced life from *outside*."[15] "Impoverishing" theories of expressive aesthetics (Hegel and Schlegel are mentioned) elide this interdependence, whereas exotopic aesthetics preserves the place from which the aesthetic moment may be "completed." Nevertheless, "impressive" aesthetics assigns prominence to the self-activity of the artist, and, reading this section of Bakhtin's essay, one may wonder whether he is trying to have his cake and eat it too.

Such doubts are only compounded when Bakhtin lauds the importance of "concrete lived experience" in his aesthetics while simultaneously invoking the soul (e.g., in relation to the temporal problematic of the hero). Significantly, he maintains that the soul, as it comes to exist in time, is a gift of the other: "The soul is spirit the way it looks *from outside*, in the other."[16] For Bakhtin, the soul is not a problem for psychology, ethics, epistemology, or idealism, nor does it exist for the individual. The soul is produced, saved, preserved outside itself *as* individual. A lived experience of the other entails an "inner exterior," an oxymoron necessary to describe the "inner countenance" directed to the "I." Once more, however, the apprehension of the "inner exterior" depends on what is "intuitively palpable" and the soul emerges within a contradictory logic of self-appreciation or subjectivism. As several of Bakhtin's critics have noted, there is no way of reconciling these inconsistencies in his thought without employing either the violence of monologism or the equally destructive force of rampant relativism.[17] The critic of Bakhtin's aesthetics is therefore invariably speaking of the plural and the incommensurate. The question for literary criticism, however, is whether this plurality facilitates the reproduction of well-worn reactionary ideologies, including, as noted, the perennial patriarchs of author and hero. This is a difficult call because of the fluctuations in Bakhtin's thought, with the privileged authority of the author apparently displaced, on the one hand, and a (for instance) masculinist logic recuperated by making the author/hero relationship an exchange either between men or between an active man and a passive woman, on the other. If masculinism is integral to the aesthetic process Bakhtin describes, then Holquist's point about discarding "previous opinions" is an important one for criticism. Indeed, this reading of Bakhtin hinges on the idea that *Author and Hero* might provide a litmus test for further Bakhtinian work, including specifically feminist readings.[18]

Having sketched the logic of I/Other relations, Bakhtin then uses this grid to examine biography and autobiography for a possible coincidence of author and hero as well as the special character of the author in this relationship. Bakhtin's interest initially appears to be spurred by the idea that the hero of a life may also become its narrator (yet another way to interpret Bakhtin's own biography as author). Ever sensitive to the need for categorization (see, e.g., the discourse chapter in the Dostoevsky book[19]), Bakhtin distinguishes between two forms of biography, the "adventurous-heroic" (in which the subject has the "will or drive to be a hero," the "will to be loved," and the "will to live life's 'fabular' possibilities") and the "social-quotidian" (in which "history" as such "is not present as a life-organizing force" and the narrating is "more individualized"). The social-quotidian biography, marked by "its everyday details" of "workaday existence," is interested not in *being* in the world but in being *with* the world. (This defines its "axiological center" of "social values"; in adventurous-heroic biography, the specificity of value resides with the hero her/himself.) Whatever the type, Bakhtin's point is that "in biography, we do not go outside the bounds of the world of *others*"; "the act of biography is somewhat one-sided: there are two consciousnesses, but they do not represent two . . . human beings, except that they are not the *I* and the *other*, but—two others."[20] (The implications of this "philosophy of two others" are consonant with the central tenets of dialogism and the Bakhtin/"Bakhtin" principle that I am forwarding.[21]) Bakhtin's argument then shifts briefly to the question of character, which, like biography, is of two types (in this case, classical and Romantic). But whereas biography is linked to the axiological importance of the other, character is important to the author/hero relationship because it is what produces the whole of a hero. It is with these twin concepts of "otherness" and "wholeness" that Bakhtin then confronts the problem of the author.

Clearly, Bakhtin's conception of the other sanctions the bold declaration that "for myself, I am aesthetically unreal." Rather than positing a Romantic notion of the artist at the godlike center of the aesthetic act, Bakhtin proposes that "the divinity of the artist consists in his partaking of the supreme outsideness" (although the degree of proselytizing suggests that this conversion retains some vestiges of a former faith). "Aesthetic activity" proper "collects the world scattered in meaning and condenses it into a finished and self-contained image." Now, this would be a major capitulation for Bakhtin if the matter rested with the author/artist and his/her words. But again, what saves the aesthetic act, if not the day, is that the "primary relationship" is *contextual*—a relationship "to the immediate givenness of a lived life and the world of that life." Furthermore, Bakhtin even argues, against the primacy of the literary tradition (as a set of predetermined characteristics), for "the more fundamental position of the author in the event of being, in the values of the world." When he maintains that "there can be, of course, no objective, universally valid, criteria for identifying aesthetic objectivity: this is inherently a matter of intuitive cogency alone," however, the argument once more appears to collapse back upon itself.[22] If the author is axiologically dependent on the other, where does this intuition arise? If the author is the source of intuitive cogency, then the other is a bystander, while if the other retains this faculty, then how can the author intuit it? The role of intuition places a heavy burden on "co-experiencing," for it suggests that the aesthetic act is merely an expression of a mutually agreed perception that this is the way it should be. (Of course, this mutual agreement goes to the heart of the problem of the comprehensive Bakhtin.) If author and hero cannily (though not subtly) merge under the banner of "intuition," then the principle of answerability is undermined because even if the author appears to defer to the other, there is no way (at the level of intuition at least) to prove that the author is not simply answering to him/herself.

As I have suggested elsewhere, there is a certain naiveté in Bakhtin's early writing such that he believes he can take almost any aspect of conventional aesthetics and recast it to the power of two.[23] Nevertheless, *Author and Hero* does not finish on this note, but rather with a supplement in which Pushkin's poem "Parting" is analyzed (an obvious surprise, given this critic's later privileging of the novel). Clearly, Bakhtin's reading is not designed to bear the full weight of the preceding theoretic discourse (which the editing process again underscores). It does, however, provide an interesting gloss on answerability in action, addressing such major components of the author/hero relationship as the architectonic (the making process), the axiological center (the level of value), empathy and exotopy (the contours of outsideness), and the concrete moment itself (the eventness of the poem and its critique). Interestingly, the poem he has chosen addresses the relationship between two heroes and the geographical and emotional boundaries that separate them (the form and content conspiring, as it were, with the critical apparatus applied). Bakhtin's thesis is that "all of the concrete and unique elements of the poem as well as the architectonic ordering of them in a unitary artistic event are actualized around the axiological center constituted by a human being *qua* hero." This has been "rendered totally human" in a "once-occurrent event."[24] One problem is that asserting the determinate nature of the lyric as form makes the efficacy of the architectonic process difficult to generalize. There is something hollow in this "wholeness" if the "totally human" can be so easily represented. Simply put, this particular analysis begs the question of the "other" and the complex co-experience that it entails. (One is left wondering whether a notebook or two of *Author and Hero* might indeed be missing.)

It is in this light that I wish to consider for a moment the answerability—and the answers—of some leading Bakhtin critics, who together suggest why the various turns of *Author and Hero* must be carefully analyzed if Bakhtinians are to avoid reconstellating the restrictive logics they purport to oppose. Holquist's nuancing of "consummation" for the wholeness of aesthetic activity is highly contentious relative to both answerability and aesthetic theory in general: "Wholeness is a kind of fiction that can be created only from a particular point of view," a characteristic that places consummation "almost literally in the eye of the beholder."[25] While this is in keeping with the general nature of answerability, it is a principle which cancels through the "event" of Holquist's argument itself, since whatever wholeness emerges must be, ipso facto, the fiction of a beholder with a particular point of view. As I have already suggested, Holquist's contention that Bakhtin is not here *yet* puts the burden of delivery, if not of proof, on him. His introduction to *Art and Answerability* does not, however, aim to answer Bakhtin by consummating him, but is more intent on casting him into the main currents of modern thought—a politico-philosophical heteroglossia—in order to gauge something of the "Bakhtin" of the Bakhtin school. (As noted, this is a wholeness whose fiction has been the subject of heated Bakhtinian debate.[26]) Holquist's thoughts on the authorship debate are well-known and have been continually challenged. The status of these early essays in relation to Marx, Marxism, and *Marxism and the Philosophy of Language* would ostensibly provide grist for the opposing camp (with religiosity a major problem in particular). Undaunted, however, Holquist takes the position that "Bakhtin himself was wrestling with many of the same questions that preoccupied Marx, as these early essays make clear," and concludes: "If there is to be any productive cross-fertilization between Bakhtin and Marx, it would now seem to have to assume the form of inscribing a Marxist emphasis on politics, economics, and social theory into dialogism's obsession with the personhood of individuals and the metalinguistics in which utterance is a deed. With these essays, at least the tools for such a labor become available."[27] Clearly, there are Bakhtinians in this collection who have taken up this challenge, but this does not preclude other forms of the production of otherness as "Bakhtin."

In summarizing the same essay and argument, Morson and Emerson note, "As author I am always 'not yet,' and thus my task *as* author is 'to find a fundamental approach to life from without.'" Later, they again paraphrase in the first person: "The surplus allows me to finalize and complete an image of you, to create a finalizing environment in which you are located for me. Whereas my own totality is open and 'my position must change every moment and I cannot linger or relax,' I can relate to you as an author relates to a hero, for I provide form and create an image of you."[28] Although not as bold as Holquist's reading, theirs conveys the same sense by underlining that the author is incomplete—in this case, to himself. Neither reading is incorrect, but we should keep in mind that *critical* authoring is not the same as *aesthetic* authoring or indeed *biographical* authoring. (As Morson and Emerson also aver, "Lives are not works of fiction."[29]) Using Bakhtin's theory of authorship suggests that the author "Bakhtin" can never be completed by the critic who contemplates him, for that would be to aestheticize him, to make him the hero of an aesthetic act—a dangerous gambit (unless we desire a Bakhtin who is merely the subject of what he describes as "adventurous-heroic" biography). The crux, however, is that the logic of Bakhtin's argument reveals a compulsion to "provide form and create an image of you"; otherwise the other of the author's gaze (or the "excess of his seeing") will disintegrate, cease to have meaning. We may hope that a "meaningful" Bakhtin can be produced without aestheticization, but there are enough convolutions in *Author and Hero* alone to indicate that Bakhtin himself was not so sure. Will critics settle for a "not yet" or "not all" Bakhtin, or will they insist that "their" Bakhtin is complete according to the excess of their seeing?

Having sketched some of the salient aspects of this early essay, with its various nods to Christianity, Kantianism, romanticism, and (in Holquist's provocative reading) Marxism, I want to recontextualize them in light of the Bakhtin/"Bakhtin" problematic. We have already remarked, for instance, that the danger of the author/hero nexus or the self/other "exchange" is not that it might be reinscribed as Marxist (a danger worth pursuing, despite fears of anachronism), but that it might broker a deeply conservative transaction intent on preserving authorial privilege beyond the other that is integral to the author's very possibility.

Even when, in *Author and Hero*, the being, other, and hero of Bakhtin's aesthetics "open up" before him in "feminine passivity," the logic of his argument suggests a contradictory and disjunctive order of aesthetic experience. Similarly, those occasions when Bakhtin inscribes a masculinist exchange between author and hero in the aesthetic act are disarticulated by moments of "active otherness" which challenge the epistemological claims of the all-knowing, all-seeing, all-male "I." Nevertheless, despite the axiological character of the other in the aesthetic act, at this early point in Bakhtin's thinking there is a little too much authority in the author (a little too much male, a little too much god), which makes for more of a contradictory phenomenological spirit than, say, a materialist one. There is the notion of answerability (responsibility), but its implications are not adequately elaborated until the linguistic turn in Bakhtin's work, the moment of dialogism. For critics interested in developing methodologies in and around Bakhtin, this suggests an interesting if problematic evaluative formula. Bakhtinians who stress the formative role of the author/hero essay tend to be more interested in authorizing *a Bakhtin* (where signifier and signified might comfortably meet). The critic in this operation occupies the position of the author in relation to the critical act, and Bakhtin is the hero who consummates this act. Bakhtinians who read the works of the Bakhtin Circle back into that essay, however, tend to be more interested in the destabilizing influence of the other, whose "heroic" deed is to question the authority of the author. Criticism in this case is marked less by an act of authorization than by a self-reflexive move toward the position of the "hero" that opens up a much broader field of analysis than aesthetics, or at least Bakhtin's version of the same, can conceptualize.[30] Obviously, the problem of authoring and authority does not disappear, but it is made answerable to the social and public spheres, which are arenas of ethico-political struggle. Again, the point is not that one position is more "Bakhtin" or more Bakhtinian than another but that the question of authenticity itself goes to the heart of many debates in contemporary cultural criticism: Who is the other? Is the other spoken for? Who or what authors the world? What is at stake in literary criticism's claims to authority?[31] Bakhtinians need not save Bakhtin from himself in this regard, yet I hope this sketch of the author/hero essay will open up a more thoroughgoing conceptual critique in Bakhtinian debate. In short, there is certainly a verifiable Bakhtin, but to cast an interpreted "Bakhtin" in this role is to confuse I/Other and author/hero in a move that allows Bakhtin to authorize (apparently) himself. And there is nothing particularly radical in that.

Perhaps we need a "critic of answerability" to legislate the conflicting constituent features of the "author," but Bakhtin, though eminently qualified, made only a beginning in that regard. As Ken Hirschkop notes, "What is lacking is an account of some figure comparable to the novelist, whose job it is to rework the local materials of everyday life into a 'participatory description' of the world, one capable of reconnecting the obligations and commitments of the everyday world to the necessarily more abstract processes of public historical life."[32] In general, one must say that it is the work of Bakhtinians to make these "reconnections" because of, and despite, the paradox of "Bakhtin." While the contributors to this volume certainly do not agree on the process of this act, they do understand the difficulties of placing aesthetics in the service of an authentic sense of self and authorship. And these, after all, were complex issues that Bakhtin devoted much of his life to engaging, if not resolving.

In general, I would say that every essay in this collection speaks to the conflicts of Bakhtin/"Bakhtin," so my brief comments here on only a few of them are intended as signposts rather than a fully formed cartography of those conflicts. Brian Poole's "Bakhtin and Cassirer: The Philosophical Origins of Bakhtin's Carnival Messianism" is controversial, and necessarily so, for just when Bakhtin is being admitted to the pantheon of the twentieth century's great thinkers, Poole offers detailed evidence that some of his laurels may have been unjustly earned. If, as I have argued, the articulation of "Bakhtin" demystifies and demythologizes the perquisites of Bakhtin as author, then what Poole presents us with is one of the ways in which that dissimulation was achieved. Certainly, his argument about Bakhtin's plagiarism of Ernst Cassirer shatters the conventional wisdom regarding the "originality" of the former. Although Poole is unambiguous about the ethical issue, as an ardent researcher of the Bakhtin archive, he knows that the ambiguity of authorship (in theory and in fact) with which Bakhtinianism is riddled already answers, if it does not vindicate, this extraordinary act of intellectual piracy. Of course, when Bakhtin argued that the word was always "half someone else's," it did not quite prepare us for this more literal assertion of proprietary rights over language.

Two key aspects of Poole's carnivalized or uncrowned Bakhtin pertain to the problem of authorship that is central to Bakhtinian studies. First, in distinguishing between Bakhtin's adopting matter and his adapting method, Poole argues that he not only plagiarized the content of Cassirer's main texts, but also took on the mantle of Cassirer's technique. Whether purloining from *The Philosophy of the Enlightenment, Goethe und die geschichtliche Welt, The Platonic Renaissance in England*, or, most stunningly,

The Individual and the Cosmos in Renaissance Philosophy (so flagrantly plagiarized that Cassirer's German text can be used to correct its Russian—and English—translation in *Rabelais and His World*), Bakhtin's reading is in step with the twists and turns of his German counterpart. Poole shows, for instance, how Bakhtin's interpretation follows the shifting registers of Cassirer's analysis of the function of comedy in Renaissance thought. That Bakhtin understood Cassirer's argument well enough to follow its development does not make his "act" any more honorable, but it does render it more answerable. How so? Bracketing the authentic Bakhtin from the fragmentary "Bakhtin" available in the extant texts makes Bakhtin quite simply a fraud. The purity of this "original" figure can be defended only by eliding the ambivalent conception of authorship that his work often betrays. And yet, of course, there are appreciable differences between Bakhtin and "Bakhtin" that warrant just this mark of authenticity. The task, however, comes with the paradox elaborated earlier, for to be "true" to Bakhtin's theorization means decentering Bakhtin as an author—the Bakhtin/"Bakhtin" schism again.

A reminder about the difference between an author and a theory of the author, far from constituting a philosophical sleight of hand, serves as an a priori in Bakhtin's emerging translinguistics. Poole's approach to this paradox is not to dismiss Bakhtin's originality, but to urge that we hold to Bakhtin's process of "reciprocal illumination" in adjudicating it. That process is exemplified by a less than reciprocal activity: Bakhtin's borrowing of Cassirer's reading of Nicholas of Cusa's description of Rogier van der Weyden's self-portrait (reproduced with Poole's essay). The point, however, is the portrait itself, the eyes in which seem to follow the beholder from any angle of the gaze. To be answerable, in this sense, is not just to come to terms with the space/time of Bakhtin in relation to that of "Bakhtin" (the one reciprocally illuminated here), but to wrestle with the fundamental disjunction of the general time/space in which Bakhtin is now made manifest. This means both nodding to deconstruction and the notion of *differance* (a valid reference point in the "fix" of this discussion) and recognizing a Bakhtin whose complex reciprocity makes Bakhtinian studies a shifting center of the present—a superaddressee of contemporary thought.

The second point about Poole's intervention spills out of the first (and both, no doubt, part company with his politics of reading). Here I would suggest that the value of Poole's interpretation lies in his close attention to Bakhtin's fascination with symbolic knowledge and absolute being. The strong reading of authorship makes Bakhtin an expression of the latter even as his arguments extol the situatedness of the former. (From the cognitive contextuality of the early philosophical essays to the ambiguous unfinalizability in the study of Dostoevsky, the authority of the author is decentered.) But there is also a sense that the fidelity to the symbolic is undermined to a certain extent by the mimetic urge of plagiarism. This is a complex issue, and one to which I can only allude here, but two forms of politics and philosophy are implied in the difference between symbolic knowledge and mimesis. If, for instance, the names of Medvedev, Vološinov, and Kanaev were convenient masks for Bakhtin, then he mimicked them without enveloping them; in plagiarizing the appearance of their argumentation without grasping its essence, he imitated them. Symbolic knowledge, however, reciprocally illuminates both sides of the I/Other nexus (subject/object, author/hero, addresser/addressee). It does not simply reproduce the image of the knowledge at issue, but animates it according to the living contexts (or angles, to recall the pictorial correlative) that might perceive it. Here, then, I disagree with Poole, who, at the end of his argument, reveals a scandal of his own (which I won't repeat in order to preserve something of its surprise). Surely, this is to imitate Bakhtin rather than to illuminate him?

Like Poole, Anthony Wall ("A Broken Thinker") provides an extended rumination on the status of Bakhtin, albeit with very different points of reference and methodology (the contrast here being between philology and philosophy). Regarding Bakhtin as a "broken thinker" stresses the fragmentary nature of his concepts, while, importantly, not viewing them as isolated wholes. Clearly, there is a strain of Bakhtinian scholarship that lauds the individuality and individualism of Bakhtin's thought; indeed, we should not be surprised to see this view strengthen in Russian Bakhtinian debates for reasons already outlined. But, as Wall argues, the part cannot stand for the whole, nor can these fragments be pieced together to form a whole—as if, as he pithily puts it, Bakhtin were a game of philosophical Humpty-Dumpty. What Wall's polemic accentuates rather is the liminality of the fragment in Bakhtin's thinking: the edges are not lined up in sharp contradistinction to other modes of thought, but rather form the contact zones, or the in-between, that imbricate without conflating otherwise disparate arenas of thought. Perhaps this explains why Bakhtin has become a key figure in new modes of interdisciplinary thinking. Wall has a different argument in mind, however. Part of what we mean by the dialogic is the relationship of part to whole—the way the utterance, for instance, exceeds itself, and is exceeded, in human interaction. If that in-between is the incommensurable, as I have maintained, it is nevertheless a vital space in Bakhtinian studies for generating new thinking (new ways to reciprocate, as Poole usefully brings out). Again, one could argue that this collection "as a whole" demonstrates the agonistic epistemology of the fragment. As Wall shows, however, the editing of Bakhtin's papers alone proves that when it comes to integral publishing projects the incommensurable can in fact become submerged.

Seeking to counter the mode of reifying Bakhtin and Bakhtinian thinking through the deployment of superconcepts, Wall ardently and eloquently answers this unitary notion even as he highlights the paradox of *a "Bakhtin,"* the comprehensive Bakhtin apposite with the conditions of mass academic consumption. He goes on to explore whether the in-between, the unique ongoing eventness of being, in the early "Toward a Philosophy of the Act" is a clue to understanding the "active unique places" that distinguish the later works. For Wall, Bakhtin's methodology eschews the logic of replaceable parts for the potential multiplicity in any one fragment. The stress is on connectivity rather than metonymy, and while this might be dystopian where the being of individualism is concerned, it has significant implications for Bakhtinian scholarship—indeed, for any serious engagement with the philosophical processes of Being that now seem possible.

"A Broken Thinker" ends on a note about the relationship of memory to the body which not only suggests a useful way of rereading the grotesque in Bakhtin's formulations, but also forms a coda on sense and the suprasensible in the production of everyday life (or the semantic and the somatic, as Wall puts it). Again, while not fully developed in Bakhtin's work, this is a position that has often encouraged attempts to orient Bakhtin within a practical politics in the social sciences, a space where real and fictional bodies are constructed and legislated.

Maroussia Hajdukowski-Ahmed has been concerned for some time with exploring this space, and her "Bakhtin without Borders: Participatory Action Research in the Social Sciences" is very much in the spirit of a "Bakhtin" caught between theory and practice without reenacting that binary. For her, dialogism is a form of practical activity, one that links the researcher to her activity, indeed one that makes the "act" of research answerable. This particular aspect of our "non-alibi in Being" (as Bakhtin terms it) is not always brought to the fore in academic work; as Hajdukowski-Ahmed argues, the structure and procedures of the academic institution screen out a good deal of disciplinary openness (the dialogism of the disciplines) and their collective reciprocity (their reciprocal illumination) with the social production of everyday life. Ultimately, however, "Bakhtin without Borders" is not simply a plea for greater practical interdisciplinarity, nor is it a basic broadside against the function of the university as an "ideological state apparatus" (although these remain key areas in which Bakhtin may be polemicized). Instead, dialogism is taken precisely according to the terms of its logic so that participatory thought and action can be made more clearly intrinsic to the "act" of academic research itself. For those whose participatory thinking is often a (Bakhtin-like) lonely labor, this comes as a refreshing argument. The task, obviously, is not to berate those thinkers whose cerebration for the social sciences did not extend to conventional participation (for this would only reproduce the nefarious dichotomy between mental and manual work). But Hajdukowski-Ahmed does emphasize that "usefulness" is not an empty gesture where meaning and experience are at stake, a lesson she applies to key issues in the lives of immigrant women in Canada.

By taking on vital elements of a Bakhtinian approach—questions about what constitutes voice and double-voicing, chronotope, hybridity—Hajdukowski-Ahmed implicates "Bakhtin" in a politics of research and analysis of the production of others in a specific society. That this goes against Poole's interpretation of Bakhtin's idealism is abundantly clear, but we are still learning to read these differences constructively in the worlds which separate Bakhtin's archivists from his interpreters across the disciplines. Again, the inevitability of the incommensurable is not the key issue: the dissimulation of "Bakhtin" is also a consequence of the agonistic machinery of the architectonic. I define an un-Bakhtinian reading as one that works to suppress the internal conflicts which necessarily structure Bakhtin's methodology. In this light, perhaps Hajdukowski-Ahmed's conclusion is too optimistic, with the impurities of Bakhtin's thought, and even his personal politics, circumscribing her best intentions. Nevertheless, her argument demonstrates one of several formidable futures for Bakhtinian scholarship—in this case, whether he oils or retards what constitutes academic research in the social sciences.

That the "Bakhtin" in these studies is profoundly *unheimlich* is part of their value and his provocation. Just as Poole's carnivalized Bakhtin is a tribute to the latter's critique of the mythic as its own reward, so do many of the other contributors destabilize summary notions of what constitutes the Bakhtin of Bakhtinian studies by carefully elaborating the conceptual logic of his approaches. This requires a sense both of play and of commitment, and it is on this note that I want to conclude with Vitalii Makhlin's "Questions and Answers: Bakhtin from the Beginning, at the End of the Century," which dramatizes in a profound way the current productive tension between Bakhtin and "Bakhtin," and the provocative liminality of a Russian Bakhtin in particular. Beginning, like many other essays in this collection, with the authorship question, Makhlin's contribution treats authorship as a profoundly theoretic issue of what can and cannot live on within modernity. While I share his take on a Bakhtinian studies that is in a "crisis" of sorts, the texture of this crisis is perceived by Makhlin from a very different philosophical conceptual apparatus. Against the ultimately centrifugal and fragmentary pressures on authorship, he argues for the necessity of reintegration, which would indeed mark a new phase in Bakhtinian scholarship. Scandalously, perhaps, Makhlin rests his case on the reclamation of a specific "authorial intent"—that "active understanding" is motivated and its motivation is the elaboration of the speaker's will or intent.

Here, I would say, we are in the realm of the "intuitively palpable" that I outlined earlier. Who adjudicates this "active understanding"? And where exactly does Bakhtin's "authorial intent" end? Makhlin's focus on the Rabelais book is both brilliant and symbolic. The brilliance lies in his daring exposition of "open seriousness," which has now been thrown down like a gauntlet before non-Russian and non-Slavicist Bakhtinians. The symbolism manifests itself in a couple of ways: (1) the fact that Makhlin is one of the world's leading Bakhtinian scholars cannot be separated from the concrete conditions of Russian intellectual life—a concreteness that, I would say, makes Makhlin's horror at the modern/postmodern logically consistent; and (2), more importantly, his approach evokes a specific symbolic time/space. While Bakhtin struggled to defend his dissertation on Rabelais in 1946–47 (as the clouds of the Cold War were gathering over the social function of the intellectual in Soviet Russia), W. K. Wimsatt (in collaboration with Monroe C. Beardsley) published that celebrated essay "The Intentional Fallacy." It was arguably also part of a Cold War ethos, one in which faith in the author and the critic (like that in the government) was unhinged by an aesthetics of doubt and displacement. At the very moment when Makhlin would have us reconstruct Bakhtin's intent, history—and even some theory—was rendering it a little less than accessible. Our *questions* about Rabelais now will be better for Makhlin's salutary warnings against our will to *answer* everything with more speed than reflection. But again, if the arbiters of "Bakhtin" are obviously in the wrong here, then the recourse to Bakhtin is no more or less suspicious. My answer is not that we revel in a trenchant undecidability—the nexus of Bakhtin/"Bakhtin"—but that we build on its recognition. Makhlin is right to admonish us to "think twice." Yet just as our answerability must exceed ourselves in the active participation of the other, so must we also be overreached by the new contexts in which Bakhtin becomes possible. From the evidence of this collection, it would seem that the nature of answerability itself is regenerating Bakhtin and Bakhtinian studies.

Notes

1 See Michael F. Bernard-Donals, *Mikhail Bakhtin: Between Phenomenology and Marxism* (Cambridge, 1994), especially the preface.

2 Caryl Emerson, "Introduction: Dialogue on Every Corner, Bakhtin in Every Class," in *Bakhtin in Contexts: Across the Disciplines*, ed. Amy Mandelker (Evanston, 1995), 1–30; quotation from 1. While I agree with Emerson's acknowledgment of this difference, I have strong misgivings about the interpretation she draws of Russian scholarship. I should add, however, that Emerson's elaboration of the contexts at issue is far more substantial than my comments here suggest; see, in particular, her *First Hundred Years of Mikhail Bakhtin* (Princeton, 1997), especially the introduction and chapter 1.

3 See Peter Hitchcock, "Bakhtin, Marx and Worker Representation," in *Face to Face: Bakhtin in Russia and the West*, ed. Carol Adlam, Rachel Falconer, Vitalii Makhlin, and Alastair Renfrew (Sheffield, UK, 1997), 81–92.

4 M. M. Bakhtin, *Author and Hero in Aesthetic Activity* (c. 1920–23), in *Art and Answerability: Early Philosophical Essays*, ed. Michael Holquist and Vadim Liapunov, trans. Vadim Liapunov (Austin, 1990), 4–256.

5 The following discussion elaborates my "Bakhtin/'Bakhtin,'" *Discours social/Social Discourse* 5 (1993): 172–80, esp. 173.

6 Michael Holquist, "Introduction: The Architectonics of Answerability," in *Art and Answerability*, ix–xlix; quotations from xvii and xviii–xix.

7 Ibid., xxiii.

8 Ibid., xxvi, xxxii.

9 The infamous scare quotes seem wholly appropriate for "hero" as it appears in Bakhtin's essay. I am using them here to flag a familiar masculinism in Bakhtin's notion, and one need not make the usual references from Homer to Carlyle to see how this might arise. The quotation marks serve a second function, however, which is to suggest that Bakh-

tin's hero is not altogether so and that the "co-authoring" inscribed in the aesthetic act offers another definition, such as this one by Berenice Fisher (in "Who Needs Woman Heroes?," *Heresies* 3 [1980]: 10–13): "The genuine hero helps her friends and comrades by teaching them directly or indirectly what she has learned from experience, and how she has applied theoretical and practical knowledge to specific situations" (12).

10 Bakhtin, *Author and Hero*, 7, 10.

11 Ibid., 22.

12 Ibid., 24.

13 Ibid., 52, 55.

14 See especially "The Lesbian Phallus and the Morphological Imaginary," chap. 2 of Judith Butler, *Bodies that Matter: On the Discursive Limits of "Sex"* (New York, 1993), 57–91.

15 Bakhtin, *Author and Hero*, 83.

16 Ibid., 100.

17 See, for example, Michael Holquist, *Dialogism: Bakhtin and His World* (London, 1990); and *Bakhtin and Cultural Theory*, ed. Ken Hirschkop and David Shepherd (Manchester and New York, 1989), both of which contest attempts to homogenize Bakhtin's thought. (The forthcoming second edition of the latter is discussed in my interview with Shepherd.)

18 Ann Jefferson's "Bodymatters: Self and Other in Bakhtin, Sartre and Barthes" (in Hirschkop and Shepherd, eds., *Bakhtin and Cultural Theory*, 152–77) shows more than any other recent Bakhtinian scholarship how an informed politics of reading can make even the vagaries of *Author and Hero in Aesthetic Activity* productive for a feminist politics of culture. Body politics have already played an important role in feminist readings of Bakhtin; however, up to now most of these have centered on the pleasures of the (excess) text in *Rabelais and His World*; see, for example, Mary J. Russo, *The Female Grotesque: Risk, Excess, and Modernity* (New York, 1995).

Jefferson also uses the Rabelais book to trace a certain masculine insistence in self/other relations from Bakhtin to Barthes, but she locates the structural logic of this argument in *Author and Hero*. The will to authority in that essay is produced through a sexist division of the creative act: simply put, the author is masculine, the "hero" is feminine, and the I and the Other are explained on this basis.

Bakhtin opines: "In the *other* . . . the determinateness of interior and exterior being is experienced as a pitiful, indigent passivity, as a defenseless movement toward being and eternal abiding that is naive in its hunger at any cost to *be*. The being which lies outside me is, as such, only naive and femininely passive even in its most outrageous pretensions, and my aesthetic self-activity gives meaning to its boundaries, illuminates them, gives them a form—from outside, and thus consummates it axiologically." And "*already-to-be* is to be in a state of need: to be in need of affirmation from outside, in need of affection and safeguarding from outside; to be *present-on-hand* (from outside) means to be feminine for the pure and affirming self-activity of the *I*. But in order that being should open up before me in its feminine passivity, I must take a stand totally outside it and must become totally active" (*Author and Hero*, 125, 136).

Although the author/hero relations sketched here are developed in terms of love, it is not hard to see toward whose interest they are geared. The sexism aside, Jefferson shows how Bakhtin makes two categorical errors: first, by conceiving aesthetics outside the social construction of language (a problem obviously remedied to a great degree in the later work); and second, by assuming that "love is the culmination—or even the condition—of the aesthetic" ("Bodymatters," 155). Jefferson is not claiming, quite rightly, that author/hero and I/Other always line up on the same side of things (since they do not, as Bakhtin's discussion of the spatiality of the hero amply shows); she claims, rather, that feminist readings (among others) can emerge in Bakhtinian analysis only when the masculine model of love, which Jefferson calls the "sweetness and light" version of the aesthetic (156), breaks down, as it does in *The Dialogic Imagination* and *Rabelais and His World*. In the later work, then, the body goes public, as it were, and the dialogic conception of language blasts away the masculine soul-searching of *Author and Hero*, leaving us with what can only be described as a conflictual model of social interaction. Thus the body politics of today can indeed use the author/hero configurations of Bakhtin's early "philosophical" period, but only by reinvesting the "other" with a sense of activity within the "I" that, though unable to ensure outcomes, can certainly give voice to pressing political debates.

19 M. M. Bakhtin, *Problems of Dostoevsky's Poetics*, ed. and trans. Caryl Emerson (Minneapolis, 1984), 181–269.

20 Bakhtin, *Author and Hero*, 155, 160–61, 164.

21 On one level, dialogism describes the mutual negotiation of the "other" within the "I" that is necessary for any communicative relation to occur; on another, "two others" suggests dialogism's departure from the diametric diachrony of subject/object philosophies toward a more nuanced and politically productive concept of a (con)textualized subject.

22 Bakhtin, *Author and Hero*, 188, 191, 195, 197, 200.

23 See Peter Hitchcock, *Dialogics of the Oppressed* (Minneapolis, 1993), 2–8.

24 Bakhtin, *Author and Hero*, 227.

25 Holquist, "Introduction," in *Art and Answerability*, x.

26 See Hitchcock, "Bakhtin/'Bakhtin,'" 173–74.

27 Holquist, "Introduction," in *Art and Answerability*, xl, xlv.

28 Gary Saul Morson and Caryl Emerson, *Mikhail Bakhtin: Creation of a Prosaics* (Stanford, 1990), 76–77, 185.

29 Ibid., 3.

30 Ironically, identifying with the hero rather than the author in this theoretical model actually challenges the masculinist logic that produces the hero in the first place.

31 See Hitchcock, "Bakhtin/'Bakhtin,'" 178.

32 Ken Hirschkop, "Introduction: Bakhtin and Cultural Theory," in Hirschkop and Shepherd, eds., *Bakhtin and Cultural Theory*, 1–38; quotation from 35.

Brian Poole

Bakhtin and Cassirer: The Philosophical Origins of Bakhtin's Carnival Messianism

The 1995 centennial of Bakhtin's birth marked yet another high point of his international fame, particularly in the Anglo-American world, while in Germany that same year marked the fiftieth anniversary of Ernst Cassirer's death and occasioned much reflection on the first Jewish rector of a German university. As will become evident here, a deeper relationship links these two thinkers. Although identifying the philosophical sources of Bakhtin's theory of laughter helps to clarify the nature of his originality, it also contradicts the current, widely held belief that he parted company with the philosophy of the Marburg school at the beginning of his career.[1] Bakhtin's two most mature works—"Forms of Time and of the Chronotope in the Novel" (from his manuscripts on the bildungsroman) and *Rabelais and His World*—put him somewhat closer to Cassirer than has hitherto been suspected.

The contrasting forces of serious dogma and carnival laughter are familiar to every reader of Bakhtin's works. The spirit of this confrontation is easy to reformulate in Shakespearean charac-

The *South Atlantic Quarterly* 97:3/4, Summer/Fall 1998.

ter. In *Twelfth Night* (2.3), Sir Toby Belch does a fine job in his verbal feud with the puritan Malvolio: "Dost thou think that because thou art virtuous, there shall be no more cakes and ale?" The quip does not at first seem to address the full range of concerns that cluster around the concept of carnival, namely, the toppling of the Aristotelian cosmos and the moral hierarchy appended to it during the Middle Ages. And yet Sir Toby Belch, whose surname recalls part of what Bakhtin termed the body's "lower stratum," has just learned from Sir Andrew Aguecheek that there is an *alternative* to the Aristotelian universe and the medieval hierarchy:

> Sir Toby: Does not our life consist of the four elements?
> Sir Andrew: Faith, so they say; but I think it rather consists of eating and drinking.
> Sir Toby: Th'art a scholar; let us therefore eat and drink. Marian, I say! a stoup of wine![2]

Sir Toby's festive exhortation is followed by a salute to an aspect of Sir Andrew's character that we are not at liberty to overlook: Sir Andrew is a *scholar* citing a scholarly argument, although he does not name his sources. (We shall return to "the four elements" and their philosophical source in due course.) This passage can be considered a Renaissance comic challenge to the conservative "Elizabethan world picture," initiating a smooth transition from the hierarchical medieval cosmos Tillyard describes to the carnivalized alternative cosmos located—to use Bakhtin's terminology—in the material zone of familiar contact.[3] Sir Toby's winning argument against the censorious puritan Malvolio is thus his first application of a carnivalesque inversion explicitly related to the rejection of the dominant medieval cosmology and its implicit fear-ridden metaphysics.

Let us briefly recall the major points in Bakhtin's theory of carnival laughter. His conviction is that "Rabelais, Cervantes, and Shakespeare represent an important turning point in the history of laughter," dividing the literature of the Renaissance not only from the Scholasticism of the Middle Ages but also from the waning universalism in the comedy of later epochs. "The sixteenth century," so Bakhtin's conviction, "represents the summit in the history of laughter."[4] His approach to epochs is certainly idealistic. He defines periods with categories of style and with their changing ideas, not with their materialistic determinants.[5] The history of ideas provides him with a cogent framework in which periodization can be obtained. This is particularly the case in his broad historical approach to laughter: "The Renaissance conception of laughter . . . has a deep philosophical meaning, it is one of the essential forms of the truth concerning the world as a whole, concerning history and man; it is a particular universal point of view on the world; the world is seen anew, no less (and perhaps more) profoundly than when seen from the serious standpoint. . . . Certain essential aspects of the world are accessible only to laughter."[6] These large claims balance the cognitive and epistemological qualities Bakhtin ascribes to laughter. We encounter the cognitive function again and again in the many aspects of life which laughter reveals to us. Thus comic forms express a "historical awareness," opening "men's eyes to that which is new, to the future."[7] The epistemological function is related to laughter's critical resistance to dogma and the pretensions of the official world. Laughter is the test of truth. Laughter also liberates man from medieval eschatology and its "cosmic terror," from the feeling of helplessness in the face of natural forces.[8]

Stressing this philosophical approach to laughter allows us to avoid the inflationary application of the tiresome epithet "carnival." Bakhtin often uses such alternatives as *prazdnik* (festival) and *pir* (symposium) in conjunction with his descriptive approach to the temporal and spatial contingencies of laughter.[9] In the second edition of his classic study of Dostoevsky, Bakhtin describes the dynamic force of carnivalization in literature as a manifestation of *folklore*. When speaking of its tradition, Bakhtin associates *carnivalized* genres with "a special realm of literature, which the ancients themselves . . . called *σπουδογέλοιον*, that is, the realm of the serio-comical"; he singles out Socratic dialogue and Menippean satire as "two genres from the realm of the serio-comical" which obtained "definitive significance" in the carnivalesque dialogues of Dostoevsky's novels.[10] Elsewhere, Bakhtin traces the folkloric origins of holiday culture "to a preclass, agricultural stage in the development of human society," when the cycle of "holidays and ceremonies" was still bound up with "the agricultural labor cycle, with the seasons of the year, the periods of the day, the stages in the growth of plants and cattle."[11] It is here, he suggests, that we may unearth folk culture's most ancient motifs and plots. Bakhtin's varying definitions of *carnival* (holiday time, festival, popular laughter, and so on) are themselves definitive of primordial *genre*, a case in point. The cultural *and* anthropological underpinnings of cult and art render the comparison plausible.[12]

In his *Problems of Dostoevsky's Poetics* Bakhtin offers a definition of genre that is both informed by his study of carnivalesque laughter and directed toward modern manifestations of archaic forms. Generic and anthropological theories are combined in a diachronic approach to literary form that ranges from archaic genres to the twentieth-century novel:

> A literary genre, by its very nature, reflects the most stable, "eternal" tendencies in literature's development. Always preserved in a genre are undying elements of the *archaic*. True, these archaic elements are preserved in it only thanks to their constant *renewal*, which is to say, their contemporization. . . . Genre is reborn and renewed at every new stage in the development of literature and in every individual work of a given genre. This constitutes the life of the genre. Therefore even the archaic elements preserved in a genre are not dead but eternally alive. . . . Genre is capable of guaranteeing the *unity* and *uninterrupted continuity* of this development. For the correct understanding of a genre, therefore, it is necessary to return to its sources.[13]

This is our cue. As with genre, for the understanding of the *philosophical* aspects of carnival laughter it is necessary to return to its sources: a difficult task, since we know little more about Bakhtin's sources than we do about Sir Toby's and Sir Andrew's, although their positions seem to coincide. Bakhtin's appreciation of literary forms is flanked by philosophical considerations. We must therefore be in a position to describe his method in terms of a specific philosophical tradition. From the perspective of German philology, there may be surprisingly little originality in the historical material Bakhtin musters to illustrate the development of comic genres.[14] His originality appears to be *indisputable*, however, when he applies a specific tradition of idealism in his own formulation of the *philosophical function* of seriocomic genres and of carnival laughter.

Bakhtin raises comedy, carnival laughter, popular holiday culture—whatever we prefer to call it—to the status of a cultural philosophy *in nuce* possessing specific epistemological and cognitive characteristics. Fervently believing that "the main point of Rabelais's laughter [is] its universal and *philosophic* character," he scolds other scholars for not understanding "that a *philosophy of laughter*, a universal comic aspect of the world, [is] possible."[15] Furthermore, Bakhtin insists upon a relationship between laughter and the body which is mediated by astrological thought (the relationship between medicine and astronomy, between microcosm and macrocosm);

he suggests that the correlation between man's physical body and the universe is deeply rooted in the humanist revision of the body/soul dualism and the corresponding (or resulting) liberation from medieval hierarchical narrowness personified by Aristotelian cosmology. Without this historical correlation Bakhtin's analysis of Renaissance imagery of the "grotesque body" would seem little more than an interpreter's willful metaphor; with it he justifies his application of philosophical concerns to Rabelais's comic art and proves, we might add, that Sir Toby and Sir Andrew are behaving as they should be: they are Renaissance men. (As we shall see, Bakhtin's text does indeed address the undocumented humanist sources of their festive good nature.)

Such "good-natured" humanism is one of the salient features Bakhtin discovers in Rabelais's work. For despite all its dung-slinging, farting, and evisceration, Bakhtin dismisses the cynicism and vituperativeness others have sensed in Rabelais's grotesque imagery by pointing to the benevolent relativity of the humanist cosmos, its universalism and openness to becoming, and its inherent opposition to the asceticism and eschatology of the Middle Ages. Here, Bakhtin claims, "Man was, as it were, born again for new, purely human relationships. *Estrangement temporarily disappeared.*"[16] In the festive celebration of the sensual world—the boisterous apologia of man's body and our earth, the fruits it bears and the appetites we have—man was liberated from the domination of celestial powers (Bakhtin's "cosmic terror"), but only insofar as the individual could be seen as an analogue of a new map of the universe. With this analogue in place Bakhtin moves strategically from Rabelais to Pico's *De hominis dignitate* (*On the Nobility of Man*), where the polarity in the relationship between the macrocosm and the microcosm is reversed so that man's dignity and autonomy become the metonymic source for the grandeur of the heavens.[17] Far from being atheistic and yet far more idealistic than religious, this argument, by eschewing dualism, returns the creative and procreative manifestations of religious energy to their source in the body and the mind. Where does this complex philosophical argument come from?

Bakhtin's paradigmatic argument appears in a theoretic formulation that deserves special attention.[18] He characterizes Rabelais's age as a period "when medicine was the center not only of the natural sciences, but also of the humanities," the "only age that attempted to orient the entire picture of the world toward medicine."[19] He cites Paracelsus as representative of the undifferentiated concerns of philosophy and astronomy: "The first foundation of medicine, according to Paracelsus, is philosophy, the second is astronomy."[20] Man is a mirror image of the universe, the stars themselves a map of his anatomy: "The starry sky is also contained in man himself, and the physician who ignores the sky cannot know man."[21] Bakhtin thus postulates that "the basis of Paracelsus' entire medical theory and practice lay in the complete correspondence of the macrocosm (the universe) and the microcosm (man)."[22] This correspondence leads Bakhtin to redefine the cosmic dimensions of "high" and "low" in relation to the body. But he is equally concerned with the philosophical tendencies underlying and unifying this image, tendencies which rejected the body/soul dualism of the Middle Ages; he thus draws our attention to the two outstanding centers of Renaissance scholarship: the Paduan and Florentine schools.

Beginning with the relationship of Rabelais's philosophical thought to "the Paduan school of Pomponazzi," Bakhtin offers a brief summary of Pomponazzi's major work: "In his treatise 'Of the Soul's Immortality' (*De immortalitate animi*), Pomponazzi proved the identity of body and soul. The soul cannot be separated from the body that creates it, individualizes it, directs its activity, lends it content. Outside the body the soul would be completely empty. In Pomponazzi's mind the body is a microcosm that assembles in one single entity all that is scattered and alienated in the rest of the cosmos."[23] Bakhtin concludes that "the human body was the center of a philosophy that contributed to the destruction of the medieval hierarchic picture of the world and to the creation of a new concept." In the ensuing paragraph we at last find a detailed description of the medieval hierarchic cosmos that the "scholars"—Sir Andrew and Bakhtin—oppose to their own liberating cosmos of "eating and drinking" (a theory quickly enlisted by Sir Toby, as we have seen, to combat Malvolio's puritan dogma):

> The medieval cosmos was built according to Aristotle. It was based on the precept of the four elements (earth, water, air, and fire), each of which had its own spatial and hierarchal position in the structure of the universe. According to this theory all the elements were subject to a definite order from top to bottom. The nature and the movement of each element were determined according to its position in relation to the center of the cosmos. Nearest of all to this center is the earth, and any part separated from the earth tends to move back to the center

> along a straight line; that is, it falls to earth. Fire moves in the opposite direction; it continually tends upward and therefore away from the center. The realms of water and air lie between the realms of earth and fire. The basic principle of all physical phenomena is the transformation of one element into the element nearest it. Thus fire is transformed into air, air into water, water into earth. This reciprocal transformation is the law of creation and destruction to which all earthly things are subject. But above the earthly world there rises the world of celestial bodies, not ruled by this law of creation and destruction. The celestial bodies are composed of a special kind of matter, *quinta essentia*. This matter is not subject to transformation; it is capable only of pure motion, that is, movement from place to place. Celestial bodies, as the most perfect, are endowed only with the most perfect movement, the circular movement around the center of the earth.[24]

This detailed description of the elaborate cosmic structure that Sir Toby addresses also shows us something else Bakhtin has in common with the scholar Sir Andrew: he does not name his sources. The passage above is Bakhtin's verbatim translation of over half a page of Cassirer's *Individual and the Cosmos in Renaissance Philosophy*.[25] Bakhtin's translation is so accurate that it is indeed possible in places to correct the errors of the Russian–English translation by using Cassirer's text. We are less concerned with the ethical questions this raises. (Bakhtin *never* cites Cassirer in his work on Rabelais.) More important: the example simplifies the tedious task of demonstrating word for word that what we have in this seminal portion of Bakhtin's work—his philosophical analysis of the grotesque body and the significance of its imagery—is about five pages of Cassirer punctuated intermittently with quotations from Bakhtin.[26] (These passages, considered central to Bakhtin's oeuvre, have recently been anthologized in a reader entitled *Bakhtinian Thought*.[27]) Here, with Cassirer's words, the "high" and the "low" ("stratum" is often added in the English translation) are given their cosmic significance as correlates; and here the alternative cosmic order that reorganizes the medieval hierarchy on a horizontal axis marks the beginning of a philosophy of history initiated by the Florentine academy. Pico's *De hominis dignitate* in particular is eulogized for its formulation of the microcosm motif in which man's historical becoming and his autonomy find their adequate expression: "Man is not something closed and ready-made, he is incomplete and open: such is Pico della Mirandola's basic idea."[28] The ensuing discussion of Pico's *Apologia* and the microcosm theme, as well as the themes of "natural magic," "astrology," and "sympathy" in Renaissance thought, their expression in the works of Giambattista Porta, Giordano Bruno, and Tommaso Campanella, and their "role in destroying the medieval notion of hierarchical space," stems from just a few pages of Cassirer's classic study of Renaissance thought.[29] On the corresponding pages of Cassirer's text we also find the verbatim source of Bakhtin's formulation of Ficino's concept of "universal animation."[30] On this same page of *Rabelais*, Bakhtin refers to Patrizzi's *Panpsychia* and makes a passing allusion to Cardano's natural philosophy, complete with a quotation from the latter's *De subtilitate* ("Metals are 'buried plants' and stones experience youth, growth and maturity"), for which his source is again Cassirer.[31]

Finally, we arrive at the proverbial "bird's-eye view" conclusion for which Bakhtin is so famous:

> For all the Renaissance philosophers mentioned previously—Pico della Mirandola, Pomponazzi, Porta, Patrizzi, Bruno, Campanella, Paracelsus, and others—two tendencies appear characteristic. First is the tendency to find in man the entire universe with all its elements and forces, with its higher and lower stratum; second is the search for this universe in the human body, which draws together and unites the most remote phenomena and forces of the cosmos. This philosophy expressed in theoretical terms the *new sense of the cosmos* as *man's own home, holding no terror for him*. It was reflected by Rabelais in the language of images and on the plane of laughter.[32]

Again, we must forgo any discussion of the issue of Bakhtin's bird's-eye view (i.e., its often being entirely dependent on secondary sources), for there is a *philosophical* issue here of greater importance, namely, Bakhtin's own philosophical tradition. What we find in the preceding passages exemplifies the way in which Bakhtin's most prominent theoretic terms reflect his debt to Cassirer: it is in *Cassirer's* cosmos that Bakhtin finds "man's own home, holding no terror for him." In the wake of the Stalinist purges and on the eve of the Holocaust, Bakhtin turned to the placid German Jew whom Husserl, in a letter to Paul Natorp of 29 June 1918 (thus *before* Cassirer's most famous works appeared), called "the only truly significant scholar of his entire generation."[33]

Cassirer had a seminal influence on two of Bakhtin's three major works: his book on Rabelais and his study of Goethe and the bildungsroman (which includes the essay on the chronotope). These works are related by Bakhtin's decisive turn to the study of genres—their prehistoric origins and historical development—and by the privileged role each text gives to the comic. Together, these elements appear in *Rabelais and His World* in a form entirely different from Bakhtin's earlier works. For even in "Discourse in the Novel," Bakhtin refers to the traditional rhetorical categories of travesty, parody, and stylization—but not to the philosophical dimensions of comedy—when discussing Rabelais, whom he places in a tradition of "radical skepticism . . . bordering on rejection of the very possibility of straightforward discourse at all that would not be false."[34] The effect of Rabelais's comic novel is purely negative, with no epistemological or cognitive advantages:

> Turning away from language (by means of language, of course), discrediting any direct or unmediated intentionality and expressive excess (any "weighty" seriousness) that might adhere in ideological discourse, presuming that all language is conventional and false, *maliciously inadequate* to reality—all this achieves in Rabelais almost the maximum purity possible in prose. But the *truth* that might oppose such falsity *receives almost no direct intentional and verbal expression* in Rabelais, it does not receive its own word—it reverberates only in the parodic and unmasking accents in which the lie is present. Truth is restored by reducing the lie to an absurdity, but truth itself does not seek words; she is afraid to entangle herself in the word, to soil herself in verbal pathos.[35]

This is a far cry from the ambivalence of humor, from the "triumphant, festive principle" of the grotesque, and from the utopianism of carnival. In "Discourse in the Novel" Rabelais belongs to a narrow tradition of novelistic satire; in Bakhtin's later works, Shakespeare takes the place of Scarron as a parallel to Rabelaisian humor, and parody and travesty become *comic* laughter, wrought with *constructive* and not just destructive powers, for (as already noted) this laughter "is one of the essential forms of truth." By contrast, "bare negation is completely alien to folk culture."[36] How do we account for Bakhtin's truly radical change in course? And what relationship does it have to his reading of Cassirer?

Bakhtin began to study Cassirer before 1936 and continued to do so after 1938, when he was still engaged with his work on the bildungsroman and contemplating another one on Rabelais. His synopses of Cassirer's *Individual and the Cosmos in Renaissance Philosophy* and the second (1925) volume of *Philosophy of Symbolic Forms*[37] offer substantial evidence of his close reading of them, while later works by Cassirer also proved important to the development of Bakhtin's theories of genre and laughter. In the early 1930s, Cassirer reached the peak of his productivity, publishing an astounding three books in 1932 alone, and it is clear that all three—*Goethe und die geschichtliche Welt* (Goethe and the Historical World), *The Philosophy of the Enlightenment*, and *The Platonic Renaissance in England*[38]—had a profound influence on Bakhtin's studies of the novel and of Rabelais, and explain the radical change in his approach to comedy generally and to Rabelais in particular.

Although Bakhtin cited the second volume of Cassirer's *Philosophy of Symbolic Forms* in the manuscript of "Discourse in the Novel" (the reference having been removed when the essay was prepared for publication),[39] his first attempt to apply Cassirer's philosophy to the study of literature came later with his published fragment on the bildungsroman. There, Bakhtin organizes the novel genre as a sequence of temporal categories: the picaresque novel is marked by an "absence of historical time" and the novel of ordeal by its "deviation from the normal social and biographical" time, by "adventure time" or "fairy-tale time," while the "biographical" novel builds a bridge to the bildungsroman. In outlining the application of his terms, Bakhtin explicitly notes his criterion for distinguishing these generic divisions: "Everything depends upon the degree of assimilation of real historical time."[40] This in turn informs his treatment of the Enlightenment and his analysis of Goethe, both being characterized by their "assimilation of historical time." We know that Bakhtin's theory of the assimilation of time by language and myth is directly related to Cassirer's anthropological and cultural thought, since in his essay on the chronotope Bakhtin explicitly refers his reader to "the appropriate chapter in Cassirer's work (*The Philosophy of Symbolic Forms*)" for "the assimilation of time by language."[41] Bakhtin was not only *adopting* names and philosophical details from Cassirer's work, however; he was also *adapting* method.

The "assimilation" (occasionally verbatim) of Cassirer's *Philosophy of the Enlightenment* and *Goethe und die geschichtliche Welt* in Bakhtin's incomplete monograph on the bildungsroman (into which I cannot go in detail here) indicates one direction taken by his development of Cassirer's thought: historicism (a weakness in Bakhtin's works from "Toward a Philosophy of the Act" to the first edition of his study of Dostoevsky). But in his interpretation of grotesque imagery in *Rabelais* Bakhtin applies the "assimilation of time by language" to larger anthropological considerations; here the major semantic unit is not the word but the body. This development in Bakhtin's interests from the chronotope to Rabelais's imagery parallels the span of Cassirer's *Philosophy of Symbolic Forms*, from volume 1 (on language) to volume 2 (on myth). But what is the evidence for this contention?

In *Rabelais and His World* Bakhtin traces a curious pattern of images surrounding the grotesque body and its dismemberment, specifically, the "influence on the grotesque concept of the body . . . exercised by relics" and the medieval literature on the dismembered bodies of the saints as "an occasion for grotesque images and enumerations." In the Middle Ages, Bakhtin contends, "there was no small church or monastery that did not preserve a relic, at times a quite unusual one. . . . Arms, legs, heads, teeth, hair, and fingers were venerated. It would be possible to give a long grotesque enumeration of all these parts of a dismembered body."[42] The parodies arising from this dismemberment are Bakhtin's immediate concern. His examples ("The Treatise of García of Toledo," "The Ass's Will," "The Pig's Will") come from Paul Lehmann's study of parody in the Middle Ages;[43] his interpretation does not. "The dismemberment here," Bakhtin writes in his commentary on "The Ass's Will," "corresponds to the divisions of the social hierarchy: the ass's head is for the Pope, the ears for the cardinals, the voice for the choir, the feces for the peasants, etc. The source of this parody is very ancient." Noting the popularity of "The Pig's Will," Bakhtin continues: "In these satires it is interesting to note the combination of the dismemberment of the body and of society. This is a travesty of the widespread mythical concept of the origin of various social groups from various parts of a god's body. (The oldest monument of this social topography is the *Rig-Veda*.)"[44] In a footnote to this discussion Bakhtin clarifies the relationship:

> The *Rig-Veda* pictures the birth of the world from the body of the man Purusha; the gods sacrificed him and cut up his body, according to the method of sacrificial dismemberment. Various social groups were thus created from the various parts of Purusha's body, as well as from certain cosmic phenomena. From his mouth appeared the Brahmans, from his arms soldiers, from his eyes the sun, from his head the sky, from his feet the earth, etc. In the christianized Germanic mythology we find a similar conception, but here the body is composed of flesh from the earth, bones from the stones, blood from the sea, hair from plants, and thoughts from clouds.[45]

The parallel with this ancient source furnishes Bakhtin with another example of the archaic roots in images of the grotesque body, roots that provide a bridge to a central motif of *Rabelais*: the theory that the "bodily topography of folk humor is closely interwoven with cosmic topography."[46] In this anthropologically informed sense of culture, and the material used to illustrate it, we discover once again the hand of Ernst Cassirer.[47] The passage on the *Rig-Veda* and subsequent comments on Germanic mythology were grafted, with very minor changes, from Bakhtin's 91-page synopsis of *Mythical Thought*,[48] the second volume of Cassirer's *Philosophy of Symbolic Forms*.

Bakhtin's notes on the *Rig-Veda*, stemming from Cassirer's chapter on the structure of space in mythic consciousness, register a fundamental change in his approach to the body in literature and indicate the seminal importance of Cassirer's work to his project of interpreting the body and its visual representation in literature in terms of its relation to time, space, astrology, and the collective.[49] All of these systemic relations arise out of the fundamental role of the body in language, an axiom on which Bakhtin follows Cassirer to the letter:

> The expressions in language of spatial orientation, the words signifying "forward," "backward," "high," "low," were assimilated from the contemplation of one's own body. The human body and its limbs serve as the system to which all other spatial distinctions refer. Myth follows the same path. It takes hold of the entirety of the world by coordinating it with the image of the human body and its organs. The external world is dismembered by analogy with the human body. Often the representation of the human body in the world as a whole determines all mythic cosmography and cosmology.[50]

These observations inaugurate a new line of thought in Bakhtin's research: "That is how the unity of the microcosm and the macrocosm was created."[51] Their unity is reflected in the fact that cosmic topography always contains within it a particular evaluative accent, an attitude toward the body.[52]

Bakhtin's tendency in his mature works to organize complex temporal forms in *visual* images is the most outstanding evidence of Cassirer's influence upon him. The temporal forms of grotesque imagery are a case in point. Open to misinterpretation, they have led some to believe that Bakhtin gives bad press to geriatrics, but, on the contrary, his sense of the ambivalence of these traditional comic motifs bestows a relativity upon the perception of age itself. Here, again, it was the visual poignancy of Cassirer's approach to forms of time and the body that literally caught Bakhtin's eye. In Cassirer's study of myth Bakhtin encountered a comparison between a Buddhist and a Greek which illustrates a new visual sense and meaning in perception of the temporal present as the "harmony of becoming." I quote Bakhtin's formulation in his synopsis, which closely follows Cassirer's:

> If, according to the Buddhist legend, Prince Siddhattha—following his first glance upon the aged, sickness and death—becomes an ascetic, then Heraclitus, upon the same occasion, holds fast to his view [of the harmony of becoming] in order to reveal within it the secret of the *logos*, which exists only because it eternally separates into contradictions. Whereas the Indian [Prince Siddhattha] senses in temporal becoming merely the suffering of discontinuity [and] non-identity, Heraclitus perceives here the great one [*velikoe edinoe*], which must divide within itself in order to find itself again. For Heraclitus, from contradictions arises the most beautiful harmony (fr. 8; 51). In the idea of a multidirected harmony lies, for Heraclitus, the secret of form, and it takes from us the burden of becoming. Time is no longer limitation and suffering, but the real life of the divine [*bozhestva*].[53]

The passage is notable for the constellation of temporal motifs, which are not so much analyzed as pictorially represented with the body in images remarkable for their relationship to a philosophical framework of temporally fixed decay and rebirth. The irksome sickness and death of age appears to be mitigated by the "beautiful harmony" of time itself within the limitless "life of the divine":

> Here a new, more full and more comprehensive and deeper view and sensation of time has been achieved; all sides (moments) are brought into balance with one another. The *plenitude of time* here is not sacrificed to the mythic *origin* of things (the absolute past), nor is it sacrificed to the prophetic *last goal* (the absolute future). There arises thus a specific *feeling of the present*: in it consciousness yields itself up to the present instant, but is not held by it and does not fall under its power; consciousness is free within it and does not allow content to dominate it; neither does it allow joy to take control of it, nor does it define itself with the aid of suffering. In this philosophical "now" the empirical differences of time are sublated.[54]

The theory espoused here spins the wheel full circle. Having begun with a glance at the aged, it returns to the image of a child representing time in Heraclitus's famous fragment, which Bakhtin noted in both Greek and Cassirer's German: "That is how one must understand Heraclitus's wonderful words: time is a boy who plays, who moves the figures hither and thither across the board, the domination is the child's." This quotation appears on four occasions in Bakhtin's study of Rabelais and serves as the epigraph to the chapter "Popular-Festive Forms and Images in Rabelais."[55] The harmony of becoming transforms not only the symbols of age, but also those of youth: "The very image of the boy . . . must be revised. [The boy] is the symbol . . . of immaturity and incompleteness. . . . Rabelais' youth is the youth of antiquity, the 'playing boy' of Heraclitus." Bakhtin interpolated this temporal axis into the carnival antics he found in other descriptive studies of grotesque comedy, using it as an exegetical tool to reveal the "element of relativity and becoming" in festive culture: "The ritual of images of the feast strove to play the role of time itself, dying and giving birth at the same time, recasting the old into the new, allowing nothing to perpetuate itself. Time plays and laughs! It is the playing boy of Heraclitus. . . . Thus were developed the rudiments that were to flower later in the sense of history as conceived by the Renaissance."[56]

The path of ideas from Heraclitus (c. 540–480 B.C.) to Nicholas of Cusa (1401–1464) and Renaissance philosophy appears to be an implausible leap over a millennium. And yet Bakhtin, in his reading of Cassirer, is fascinated by the *philosophia perennis*, the recurrence of themes and images stimulating intellectual reflection. Thus Heraclitus is significant for his advocacy of the notion that being is a mere illusion; in the seemingly stationary, substantive manifestations of nature the real essence of being as becoming is concealed. Cassirer, in his study of Greek philosophy, drew attention to the "immanence" of "becoming" in Heraclitus's thought, whereby only symbolic approximations of forever changing being are possible: "All images which are taken from material reality and its transformations [*Wandlungen*] are nothing more than symbols of a non-sensual, an unseeable 'Harmony.' . . . Life and death are never separated by rigid boundaries."[57] The Renaissance theodicy of becoming and the ambivalence of life and death that Bakhtin would find in Pico's thought was anticipated by Heraclitus. In the harmony of becoming, "opposites are connected through being different stages in a single invariable process."[58] Heraclitus contributed a number of metaphors to the Renaissance understanding of the universe and the relativity of life and death, such as "the path up and down is one and the same" (Frag. 60), and "immortals are mortal, mortals are immortal, living their death, dying their life" (Frag. 62).[59] In time itself the contradictions are sublated by the harmony of becoming; the "opposites coincide." The philosophy of Nicholas of Cusa is built upon this principle.

In Cassirer's *Individual and the Cosmos* and *Platonic Renaissance in England*, Cusa appears as the primum mobile of Renaissance thought. What qualifies him to be the "first modern thinker" is, in Cassirer's opinion, his belief in the possibility of determining a mediation between the finite and the infinite.[60] Cusa voiced his rejection of rational theology by means of his theory of the *coincidentia oppositorum*, a famous catchword for a series of complex theological arguments "diametrically opposed to scholastic thinking."[61] Although the rejection of absolute knowledge in Cusa's *Docta ignorantia* would seem to yield entirely to skepticism, Cassirer argues that its emphasis on the opposition between the absolute and every form of rational, logical, or categorical cognition entails a positive challenge. "The absolute divine being," suggests Cassirer, "demands a new manner and a new form of cognition."[62] Cusa's development of this thought appears to have inspired a shift in Cassirer's language and method from neo-Kantianism to the study of symbolic forms in language, myth, religion, and art: "The view that all finite thought and understanding are by nature symbolical . . . constitutes a new point of departure in religion. . . . Cusa does not infer the sheer impotence of the symbol and symbolic knowledge from the fact that everything transitory is but a symbol. On the contrary, he endows the symbol with new content and value. The symbol cannot be adequate for knowledge, for *dogmatic* 'precision'; it is confined within the limits of 'otherness' and 'conjecture.'"[63] Cusa's postulate (in *De pace fidei*) that the "unattainable unity of truth is known in conjectural otherness" became for Cassirer the key to the idea of tolerance characterizing humanist theology: "Since no name can apprehend the divine, or exhaust its meaning, it can therefore be conceded . . . that all names, in so far as they proceed from a genuine religious conviction and are conscious of their limited and mediate capacity, may be assured of a certain relationship to the divine."[64]

Earlier, in *The Individual and the Cosmos*, Cassirer described Cusa's *visio intellectualis* as a new organ of cognition, a manner of *seeing the intelligible*. In *The Platonic Renaissance*, however, Cassirer draws attention to yet another dimension of the *visio intellectualis*: its purely "symbolic" expression of truth provides the key to the humanist acceptance of heterodoxy, a direction of humanist thought which Cusa, in Cassirer's opinion, initiated in his *De pace fidei*. "Henceforth," declares Cassirer, "neither variety nor contradiction in religion need give offence."[65] This principle of tolerance was adopted by Marsilio Ficino, whose *De christiana religione* is quoted by Cassirer: "There is only one religion in the variety of rituals."[66] In addition to explaining the humanist openness to pagan mythology, Ficino suggests another line of thought to Cassirer with his claim that God "would rather be worshipped in any manner, be it ever so *absurd*, so long as it is human, than not to be worshipped at all on account of pride."[67] Beginning with Cusa and Ficino, Cassirer attempts to derive the origins of English humanism and those of humanist *humor* in parallel from Neoplatonic tendencies alive in Renaissance thought. Through John Colet, who studied in Italy, Cassirer demonstrates the path and development of this philosophical tradition in Erasmus's *devotio moderna*, a conception of religion that reached maturity only when Erasmus "set foot on English soil." Under this inspiration, Erasmus and Thomas More articulate the first adequate literary expression of the spirit of humorist criticism and its drive to "renew life."[68] Here we find one of the first parallels to Bakhtin's theory of Renaissance comedy: "Medieval Latin humor found its final and complete expression at the highest level of the Renaissance in Erasmus' 'In Praise of Folly,' one of the greatest creations of carnival laughter in world literature"; or, in Cassirer's words, "In his *Encomium Moriae* Erasmus introduced the literary form which was to combat dogmatic and literal religious faith most successfully."[69] Of course, in view of the vast literature both authors survey in their works, such parallels can hardly be taken as convincing examples of Cassirer's influence. We need to find the parallel in method, not just in matter.

Such a parallel in method is, however, the most obvious link between Cassirer and Bakhtin, justifying our focus not only on the isolated textual echoes in *Rabelais*, but on their significance in an organized and systematic approach to comedy that was new for Bakhtin in 1938. Remarkably, Cassirer's increasing attention to the function of humor in culture produced an entirely new accent in his own study of Renaissance thought in 1932. As in Bakhtin's later work, the theological, astrological, and philosophical thought of the period converged for Cassirer in a "new attitude towards the world" that found its purest expression in "comic" literature.[70] Beginning with the last representative of "Platonic philosophy" in England, Shaftesbury (himself thoroughly influenced by the Platonic school at Cambridge and its ties, through Erasmus and More, to the Florentine academy), Cassirer uncovered both the epistemological and the cognitive characteristics of humor that we have already found in Bakhtin's work: "Humour represents that fundamental attitude and disposition of the soul in which it is best equipped for the comprehension of the beautiful and the true. . . . The recognition of humour as a fundamental power of the soul and likewise as an objective criterion of truth and falsehood is indeed one of the most paradoxical features of Shaftesbury's world-picture." While this reflects the cognitive and epistemological concerns of humor inherent in Bakhtin's thought, Cassirer also addresses the humanist spirit with which humor is infused: "By humour, Shaftesbury does not mean purely intellectual sarcasm . . . nor does he mean purely intellectual irony, however refined. He understands humour again in the basic sense which the Renaissance had given the term, that is, as a *liberating*, life-giving, and life-forming power of the soul. Establishing this power as his standard, he is certain that nothing really genuine and vital need fear its judgment."[71] This subtle and important distinction between humor and sarcasm helps explain Bakhtin's new approach to Rabelais's humor, for just as dialogism is not opposed to a "unified" truth, nor "carnival laughter" to be confused with cynical atheism, neither is humor, to Shaftesbury,

> directed against the seriousness of knowledge or against the dignity of religion, but simply against a mistaken seriousness and an arrogated dignity, against pedantry and bigotry. To the pedant, as to the zealot,

> freedom of thought is an abomination. . . . When both entrench themselves behind a false gravity, nothing remains but to subject them to the test of laughter and so to expose them. Then only will knowledge and piety appear in their true character, which together are not inconsistent with the enjoyment of life, but are, on the contrary, the finest expression of the enjoyment of life and of the affirmative attitude toward the world.[72]

A comparison with one of the many passages in Bakhtin's *Rabelais and His World* in which the ambivalence of laughter is defined reveals the startling methodological parallel: "True ambivalent and universal laughter does not deny seriousness but purifies and completes it. Laughter purifies from dogmatism, from the intolerant and the petrified; it liberates from fanaticism and pedantry, from fear and intimidation, from didacticism, naiveté and illusion, from the single meaning, the single level, from sentimentality. Laughter does not permit seriousness to atrophy and to be torn away from the one being, forever incomplete."[73]

The importance of Shaftesbury's theory (and likely the reason Cassirer began his discussion of Renaissance comedy with it) is its parallel with Ficino's argument against dogma—an argument inspired, in Cassirer's opinion, by Cusa and developed by the Cambridge Platonists:

> Like the Cambridge Platonists, Shaftesbury finds himself confronted with the harsh seriousness no less than with the severe intolerance and the dogmatic narrowness of Calvinism and puritanism. Against both he has to carry on his struggle for a free form of religion, a form of religion which faces the world openly and enjoys the world. But if this circumstance explains his defence of the rights of humour against a gloomy and ascetic attitude toward the world, it is no less remarkable that he does not stop here, but turns from the defensive to the offensive. . . . Humour need not justify itself before religion, but religion before humour. Thus all ostensible religious revelation and ecstasy are subject to the critique of humour.[74]

Humor is thus not antireligious, not latent atheism, but rather the banner of tolerant religion, the litmus test of true tolerance.

Turning his attention in 1932 to the literature of the epoch, Cassirer extended his 1927 remarks in *The Individual and the Cosmos* and in the process revised his views on the character of Renaissance literature. In 1927, Cassirer maintained that the intellectual character uniting all the humanists of the period lay not in their individualism or their politics, nor in their strictly philosophical and theological thought, but rather in their particular "artistic sensitivity [*das künstlerische Empfinden*]."[75] And whereas, in his first study of Renaissance thought in 1906, Cassirer had focused primarily upon philosophy and the sciences as characteristic expressions of the period, in 1927 he maintained that the artistic forms and sensitivity of the Renaissance ultimately dominated the period's conceptual views of man's physical world, which in turn provided inspiration for the sciences.[76] Thus the art of the period initiated a very real advancement in man's assimilation of his environment. This new approach is typical of Cassirer's increasing tendency to break down the division between the cognitive faculties (which classic neo-Kantianism distilled into the often completely isolated branches of logic, ethics, and aesthetics) and to speak instead of an intellectual energy (*energeia*) whose classic expression is language.[77] In the wake of his theory of symbolic forms it is not at all astonishing to find Cassirer privileging the cognitive capacities of the fine arts and literature in the concluding chapter of *The Individual and the Cosmos*, where he points to the new sense of form in Dante's *vita nuova* and Petrarch's sonnets, to Leonardo's characterization of painting and its significance for the sciences, to Galileo and the relationship between the theory of experience and the theory of art, and to Bruno, whose sonnets gave expression to the idea that "in death, in abandoning one's individual form of existence, the real truth and universality of life may be grasped."[78] Of course, such views on the central role of art in Renaissance thought were common enough in Cassirer's day, and he does not pretend to be staking an original claim.[79] The most original component in Cassirer's later study of Renaissance thought is missing from *The Individual and the Cosmos*, where no mention is made of the comic in Renaissance literature or art.

While it was not until 1932 that Cassirer found, through Shaftesbury, a new interpretation of the artistic impulses inherent in the Platonic revival in England and on the Continent, the latter had figured in Cassirer's 1916 descriptive analyses of the genesis of Kant's aesthetics. In *Freiheit und Form* (Freedom and Form), Cassirer traces the path through which Platonist and Neoplatonist thought found its way into the philosophy of the German Enlightenment. "For the eighteenth century," Cassirer argues, "modern Platonism, while represented by many figures from Ficino to Giordano Bruno and Malebranche, Cudworth and Norris, is nevertheless embodied essentially by the teachings of one single thinker: by the philosophy of Shaftesbury."[80] Again, in 1918, Cassirer focused on Shaftesbury's mediating role in transporting Platonist and Neoplatonist thought from the Florentine academy to Winckelmann, Herder, Kant, Goethe, and Schiller.[81] This theme of Shaftesbury and German idealism remained a standard reference point in Cassirer's later works.[82] But in *The Platonic Renaissance* Shaftesbury is no longer just a medium for philosophical thoughts *from the past*; here Shaftesbury (1671–1713), who was tutored by Locke and whose opposition to puritanism and empiricism made him the last bastion of Renaissance thought, becomes the perfect medium through which we can look *into the past* for the historical roots of that thought and the rich tradition it inspired.[83] Cassirer's advance here—his breakthrough to a theory of comedy, inspired by Shaftesbury, and to a new conception of the Renaissance as epoch—first found its way into print in his 1930 essay on Shaftesbury and the Platonic Renaissance in England. The historically misleading title is related to Shaftesbury's status as a living anachronism, "perhaps the only English thinker in the eighteenth century for whom the antique world was still intellectually present."[84] Cassirer, to whom Shaftesbury thus seemed the heroic advocate of ideas which might otherwise have been lost to succeeding generations, pinpoints the source of his ethical and religious idealism in the most important text of the Platonic canon during the Renaissance:

> Shaftesbury is guided and dominated by the motif of the Platonic Eros. For Plato, Eros connects the divine and the human, the world of ideas and the world of appearances, the sensual and the intelligible, and thus overcomes the basic division between both, the χωρισμός between them. This division, ontically considered, cannot be eliminated from being, and yet Eros builds the bridge between both worlds. Eros is the great mediator of being, the link of being, the μέγας διάλεκτος which runs from the mortal to the immortal nature and back again.[85]

The "great dialogue" (μέγας διάλεκτος) is not only a link between the sensual and the ideal world; the dialogue of epochs is also inherent in the enrichment of the Platonic tradition with which Cassirer is concerned.[86]

Shaftesbury's theory of laughter as a "touchstone" for truth sheds new light on Renaissance comedy ranging from Ariosto and Boiardo to Rabelais and Cervantes, from More and Erasmus to Lyly and Shakespeare, according to Cassirer. "Shaftesbury's defense of humor is related to the basic forces of the Renaissance. He belongs to the few who in the eighteenth century still had a living sense of these basic powers, who still possessed an inner understanding of the world picture of an Erasmus, a Thomas More, a Shakespeare."[87] Shaftesbury's philosophy does for comedy, in Cassirer's view, what Bakhtin sees Dostoevsky's polyphony as doing for Menippean satire, namely, signaling the "general function of the comic in the construction of European intellectual life."[88]

This new angle on the Renaissance in Cassirer's work of the early 1930s was perhaps the most important source for Bakhtin's philosophical thought on comedy. Indeed, his furtive use of *The Individual and the Cosmos* makes sense only in terms of his ensuing encounter with the fully developed theory of comedy Cassirer advances in *The Platonic Renaissance*. For along with a standard discussion there of the Renaissance remapping of Augustinian theology and the Aristotelian cosmos, we find an entirely new articulation of the Renaissance "struggle for a free form of religion": "satire" and "ridicule," "invective," "witty play," and "coarse obscenity"—all somehow mitigated by the comic spirit of "reconciliation"—are revealed as inherent in the "new humanistic ideal."[89] Cassirer's conception of Renaissance comedy arose from his attempt to explain Shaftesbury's demand (in his *Letter Concerning Enthusiasm*) that "all ostensible religious revelation and ecstasy" be "subject to the critique of humour. This is indeed a strange demand," Cassirer notes, and he suggests a method for its interpretation that is entirely consonant with the approach to comic genres we have already observed in Bakhtin's work: "In order to understand it in its origin, its tendency, and its significance, one must look far afield among philosophical systems and *far back in the history of thought*. One must ask oneself the general question as to what part the various types and species of the comic have had in the formation of the modern world and what latent energies seek expression in these types."[90] The answer to this question is Cassirer's redefinition of the Renaissance:

> It is at once evident that, along with all the other fundamental powers of the intellect to which it gave new form, the Renaissance also endowed the comic with new force and new meaning. Our conception of the Renaissance would remain fragmentary and incomplete,

> if we were to forget this aspect of the comic. Ariosto and Boiardo in the Italian Renaissance, Rabelais in the French, and Cervantes in the Spanish—all have their necessary places. These names signify far more than mere details in the luminous and variegated picture of the literary Renaissance; they represent its substance and spirit in all its vigour and in its clearest expression. *It was first in the realm of the comic that this spirit celebrated its highest triumphs and won its decisive victories.* These types of the comic are most diverse; they are nationally coloured and conditioned in the extreme. But in all its variations the comic performs, nevertheless, a certain similar intellectual task. . . . Everywhere it is striving towards one principal goal, the goal of *liberation.* Renaissance emancipation from all the forces that were binding it to the past, to tradition and to authority, is really achieved only when it succeeds in reflecting these forces in the comic mirror. In this mirror Boccaccio in the *Decameron* views monasticism, and Cervantes chivalry. The Renaissance power of comic representation thus belongs inseparably and essentially to its power of action, to its vital and creative energies. Yet, if the comic thus became the strongest aggressive weapon of modern times, its effect was, on the other hand, to take away the violence and bitterness of that struggle out of which the modern era arose. For the comic spirit contains also an element of balance and reconciliation. It does not entertain feelings of hatred towards the world which its free play is destroying, which it cannot but negate; on the contrary, the comic spirit forms rather the last glorification of this decadent world. In Cervantes' *Don Quixote* the decline of the medieval chivalric world reaches its final stage, and yet from the ruins of this world emerges a heroic individual, an incomparably original character, seen with the eyes of a great poet and shaped by his noble capacity for sympathy and understanding. Thus in this power of the comic lives the power of love which will and can understand even that form of the world which the intellect must abandon and surmount. Love cannot check the process of destruction, but it retains in the image that which must perish in reality.[91]

"Love" here is obviously not a sentimental or teenage dream, but rather the translation of standard Platonic terminology into the vernacular. As a mediating power between the "high" and the "low," Plato's Eros, reinterpreted by Christian philosophers, becomes for Renaissance thinkers the link between heaven and earth.

The same idealistic comic force that expresses the mediating power of eros informs Bakhtin's conception of the "medial sphere [*promezhutok/promezhutochnaia sfera*]" as a "peculiar mid-zone."[92] Love as spiritual energy proves to be more than a link between the high and the low, the macrocosm and the microcosm, however. In *The Platonic Renaissance* Cassirer describes the same strange relativity of ages that Bakhtin notes in grotesque imagery: "In the realm of humour," Cassirer tells us, "epochs meet and intermingle in strange ways. For humour is directed both forwards and backwards; it helps to usher in the vital shapes of the future without renouncing the past."[93] *Don Quixote* is one example (to which we shall return) of this mixture of epochs familiar to Bakhtin. Another example of this principle is the scene in Shakespeare's *Henry IV, Part 1* (2.4), in which Prince Hal seems both to objectively characterize and to parody Percy, the young "Hotspur of the North" who embodies all the chivalric virtues of knighthood: "I am not yet of Percy's mind, the Hotspur of the North; he that kills me some six or seven dozen of Scots at a breakfast, washes his hands, and says to his wife, 'Fie upon this quiet life! I want work.'" As Cassirer notes in his brilliant commentary: "In this transformation of Percy into a comic actor, minds and epochs part. The heyday of chivalry must now decline as a new world emerges which is broader and freer, more elastic and uninhibited, than the heroic medieval world. . . . So throughout Shakespeare humour becomes the *touchstone* of the true and the false, of the genuine and the counterfeit, of the essential and the merely conventional. *A new mode of perception, a new knowledge of men and things*, thus emerges which finds in humour its own proper and adequate means of expression."[94] Here, in a nutshell, is the source of Bakhtin's theory of the cognitive and epistemological functions of laughter that he brilliantly developed in his study of Rabelais.

We last encountered verbatim quotations of Cassirer in Bakhtin's discussion of the reinterpretation of the Aristotelian cosmos launched by Ficino, Pico, and other representatives of the Italian Renaissance. Some forty pages later in *Rabelais*, Bakhtin reminds the reader that "in the preceding chapter we described the hierarchical character of the medieval physical cosmos (the respective positions of the four elements and their movement). Such a gradation also existed in the metaphysical and moral world order." In recalling the last large passage he pilfered from Cassirer, Bakhtin could hardly have formulated a better forward for the next:

> An important influence on the entire medieval philosophy was exercised by Dionysius the Areopagite. His works contain a complete and consistent development of the idea of hierarchy. The teaching of the Areopagite is a combination of neoplatonism and Christianity. The idea of a graded cosmos, divided into higher and lower worlds, was taken from neoplatonism. While Christianity brought the idea of redemption as an intermediary between these two levels, Dionysius offered a systematic description of his hierarchical scale, leading from heaven to earth. Between man and God there is the world of pure intelligences and heavenly powers.[95]

Here we should pause to note that the constellation we find in Cassirer's text is an inexorably dualistic cosmos. As might be expected by now, the image of a rigid, dogmatic theological hierarchy is the cue for Cassirer's interpretation of Cusa. But instead of bringing Cusa back into the scene, Bakhtin continues with an entirely redundant presentation of the implications of the vertical axis upon which the medieval universe is constructed, a universe "outside of time" and bereft of the "horizontal . . . movement, forward or backward," in history: bereft, in a word, of the humor Cassirer saw as looking "both before and after," ushering in the "future" yet "without renouncing the past."[96] Bakhtin sees in the new interpretation of the cosmos during the Renaissance the same temporal emphasis: "The accent was placed on 'forward' and 'backward.'"[97]

Cusa's absence from *Rabelais and His World* raises a serious question: How could Bakhtin have been influenced by Cassirer's two works on the Renaissance, the central figure in both of which is Nicholas of Cusa, without ever mentioning him in *Rabelais*? One simple explanation is that Bakhtin did not want to give away his source, which naming Cusa would have done.[98] But this raises another question: Did he overlook the importance Cassirer attributed to Cusa in Renaissance philosophy? Bakhtin's synopsis of *The Individual and the Cosmos* indicates that he did not.[99] Covering the philosophical sources surveyed in *Rabelais*, his synopsis of Cassirer's work places them in the orbit of Cusa's influence, referring to him more often than to any other representative of Renaissance philosophy.

Bakhtin's description of Cusa's *coincidentia oppositorum* is preceded by an outline of the influence of the Pseudo-Dionysius (Areopagite) upon medieval thought: "The Areopagite's major problem was the problem of the hierarchy. Here the idea of the hierarchy received its broad, extensive expression and metaphysical foundation."[100] In the synchronism of the late Middle Ages the Aristotelian hierarchy, reinterpreted and transformed by Christian Neoplatonists, brought the cosmic and theological dimensions of the universe together such that they inevitably coincide with and affect the relationship to the body. As Bakhtin noted, "Neoplatonism gave rise to a conception and a map of the cosmos, its division into higher and lower worlds. The idea of redemption serves as the mediator between the higher and lower worlds."[101] The medial sphere becomes an ethical problem and an object of metaphysical and theological debate. Heaven and earth, God and man, are separated by what Bakhtin refers to as a graded cosmos (Cassirer's threefold *Stufenkosmos*).[102] In the Areopagitean cosmos the medium of redemption is itself open to interpretation. Augustine proposed that redemption is purely an act of God's grace, but were this the case the path between heaven and earth, the "way up and the way down," would amount to a one-way street negating man's autonomy. Cassirer contrasts the Augustinian dogma on grace with the fundamental principles of Cusa's theology.[103] Bakhtin, noting Cassirer's characterization of "Cusa's *amor Dei intellectualis*" as a concept that unites the faculties of love and cognition, abbreviated the argument: "Love contains within itself an element of cognition; it is impossible to love that which one does not know."[104] Both cognition and love thus express and reflect "the essence of the soul, its capacity to move itself and to determine itself." Cassirer demonstrates that Cusa's dynamic interpretation of the soul represents grace as both act of God and free act of the individual. The microcosm provides for the concept of man as the "band of the world," an "affirmation of man" that yields a corresponding "affirmation of the earth"; thus "the idea of '*humanitas*' gives the macrocosm a new content and meaning."[105]

Bakhtin's synopsis follows in detail Cassirer's juxtaposition of Cusa and medieval cosmology. But whereas Bakhtin literally grafted the long passage describing the Aristotelian cosmos from his synopsis onto *Rabelais*, he left out the paragraph immediately following it. "The philosophy of Nicholas of Cusa destroyed this map of the world." In place of the "gradations of the peripatetic philosophers," Cusa "accepts the principle of Anaxagoras: 'everything is in everything.' The entire world is homogeneous." Moreover,

Bakhtin also recorded, in point form, the reevaluation of the body resulting from the homogeneity of the cosmos: "the destruction of the hierarchy; the transposition of the evaluative center into the body."[106] The evaluative coordinates dividing the sublunary from the heavenly were swept aside when an ethical and metaphysical conviction led Cusa toward a new orientation in astronomy, which explicitly challenged the geocentric model of the universe. The dominant medieval astrological and theological models of the universe and their concomitant sense of "fear" collapsed in the wake of this new idea, namely, that everything is equidistant to God. In his synopsis, Bakhtin noted that "all philosophy of nature during the Renaissance from the fifteenth century to the seventeenth was permeated by astrology," which was characterized, on the one hand, by an attempt to reveal the natural "laws of the earth" and, on the other, by fear: "fear of demons, that is, the most primitive forms of religiousness."[107] Cusa's philosophy helped to displace this medieval cosmology by laying the foundation for a new religious sentiment. These overlapping concerns influenced Bakhtin's thought in and beyond his study of Rabelais. As he noted in his synopsis: "If there is no longer an absolute high and low, then all moments of being are equally near to God. Thence a new form of religiousness. Insofar as there is no absolute center, all being and each individuality obtains its center in its very self. Thence the justification of individuality."[108]

Bakhtin's detailed notes on Cassirer's study of Cusa provided surprising material for his theory of popular culture. The dialogues in *De docta ignorantia* transported him from the silent, bookish world of scholarship into the noisy marketplace of the Renaissance. "Cusa begins to seek the truth in empirical multiplicity and diversity," noted Bakhtin. "He uses the expression that 'truth cries out in the streets.' Thus in his '*De apice theorie*' (fol. 332f)."[109] Equally important was Cusa's rehabilitation of the perspective of the common man, the unlearned interlocutor in his dialogues: "Cusa's relationship to the simple man (*Laie, Idiota*). He gave his dialogic trilogy (*De sapientia, De mente, De Staticis experimentis*) the general title '*Idiota*.' The unlearned individual knows the truth, it cries out in the streets, in the marketplaces [*bazarakh*] where the people's day-to-day affairs are transacted."[110]

In his synopsis of Cassirer's work, Bakhtin's favorite exponent of Renaissance humanism is certainly Cusa. Cassirer's observations on Cusa's defense of individuality and his "truly majestic tolerance"[111] repeatedly caught Bakhtin's attention. As he recorded (again in point form): "The justification of the diversity of confessions, rituals, and customs. For example, in *De pace fidei* the representatives of various nationalities take the stage. The deep contradictoriness of rituals and customs (in necessary abundance). And [each] cultural-historical cosmos is equidistant to God."[112] Bakhtin is referring here to a dialogic conflict in the marketplace to which Cassirer drew his attention. In Cusa's dialogue *De pace fidei*, an ambassador of the Tartars addresses an international assembly and raises doubts about the planned unification of all confessions and all peoples. How, he asks, can one envisage such a unification in the face of radically different religious convictions, rituals, and customs which are themselves inconsistent and subject to change? "I, for one, cannot understand how in all that which changes according to place and to time a unification could ever be reached. And so long as unification cannot be reached, there shall be no end to persecution. For the differences produce division and animosity, hatred and war."[113] The answer to this historical quandary (and a quandary it was during the Reformation and in Bakhtin's age) lies in Cusa's postulate of the *coincidentia oppositorum*: the content of belief remains conjecture; orthodoxy must yield to heterodoxy, since truth itself is known to us only in the symbolic alterity of conjecture.[114]

In *The Platonic Renaissance*, Cassirer notes the relationship between Cusa's dialogue on faith and the English humanist reinterpretation of Pauline doctrine that Cusa himself advocated. The reply to the reservations of the Tartarian ambassador, Cassirer believes, is suggested by Paul's well-known statement about our hope of redemption lying not in the manner of our reverence but in the sincerity of our faith. This humanist interpretation of Pauline doctrine can be associated with Ficino's defense of even absurd forms of reverence. Indeed, in Paul's defense of his apostleship we also find the theological underpinnings of Sir Toby Belch's winning argument against Malvolio: "Mine answer to them that examine me is this: Have we no right to eat and drink?" (1 Corinthians 9:3–4). Cassirer, however, is concerned with the relationship between absolute being and symbolic knowledge and with Cusa's application of it. Cassirer relates Colet's interpretation of the Pauline Epistles (via his connection with the Florentine academy) to Cusa's *De pace fidei*. What underlies their unity is the thought that confessional dogma cannot presume to knowledge; the certainty of devotion is the only—strictly *symbolic*—knowledge of the divine available to man: "The one being, the single truth, can be uttered only in the form of otherness ['*Andersheit*']." The manifold expressions of the love of God are thus for Cusa no contradiction to the unity of all confessions. "The multiplicity of rituals is no longer a barrier," Cassirer notes, following Cusa's text almost word for word, "for all the institutions and customs are only the visual signs [*signa*] for the truth of faith, and only these signs, and not that which is symbolized [*signatum*], is subject to mutation and change."[115]

Thus tolerance found its way into the theology of the Renaissance; and thus Bakhtin, like Cusa before him, goes in search of truth's alterity "crying out in the marketplace," manifesting itself in the heterodoxy of pagan and Christian ritual, and relocated in the body, now at the center of the cosmos—a theory no less revolutionary for being theological, and no less theological for being revolutionary. In this combination we find the intellectual roots of modern idealism and the source of the spiritual energy which, in Cassirer's opinion (as in Bakhtin's), toppled the medieval hierarchical cosmology. In his synopsis of Cassirer's work Bakhtin states explicitly that "Cusa was the first to find a new principle" opposing the medieval hierarchy.[116] Cusa is thus in some sense the primum mobile of Bakhtin's—and not just Cassirer's—interpretation of the Renaissance. Moreover, Cusa's opposition to Scholasticism can also be linked to a dynamic argument for tolerance which ultimately gave rise to the purest Renaissance expression of Platonist thought: the humanist theodicy of the cognitive and epistemological functions of laughter.

It was the *symbolic* expression of this central moment in Renaissance thought that most impressed Bakhtin's imagination. At the beginning of *De visione Dei*, Cusa recalls the self-portrait by Rogier van der Weyden and the peculiarity of its subject's appearing to look directly at the beholder regardless of where he or she was standing. (Again, Bakhtin's reflections were based on Cassirer's reading of Cusa's text, the portrait itself having been reproduced in the first chapter of *Individuum und Kosmos*.) If we envision the portrait hanging on the northern wall of a monastery and a group of monks (*De visione Dei* was dedicated to the monks of Tegernsee) gathered in a half circle around it, we can imagine

> that each one of them will believe that the eye of the portrait is directed straight at him. We must not only attribute to the portrait such

Self-portrait by Flemish painter Rogier van der Weyden (1399–1464) from Ernst Cassirer's *Individuum und Kosmos in der Philosophie der Renaissance*. Reproduced courtesy of Yale University Press.

> a simultaneous gaze to the south, the west, and the north, but also a threefold status of movement. For while the image seems to be at rest to the beholder standing still in front of it, the gaze follows the beholder who is not stationary, so that when one of the brethren moves from east to west, and another from west to east, the image seems to participate in both these diametrically opposed movements. . . . Here we have in this visual comparison the elementary relationship that exists between the all-encompassing being and the being of the finite, the final particular. Every particular and every individual has an immediate relationship to God. . . . But the true sense of the divine can be grasped only when our spirit no longer remains fixed to one of these relationships, nor to their mere totality, but rather when it takes the unity of this seeing [*Schau*], the "*visio intellectualis*" together.[117]

The parallels between Cassirer's formulation of the *visio intellectualis* and such central aspects of Bakhtin's mature thought as the superaddressee and the dialogism ascribed to Dostoevsky's "authorial seeing" can scarcely be ignored. The concept provides for an intersubjective common ground (the singularity and distinctiveness of the portrait), the validity and dignity of each individual "subjective" perspective (the inexorable and noninterchangeable "situatedness" of individuals), and the truth as what may ultimately be beyond all individual perspectives, although this in no sense diminishes the status of the individual whose particular vantage is part of the whole. "And thus," Cassirer sums up, "there can be no vision of God that is not conditioned just as much by the nature of the 'object' as by the nature of the subject, that does not contain within it that which is seen and the specific manner and direction of seeing."[118] The same conclusion can be drawn from Cusa's apostrophe to God, which Cassirer quotes: "Now I understand, O Lord, that your face is prior to every other face, that it is the truth and the model of all faces. Any face that gazes upon yours sees in it nothing that is dissimilar to itself, because it sees its own truth."[119]

The passage by Bakhtin to which we now turn, while demonstrating the significance for him of Cusa, and thus of Cassirer's map of the Renaissance, will not satisfy everyone's expectations of what might constitute proof of Cassirer's influence on him. The fragment in question is not cited in an effort to undermine Bakhtin's originality, however, but rather as a paradigm for understanding his dynamic mind *and* his loyalty to the Marburg school, whose influence he underscored as late as 1973.[120] This paradigm is really nothing more than the notion that when Bakhtin made all his important discoveries and developments he was standing fairly squarely on someone's shoulders. Here the shoulders belong to (1) M. I. Kagan, who first formulated in the Russian idiom the conception of the immanence of the present in the idea of modern historical time; (2) Paul Natorp, who, in creating his own dialogism, retranslated the medial sphere of the Platonic Eros into the language of both Presocratic philosophy and Einsteinian physics; and (3) Ernst Cassirer, who provided Bakhtin with, among other things, a *visual image* to which all these linguistic, ethical, historical, and spatial metaphors could be assimilated in his own definition of the Renaissance. The passage below comes from the fourth of six notebooks that together bear the title "On Questions of the Theory of the Novel."[121] Although this text was written while Bakhtin was still composing *Rabelais and His World* (with remarks running throughout these notebooks about what he wanted to include in various chapters of that book), we also find here his notes in point form which would find expression in his two remarkable lectures on the novel, "Epic and Novel" and "From the Prehistory of Novelistic Discourse."[122]

> In order that the contemporary moment (the present) could take its place at the center of literature (in order, consequently, to put an end to the projection of images into the past), it was necessary to sense one's own contemporaneity as a new beginning. This is what the Renaissance did. It restructured not only the spatial, but also the temporal cosmos. The beginning and the end lost their absolute meaning, and the center took its place "everywhere" at any point, that is, in any contemporaneity. Nicholas of Cusa. The epoch had a sense of itself at the relative–absolute center of historical time. This is not a matter of an abstract-theoretical formulation of this sense (how the term "Middle Ages" was created and so forth)—it is a matter of the praxis of literary incarnation. Cervantes transposed the heroic past of chivalric novels into his contemporary context (the result was the figure of Don Quixote). In the novelistic epoch of antiquity Lucian did the same thing with the Homeric past. Travesties do the same thing. This sort of contemporization of the past always existed: it was one of the central themes of popular laugh culture (parodies, travesties, lowerings), but it entered into great literature only in the novelistic epochs. The popular play with time (like the dialogues of ages, the old and

> the young, the winter and the summer, and so forth) in all its manifold forms was one of the most important sources of the novel. The novel is born out of the mixture of the reciprocal illumination of languages (polyglossia) with the reciprocal illumination of ages (with bi-temporalness). One's own in the light of another's, and the other's in light of one's own. The multifarious is combined with change, the polyglossic historical space of the world with the polyglossicness of historical time. Thus the chronotope of the novel (in distinction to the monoglossic and monochronic epic). What is important is that the scale for measuring and evaluating ages gives us this very contemporaneity (as the relative center of history: paraphrase of the definition of God and the image of Nicholas of Cusa).[123]

It would seem that, having begun by accusing Bakhtin of plagiarism, we have come to the conclusion that his assimilation of everything to his own context effectively recreated all the material he took from others. "Assimilation" is a good word. But it will not do to soften our language in describing what Bakhtin did with his sources; if we cannot recommend such techniques to undergraduates, we ought not to condone Bakhtin's practice as an "exception theory" to philological standards. It is certainly not the most important aspect of Bakhtin's texts, however, so neither is there any intent here to "moralize this spectacle." Nevertheless, Bakhtin's use of Cassirer lends urgency to the question of his sources in all his texts, notably, those instances where substantial portions of Bakhtin's published work are based upon German secondary literature. Although his comprehensive erudition has given rise to comparisons with Spitzer, Curtius, and Auerbach, Bakhtin rarely lived near a good library. He himself propagated the story that his friend Ivan Kanaev, who held a senior post at the library in Leningrad, sent cartons of books to him in exile, beginning in the late 1930s during the Stalinist purges and continuing through the blockade of Leningrad.[124] (The story in *The Tempest* of how Prospero got his library to the island in that "rotten carcus of a butt" is just as romantic and more credible.) We still do not know who Bakhtin was. In one of Duvakin's 1973 interviews, Bakhtin described his studies in philosophy and classics at, and his graduation from, the University of St. Petersburg, although he was never registered at the university, and for obvious reasons: he never finished high school.[125]

In Cassirer's 1932 book on Goethe and the historical world (published at the centennial of Goethe's death), we find, conveniently assembled on one page, some of Goethe's most profound thoughts on the notion of originality: "The truth was discovered long ago."[126] Nothing seemed more brainless to Goethe than to pretend to be original: "For it is unconscious arrogance not to candidly admit that one plagiarizes."[127] Of course, that is not a satisfactory explanation for plagiarism. I would like, therefore, to end this essay with a personal confession regarding the interpretation of the exchange between Sir Toby Belch and Sir Andrew Aguecheek offered at the beginning: I stole it from Ernst Cassirer.

Notes

Parts of this essay were presented at a conference on "Bakhtin's Centenary" held at the Bakhtin Centre, University of Sheffield, in the summer of 1995, and at a Yale University conference, "New Perspectives on Ernst Cassirer," 4–6 October 1996. I wish to express my gratitude for the warm hospitality extended by Professor David Shepherd, Director of the Bakhtin Centre, and by Yale Professors Cyrus Hamlin and Michael Holquist.

Translations from Russian and German sources are my own unless otherwise indicated.

1 See Sergei Averintsev's note in M. M. Bakhtin, *Toward a Philosophy of the Act*, ed. Michael Holquist and Vadim Liapunov, trans. Vadim Liapunov (Austin, 1993 [1986]). Averintsev willfully associates Bakhtin's critique of neo-Kantianism with "the direction in which Ernst Cassirer's thought developed more and more distinctly" (90–91 n. 59).

2 Of significance to those interested in applying Bakhtin to Shakespeare's comedies is that this exhortation initiates a turn stemming from the lower characters, or *Dienerkomik* (servant comedy); see Albrecht Dieterich, *Pulcinella: Pompejanische Wandbilder und römische Satyrspiele* (Leipzig, 1897), 20–54, esp. 26 (a work of which Bakhtin made detailed use in his study of Rabelais). At Sir Toby's words the clown enters the scene, whence follows dialogue full of quite literally "Rabelaisian" allusions (the use of preposterous names constructed upon pseudo-scholarly Latin roots); in the ensuing conflict with Malvolio, time is inverted (night and day reversed), Malvolio's religious seriousness is associated with the devil ("The devil a Puritan that he is"), and the "device" against Malvolio is set in motion. Such is the "motivating" force of cosmologic/comic inversion.

3 See E. M. W. Tillyard, *The Elizabethan World Picture* (London, 1943). I do not, however, share the excessive New Historicist condemnation of Tillyard's work. See the critique of "Tillyard-bashing" by Thomas Sorge, "Shakespeares Historien: Jenseits der Tillyard-Shelte?," *Jahrbuch-der-deutschen-Shakespeare-Gesellschaft* (1993): 229–34.

4 Mikhail Bakhtin, *Rabelais and His World*, trans. Hélène Iswolsky (Bloomington, 1984 [1968]), 66, 101.

5 In his incisive review of the French translation of Bakhtin's study of Rabelais, *L'oeuvre de François Rabelais et la culture populaire au Moyen Age et sous la Renaissance*, trans.

Andrée Robel (Paris, 1970), Siegfried Jüttner pointed out the lack of historical research in Bakhtin's work; see *Romanistisches Jahrbuch* 23 (1972): 243–49.

6 Bakhtin, *Rabelais*, 66; translation modified ("universal" was simply left out of the English translation); see also the original text, *Tvorchestvo Fransua Rable i narodnaia kul'tura srednevekov'ia i Renessansa* (Moscow, 1990 [1965]), 78.

7 Bakhtin, *Rabelais*, 99, 94; translation modified.

8 Ibid., 335. In distinguishing between the cognitive and epistemological functions of the intellect (however unconventional that might seem), Bakhtin associates the cognitive faculty with perceiving *more* of the world and of humanity, thanks to laughter, and the epistemological faculty with discerning the truth from the thick subterfuge of dogma and ideology.

9 The material Bakhtin culled at breakneck speed to illustrate "carnival" culture is largely secondary and rarely original; his strength lies in the anthropological and philosophical relevance of his thought. (Cf. Alexander von Gleichen-Russwurm, *Der Karnival* [Munich, 1922], a work containing scores of similar examples of carnival festivities which is, by comparison with *Rabelais*, philosophically shallow and banal.) In a notebook dedicated largely to Rabelais and labeled "Material—1938," Bakhtin refers to the "chronotope" in analyzing laughter, grotesque realism, and generic traditions in Rabelais's work; the term "carnival" is absent. Conversely, in *Rabelais and His World* "carnival" appears on almost every page, while "chronotope" is absent. What this preparatory material makes obvious is that the concept of carnival, not the term itself, is important and that the time/space neologism "chronotope" was the main analytical tool with which Bakhtin unearthed the content of the "festive" culture addressed in *Rabelais*.

10 M. M. Bakhtin, *Problems of Dostoevsky's Poetics*, ed. and trans. Caryl Emerson (Minneapolis, 1984 [1929, 1963]), 106, 109. This approach had a long tradition in the German secondary literature Bakhtin relied upon. The Greek term and the focus on the seriocomic Menippea stem from Rudolf Hirzel's 1895 *Der Dialog*, which Bakhtin discovered while reading Georg Misch's *Geschichte der Autobiographie*, Vol. 1 (Leipzig and Berlin, 1907). In the typescript of his "Discourse in the Novel," Bakhtin drew particular attention to Misch's chapter on "self-characterization in realistic forms of literature" (216–28), where Misch notes the significance of "humor" and "irony" in fictional–autobiographical forms and in first-person narratives beginning with Lucian and Petronius. Misch advances the theory that the evolution of realistic narrative which gave rise to the Spanish picaresque of the Renaissance cannot be directly traced to the Greek novel. The first-person narration of the latter is deceptive, for it "conceals the actual distance from reality" (217) peculiar to the erotic prose romance composed in the Hellenistic style (the "second sophistic"). (References to Misch and other prominent German Jewish scholars were removed from "Discourse in the Novel" when it was prepared for publication.)

11 M. M. Bakhtin, "Forms of Time and of the Chronotope in the Novel: Notes toward a Historical Poetics" (1937–38), in *The Dialogic Imagination: Four Essays*, ed. Michael Holquist, trans. Caryl Emerson and Michael Holquist (Austin, 1981), 84–258; quotation from 206.

12 In the last sentence of *Rabelais and His World* Bakhtin claims that Rabelais "so fully and clearly revealed the peculiar and difficult language of the laughing people that his work sheds its light on the folk culture of humor belonging to other ages" (474). Here, as elsewhere, Bakhtin underscores the anthropological and philosophical roots of his descriptive analyses of historically evolving generic conventions.

13 Bakhtin, *Dostoevsky's Poetics*, 106.

14 I deal with this subject in my forthcoming *Bakhtin the Philosopher: His Thought and His Sources*; see also my remarks on the relationship of M. I. Kagan's historicism and the Marburg school to Bakhtin's work in "Nazad k Kaganu," *Dialog, Karnaval, Khronotop*, No. 1 (1995): 38–126.

15 Bakhtin, *Rabelais*, 133; my emphases. Bakhtin scolds, among others, Wolfgang Kayser and Lucien Febvre.

16 Ibid., 10; translation modified. Italicized words were left out of the translation. Note that *otchuzhdenie*, which I have translated as "estrangement," could be rendered as "alienation," giving the statement a Marxist flavor.

17 See ibid., 364.

18 See ibid., 361–65; and *Tvorchestvo Fransua Rable*, 400–404.

19 Bakhtin, *Rabelais*, 359; translation modified. Bakhtin adds that medicine "was assimilated into philosophy; . . . many famous humanists and scientists of the time were physicians: Cornelius Agrippa, Paracelsus, Cardano, Copernicus."

20 Ibid., 361. Cf. Ernst Cassirer, *Individuum und Kosmos in der Philosophie der Renaissance* (Leipzig and Berlin, 1927), 117. Cassirer is here arranging quotations of Paracelsus's quaint *Mittelhochdeutsch*: "Wie die Philosophie 'der erste Grund der Arznei,' so ist die Astronomie ihr 'ander Grund.' "

21 Bakhtin, *Rabelais*, 361; cf. Cassirer, *Individuum und Kosmos*, 117. Cassirer is again quoting Paracelsus: "Erstlich sol der arzt wissen, das er den menschen in dem andern halben teil, was astronomicam philosophiam betrift, verstande und das er den menschen da herein bring und den himel in i[h]n, sonst wird er kein arzt sein des menschen, dan der himel in seiner sphaer halt innen den halben leib."

22 *Rabelais*, 361; translation modified. Cf. *Individuum und Kosmos*, 117, where Cassirer notes the correlative relationship (*Korrelationsverhältnis*) in Paracelsus's astrological thought: "Der Zusammenhang und die durchgängige Entsprechung zwischen der 'grossen' und der 'kleinen' Welt ist hier durchaus festgehalten. Er bildet für Paracelsus die Voraussetzung aller Arzneikunde."

23 *Rabelais*, 362; cf. *Individuum und Kosmos*, 144:

> Eine individuelle Seele kann als solche nur begriffen werden, wenn sie als Form eines individuellen Leibes gedacht wird. Ja, man kann geradezu sagen, dass das, was wir die Beseelung eines Leibes nennen, in nichts anderem als in dieser seiner durchgehenden Individualisierung besteht. . . . Durch sie wird er zum organischen Leib, der in seiner individuellen Bestimmtheit der Träger eines bestimmten, konkret-individuellen Lebens ist. Die "Seele" tritt demgemäss zum "Körper" nicht als ein äusserlich-bewegendes und äusserlich-belebendes Prinzip hinzu, sondern

sie ist dasjenige, was den Körper erst gestaltet, was ihn zu einem in sich unterschiedenen und in dieser Unterscheidung gegliederten Ganzen macht.

24 *Rabelais*, 362–63; translation modified (see also the more accurate German translation, *Rabelais und seine Welt*, trans. Gabriele Leupold [Frankfurt a.M., 1987], 407). Cf. *Individuum und Kosmos*, 25–26 (note that Cassirer is defining the salient characteristics of "medieval physics"):

> Diese stützt sich auf die Aristotelische Grundlehre von den vier Elementen, deren jedem im Aufbau des Kosmos ein ganz bestimmter Platz angewiesen ist. Feuer, Wasser, Luft und Erde stehen zueinander in einer fest geregelten räumlichen Beziehung, in einer bestimmten Ordnung des "Oben" und "Unten." Die Natur jedes Elements weist ihm einen bestimmten Abstand vom Mittelpunkt des Universums zu. Diesem zunächst steht die Erde; und jeder Teil von ihr strebt, wenn er einmal von seinem natürlichen Ort, von der unmittelbaren Nähe zum Weltmittelpunkt getrennt ist, in geradliniger Bewegung zu ihm zurück. Im Gegensatz hierzu ist die Bewegung des Feuers "an sich" nach oben gerichtet, so dass es sich ständig vom Mittelpunkt zu entfernen strebt. Zwischen dem Ort der Erde und dem des Feuers lagert sich dann das Gebiet, dem Luft und Wasser angehören. Die allgemeine Form des physikalischen Wirkens ist durch diese Stellenordnung bestimmt. Alle physische Wirksamkeit vollzieht sich derart, dass eine Umwandlung von einem Element in ein anderes, ihm benachbartes stattfindet, so dass Feuer zu Luft, Luft zu Wasser, Wasser zu Erde wird. Dieses Prinzip der gegenseitigen Umwandlung, dieses Gesetz des Entstehens und Vergehens, prägt allem irdischen Geschehen seinen Stempel auf. Über der irdischen Welt aber erhebt sich die Sphäre, die diesem Gesetz nicht mehr unterworfen ist, die weder Entstehen noch Vergehen kennt. Die Materie der himmlischen Körper hat ein eigenes Sein, eine "*quinta essentia*," die von der Art der vier irdischen Elemente wesenhaft verschieden ist. Ihr kommt keine qualitative Umwandlung zu, sondern sie besitzt nur noch eine mögliche Art der Veränderung: die reine Ortsbewegung. Und da von allen möglichen Formen der Bewegung dem vollkommensten Körper die vollkommenste zukommen muss, so ergibt sich, dass die himmlischen Körper reine Kreislinien um den Mittelpunkt der Welt beschreiben.

25 Ernst Cassirer, *The Individual and the Cosmos in Renaissance Philosophy*, ed. and trans. Mario Domandi (Philadelphia, 1972 [1963]).

26 There are approximately ten pages in all of *Individuum und Kosmos* in *Rabelais*. Irina Popova is preparing an authoritative and critical edition of both versions of the Rabelais study (1940 and 1965) that will include a critical assessment of Bakhtin's sources.

27 *Bakhtinian Thought: An Introductory Reader*, ed. Simon Dentith (London, 1995), 248–52.

28 Bakhtin, *Rabelais*, 364; translation modified. Cf. Cassirer, *Individuum und Kosmos*, 88–90.

29 Cf. *Rabelais*, 364; and its almost verbatim source in *Individuum und Kosmos*, 158. My quotations are from *Rabelais*, 365; cf. *Individuum und Kosmos*, 156–60.

30 Cf. *Rabelais*, 365: "the world is not an aggregate of elements but an animate being"; and *Individuum und Kosmos*, 116: "so wahr die Welt kein Aggregat toter Elemente, sondern ein beseeltes Wesen ist."

31 Cf. *Rabelais*, 365; and *Individuum und Kosmos*, 157, and 157–58 for the Cardano quotation ("Die Metalle sind ihm [Cardanus] nichts anderes als 'begrabene Pflanzen,' die ihr Dasein unter der Erde führen; die Steine haben ihre Entwicklung, ihr Wachstum und ihre Reife").

32 *Rabelais*, 365; translation modified. The emphases (almost never retained in the translation) are Bakhtin's.

33 Quoted in Ulrich Sieg, *Aufstieg und Niedergang des Marburger Neukantianismus* (Würzburg, 1994), 447–48.

34 M. M. Bakhtin, "Discourse in the Novel" (1934–35), in Holquist, ed., *Dialogic Imagination*, 259–422; quotation from 401 (cf. 275 and 309).

35 Ibid., 309; my emphases.

36 Bakhtin, *Rabelais*, 11. Cf. this statement from the next page: "The satirist, who knows only negating laughter, places himself outside the phenomenon laughed at, juxtaposes himself to it, thus the wholeness of the world's comic aspect is destroyed, and the laughable (negative) becomes a personal phenomenon" (12); translation modified.

37 Ernst Cassirer, *Das mythische Denken*, Part 2 of *Philosophie der symbolischen Formen* (Darmstadt, 1994 [1925]) / *Mythical Thought*, Vol. 2 of *The Philosophy of Symbolic Forms*, trans. Ralph Manheim (New Haven and London, 1955).

38 Ernst Cassirer, *Goethe und die geschichtliche Welt: Drei Aufsätze* (Berlin, 1932); *Die Philosophie der Aufklärung* (Tübingen, 1932)/*The Philosophy of the Enlightenment*, trans. Fritz C. A. Koelln and James P. Pettegrove (Boston, 1955 [1951]); *Die Platonische Renaissance in England und die Schule von Cambridge* (Leipzig, 1932)/*The Platonic Renaissance in England*, trans. James P. Pettegrove (Austin, 1953).

39 Had it been retained in the Russian original, the missing reference would likely have been included in note 36 of "Discourse in the Novel" (369). In the typescript the note continues: "A more fundamental connection between the problems of linguistics [i.e., the relation of myth and language] is given in Usener's study [*Götternamen: Versuch einer Lehre von der religiösen Begriffsbildung*] and, in particular, in Cassirer's work [*Philosophie der symbolischen Formen*, T. 2]." The typescript is the only extant manuscript of this essay. Lacking a typewriter with Latin-alphabetic characters, the typist left blanks where titles ought to have appeared, while typing names in Russian. It is nevertheless possible to reconstruct almost all of the missing notes on the basis of archival material. (Significantly, and for purely ideological reasons, Bakhtin's ensuing references to Marr and Dilthey were also left out of the published text.)

40 M. M. Bakhtin, "The *Bildungsroman* and Its Significance in the History of Realism (Toward a Historical Typology of the Novel)" (1936–38), in *Speech Genres and Other Late Essays*, ed. Caryl Emerson and Michael Holquist, trans. Vern W. McGee (Austin, 1986), 10–59; quotations from 11, 14, 15, 21.

41 Bakhtin, "Forms of Time and of the Chronotope in the Novel," 251.

42 Bakhtin, *Rabelais*, 349, 350.

43 Paul Lehmann, *Die Parodie im Mittelalter* (Munich, 1922), 45, 234. Bakhtin based approximately twenty pages of *Rabelais* on quotations from and observations by Lehmann, whose relatively slim study was dedicated to Karl Vossler, the twentieth-century pioneer of linguistic idealism and a favorite of Cassirer and Bakhtin.

44 Bakhtin, *Rabelais*, 351.

45 Ibid., n. 14.

46 Ibid., 354.

47 On the cultural and anthropological dimensions of Cassirer's thought, see Ernst Wolfgang Orth, *Von der Erkenntnistheorie zur Kulturphilosophie* (Würzburg, 1996).

48 Bakhtin, synopsis, 113; cf. Cassirer, *Das mythische Denken*, 112. The synopsis is contained in a 176-page notebook together with Bakhtin's notes on Georg Witkowski's *Goethe* (Leipzig/Berlin/Vienna, 1899); and O. Freidenberg's *Poetika siuzheta i zhanra* (Leningrad, 1936).

49 Attention to the body was of course not new in Bakhtin's thought of the late 1930s. But his early phenomenological analyses of the body in "Toward a Philosophy of the Act" and *Author and Hero in Aesthetic Activity* (1926?), written under the overwhelming influence of Max Scheler, have an entirely different character, lacking both the link between the body and the *historical* development of spatial and temporal perception per se and the body's correlation with the cosmos, so characteristic of myth and of Renaissance philosophy. On Bakhtin's early work, see my "From Phenomenology to Dialogue," in the forthcoming second edition of *Bakhtin and Cultural Theory*, ed. Ken Hirschkop and David Shepherd (Manchester and New York: Manchester University Press).

50 Bakhtin, synopsis, 113; cf. Cassirer, *Das mythische Denken*, 112.

51 Synopsis, 114; cf. *Das mythische Denken*, 113.

52 Bakhtin composed his synopsis of Cassirer's study of myth prior to completing "Forms of Time and of the Chronotope in the Novel" and before beginning *Rabelais and His World*. His careful Russian renderings of Cassirer's German provide a key to a number of the most perplexing formulations in both texts, for we find here a new atmosphere and a new vocabulary in which Bakhtin increasingly views the questions of meaning and genre, and of body and mind, through Cassirer's philosophy. The synopsis contains an abundance of terminology foreign to Bakhtin's earlier works but characteristic of his mature ones.

53 Bakhtin, synopsis, 146; cf. Cassirer, *Das mythische Denken*, 164 ("das grosse Eine" and "des Göttlichen" for Bakhtin's "velikoe edinoe" and "bozhestva," respectively).

54 Synopsis, 147–48 (Bakhtin's emphases); cf. *Das mythische Denken*, 165–66.

55 Cf. synopsis, 149: "Tak nado ponimat' zamechatel'nye slova Geraklita: [*αἰὼν παῖς ἐστι παίζων πεττεύων. παιδὸς ἡ βασιληίη*] (die Zeit ist ein Knabe, der spielt, der hin und her die Brettsteine setzt, eines Kindes ist die Herrschaft) (fr. 52)"; and *Das mythische Denken*, 166. See also *Rabelais*, 82, 147, 196 (chapter epigraph), and 435; and *Tvorchestvo Fransua Rable*, 95, 163, 452, 480, and, for the (translated) epigraph, 219.

56 Bakhtin, *Rabelais*, 147, 82; translation modified.

57 Ernst Cassirer, "Die Philosophie der Griechen von den Anfängen bis Platon," in *Lehrbuch der Philosophie*, ed. Max Dessoir (Berlin, 1925), 7–139; quotation from 20–21.

58 G. S. Kirk, J. E. Raven, and M. Schofield, *The Presocratic Philosophers: A Critical History with a Selection of Texts*, 2d. ed. (Cambridge, 1983 [1957]), 189.
59 Ibid., 188, 208; see also Cassirer, "Die Philosophie der Griechen," 21.
60 See Cassirer, *Individuum und Kosmos*, 10.
61 Cassirer, *Platonic Renaissance*, 13.
62 Cassirer, *Individuum und Kosmos*, 14.
63 Cassirer, *Platonic Renaissance*, 14; my emphasis.
64 Ibid.
65 Ibid.
66 Ibid., 15 (*una est religio in rituum varietate*); translation modified.
67 Ibid., my emphasis.
68 Ibid., 17, 18.
69 Bakhtin, *Rabelais*, 14; Cassirer, *Platonic Renaissance*, 21.
70 Cassirer, *Platonic Renaissance*, 111.
71 Ibid., 168, 183; my emphasis.
72 Ibid., 183–84; translation modified.
73 Bakhtin, *Rabelais*, 122–23; cf. 64. (Note the resemblance of Bakhtin's "one being, forever incomplete," to the Heraclitian notion of a continually becoming "great one" which Bakhtin found in Cassirer's *Mythical Thought*.)
74 Cassirer, *Platonic Renaissance*, 169–70; translation modified.
75 Cassirer, *Individuum und Kosmos*, 170.
76 Cf. Ernst Cassirer, *Das Erkenntnisproblem in der Philosophie und Wissenschaft der neueren Zeit*, Vol. 1 (Darmstadt, 1995 [1906]); and *Individuum und Kosmos*, esp. 170ff., 198, 200.
77 See Ernst Cassirer, *Die Sprache*, Part 1 of *Philosophie der symbolischen Formen* (Berlin, 1923), 105; and *An Essay on Man: An Introduction to a Philosophy of Human Culture* (New Haven and London, 1944), 121.
78 Cassirer, *Individuum und Kosmos*, 200; see also 169, 170, and 175.
79 Cassirer (ibid., 170 n. 1) cites the inspiring research of Ernst Walser, *Studien zur Weltanschauung der Renaissance* (Basel, 1920).
80 Ernst Cassirer, *Freiheit und Form: Studien zur deutschen Geistesgeschichte* (Darmstadt, 1991 [1916]), 83.
81 See Ernst Cassirer, *Kants Leben und Lehre* (Berlin, 1918), 297. In a 1923 essay on Kant's philosophy of aesthetics, M. I. Kagan, Bakhtin's closest friend, drew attention to both these early references by Cassirer to Shaftesbury. We may therefore assume that Kagan would have immediately recognized the new dimension in Renaissance art and literature that Cassirer profiled in *The Platonic Renaissance* with Shaftesbury as his guide, namely, the role of comic laughter and humor. Kagan, who studied with Cassirer in Berlin, followed his publications closely and corresponded with him as late as 1927. Reporting in a letter of 7 August 1937 to his wife that Bakhtin had arrived unexpectedly in Moscow and discussed with him his "almost complete book," Kagan added that "in general, much in [Bakhtin's] work coincides with my own thoughts, but in certain questions he will have to make some changes of a fairly principal character following our conversations"; see Yu. M. Kagan, "O starykh bumagakh iz semeinogo arkhiva (M. M.

Bakhtin i M. I. Kagan)," *Dialog, Karnaval, Khronotop,* No. 1 (1992): 60–88. (I assume that the change in Bakhtin's approach to Rabelais began in 1937 at the latest.)

82 See Ernst Cassirer, "Schiller und Shaftesbury," *Publications of the English Goethe Society,* n.s., 11 (1935): 37–59.

83 On Shaftesbury's ethical idealism and his opposition to Locke, see Cassirer, *Platonic Renaissance,* 188–91; and, on Shaftesbury's opposition to puritanism and empiricism, "Shaftesbury und die Renaissance des Platonismus in England," *Vorträge der Bibliothek Warburg* 9 (1930–31): 136–55, esp. 138–40.

84 Cassirer, "Shaftesbury und die Renaissance des Platonismus," 141.

85 Ibid. For Cassirer's parallel analysis of Cusa's thought, see *Individuum und Kosmos,* 21–25.

86 For his most extended discussion of the Renaissance as a historical period characterized by the dialogue of epochs, see Ernst Cassirer, *Zur Logik der Kulturwissenschaften,* 6th ed. (Darmstadt, 1994 [1942]), 110–13.

87 Cassirer, "Shaftesbury und die Renaissance des Platonismus," 146; cf. Bakhtin, *Rabelais,* 118–19.

88 Cassirer, "Shaftesbury und die Renaissance des Platonismus," 146.

89 Cassirer, *Platonic Renaissance,* 168, 169, 170–72. Oswald Schwemmer, in his otherwise admirable *Ernst Cassirer: Ein Philosoph der europäischen Moderne* (Berlin, 1997), fails to state the obvious in his chapter "Cassirer's Image of the Renaissance" (221–42), mentioning neither Cassirer's defense of Renaissance tolerance nor his theory of comedy. For a suggestive application of Cassirer's thought, see Walter Kaiser, *The Praisers of Folly: Erasmus, Rabelais, Shakespeare* (Cambridge, MA, 1963).

90 Cassirer, *Platonic Renaissance,* 170; my emphasis. Cf. Bakhtin's definition of genre in *Dostoevsky's Poetics,* 106.

91 Cassirer, *Platonic Renaissance,* 170–72; my emphases.

92 Bakhtin, *Tvorchestvo Fransua Rable,* 13; *Rabelais,* 8. Cf. Cassirer's "middle realm [*mittleres Reich des Seins*] between the divine and the human, the intelligible and the sensual world" (*Individuum und Kosmos,* 139).

93 Cassirer, *Platonic Renaissance,* 179; translation modified. (Cf. *Die Platonische Renaissance,* 125.)

94 Cassirer, *Platonic Renaissance,* 180–81; translation modified, my emphases.

95 Bakhtin, *Rabelais,* 400–401. (The passage closely follows Bakhtin's synopsis of *Individuum und Kosmos,* to which we will return.) Bakhtin's nonchalant bird's-eye view of "the teaching of the Areopagite" as having "had a great influence on Erigena, Albert the Great, Thomas Aquinas, and others" (*Rabelais,* 401) is likewise rendered in a one-sentence summary by Cassirer (*Individuum und Kosmos,* 8).

96 Bakhtin, *Rabelais,* 402, 401; Cassirer, *Platonic Renaissance,* 179.

97 Bakhtin, *Rabelais,* 363.

98 In Germany Cassirer was instrumental to the rediscovery of Cusa's prominent role in Renaissance philosophy (as Paul Oskar Kristeller, among others, has noted), with *Individuum und Kosmos* serving as a 200-page forward to a Latin–German edition of *De mente* (bk. 3 of *De docta ignorantia*). See the second edition of Cassirer's *Erkenntnisproblem* (Berlin, 1910), 1: 21–61.

99 Bakhtin's synopsis (23 ms. pages extending over two undated notebooks) is one of two synopses of *Individuum und Kosmos* in the Bakhtin archive. The second synopsis is not in the handwriting of either Bakhtin or his wife; while I am not a graphologist, judging from a comparison with a fall 1921 letter to Kagan from Valentin Vološinov, the second synopsis is in a hand that appears to resemble the latter's. Subsequent citations of the two notebooks begin with the notebook number (1 or 2) followed by the notebook page number.

100 Bakhtin, synopsis, 1: 11; cf. Cassirer, *Individuum und Kosmos*, 9.

101 Synopsis, 1: 12; cf. *Individuum und Kosmos*, 9.

102 See *Individuum und Kosmos*, 9–10. Cf. Bakhtin's synopsis, 1: 11–12; but see also *Rabelais*, 443.

103 On the relationship between ethical freedom and the rejection of Augustine's theory of grace during the Renaissance, see Cassirer, *Individuum und Kosmos*, 69.

104 Bakhtin, synopsis, 1: 12 ("liubov' neobkhodimo vkliuchaet v sebia moment poznaniia; nel'zia liubit' nezaemoe"); cf. Cassirer, *Individuum und Kosmos*, 13.

105 Cassirer, *Individuum und Kosmos*, 69, 68, 71.

106 Bakhtin, synopsis, 1: 15; cf. Cassirer, *Individuum und Kosmos*, 26–27, 28–29.

107 Synopsis, 2: 1; cf. *Individuum und Kosmos*, 111.

108 Synopsis, 1: 15; cf. *Individuum und Kosmos*, 29–30.

109 Synopsis, 1: 17; cf. *Individuum und Kosmos*, 38.

110 Synopsis, 1: 18; cf. *Individuum und Kosmos*, 52–53.

111 Cassirer's phrase is "wahrhaft grossartige Toleranz" (*Individuum und Kosmos*, 31).

112 Bakhtin, synopsis, 1: 15–16; cf. *Individuum und Kosmos*, 31–32.

113 Quoted in Cassirer, *Individuum und Kosmos*, 31. While reworking his dissertation on Rabelais during the 1940s, Bakhtin referred (in point form) to this scene in his notes: "Nicholas of Cusa a representative of both the people and the market square, as protagonist of his dialogues"; see M. M. Bakhtin, "Dopolneniia i izmeneniia k 'Rabelais's" (Additions and Changes to Rabelais), *Voprosi filosofii*, No. 1 (1992): 134–64; quotation from 152.

114 See Cassirer's quotations from *De conjecturis* 1.13, in *Individuum und Kosmos*, 31 and 24.

115 Ibid., 31, 31–32.

116 The synopsis that is not in Bakhtin's handwriting includes the following statement in reference to *Individuum und Kosmos* (136–37): "Cusa was the first to find, philosophically, a new principle against Averroism: he negated the absolute rift between the intellectual and the sensual; the former requires the latter for its own complete actualization."

117 Cassirer, *Individuum und Kosmos*, 33.

118 Ibid. (It is worth underscoring here that Cassirer's work appeared two years before the first edition of Bakhtin's book on Dostoevsky.)

119 Ibid., 34.

120 During Viktor Duvakin's 1973 interviews with him, Bakhtin admitted to his "partiality for the Marburg school," citing Hermann Cohen's major works, Natorp's *Philosophische Propädeutik*, and Cassirer's *Philosophy of Symbolic Forms*; see *Besedy V. D. Duvakina s*

M. M. Bakhtinym (Moscow, 1996); and my forthcoming translation, *M. M. Bakhtin in Dialogue with V. D. Duvakin* (Austin: University of Texas Press).

121 The complete Russian text is forthcoming in my edition of the manuscripts of Bakhtin's study of the bildungsroman and his fragments on the theory of the novel in Vol. 3 of M. M. Bakhtin, *Sobranie sochinenii v semi tomakh* (Collected Works in Seven Volumes), ed. S. G. Bocharov and L. A. Gogotishvili (Moscow: Russkie slovari).

122 M. M. Bakhtin, "Epic and Novel" and "From the Prehistory of Novelistic Discourse," in Holquist, ed., *Dialogic Imagination*, 3–40 and 4–83, respectively.

123 Bakhtin's reference to Cervantes directly parallels Cassirer's interpretation of how "two epochs" (one dying and the other just being born) are combined in a single image in comic literature, namely, Don Quixote (*Platonic Renaissance*, 171).

"Contemporization [*osovremenenie*]" here is, I believe, the first appearance of Bakhtin's neologism, which would reappear in the second edition of his Dostoevsky study (see *Dostoevsky's Poetics*, 106); the term describes what Cusa did for Platonic thought (and for Heraclitus's theory of the coincidence of opposites) and what Shaftesbury did for Platonism and the theory of laughter, that is, showing its contemporary relevance.

For Bakhtin's broad application of the temporal categories with which he defines the Renaissance in this passage, see the penultimate paragraph of "Epic and Novel," 39–40.

124 See Bakhtin's comments in *Besedy V. D. Dubakina*, 211.

125 See the excellent essay by N. A. Pan'kov, "Zagadki rannego Bakhtina," *Dialog, Karnaval, Khronotop*, No. 1 (1993): 74–89.

126 "Das Wahre war schon längst gefunden / Hat edle Geisterschaft verbunden / Das alte Wahre fass es an!" (quoted in Cassirer, *Goethe und die geschichtliche Welt*, 25). Cassirer uses this same poem by Goethe ("Vermächtnis") to underscore the lack of any concept of personal originality in the work of Pico della Mirandola: "If we understand by 'originality' the individual's ability to break through in his thinking and action the limits of what has already been achieved, we cannot in Pico's case look for even the disposition or the will to attain such originality"; Ernst Cassirer, "Giovanni Pico della Mirandola: A Study in the History of Renaissance Ideas," *Journal of the History of Ideas* 3 (1942): 123–44 and 319–46; quotation from 124.

127 Cassirer, *Goethe und die geschichtliche Welt*, 25 (quoting Goethe's *Maximen und Reflexionen*, 1146).

Ken Hirschkop

Bakhtin Myths, or, Why We All Need Alibis

We know a lot less about Bakhtin than we thought we did. For example, it had long been assumed that he was descended from gentry who had lost most of their land and wealth a generation before his own and that the bank at which his father worked had actually been founded by his grandfather. Bakhtin himself related the story of how the land was lost and the bank founded, in great detail, in his 1973 interview with Viktor Dmitrievich Duvakin, whom he also informed that his great-great-grandfather had founded a cadet corps at the time of Catherine the Great.[1] Unfortunately, it appears that none of this is true: Research in the relevant regional archive has revealed that there were no familial connections between the Bakhtins who interest us and the noble Bakhtins who founded cadet corps and the like. (In fact, the noble Bakhtin who founded the corps, far from being Bakhtin's great-great-grandfather, died childless.) Moreover, Mikhail's grandfather was a merchant hardly in a position to have founded a bank.[2] Where did the myth of noble origins come from? One of the authors of the first biographical note on Bakhtin's life

The *South Atlantic Quarterly* 97:3/4, Summer/Fall 1998.

revealed that it came not from Mikhail himself but from a biographical note on his brother Nikolai. The latter, to whom Bakhtin had once been very close, left Russia in the wake of the civil war and eventually ended up, following stints in the French Foreign Legion and at the Sorbonne, in the linguistics department at the University of Birmingham. After his death, a collection of his essays was published by that university with a brief biographical introduction, presumably based on Nikolai's own testimony, in which these noble family origins were outlined.[3] It is, of course, odd that he should have been so mistaken about his family origins (assuming that it was Nikolai who provided the information and that he was, in fact, mistaken), but it is much odder that Mikhail should have repeated it, adding, "I was not interested in this, but my brother was interested in it, he knew about it."[4] Bakhtin cites his brother's account, which, being false, he must have learned of from its appearance in the later biographical note devoted to himself, but for reasons we can only speculate about. It may have been indifference or a desire not to rock the biographical boat, or it may have been that Bakhtin willingly seized an opportunity to trade in his petit-bourgeois origins for noble "cultured" ones. (While the Russian people benefit from the fact that their name, *narod*, is also the word for "nation," their petite bourgeoisie suffer from the fact that their name, *meshchantsvo*, also signifies philistinism.[5])

Petit-bourgeois or not, Bakhtin was a member of the formally educated minority of Russian society. In 1905 his family moved to Vilnius (Lithuania), where he enrolled in one of the city's gymnasiums, after which they moved to Odessa, apparently in the middle of 1911.[6] Then, more ambiguity, and a bolder kind of citation: in the Duvakin interview Bakhtin claimed (as he had done on other occasions) that he had been enrolled at Novorossiskii University in Odessa for a year (presumably 1912–13) and then transferred to the University of St. Petersburg, from which he graduated in 1917. Recent work on university records, however, reveals that this path was the one taken not by Mikhail but by Nikolai; there is no record of Mikhail's having been registered at either university.[7] This may reflect a casual approach to the formalities, but at first glance it appears, as has been suggested, that Bakhtin "was able to 'borrow' certain biographical episodes from his older brother" (as Pan'kov delicately puts it) in order to provide what was in effect self-education with an official veneer.[8] As before, Bakhtin drops a hint: "But, I have to say, that nevertheless, although I have no complaints about either gymnasium or university, I acquired the foundations by independent study. Because any official educational establishment, by its very essence, cannot provide the kind of education which can satisfy a person."[9] In actual fact, it would appear he moved to Petrograd a year after his brother in 1914, together with the rest of his family, and attended the university there without actually registering.

We know less about the facts of Bakhtin's life, but perhaps we know more about Bakhtin himself as a consequence, such as that he was perfectly willing to go along with myths already in circulation. Naturally enough, this applies to the most consequential area of the mythology—the matter of the "disputed texts" by Vološinov and Medvedev, claimed for Bakhtin by several critics and biographers. When Bakhtin confessed to his friend (and later, his literary executor) Sergei Bocharov that he had written the disputed texts, was he again going along with a myth he had no interest in rebutting? Even Bocharov admits we can never know decisively, given that Bakhtin *denied* authorship on other occasions. But Bocharov added a telling afterthought on the matter: "There is no proof and most probably there will never be any. . . . There is already more than a little *testimony*, but it cannot be *proof*"—a concession that is then followed by quotations from Bulgakov (a heroic figure for the Russian intelligentsia) and Dostoevsky in which the desire for proof of the existence of God is mocked for its narrow, scientistic pretensions.[10] While we can have no proof, no visible evidence, the truth is still there for those who are willing to look deep into the heart of things, who will read between the lines and recognize the larger human situation only ever partially rendered in the visible and apparent.[11] Bakhtin may or may not have been the author of the disputed texts attributed to him; what's interesting in any case is the belief that the question ought to be settled by a truth embodied not in evidence but in the person of Bakhtin himself.

For this truth depends upon the most audacious and fundamental myth of all, in which I think Bakhtin believed and on which his entire intellectual position depended: the myth of a sphere of truth and responsibility "above" the concerns and problems of historical, secular existence. Another of Bakhtin's editors and followers, Sergei Averintsev, defined this precisely in an early polemic, where Bakhtin was congratulated not for his contributions to scholarly knowledge, but for his ability to rise above the tortured sphere of scientific argument: "The essence of Bakhtin's position always consisted not of 'against' but of 'for,' not of argument or of rejection but of affirmation, in defense of the rights of the whole in the face of the unjustified pretensions of the part."[12] To "drag Bakhtin into the dualism of arguments between circles" was to do an injustice to his philosophizing, which traded in goods far more valuable than mere empirical truth and falsity. For Bakhtin aimed at truths transcending the fallible judgments of mortal human beings, which were prone to historical revision, and at a perspective from which every error would be forgiven.

It is worth pointing out, parenthetically, that this metaphysical conception of the true, rather than Marxism, is what critics have used to distinguish Bakhtin from his friends Vološinov and Medvedev. In nearly all Russian works discussing the authorship question, the issue is not particular Marxist or non-Marxist positions (about which very little is usually said), but the relative degree to which these three scholars were engaged with the cultural institutions of the new Soviet order. Medvedev and Vološinov, particularly the former, stand convicted not of any specific intellectual crime, but of having taken seriously the institutions of Soviet cultural life and thus of having failed to keep a philosophically sanctioned distance from the actually existing situation. That their work was published in the journals of the day is taken as evidence of an apparently disreputable concern with secular results and earthly success, a concern confirmed by the so-called sociological flavor of these texts. Those wishing to recuperate the philosophical content of the disputed texts retain a belief in a metaphysical conception of the philosophical task, in which insight into the true nature of things (hidden, of course, from the social sciences) is the only source of reliable moral truth. And a metaphysical conception of the philosophical task demands a metaphysical conception of the philosopher, who must steer clear of the secular and strife-ridden world if he or she is to maintain his or her moral bearings. Rarely does anyone accuse Vološinov or Medvedev of being wrong; the accusation is rather of a certain secular vulgarity, a willingness to engage in a game that is itself part of the problem and from which nothing valuable could ever come.[13]

In short, Bakhtin's casualness with historical facts may reflect not carelessness but a sincerely held belief that one cannot put too much faith in them. Facts are historical facts, all values historical values; they are subject to incessant change, and the individual who expects them to ground his or her life is doomed to an "infinite discontent" capped by a meaningless death. This, of course, is the very principle of the popular culture of "laughter" which so enthused Bakhtin in his study of Rabelais:

> The ruling power and the ruling truth cannot see themselves in the mirror of time, therefore they do not see their own beginnings, boundaries, and ends; they do not see their old and ridiculous face, the comic character of their pretensions to eternity and immutability. And the representatives of the old power and the old truth finish playing their roles, in serious tones and with very serious faces, after their audience has already been laughing for a long time. They continue to speak in the serious, majestic, threatening, terrible tone of kings or heralds of "eternal truths," not noticing that time has already rendered this tone ridiculous in their mouths and transformed the old power and truth into a Shrovetide carnival dummy, into a comic scarecrow which the people tear to pieces with their laughter in the public square.[14]

Passages such as this one have made carnival the darling of many critics on the Left, even though its argument is little more than a popular rewrite of *sic transit gloria mundi*. But the culture of laughter, far from representing some sudden veer into vulgar sociologism, is utterly congruent with the myth of a metaphysical perspective which will redeem all. In notes Bakhtin made in the early 1940s, at the same time he was revising the Rabelais text for publication (yes, *pace* some of his devotees, he was very interested in the earthly success represented by publication), he consciously identified the system of popular images with a disinterested, suprahuman perspective, as if the steady flow of collective usage wore away every pragmatic consideration:

> The system of folkloric symbols laid down over the millennia, which gave form to the ultimate whole. In them one finds the great experience of humanity. In the symbols of official culture one finds only the petty experience of a specific part of humanity (at a given moment, interested in its stabilization). Characteristic of these petty models, created on the basis of petty and private experience, is a specific pragmatism, a utilitarianism. They serve as a scheme for the practically interested action of a person; in them, actually, practice determines

> thought. Therefore in them one finds deliberate concealment, falsehood, salvational illusions of every kind, the simplicity and mechanistic quality of a scheme, a literalness and one-sidedness of evaluation, one-dimensionality and logicality (directly linear logicality). They are interested, least of all, in the truth of the all-embracing whole (this truth of the whole is nonpractical and disinterested; it is indifferent to the temporal fates of the partial).[15]

One finds here the classic populist move, but with a metaphysical twist. The writer credits "the people" and their culture with the perspective which he would like them to have: his perspective, presented not as the product of research and argument but as the spontaneous yield of their everyday life. One need not, according to Bakhtin, engage in metaphysical speculation or devote oneself to religion in order to understand that there is a sphere of values transcending the pragmatic and historical concerns of immediate life; one need only be a peasant and do what comes naturally. Bakhtin therefore hoped to find anchorage in the history of European culture for the point of view which he himself had worked out in response to the crisis of European culture. But to understand how the medieval European peasantry ended up assuming these awesome metaphysical burdens, we ought to go back to the beginning and trace Bakhtin's interest in the all-embracing whole from its philosophical beginnings to its would-be carnival finale.

As a fledgling member of the Russian intelligentsia and privileged recipient of a gymnasium education as well as the attentions of a personal tutor, Bakhtin was well acquainted with both the breadth of early twentieth-century European intellectual culture and the sense of crisis which pervaded it. He would have known that European achievement in the arts, in philosophy and science, in law and government, was impressive in a technical sense and a complete failure in a moral sense, having led inexorably to a horrific war and an apparently endless series of social crises and conflicts. Bakhtin did not, however, turn to either sociological or political analysis, but to philosophy, for an explanation of this failure. In fact, he went even further: he argued that it was the forgetting of philosophy, its displacement by the methods of natural science, which lay at the bottom of the crisis to begin with. In his earliest extant essay, "Toward a Philosophy of the Act," he claimed that the problem with all existing moral theory was that it trusted culture to create a sense of obligation, of "oughtness," in relation to its norms and values. One could not, however, instill obligation by means of rational argument or scientific proof: "I can agree with this or that position as a psychologist, a sociologist, a jurist ex cathedra, but to claim that by this alone it becomes a norm for my act is to leap over the fundamental problem. Even for the very fact of my actual assent to the validity of a given position ex cathedra—as *my act*—the validity of the position and my psychological faculty of representation are not enough; something more must come from me, precisely the ethically obligating position of my consciousness in relation to a position which is itself theoretically valid."[16] The essential point is that one cannot derive such an "ethically obligating position," the sense of oughtness which turns a norm or value into something compelling, from a demonstration or proof that something is right, for a proof can only justify something that is objectively right, and objective norms—laws, we might well call them—always provide escape hatches for subjects because they apply to people in general and to no one in particular. Law provides people with reasons but not with conscience, and only the latter makes one truly responsible in thought and deed.

And how do we acquire a conscience? From, it appears, an understanding of the uniqueness of our place in the world, the realization that we do not inhabit—as laws imply, by their very abstractness—an individual place more or less exchangeable with everyone else's, but rather a place in which everyone else confronts us in the form of *others*. By this Bakhtin meant something comparatively simple. He meant that for every person consciousness does not appear as something we have and that others have in the same way we have it; it is something which exists in two, absolutely distinct registers: consciousness is either our consciousness, the consciousness of the *I*, which imposes a certain structure on time and space, on values and feelings, or the consciousness of *others*, which we always experience as something expressed—as bounded in time and space, surrounded by things and with a physical embodiment. There is no such thing as a person in general, for we experience our own person and our own life in an absolutely different manner from the way we encounter other persons and lives. To take the obvious illustration, the death of other consciousnesses is an event utterly different in its consequences, meaning, and even tonality from the death of our own.

Thus the world is, in its most basic constitution, an ethical space, a space structured by an irreducible difference between *I* and *other*. One's place is unique not on account of its particular spatial or temporal location—not unique physically—but insofar as one experiences it as the unique space of an I which confronts others. "Responsibility" means grasping this uniqueness and the obligation to act toward others that flows from it. It therefore distinguishes itself from Kantian, lawlike "morality" as

> *conscience*, that is, not moral but unique obligation: no one in the entire world except myself can accomplish what I must accomplish. By contrast, moral obligation is the obligation to conform to a law. In the present case obligation issues only from unrepeatability, and conscience torments one not for insubordination to a law but as a result of a unique orientation. From this flows the impossibility of generalizing the religious norm; from this stems the Christian's demand, not understood by Feuerbach, for the Cross for himself and happiness for others.[17]

When conscience speaks, there is no ambiguity about the addressee—it speaks to you as the only person who could do what you ought to do, and this is its power. And because it speaks to you alone, it leaves you with (as Bakhtin famously put it) "no alibi in being." There is no limit to your responsibility, nor can you justify your acts by reference to some formal identity or any other quasi-legal consideration. Once you have grasped the architectonics of the world, its ineluctable division into *I* and *other*, you become responsible, obligated, because you simultaneously grasp the fact that your *own* consciousness can neither satisfactorily ground your acts nor provide your life with certain meaning and significance. For that, you must depend on the community of *others* around you and on the faith that they will sense their obligations toward you as surely as you acknowledge your obligations toward them. With the end of solipsistic individualism comes, so Bakhtin believed, the beginning of an ethical life.

The final twist: "This fact of my *non-alibi in being*, lying at the base of the very concrete and unique obligatoriness of the act, is not known and not cognized by me, but recognized and asserted by me in unique form."[18] The distinction between knowing something and recognizing it, which in Russian comes down to a difference of verbal prefix, is crucial, for Bakhtin aligns it with the distinction between the historically bound knowledge yielded by science and the moment of insight offered by what he calls "first" or "primary" philosophy. The architectonics of the actual world is not something that research and analysis can determine; its description is the task of philosophy alone, for philosophy—real philosophy, in Bakhtin's eyes, not the stuff corrupted by the partial concerns of science or religion—is alone devoted to the perspective of the ultimate whole.

Had Bakhtin left it at that, he would not have had much of a career, since at some point later in the 1920s—for reasons still being debated by his biographers—Bakhtin decided he could no longer do philosophy. Another route to the world of responsibility had to be found, and another was. For the world of responsible acts was also, as Bakhtin himself had put it, "the world of proper names, of *these* objects and of the specific chronological dates of a life."[19] In what kind of prose do we find a world with both general relevance and this kind of particularity? In the modern European novel, of course. According to his notes from around 1944–45, "all the [classical] genres are oriented to myth (as the ultimate whole), the novel to philosophy (and science)." Bakhtin therefore asked the novel to take on the task originally assigned to "first philosophy," the task of describing the world as it actually is: "We do not know what kind of world we live in. The novel wants to show it to us."[20]

A strange idea: the novel as representing a world of absolute responsibility. For is not the modern novel the most fertile begetter of excuses, its empirical density and wealth of historical description providing endless alibis for the actions of its characters? Does not the "realism" of the modern novel describe a world available to all through experience rather than one that is split between *I* and *other*? Bakhtin did not dissent from the usual list of defining features; he emphasized the novel's interest in the detail and the language of everyday life, its concern with social typicality and description, its strong investment in irony, and its drive to represent the world as something historical, a human creation. Again conventionally, these features derived, for Bakhtin, from the modern novel's historicizing impulse, its reconstitution of the world as a historical fact or a concatenation of historical facts. The ethical key lay in his sense of what it means for the world to be historical. That depends, he believed, on a redrawing of the relationship between time and the future. "For artistic-ideological consciousness, time and the world become for the first time historical: they are disclosed, even if at the beginning unclearly and hazily, as becoming, as an unbroken movement into a real future, as a unified, all-embracing, and unconsummated process."[21] In itself, this vision of the present as historical, its meaning as yet undetermined, its orientation being to the future rather than the past, is also conventional, the usual account of what we call European "modernity."[22] But it will have unforeseen consequences.

For the "orientation to the future" which makes the world historical is not an empirical fact that novels merely register, but an ethical one, which changes everything for the subject. If we thought of novels as purely representational vehicles, then we might conclude that the historicism of novelistic narrative reflects its faithfulness to an endless history. Novels, however, embody temporality as historical and unfinished not in order to represent an external history, but to make an inner one possible. A world moving into the future constitutes an "unconsummated present" in which everything is up for grabs and the subject has no choice but to act. In Bakhtin's various accounts of the novel, therefore, the responsibility of the hero is in direct proportion to the historicity of his or her surrounding world. Only in a world that has been "set as a task [*zadan*]" can the subject construct a life for itself in a truly ethical spirit, for if everything is unfinished and its meaning dependent on the future, then the hero has no "alibi in being," that is, no dogmatically given facts or conventions to which it can turn to justify its actions. The novel must display a completely historical culture in which the future presses unceasingly upon the present not because time goes on and on, but because the inevitability of acting and of creating the future is what forces the subject to assume full responsibility for its life. Or, to put it differently, Bakhtin believed in Dostoevsky's claim to have invented a "realism in a higher sense." Novels are realistic less in Ian Watt's sense of their representing the physical appearance of an everyday world than because they can represent the human soul in a manner adequate to *its* reality. Were the novelistic hero to be represented as an individual, driven by self-interest and occasional acts of sympathy, he or she would be misrepresented, for the fact is that humans are fundamentally *I* and *others*. To represent the hero realistically is therefore to represent an *other*, a human being whose life can be narrated, whose boundaries and surroundings can be delineated, from outside, as it were, but whose own ceaseless striving has to be acknowledged and redeemed. Novels are themselves ethical acts—they "save" their heroes—and this makes them more, not less, realistic, insofar as the primary reality of human existence is the ethical reality I described above.

If the world as a whole has ethical significance, then its most realistic representation is one in which it exists not as a backdrop to, but as the substance of, ethical activity. In the ideal novel, therefore, nothing exists as ratified in itself and "the hero *becomes together with the world*; he reflects in himself the historical becoming of the world. . . . The issue here is precisely the development of a new person; the organizing force of the future is therefore extraordinarily great, and it is, of course, not a private-biographical future but a historical future."[23] The novel gives birth to a new kind of world in order to make possible a new kind of person, a responsible person. (In a 1961 letter, Bakhtin affirmed that the novel prepared the way for a "new *being* of the person."[24]) Within its bounds, the environment exists not as the dead hand of an inert world, but as something that the novelist forces to "speak." History, far from offering the subject an endless source of secular alibis, turns out to be an even sterner judge than the divine creator it has displaced. (In the words of Schiller's well-known claim, "Die Weltgeschichte ist das Weltgericht" [world history is the final court of judgment].)

Because judgment, in the end, will not go away, Bakhtin quite shrewdly regarded the modern vision of a secular world history as a reintegration, not a liquidation, of salvational energies and hopes. The question of the meaning of history did not go away when the gods tumbled; it simply changed its geometry, shifting from the vertical to the horizontal axis of existence. For the world as such to acquire meaning, the whole practice of medieval symbolism had to be abandoned. Before modernity,

> the addition of the otherworldly broke down and decomposed the real compactness of the world; it impeded the bringing together of the real world and real history into a unified, compact, and full whole. The otherworldly future, torn from the horizontal of earthly space and time, was raised up as an otherworldly vertical to the real flow of time, bleeding white the real future and earthly space as the arena of this real future, endowing everything with symbolic meaning, devaluing and rejecting everything that did not submit to symbolic interpretation.
>
> In the epoch of the Renaissance the "whole world" began to coalesce into a real and compact whole.[25]

When places become part of a determinate geographic reality ("part of *this* world") and events become part of an irreversible human history ("a moment which cannot be transferred in time"), then the world undergoes a qualitative change: "It coalesces, is embodied and filled up by the creative possibilities of further endless *real* becoming and development."[26]

Bakhtin rightly saw that every eschatology, or anticipation of the end of time, would devalue the ethical substance of the present, but he framed the alternative as a different kind of faith rather than as the skeptical refusal of faith: "Not faith (in the sense of a definite faith in Orthodoxy, in progress, in man, in revolution, etc.), but the *feeling of faith*, that is, an integral relation (of the whole person) to a higher and ultimate value."[27] This distinction, made in the course of discussing Dostoevsky, reflects an apparently continuing belief that the forward movement of history has to be grounded in an unredeemable anticipation of redemption. In the context of Bakhtin's philosophy of language, this faith appears as the immanent orientation of every utterance to what he called "a higher 'superaddressee' ('a third'), an absolutely just answering understanding,"[28] which, of course, never actually arrives. (One might describe this as a desecularized version of the "unavoidable idealization" that Habermas once called "the ideal speech situation."[29]) In the context of Bakhtin's theory of novelistic narrative, it means that subjects become responsible to the degree that they believe their history has a point.[30]

All very attractive, of course, and in large part convincing, even for atheists. Historical subjects demand not only material goods and certain abstract things like justice and dignity, but also a sense that their roles, desires, and acts add up to something coherent and meaningful. There is a fly in the ointment, however: the paradox that the more a subject acts with the faith that history as a whole has some meaning, the less able it is to make history. For if the question is whether human history in its entirety, which Bakhtin grandly called the "all-embracing whole," means anything, then we already know two things about the answer: first, only a subject who is in some sense *outside* that history can decide what it is worth (and we all know who that will be); and second, the answer will not really be a matter of judgment at all, but an act of divine benevolence, a redemption of all of history's mistakes as well as its successes that could not possibly be motivated by anything so banal as an argument. As I show elsewhere, both features stem from the fact that in Bakhtin's theories the self or subject per se is deemed incapable of narrating its own life story, requiring an *other* that can do it, to grasp its life as something with a plot—a beginning and an end, an environment and events, characters and projects.[31] For our purposes here, it will suffice to acknowledge that if all narrative depends upon an *other* beyond the self, then narrative has the status, as Bakhtin put it, of a "gift," an act of unmotivated love.[32] (At which point it may be worth recalling Averintsev's description of Bakhtin's position as always consisting "not of 'against' but of 'for,' not of argument or of rejection but of affirmation, in defense of the rights of the whole in the face of the unjustified pretensions of the part." Who could love history as a whole? Someone like Bakhtin.)

The price of that love is a responsibility without any excuses. The subject that hopes to have its own history affirmed must listen to its conscience rather than adhering to law or social convention. It has to act without reference to the requirements of law or custom, where responsibilities frequently have limits, for it knows that these are merely human conventions destined to pass away on the path of history. What inspired Bakhtin about the culture of laughter exemplified in carnival was the violence it did to formal roles and responsibilities, the way in which, from the larger perspective it enforced, each of these was revealed as a mere mask, a role that disguised the human being behind it. From the perspective of carnival, the Emperor has only clothes, all the world's a stage, and anyone who identifies too closely with his or her costume will be sorely disappointed when the play's over and the lights come up. Better to place your faith in the meaning of history as a whole than to identify yourself with merely earthly, historically finite roles and powers.

The problem, of course, is that the modern concept of history, on which Bakhtin relies in his praise of the novel, requires a modern concept of responsibility, and the latter entails not only acting out of a deeply felt sense of obligation, but acting autonomously. You cannot be accountable for your own actions until you have constituted them *as* your own, and this demands a prior narrativization of your life story, in which others are presented with your claim to be, as the saying goes, your own person. Habermas has reminded us of just what being a thoroughly modern individual involves: "Once the vertical axis of the prayer has tipped into the horizontal axis of interhuman communication, the individual can no longer redeem the emphatic claim to individuality solely through the reconstructive appropriation of his life history; now the positions taken by others decide whether this reconstruction succeeds."[33] Since Kant and Fichte, Habermas argues, individuality (the unique, irreplaceable personality) has not been a *property* of persons to be acknowledged from on high, but has been indissolubly tied to the act of self-constitution and the claim to the autonomy of an ego.[34] To be an individual, or a unique personality, means to be accountable, responsible, for one's own actions, and this self-accountability is a claim made in the first person within a community of other individuals. Although no one else can grant the continuity that comes from the desire to be autonomous, it rests upon a claim made to, and ratified by, others.

Which is to say that it depends upon whether one fulfills responsibilities made by human hands. The life story one composes in the glaring light of historical day will consist of obligations incurred and discharged, but these obligations will be made of the limited, finite temporal stuff that carnival throws to one side. Whether one has made history, and made it well or screwed it up, will be decided by others with reference to the humanly fashioned roles and responsibilities that define one's moral choices. While a life can be assessed from the point of view of its *absolute* responsibility toward others, this would be less a historical evaluation than one geared toward candidacy for sainthood. And if the ultimate court of authority is the sphere of human judgment, then the very condition of argument that Averintsev sought to displace returns with a jolt, since we do not agree either on people's responsibilities or on whether they have acted responsibly. A history that depends on fallible human judgment is a history with plenty of mistakes in it. "Life as utter error," Bakhtin wrote, "is the essential theme of the European novel."[35] True, insofar as in novels even the mistakes contribute to the meaning of the whole. But outside of novels the mistakes remain mistakes, and history as a whole remains unredeemable.

Historical origins entail historical limits as well: if the subject's ability to act responsibly, to accept or acknowledge its responsibility, depends upon an accountability recognized by others, then responsibility is an *achievement* rather something which any subject can accomplish, regardless of circumstances. In his earliest philosophy Bakhtin expressed the hope that subjects could be persuaded to acknowledge a responsibility which was, in a sense, theirs already, but his hope was based on the conviction that this was no more than the God-given possibility of every Christian soul—that this was what made it a Christian soul. But responsibility can *fail*, and not because a subject lacks the requisite devotion, but because the intersubjective community—more precisely, the distribution of authority and power within it—makes it impossible for that subject to act responsibly. If Bakhtin's subjects take no such risk, it is because he has stacked the deck in their favor by subtly conflating two senses of "responsibility." One can be responsible as a minimal condition for the existence of a self or ego, in the sense of recognizing the decisions one has to make as *one's own*, no matter what the external circumstances. However, if "historical development" implies a "hero who *becomes together with his world*," then it requires not only autonomous intentions but the power to fulfill them; otherwise, responsibility is as otherworldly and invisible, and as unlikely to make its mark in history, as the mythical activities it is meant to displace. Responsibility in the latter sense means not only making decisions, but taking part in those particular decisions that shape a historical world. Men make history, as the old adage goes, but not in circumstances of their own choosing. And indeed, those who make history often do so by making others make it for them.

If the point of being responsible is to seek salvation or redemption, then the degree to which one is "in effect" responsible does not matter. Before God, one is a unique individual, whose responsibility should transcend the particular positions or roles one occupies in a given social formation. But if we do not want to stake all on redemptive possibilities, then responsibility cannot be disentangled from the roles we play in an actual social world, roles or formal positions that determine the depth and limits of our responsibilities. It was, of course, precisely this legal/juridical concept of responsibility which Bakhtin sought to supplant.[36] He sought a responsibility "with no excuses," knowing that the legal/juridical concept set limits to what a subject could be held responsible *for*. Responsibilities that have limits set by human agreement, by law or custom, or a tacit recognition of roles, draw a line beyond which, if something goes wrong, it is really not your fault. (Thus, for example, the modern concept of negligence defines just when it is that you are responsible for the suffering of another and when it is that you are not, even though your actions may have directly led to the suffering in question.)

It may sound unchristian, but the modern concept of history, so important to Bakhtin's interpretation of the novel, includes the notion of suffering for which one is not responsible, however much one may regret it. But is this a recipe for political quietude, or the bad-faith insistence that if you do your job, it is no concern of yours what the consequences are?

The interest and value of Bakhtin's account of modern European culture is his insistence on a role-transcending responsibility, an ability to live both within and beyond the concrete obligations assigned to one by a particular, historically finite social order. Characteristically, Bakhtin found models for this role transcendence in three figures from early modern popular culture: the clown, the fool, and the rogue. These figures "can exploit any position in life only as a mask,"[37] which is to say that they occupy social roles in a new, peculiarly indeterminate fashion. On the one hand, they have no existence save that of the social role they mimic—they lack an inner self; on the other hand, they treat that role precisely as a role, something to be performed and thus held at a slight distance. Bakhtin did not regard this role-playing as mere play, but as an idealized form of ethical life and a model for the position that novelists should adopt.

For an equivalent to the role-playing of the clown or fool, I think we must look not to modern versions of carnival, as is the current fashion, but to the modern concept of politics. When human societies assumed responsibility for their history, they also assumed responsibility for their politics, that is, they acknowledged that the design of social orders was a matter of human invention, a "science of politics," and that anything wrong with them was due to poor judgment rather than Original Sin or corruption. Social orders, with their laws and customs, define responsibilities and obligations, and social orders that lead to unnecessary suffering can be redesigned. One's responsibility therefore transcends immediate obligations precisely to the extent that one is responsible for the social order as a whole. To put it simply: one transcends one's formal responsibilities not through religion but via politics.

Politics, however, was precisely the sphere in which Bakhtin had the least faith, since it was "not illuminated by truth."[38] By his own account, while 1917 raged around him, he sat reading in the library.[39] He preferred the myth of a position above such struggles and was happy to collude in the myth that both his own work and his own life transcended the sphere of "for and against," of mere historical argument, teaching by example rather than by contention. Bakhtin, it strikes me, was a very bad example, though one with some very good arguments. He can be forgiven for believing in a kind of history different from the one he lived through and for not caring much about the details of his personal history. But those who would elevate adaptation to circumstances to a model for life forget that it is we who, having evaluated the facts, decide when and when not to forgive. The person who forgives too much is not only ignorant of history, but dedicated to its eradication: he or she refuses the unforgiving responsibility of making judgments.

Notes

1 See "Razgovory s Bakhtinym," *Chelovek* 4 (1993): 141–54, esp. 141–42. All translations from Russian are my own, but in cases where quoted material can also be found in a published translation, it is cited as well.

2 S. S. Konkin first suggested this in the biography he coauthored with L. S. Konkina, *Mikhail Bakhtin: Stranitsy zhizni i tvorchestva* (Saransk, 1993); for further details, see also his "Pora zakryt' vopros o rodoslovnoi M. M. Bakhtina," *Dialog, Karnaval, Khronotop*, No. 2 (1994): 119–23; "Posleslovie k stat'e 'Pora zakryt' vopros o rodoslovnoi M. M. Bakhtina,'" *Dialog, Karnaval, Khronotop*, No. 3 (1994): 135–37; and "Esli obratit'sya k pervoistochnikam . . . (k rodoslovnoi M. M. Bakhtina)," in *The Seventh International Bakhtin Conference*, 2 vols. (Moscow, 1995), 2: 244–50.

3 See Francesca M. Wilson, "Biographical Information," in *Nicolas Bachtin: Lectures and Essays* (Birmingham, 1963). This was the source of the story in V. V. Kozhinov and S. Konkin, "Mikhail Mikhailovich Bakhtin—kratkii ocherk zhizni i deyatel'nosti," in *Problemy poetiki i istorii literatury: Sbornik statei*, ed. S. Konkin (Saransk, 1973), 5–15. For his (admirably open) discussion of his use of this source, see V. V. Kozhinov, "Kak pishut trudy, ili Proiskhozhdenie nesozdannogo avantiurnogo romana," *Dialog, Karnaval, Khronotop*, No. 1 (1992): 110–11. Katerina Clark and Michael Holquist, presumably also relying on Nikolai's biography as a source, presented the same account in *Mikhail Bakhtin* (Cambridge, MA, 1984), 16.

4 Quoted in N. A. Pan'kov, "Predislovie k zapozdavshemu 'Poslesloviyu . . .' S. S. Konkina," *Dialog, Karnaval, Khronotop*, No. 3 (1994): 130–34; quotation from 133.

5 Nikolai Pan'kov, in a typically shrewd response to Konkin, suggested that indications of Bakhtin's awareness that he was playing a game, which Duvakin mischievously pushed along, can be found in the latter's interview. Pan'kov also mentions the conviction among Bakhtin's friends of his aristocratic background (based on his bearing) and the possibility "that at a certain period in his life a substantial concept of the distance between a certain 'elite' and the mass 'mob' may have meant a great deal to him" (ibid.).

6 The exact dates of the family's movements and Bakhtin's secondary education are now the object of rather intense scrutiny. Pan'kov, on the basis of school records, has provided a hypothetical sketch of Mikhail's and Nikolai's schooling in "Zagadki rannego perioda (Yeshche neskol'ko shtrikhov k 'biografii Bakhtina')," *Dialog, Karnaval, Khronotop*, No. 1 (1993): 74–89.

7 Ibid., 80–86.

8 Ibid., 85.

9 "Razgovory s Bakhtinym," 150.

10 S. G. Bocharov, "Ob odnom razgovore i vokrug ego," *Novoe literaturnoe obozrenie*, No. 2

(1993): 70–89; quotation from 73; see also 79. See also the abridged translation of this article (without the Bulgakov and Dostoevsky quotations), "Conversations with Bakhtin," trans. Stephen Blackwell and Vadim Liapunov, *PMLA* 109 (1994): 1009–24.

11 So, for example, the following letter from Bakhtin to Kozhinov of 10 January 1961 (though published only a few years ago) is read against the grain by Bocharov ("Ob odnom razgovore," 76) as *support* for Bakhtin's authorship:

> The books *Formal Method* and *Marxism and the Philosophy of Language* are very well known to me. V. N. Vološinov and P. N. Medvedev were my dear friends; in the period of the creation of these books we worked in the closest creative contact. Even more, at the base of these books and my book on Dostoevsky there lies a *common* conception of language and the production of speech. In this respect V. V. Vinogradov [the source of the information for Kozhinov] is completely right. One should point out that the presence of a common conception and contact in work does not reduce the self-sufficiency and originality of any of these books. Regarding the other works of P. N. Medvedev and V. N. Vološinov, they lie on a different plane and do not reflect a common conception, and I did not participate in their creation in any way.

Bocharov interprets "common" conception and "different plane" as signals of differing authorship: a possible reading, but one which depends on a prior conviction or decision that the truth is to be found via a symbolic reading of the available evidence. The issue of authorship is thus inextricably bound up with a concept of truth attached to the person of Bakhtin himself, whose polemics with positivism are applied reflexively to the authorship question. Bocharov appeals to the inwardness of conviction against the surface meanings of text and proof, a contrast that neatly corresponds to the inwardness or separation which Bakhtin apparently maintained in relation to the "official" social and political world beyond him.

12 Sergei Averintsev, "Lichnost' i talant uchenogo," *Literaturnoe obozrenie*, No. 10 (1976): 58–61; quotation from 59.

13 No other explanation accounts for the curious imbalance one finds in the assessment of relative tragedy in the lives of these three intellectuals. Those inclined to represent Bakhtin as the tragic figure among them either forget or ignore the fact that he died in bed, while it was Medvedev who was shot shortly after having been arrested. On any ordinary estimation, one would expect the hero's laurels to fall to the latter. That they have not reflects no ill will or personal enmity, but, as it were, the conviction that Bakhtin's path was somehow both more proper and more difficult. As an intellectual whose freedom depended on a self-conscious distance from "results," he refused—or so we assume—to be guided by the expectation of earthly reward or social and political success (hence the myths, also recently disproven, of Bakhtin's indifference to the prospect of publication). By contrast Medvedev's and Vološinov's participation in public life and interest in Marxism (in however original or unorthodox a fashion) reflected a belief in the truth-value of the secular, which Bakhtin devotees cannot countenance.

14 M. M. Bakhtin, *Tvorchestvo Fransua Rable i narodnaya kul'tura srednevekov'ya i Renessansa* (Moscow, 1990 [1965]), 236; see also *Rabelais and His World*, trans. Hélène Iswolsky (Cambridge, MA, 1968), 213.

15 M. M. Bakhtin, "K voprosam samosoznaniya i samootsenki" (Toward Questions of Self-Consciousness and Self-Evaluation), in *Raboty 1940-kh–nachala 1960-kh godov* (Works from the 1940s to the Early 1960s), Vol. 5 of *Sobranie sochinenii v semi tomakh* (Collected Works in Seven Volumes), ed. S. G. Bocharov and L. A. Gogotishvili (Moscow, 1996), 72–79; quotation from 77.

16 M. M. Bakhtin, "K filosofii postupka," in *Filosofiya i sotsiologiya nauki i tekhniki* (Moscow, 1986), 80–160; quotation from 99. See also *Toward a Philosophy of the Act*, ed. Michael Holquist and Vadim Liapunov, trans. Vadim Liapunov (Austin, 1993), 23–24.

17 M. M. Bakhtin, "Problema obosnovannogo pokoya—doklad M. M. Bakhtina" (The Problem of Grounded Peace: A Lecture by M. M. Bakhtin), from "Lektsii i vystupleniya M. M. Bakhtina 1924–1925 gg. v zapisyakh L. V. Pumpyanskogo" (Lectures and Interventions by M. M. Bakhtin in 1924–25, from notes by L. V. Pumpyansky), ed. N. I. Nikolaev, in *M. M. Bakhtin kak filosof*, ed. L. A. Gogotishvili and P. S. Gurevich (Moscow, 1992), 221–52; quotation from 235.

18 Bakhtin, "K filosofii postupka," 112; see also *Philosophy of the Act*, 40.

19 Bakhtin, "K filosofii postupka," 122.

20 M. M. Bakhtin, "K stilistike romana" (Toward a Stylistics of the Novel), in Bocharov and Gogotishvili, eds., *Raboty 1940-kh–nachala 1960-kh*, 138–40; quotations from 138 and 139.

21 M. M. Bakhtin, "Epos i roman," in *Voprosy literatury i estetiki* (Moscow, 1975), 447–83; quotation from 473; see also "Epic and Novel," in *The Dialogic Imagination: Four Essays*, ed. Michael Holquist, trans. Caryl Emerson and Michael Holquist (Austin, 1981), 3–40, esp. 30.

22 The most acute account of the emergence of the modern concept of history is contained in the essays of Reinhardt Koselleck in *Futures Past: On the Semantics of Historical Time*, trans. Keith Tribe (Cambridge, MA, 1985).

23 M. M. Bakhtin, "Roman vospitaniya i ego znachenie v istorii realizma," in *Estetika slovesnogo tvorchestva*, 2d ed. (Moscow, 1986), 199–249; quotation from 214; see also "The *Bildungsroman* and Its Significance in the History of Realism" (Toward a Historical Typology of the Novel)" (1936–38), in *Speech Genres and Other Late Essays*, ed. Caryl Emerson and Michael Holquist, trans. Vern W. McGee (Austin, 1986), 10–59, esp. 23–24.

24 Letter to V. V. Kozhinov, 1 April 1961, in "Pis'ma M. M. Bakhtina," *Literaturnoe ucheba*, Nos. 5–6 (1992): 146–47.

25 Bakhtin, "Roman vospitaniya," 237; see also "The *Bildungsroman* and Its Significance," 43.

26 Bakhtin, "Roman vospitaniya," 245; see also "The *Bildungsroman* and Its Significance," 50.

27 M. M. Bakhtin, "1961 god. Zametki," in Bocharov and Gogotishvili, eds., *Raboty 1940-kh–nachala 1960-kh*, 329–60; quotation from 352; see also "Toward a Reworking of the Dostoevsky Book" (1961), in *Problems of Dostoevsky's Poetics*, ed. and trans. Caryl Emerson (Minneapolis, 1984), 283–302, esp. 294.

28 Bakhtin, "1961 god. Zametki," 337; see also "The Problem of the Text in Linguistics, Philology, and the Human Sciences," in Emerson and Holquist, eds., *Speech Genres*, 103–31, esp. 126.

29 Jürgen Habermas, *Legitimation Crisis*, trans. Thomas McCarthy (London, 1976 [1973]), 110. Perhaps entirely characteristically, some readers of Habermas persistently treated the "ideal speech situation" precisely as a mythical image of a possible real future, and then proceeded to denounce it as such. Although it is clear from the outset that Habermas has nothing like this in mind, he later conceded that his choice of words was a hostage to fortune; see "Discourse Ethics, Law and *Sittlichkeit*," in *Autonomy and Solidarity: Interviews with Jürgen Habermas*, ed. Peter Dews, rev. ed. (London, 1992 [1986]), 245–71, esp. 260.

30 Another way to sum up Bakhtin's position is to say that he still believed in the philosophy of history, insofar as he thought it necessary to explain why there *was* history. In this respect, the trilogy of articles by his close friend Matvei Kagan—"O lichnosti v sotsiologii" (On the Personality in Sociology [1918–19]), "Kak vozmozhna istoriya?" (How Is History Possible? [1919]), and "'O khode ostorii" (On the Course of History [1920])—were probably quite influential. The second of these was published in *Zapiski Orlovskogo gosudarstvennogo universiteta, seriya obshestvennykh nauk*, No. 1 (Orel, 1921): 137–92; all three are to be included in a forthcoming collection of Kagan's writings edited by Brian Poole.

31 See the "Narrative" chapter in my *Mikhail Bakhtin: An Aesthetic for Democracy* (Oxford: Oxford University Press, forthcoming).

32 See M. M. Bakhtin, "Avtor i geroi v esteticheskoi deyatel'nosti," in *Estetika slovesnogo tvorchestva*, 9–191, esp. 95; see also *Author and Hero in Aesthetic Activity*, in *Art and Answerability: Early Philosophical Essays*, ed. Michael Holquist and Vadim Liapunov, trans. Vadim Liapunov (Austin, 1990), 4–256, esp. 100.

33 Jürgen Habermas, "Individuation through Socialization: On George Herbert Mead's Theory of Subjectivity," in *Postmetaphysical Thinking: Philosophical Essays*, trans. William Mark Hohengarten (Cambridge, 1992 [1988]), 149–204; quotation from 167.

34 Ibid., 158–70.

35 M. M. Bakhtin, "K voprosam teorii romana," in Bocharov and Gogotishvili, eds., *Raboty 1940-kh–nachala 1960-kh*, 48–49; quotation from 48.

36 See Nikolaev, ed., "Lektsii i vystuplenii," 226–27.

37 M. M. Bakhtin, "Formy vremeni i khronotopa v romane," in *Voprosy literatury i estetiki*, 234–407; quotation from 309; see also "Forms of Time and of the Chronotope in the Novel: Notes toward a Historical Poetics" (1937–38), in Holquist, ed., *Dialogic Imagination*, 84–258, esp. 159.

38 Quoted in Bocharov, "Ob odnom razgovore," 82.

39 "Razgovory s Bakhtinym," 60.

Galin Tihanov

Vološinov, Ideology, and Language: The Birth of Marxist Sociology from the Spirit of *Lebensphilosophie*

Valentin Vološinov's and Mikhail Bakhtin's views of ideology and language in the late 1920s, articulated in their major work, *Marxism and the Philosophy of Language*, enable us to "place" the concept of ideology in the dialogue between Russian Marxism and other philosophical schools, mainly *Lebensphilosophie* (philosophy-of-life).[1] While the peculiar position of Vološinov in the Marxist debates on ideology has clearly been pointed out by several scholars,[2] little has been done to explore the roots of his ideas. As I argue here, Vološinov's (and Bakhtin's) writings on ideology and language figured in a complex effort to reformulate and translate ideas from *Lebensphilosophie* and neo-Kantian philosophy into the language of Marxism so that they could become instrumental in its sociological project. In reading the Bakhtin of the second half of the 1920s as alternatively a philosophy-of-life, neo-Kantian, or Marxist thinker, we fail to do justice to his organic, if temporarily limited (in the case of his dealings with Marxism), participation in all three traditions. Stimulated by his communication with Vološinov, Bakhtin's participation never amounted to full belonging, and his pre-

The *South Atlantic Quarterly* 97:3/4, Summer/Fall 1998.

sumed originality in the late 1920s should be traced to his ability to subject those three approaches to a mutually challenging examination. From this point of view, it would be as unsupportable to claim that Marxism was for Bakhtin merely rhetoric under which his allegedly heretical thoughts could remain hidden as it would be to consider him a consistent Marxist theorist. The history of ideas offers more stories of continuity and mixture than of radical breaks, neat divisions, and innocent conceptions. Vološinov and Bakhtin's book would seem to be a strong case in point: their writings on ideology and language reveal, beneath the Marxist sociological project, fascinating palimpsests of *Lebensphilosophie* and neo-Kantianism.

The endeavor to bring Kantianism and Marxism together has been a significant element of Russian intellectual life ever since the latter half of the nineteenth century. By 1909–10, S. L. Frank, himself suspicious of the value of these efforts, had nevertheless affirmed the question of their relationship as a traditional philosophical and social concern in Russia.[3] By the time Vološinov and Bakhtin undertook their work on ideology and language, such neo-Kantian or philosophy-of-life thinkers as Hermann Cohen, Georg Simmel, and Ernst Cassirer were well-known in the Bakhtin Circle to M. I. Kagan, L. V. Pumpyansky, and Vološinov and Bakhtin themselves, all of which tends to reinforce the argument for interpreting their views on ideology and language in the triple clef of Marxism, *Lebensphilosophie*, and neo-Kantianism.[4] Historically, *Lebensphilosophie* was not insulated from the ongoing debates in German philosophy, and it had recognizable points of intersection with neo-Kantianism. Despite all the differences and polemics between the two trends,[5] both were hostile to positivism and willing to admit that the source of value lay in the singularity of individual phenomena rather than in abstract general laws. The intellectual biography of Georg Simmel (who, as Thomas Willey has demonstrated, was informally associated with the Baden school[6]), including the fact that he made the neo-Kantian fact/value split the controversial premise of his own theory of culture, furnishes sufficient proof that these were two different yet not isolated trends in the eyes of those who were exposed to their impact.

As for where to place Vološinov's concept of ideology in the then existing Marxist paradigm, Raymond Williams summarizes three different conceptual versions of ideology in the Marxist tradition: "(1) a system of beliefs characteristic of a particular class or group; (2) a system of illusory beliefs—false ideas or false consciousness—which can be contrasted with true or scientific knowledge; (3) the general process of the production of meaning and ideas."[7] Terry Eagleton's more nuanced analysis of the concept also singles out, among others, the meanings pointed to by Williams.[8] Eagleton's and Williams's typologies overlap in the way they define points (1) and (3), but Eagleton is subtler in outlining the possible ramifications—and through them the essence—of ideology as captured in point (2). Despite their differences, these two typologies do offer a safe ground on which to describe the concept of ideology in early Soviet Marxism as favoring a combination of senses (1) and (3) and far less obsessed with sense (2) than the later official doctrine. (Even Lenin, in *What Is to Be Done?*, regards the ideology of the proletariat as undergoing "the general conditions of birth, development and consolidation of any ideology.") The general laws governing the rise and workings of any ideology are precisely what lies at the heart of the writings of Plekhanov, Bukharin, and Vološinov himself. While agreeing on the nature of ideology as a superstructural phenomenon, they were not unanimous on how ideology is connected with the other elements of the superstructure and with language (the two problems on which my discussion of Vološinov's ideas here is centered).

My starting point is Nikolai Bukharin's 1921 *Historical Materialism*, which, despite the fact that Vološinov never explicitly mentioned it, was one of the most influential works in postrevolutionary Russian Marxism. (In "Po tu storonu sotsial'nogo" Vološinov polemicizes with another work by Bukharin, his article "Enchmeniada," without, however, mentioning Bukharin's name.) While Bukharin remains predictable and orthodox in the way he splits society into base and superstructure, he does offer a truly intriguing picture of the internal divisions within the latter. The need to outline this division is anticipated in his rather broad definition of the superstructure: "We shall interpret the word 'superstructure' as meaning any type of social phenomenon erected on the economic basis: this will include, for instance, social psychology, the social–political order, with all its material parts (for example, cannons), the organization of persons (official hierarchy), as well as such phenomena as language and thought. The conception of the superstructure is therefore the widest possible conception."[9] Even without his own inference, it is not difficult to see Bukharin's definition as overly inclusive. Superstructure to him designates a vast field of human activities which can be shown to be as wide, vibrant, and fluctuating as culture is in the philosophy-of-life tradition, especially with

Simmel. Both superstructure and culture, because of their dynamic and all-embracing nature, seem necessarily to defy a more rigid definition. Against the background of these problems of determining what superstructure is, it comes as no surprise that the center of Bukharin's analysis is shifted toward questions of internal morphology: what cannot be defined as a whole should be approached and interpreted in terms of the elements which constitute it.

Bukharin distinguishes two major entities within the superstructure: social ideology and social psychology. This internal division, foreshadowed in Marx's *Eighteenth Brumaire of Louis Bonaparte*, was established by Plekhanov, whom Vološinov explicitly mentions in his discussion of the concept of social psychology.[10] In his 1908 *Fundamental Problems of Marxism*, Plekhanov, while complaining that Marxism is "still far from being always capable of discovering the causal link between the appearance of a given philosophical view and the economic situation of the period in question,"[11] already questions this possibility by arguing that the base and the different ideologies are bound not in a direct cause/effect relationship, but rather in one that is mediated by people's mentality, or, as he renders it, by "the psychology of the epoch." It is the properties of that mentality (psychology)—and not the base itself and its respective sociopolitical system—that are reflected by the various ideologies.[12] Although anticipating the important debates on how the superstructure is structured, Plekhanov remains primitively confined to the traditional Marxist idea that the "psychology of the epoch," the zeitgeist, is always to be understood as the psychology of a given class only. In the earlier "Materialist Conception of History," the tensions within Plekhanov's ideas of ideology are evinced more saliently: "What is known as ideologies is nothing but a multiform reflection in the minds of men of this single and indivisible history."[13] In a rather contradictory manner, Plekhanov reinforces the reflectionist view of ideology, while at the same time positing as the object of reflection the challenging whole of history at large. He does not confine himself to the base/superstructure dichotomy, in which the superstructure reflects the economic foundations of society, but tries to replace it with a notion of history that would hold together both the economic and the cultural aspects of social life.

Plekhanov's concept of ideology crystallized in the process of his appropriation of the work of Antonio Labriola, the French edition of whose *Essays on the Materialistic Conception of History* Plekhanov had reviewed in "The Materialist Conception of History."[14] With Labriola one can already discern the strategy of viewing history as an organic whole and of ascribing to social psychology a mediating function in the recognition of this whole: "Passing from the underlying economic structure to the picturesque whole of a given history, we need the aid of that complexus of notions and knowledge which may be called, for lack of a better term, social psychology." Labriola insists on describing social psychology as the locus in which the basic experience of the social conditions of human life is being restructured into different ideologies: "Before attempting to reduce secondary products (for example, art and religion) to the social conditions which they idealize, one must first acquire a long experience of specified social psychology, in which the transformation is realized." Again, we are confronted here with the vacillations typical of the still productive and unorthodox forms of both Western and Russian Marxism. The understanding of ideology is suspended between its realization as a secondary product and its power not simply to reflect, but also to idealize, as a product which produces. Being a painstaking method of deciphering the formation of ideology, historical materialism, according to Labriola, should nevertheless not be equated with "a particular case of a generic sociology" and should work to preserve its nature as a philosophy of history.[15]

By the time Bukharin developed his own project, Plekhanov's ideas of social psychology had already become classic and been subjected to a number of different uses serving different purposes.[16] Moreover, throughout the 1920s, despite all the new aspects introduced by Bukharin in the interpretation of superstructure, social psychology, and ideology, he seems to have abided in the shadow of Plekhanov's popularity. The latter's ideas, which were gradually gaining the shape of a dogma, had already been reduced by the late 1920s to the almost magic formula known then as *pyatichlenka* (a five-point formula), and his authority was often appealed to when a simplified picture of society as a whole was needed. The five elements of Plekhanov's formula were the means of production, the economic relations, the political order, the social psychology, and the various ideologies reflecting the peculiarities of that psychology. In the early 1930s, however, the climate of opinion changed, and Plekhanov's legacy acquired the stigma of a mechanistic account of society that was, moreover, intoxicated with Kantianism.[17]

Bukharin's advance over both Plekhanov and Labriola consisted in posing the relationship of the superstructure to the respective ideologies as a sociological problem (as witness the suggestive subtitle of his book: *A System of Sociology*). No longer committed to the understanding of ideology as the exclusive product of classes, Bukharin sought instead to grasp its existence as nurtured by a wider range of social formations. In addition, he strived for a more adequate and elaborate picture of the morphology of the superstructure, that is, of the differences between ideology and social psychology. Describing ideology as a "unified, coordinated system of thoughts," or of "feelings, sensations, forms," exemplified by science, art, religion, philosophy, or morality, Bukharin also noted that, because "we live in 'every-day' life," we constantly produce and encounter "a great mass of incoherent, non-coordinated material, by no means presenting an appearance of harmony." This is the material from which the realm of social psychology—"the non-systematized or but little systematized feelings, thoughts and moods found in the given society, class, group, profession, etc."—is constructed.[18] The difference between social psychology and ideology, contends Bukharin, lies "merely in their degree of systematization." He compares social psychology to "a sort of supply-chamber for ideology," or a "solution out of which ideology is crystallized." Ideology, Bukharin goes on to say, "systematizes that which has hitherto been not systematized, *i.e.*, the social psychology." Now, the status of the different ideologies proper is ambiguous, for they amount to "*a coagulated social psychology*," which clearly suggests that they are regarded as hierarchically higher and more elaborated phenomena.[19] On the other hand, however, ideology is static and petrified, relying on social psychology to provide it with material and incentives for change. Thus ideology is at once superior and inferior to social psychology, both erected above it and grounded or dependent on it. The binomial partitioning of the superstructure into one region of constant change and flux and another which cannot move and subsist on its own closely follows (Simmel's) philosophy-of-life visions of culture, where the forces of organic growth, creation, and shift are in conflict with the forces of solidification and consolidation.

Vološinov retains this division, yet he also departs from it on two significant points. First of all, he chooses to speak not of "social psychology" but of "behavioral ideology." This is an unambiguous insistence on the essentially common nature of ideology proper and "behavioral ideology" as components of the superstructure. The idea of their unity goes back to

Vološinov's *Freudianism* of 1927, where he emphatically claims that "the haziest content of consciousness of the primitive savage and the most sophisticated cultural monument are only extreme links in the single chain of ideological creativity."[20] Unfortunately, "behavioral ideology" does not adequately render the Russian *zhiznennaia ideologia* ("life-ideology") and blurs the considerable impact of Simmel's *Lebensphilosophie* on Vološinov's views.[21] The way he defines "life-ideology" (or "behavioral ideology" here) heavily stresses the vigor and mobility of life, just as in Bukharin:

> To distinguish it from the established systems of ideology—the systems of art, ethics, law, etc.—we shall use the term *behavioral ideology* for the whole aggregate of life experiences and the outward expressions directly connected with it. Behavioral ideology is that atmosphere of unsystematized and unfixed inner and outer speech which endows our every instance of behavior and action and our every "conscious" state with meaning. Considering the sociological nature of the structure of expression and experience, we may say that behavioral ideology in our conception corresponds basically to what is termed "social psychology" in Marxist literature.[22]

A comparison with the Russian text would single out some vital nuances relevant to the philosophy-of-life subtext of Vološinov's argument. The original *stikhia* (rendered as "atmosphere") conveys the philosophy-of-life understanding of being as an undifferentiated and unstoppable process evolving in more than one direction. Moreover, in rendering *postupok*—a notion central to neo-Kantian ethics and a key concept (*filosofiia postupka*) in Bakhtin's early "Toward a Philosophy of the Act"—as "instance of behavior," the translation unduly emphasizes the psychophysiological dimensions of the act rather than its ethical coloration and value.

By speaking of "life-ideology," Vološinov not only underlines the common nature of ideology and of what Bukharin and Plekhanov call "social psychology," but also makes a much stronger case for their mutual dependence. While Bukharin regards them as exhibiting a one-way connection ("a change in the social psychology will . . . result in a corresponding change in the social ideology"[23]), Vološinov envisages the two as necessarily interacting. The firmly structured ideological modes of expression (science, art, religion, etc.) exert "a powerful, reverse influence on experience" (*perezhivanie*); they begin "to tie inner life together, giving it more definite and lasting expression," even setting the tone for life-ideology.[24] This statement, again, concedes that ideology proper should be considered as occupying a higher hierarchical position than life-ideology. Yet, as we shall see, Vološinov does not fail to point out that this is only one side of the coin and thus argues for the ambiguity of ideology proper. What is of the greatest importance, however, is the fact that Vološinov takes further and disambiguates Bukharin's occasional hints that ideology proper does not emerge from the economic base. In a bold and defiant move that distances him from the prevailing Marxist tenets, Vološinov sees it instead as born from the womb of just another type of ideology and governed by it all along. It was Vološinov's polemic with Freudianism that, together with Plekhanov's and Bukharin's work, made him alert to everyday life as the initial source of ideological meanings which are then reshaped and structurally upgraded to products of ideology proper.[25]

Vološinov's second significant departure from Bukharin's model consists in the different place he assigns to language. For Bukharin, language is unequivocally an element of the superstructure,[26] as is thought, a category that remains obscure and so broad as to appear stripped of any real meaning. Both thought and language create problems for Bukharin; since everything can be said to be a manifestation of them, their definition as specific elements of the superstructure becomes suspect. Hence the inconsistency in Bukharin's views of the evolution of language: "If, as a result of enhanced productive forces, a huge and complicated ideological superstructure has been erected, language will of course embrace this superstructure also."[27] Language is shown here to be not only an element of the superstructure, it is at the same time a modus/locus operandi of the superstructure as a whole.

The same difficulty faces Vološinov. His project, not unlike Bukharin's, is sociological: he derives language from the primordial fact of social intercourse. First, "*social intercourse is generated* (stemming from the basis); *in it verbal communication and interaction are generated; and in the latter, forms of speech performances are generated; finally, this generative process is reflected in the change of language forms.*"[28] This statement could be considered the one major concession made by Vološinov to the vulgar Marxist view of language; note that social intercourse is for him pre-linguistic (occurring prior to, and outside, language). Unlike Bukharin, however, Vološinov never identifies language as an element of the superstructure or of ideology, since language partakes of ideologies without being an element of any particular ideology. It is, Vološinov believes, "neutral with respect to any specific ideological function. It can carry out ideological functions of *any* kind—scientific, aesthetic, ethical, religious." The vague idea that language could possibly reconcile the status of an element of ideology with the status of an indispensable condition for the existence of ideology is couched in a self-contradictory formulation: "*The word functions as an essential ingredient accompanying all ideological creativity whatsoever.*"[29] The original Russian formulation—"Slovo soprovozhdaet kak neobkhodimyi ingredient vse voobshche ideologicheskoe tvorchestvo"[30]—makes the contradiction even more palpable: language is meant to play only an accidental, accompanying role and to be at the same time a necessary element of all ideologies. His attempt to find a way out of this discrepancy leads Vološinov to credit language with the no less contradictory status of an active vehicle through which all ideological creativity is not simply carried out but also commented on—socially evaluated—and thus accomplished. Language becomes the milieu in which the interaction with all other sign systems proves possible and, moreover, inevitable: "All manifestations of ideological creativity—all other nonverbal signs—are bathed by, suspended in, and cannot be entirely segregated or divorced from the element of speech."[31] Having set out to cope with the difficulties arising from the attempt to locate language in the superstructure, Vološinov ends up anticipating a totally different solution to the problem; having laid bare the impasse created by the unduly sharp juxtaposition of base and superstructure, he gradually moves on to a different frame where language is theorized as a master code through which all other sign systems become mutually translatable.

What is of more interest to us here than the semiotic tendencies in Vološinov's work is his attitude toward *Lebensphilosophie* and neo-Kantianism. To begin with, the very "study of ideologies" (*nauka ob ideologiakh*) can be recognized as a pendant of, and materialist alternative to, the neo-Kantian "idealistic philosophy of culture."[32] To Vološinov, "the domain of ideology coincides with the domain of signs."[33] This is precisely a definition of ideology as broad as Bukharin's definition of the superstructure. The crucial difference is that whereas Bukharin highlights the superstructure against the background of the base, Vološinov chooses to contrast ideology—through the sign—to nature and only inconsistently to what Simmel calls "objective culture."

Simmel elaborates on the distinction between subjective and objective culture in his 1908 essay "On the Nature of Culture."[34] Objective culture for Simmel is the domain of artifacts which are meant to be instrumental in promoting the spiritual cultivation of the individual, of his/her subjective culture. Beginning with the neo-Kantian doctrine of the world as disintegrated and poised between a realm of facts and a realm of values (hence also the splitting of knowledge into *Naturwissenschaften* and *Geisteswissenschaften*), Simmel goes on to radicalize this doctrine, arguing that even within culture (the realm of values) there are two different worlds which, initially coexisting in peace and harmony, are doomed eventually to drift apart. Simmel's later studies of the conflicts of modern culture picture the process of growth and development as a constant struggle between the subjective culture of individuals and the objective culture of the artifacts that they themselves produce. At the root of this conflict lies the formative principle of objectification, which is absolutely indispensable for the rise and progress of human culture. The natural development of life, however, informed by the principle of objectification, necessarily endows cultural forms with an autonomous existence and transforms creative impulses into stiff and lifeless products: "It is the essential nature of life to transcend itself, to create from its own material what no longer qualifies as life."[35] While optimistic at times and seeing in this process a sign of the omnipotence of life,[36] Simmel remains more often than not wistful in the face of the increasing expansion of objective forms and artifacts to the detriment of organic life-contents. This is unfortunate, as Simmel perceives it, for it evinces a clear asymmetry: the subjective culture of the individual never ceases to be dependent on the objective culture of artifacts, while the domain of artifacts grows independent and over time even imposes itself on the subjective culture of the individual without any longer assisting its development. The problem which torments Simmel is whether the propitious work of the form-giving factors can be reconciled with the danger of its inevitably promoting the gradual domination of culture by ready-made and independent forms.

Vološinov's definition of ideology as "the world of signs" remains slightly ambiguous because it seems to accommodate both subjective and objective culture: "Any item of nature, technology, or consumption can become a sign, acquiring in the process a meaning that goes beyond its given particularity."[37] It is quite revealing, however, that Vološinov, unlike Bukharin, speaks of "ideological creativity" and not simply of "ideological production." It is "creativity" precisely that conveys the originality and the redeeming character of ideology proper as subjective culture, in contrast to its traditional reflectionist understanding in Marxism. That "ideological creativity" is conceptually opposed to ideology viewed as false consciousness could be inferred from its capacity to accommodate religion on an equal footing with art and science.[38]

The differences between subjective and objective culture, which are somewhat blurred in Vološinov's definition of ideology as an indiscriminate world of signs, are resolutely restored and fortified by stressing the importance of "life-ideology" for the products of ideology proper. The works of all fields of ideological creativity must prove their right to exist by being subjected to the test of different social groups at different times in their everyday life. The very idea of transferring elements from the world of ideology proper back into the organic world of everyday life-ideology is strongly reminiscent of Simmel's drive to protect subjective culture from the encroachments of objective culture by trying to impute to the latter a renewed commitment to the organic characteristics and demands of the former. Bukharin, whose *Historical Materialism* is scattered with (positive) references to Simmel, confronted the issue of the necessary "translatability" between the spheres of life-ideology and ideology proper earlier than Vološinov. But Bukharin remained blissfully nonchalant vis-à-vis Simmel's awareness of the problems such a transition entails. While he admitted that ideology proper is "*crystallized or congealed in things which are quite material*," this seemed to him not a perilous lapse into the province of artifacts, but rather a cause for celebration because such artifacts enable us "to judge the psychology and ideology of their contemporaries with precision."[39]

For Vološinov, however, the products of ideology proper, contrary to the undefinable stream of everyday life-ideology, were not immune to the danger of ceasing to exist as phenomena of subjective culture. If we now recall Bukharin's views of social psychology, we will be able to appreciate yet another aspect of Vološinov's advance on him: Vološinov recognized that outside the element (*stikhia*) of life-ideology the already formalized products of ideology proper would be dead. For Bukharin, social psychology was active only prior to ideology's crystallization of its scattered impulses, while Vološinov saw life-ideology as coming back on stage after the products of ideology are a fact to endow them with life. Indeed, the creation of ideological forms cannot be accomplished before they have reestablished their connection to life-ideology. This move in Vološinov's argumentation opens up a totally new perspective: the flexible, bilateral contact between the different forms of everyday experience and of ideology proper is fully realized only in the reception of the works of ideology proper by the social milieu set by life-ideology. Because life-ideology alone (thanks to its versatile nature and immediate proximity to the base) "draws the work into some particular social situation . . . in each period of its historical existence, a work must enter into close association with the changing behavioral ideology, become permeated with it, and draw new sustenance from it. Only to the degree that a work can enter into that kind of integral, organic association with the behavioral ideology of a given period is it viable for that period (and of course, for a given social group)."[40] It is clear to Vološinov that the products of ideological activity cannot be born "*outside objectification, outside embodiment in some particular material,*" but it is equally clear to him that absent their connection with life-ideology these products would cease to exist or "to be experienced as something ideologically meaningful."[41] They would remain dead monuments of civilization if they were not reintroduced into the formless flux of life.[42]

That this "perception, for which alone any ideological piece of work can and does exist,"[43] is communicable only in the language of life-ideology (i.e., in the language of organic, still unformed and unorganized human experience) creates a problem with Vološinov's idea. Obviously, it precludes any possibility of one product of ideology proper (e.g., art) being evaluated by means of the highly organized discourse of another (e.g., science). (The fear that judgments about art made in the terms of scholarly discourse will inevitably end up judging art by criteria that are external to it can be traced to Simmel's belief that, as different cultural forms gradually claim and attain complete independence, they should be thought of as incommensurable.) In deliberately placing the entire process of evaluation in the field of life-ideology, Vološinov seems to be suggesting that the creation of culture is a self-sufficient activity which proceeds only within the limits, and between the different levels, of the superstructure. Hence the creative impulses originating in life-ideology are shaped by the steadfast forms of ideology proper, which in turn, far from petrifying into lifeless products, are endowed with genuine existence through the evaluative reception taking place in the everyday manifestations of life-ideology.

How is this circular exchange possible, and to what is the miracle of self-sufficiency bestowed upon ideology to be ascribed? For Vološinov and Bakhtin, the implicit solution to the neo-Kantian dilemma of fact versus value and culture versus civilization becomes language. It is to language that they look to provide the glue that can bond the different levels of the superstructure together, for language never ossifies and never ceases to move within and between the social groups which employ it. Never fully detached from its possible materializations, language is never fully embodied in them either. There is always some unrealizable potential to language that saves it from petrification and exhaustion, and this makes language the great redeemer which can objectify our creative impulses without ever deadening them. It stabilizes and brings to fruition a writer's ideas in a literary work, but then conveys those ideas to a living world of everyday reception and thereby destabilizes them, shattering in a wholesome way the work's finishedness and abstractness as fact and clearing a path for its varied accomplishment as value through its numerous instances of social appropriation and evaluation. In order to be able to shuttle continually between the realm of forms and the realm of life, between life-ideology and ideology proper, language must preserve its freedom to partake of all ideologies proper without identifying itself with any one ideology in particular. Vološinov formulates this mandate in terms of a law: "*Linguistic creativity*" (*tvorchestvo yazyka*) "*does not coincide with artistic creativity nor with any other type of specialized ideological creativity.*"[44]

Given this view of language as nonidentical with any of the elements of the superstructure, we are now better able to grasp the roots of the disagreement of Bakhtin and his colleagues with the Russian Formalists—roots that evidently went much deeper than purely literary disputes and into philosophical and sociological principles. What was at stake in the debate with the Formalists was not merely the question of form/content precedence, as has often been asserted. The true apple of discord was the nature of language as a social phenomenon. Vološinov and Bakhtin refrained from identifying language and art (literature) not because they thought that the art of literature was not linguistically bound and determined, but because they believed the essence of language to rule out its identification with any one product of ideology proper. Their reasons for deploring the Formalists' identification of literature with a specific, prevailing function of language are impossible to understand outside the neo-Kantian approach to language and culture. In severing language from literature, they were undoubtedly following Cassirer, the first (1923) volume of whose *Philosophie der symbolischen Formen* deals with language and was known to Vološinov.[45] There, in contemplating the status of linguistics and opposing Croce's and Vossler's view that it should be subsumed under aesthetics as a science of expression, Cassirer concludes: "If language is to be singled out as a truly autonomous and original energy of the spirit, then it should be incorporated with the whole of these forms without ever coinciding with any of the already extant elements of that whole. So within the whole, language should be assigned a place in accordance with its specific nature and thus its autonomy should be secured, despite all systemic connectedness with logic and aesthetics."[46] Vološinov was clearly attempting to modify Cassirer's views and to translate them into Marxist parlance. Language, though not identifiable with any branch of ideology, is replete with ideological meaning, which for Vološinov (here departing resolutely from Cassirer) is socially produced and grounded in the specific power of language, thanks to its mobile position, to *refract* reality. It is important to note that endowing language (and hence literature) with the power to refract, not merely to reflect, reality signifies a major departure from the prevailing Marxist view of that time, in which language and the superstructure were afforded a largely passive status in society.

We find the refraction doctrine clearly formulated as early as 1928 in Medvedev and Bakhtin's book on the Formalists. Still inconsistently espousing their own innovation, however, they contend that literature, like any other ideology, both refracts and reflects the world, and they do not seem to see any irreconcilability between these two essentially different acts.[47] On the contrary, Medvedev and Bakhtin seem to be endowing language and its products with a twofold power to provide both an *objective reflection* and a socially and class-determined *subjective refraction* of reality. Then, in the slightly later *Marxism and the Philosophy of Language*, we find a predominant, if not exclusive, emphasis on refraction that evinces a determination to advance a broader sociological approach to language and art.[48]

If language renders any superstructural component equally capable of refracting the existing reality, then there is also a master component—literature—which refracts the refractions of all other ideological spheres.[49] It is of particular importance to recognize the neo-Kantian tenor behind this proposition. Medvedev and Bakhtin specifically identify Hermann Cohen's aesthetics as a source for this privileged status of art which they see embodied in literature: "Cohen understands 'the esthetic' [*das Ästhetische*] as a kind of superstructure over other ideologies, over the reality of cognition and action. Thus, reality enters art already cognized and ethically evaluated."[50] Although Medvedev and Bakhtin criticize Cohen for not paying attention to exactly how the worlds of ethics and cognition enter the world of art, they nevertheless remain committed to his general conclusions about the special relevance of art (literature) as a refractor of all other ideologies. Vološinov and Bakhtin's arguments in *Marxism and the Philosophy of Language* can thus be seen as evolving in two steps: first, in a forceful and nontraditional way, they grant all ideologies the power to refract rather than reflect reality; second, by seeing in the verbal art of literature the master ideology which refracts all other ideologies, they seem to fall back on a neo-Kantian philosophical framework for discussing art. One could even argue that, despite all their disagreements, the Bakhtin Circle and the Formalists finally come to endorse the same conclusion: literature is not just one art among others, but is to be celebrated as a model on which all other aesthetic appropriations of reality can be based and interpreted. The Formalists drew their arguments from an anticipatory glorification of language as a universal semiotic pattern (master code); the Bakhtin Circle, while not entirely averse to this line of thought, reshaped it by foregrounding a powerful combination of neo-Kantian and Marxist reasoning about art as superideology (master refractor).

It is essential to recognize that for Vološinov language is not only the mechanism by which all ideology is produced and stratified, but also the site of all developments crucial to social change. Like *Marxism and the Philosophy of Language*, his *Freudianism* emphasizes the process of transformation of the amorphous life-ideological elements into solid ideological forms (e.g., the rise of literary genres from everyday speech genres[51]). But *Freudianism* also stresses the subversive actions of life-ideology by which the existing ideology proper is ultimately destroyed. Ironically enough, on closer inspection Vološinov's reasoning proves to be modeled on the Freudian conscious/unconscious dichotomy, which he himself is quick to declare untenable. However, Vološinov then replaces Freud's binarism with that of an "official" and an "unofficial" conscious. The latter is located predominantly (but not exclusively) in the depths of life-ideology, while ideology proper is, predictably, the abode of the "official" conscious. The different aspects of language cover both the unofficial, but often free, work of life-ideology and the censored work of ideology proper. Thus, in a second move, Vološinov identifies life-ideology with "inner speech" and ideology proper with "outward speech," claiming that the former's unimpeded transition to the latter is directly dependent on the proximity between these divided forms of the conscious: "The wider and deeper the breach between the official and the unofficial conscious, the more difficult it becomes for motives of inner speech to turn into outward speech . . . wherein they might acquire formulation, clarity, and rigor."[52] As the Russian text implies, this is a desirable change, the obstacles to which are regrettable. The volatile contents of inner speech/life-ideology, refused the chance to enter the realm of articulation and stability, are assigned instead to the outcast who works to erode the established regime of ideological production from below: "At first, a motive of this sort will develop within a small social milieu and will depart into the underground—not the psychological underground of repressed complexes, but the salutary political underground. That is exactly how a *revolutionary ideology* in all spheres of culture comes about."[53]

The activist metaphor of the underground should not mislead us into interpreting Vološinov's texts in strictly Marxist terms.[54] When he asserts that "in the depths of behavioral ideology accumulate those contradictions which, once having reached a certain threshold, ultimately burst asunder the system of the official ideology,"[55] he is clearly drawing on Marx's explanation of the way new relations of production are substituted for the outdated ones when demanded by the growth of productive forces. The point, however, is that this extrapolation, ascribing superstructural changes to the stimulation/suppression of certain speech activities and to the conflict between fluctuating content and rigid forms taking place simultaneously and indiscriminately across the organic whole of life (an unmistakable philosophy-of-life motif), erases the distinction between primary base and derivative superstructure.[56] Vološinov's disclaimer that these changes can take place only when based on the economic interests of a whole social group[57] appears so remote from the rest of his argument that it scarcely succeeds in challenging the idea that the superstructure has its own self-sufficient mechanisms of development and modification. No less important is that this argument seems to work against Vološinov's case for exclusive scientific rationality by suggesting that as the product of the unofficial conscious—of its scattered, undifferentiated, and elusive forces—the rise of new ideological phenomena can never be fully explained in objective terms. His discourse thus effectively corroborates the apprehensions of early Western Marxism that the formation of ideologies would prove to be a "very complicated, often subtle, tortuous and not always legible" process.[58]

It seems that Vološinov's ambition to represent a gradual organic change starting in the base and moving through the lower strata of ideology up to its stabilized forms yielded a result beyond his own expectations. His power as a Marxist sociologist can be seen in his innovative identification of ideology with culture at large and, more specifically, with the processes of signification, which he believed to be the superstructure's principal mode of existence and operation. Even more importantly, recognizing the role of language and signification in human labor strongly relativized the base/superstructure dichotomy and thus deconstructed the classic notion of superstructure. Asserting that signs, and hence signification, have a material nature was not enough to restore the balance. Vološinov ended up reducing culture to a single—ideal—mode of existence and ignoring those aspects that rest on practices entailing explicit domination (politics, law, etc.). This choice made Vološinov's construction implicitly capable of accounting only for those social phenomena which did not contradict his stipulation that language had a conspicuous and autonomous role in the formation of social life. Thus, while avoiding a Formalist position on literature, Vološinov pursued a language-centered type of theorizing in the field of social thought.

In synthesizing philosophy-of-life and Marxist traditions of thought, Vološinov and Bakhtin identified two different strata within the superstructure—life-ideology and ideology proper—and the substantial differences between them. But they also insisted on the essential unity of those strata, on their being bound together by the workings of language (Cassirer's neo-Kantian understanding of language being decisive here). Given the ambivalent picture they drew of the relations between life-ideology and ideology proper (official ideology), it is now possible to see why over time Bakhtin became so preoccupied with celebrating the power of noncanonical culture to create works of art that could evade the relentless grip of form and rigidity (the novel) and with extolling the vigor of life-ideology in popular culture (carnival). His 1930s essays on the novel and his *Rabelais* were not a departure from but an organic continuation of the Bakhtin

Circle's 1920s work on ideology and language, which was in turn a continuation of his early writings on artistic creativity.[59]

Thus we may argue that what links the seemingly disparate writings of the early, mature, and late Bakhtin is the philosophy-of-life concern with the interrelationship of life and culture (forms). In his early essay on the author and hero, Bakhtin was already passionately declaring that "life tends to recoil and hide deep inside itself, tends to withdraw into its own inner infinitude, *is afraid of boundaries*, strives to dissolve them," and was trying to reconcile this insight with his view of "aesthetic culture" as "a culture of boundaries."[60] His attempts to argue for the existence of art as more than a mere philosophical paradox led him into an exploration of art's place in culture during the 1920s and of how artistic forms (e.g., the novel) could appropriate life, without violating its versatile and dynamic nature, during the 1930s. The sociological project of the late 1920s, which took shape in an intensive affiliation and critical dialogue with Marxism, did not cancel out the neo-Kantian ground of Bakhtin's and Vološinov's philosophizing. In addition to preserving it, Vološinov and Bakhtin also transformed the basic categories and propositions of *Lebensphilosophie* so that these could broaden the horizons of their own sociological project.

Notes

1 I leave aside the problems of authorship here. The present state of the discussion clearly suggests that *Marxism and the Philosophy of Language* (trans. Ladislav Matejka and I. R. Titunik [New York and London, 1973 {1929}]) was written by Vološinov and Bakhtin rather than by Vološinov/Bakhtin. While Bakhtin confirmed his participation in the creation of the book in a letter of 10 January 1961 to Vadim Kozhinov (*Moskva* 12 [1992]: 176), he refused to claim the copyright, so I shall use only Vološinov's name here. The same holds true (see the same letter to Kozhinov) for Medvedev and Bakhtin's *Formal Method in Literary Scholarship: A Critical Introduction to Sociological Poetics* (trans. Albert J. Wehrle [Baltimore and London, 1978 {1928}]).

2 See, among others, Raymond Williams, *Marxism and Literature* (Oxford, 1977), 70–71; and Samuel M. Weber, "The Intersection: Marxism and the Philosophy of Language," *diacritics* 15 (1985): 94–112, esp. 95–96.

3 S. L. Frank, *Filosofiia i zhizn': Etiudy i nabroski po filosofii kul'tury* (St. Petersburg, 1910), 348.

4 See, among other sources, N. Nikolaev, "Lektsii i vystupleniia M. M. Bakhtina 1924–1925 gg. v zapisyakh L. V. Pumpyanskogo," in *M. M. Bakhtin kak filosof*, ed. L. A. Gogotishvili and P. S. Gurevich (Moscow, 1992), 221–51; and Yu. M. Kagan, "O starykh bumagakh iz semeinogo arkhiva (M. M. Bakhtin i M. I. Kagan)," *Dialog, Karnaval, Khronotop*, No. 1

(1992): 60–88; see also, most recently, V. D. Duvakin, *Besedy V. D. Duvakina s M. M. Bakhtinym* (Moscow, 1996).

On the Bakhtin Circle and neo-Kantianism, see Katerina Clark and Michael Holquist, "The Influence of Kant in the Early Work of M. M. Bakhtin," in *Literary Theory and Criticism: Festschrift Presented to René Wellek in Honor of His Eightieth Birthday*, 2 vols., ed. Joseph Strelka (Bern and New York, 1984), 1: 299–313; Matthias Freise, *Michail Bachtins philosophische Ästhetik der Literatur* (Frankfurt a.M. and New York, 1993), 58–59 et passim; Brian Poole, "'Nazad k Kaganu': Marburgskaia shkola v Nevele i filosofia M. M. Bakhtina," *Dialog, Karnaval, Khronotop*, No. 1 (1995): 38–48; and "Rol' M. I. Kagana v stanovlenii filosofii M. M. Bakhtina (ot Germana Kagana k Maksu Sheleru)," in *Bakhtinskii sbornik*, Vol. 3, ed. V. Makhlin (Moscow, 1997), 162–81; Deborah J. Haynes, *Bakhtin and the Visual Arts* (Cambridge and New York, 1995), 37–44. While these publications pay considerable attention to Cohen (and to Th. Lipps), the crucial impact of Simmel remains largely unexplored. Exceptions are N. K. Bonetskaya's comments on the author and hero essay in *Bakhtinologia*, ed. K. G. Isupov (St. Petersburg, 1995), 239–87; and Yu. Davydov, "Tragedia kul'tury i otvetstvennost' individa (G. Zimmel' i M. Bakhtin)," *Voprosy literatury*, No. 4 (1997): 91–125.

5 The most important document of the neo-Kantian attack against *Lebensphilosophie* is Heinrich Rickert's *Die Philosophie des Lebens: Darstellung und Kritik der philosophischen Modeströmungen unserer Zeit* (Tübingen, 1920), where vestiges of the philosophy-of-life attitude are identified even in the thought of Husserl and Scheler (29–30), two thinkers of extreme importance to Bakhtin. On Vološinov's ambivalent attitude toward Rickert's book, see *Marxism*, 32 n. 10.

6 See Thomas E. Willey, *Back to Kant: The Revival of Kantianism in German Social and Historical Thought, 1860–1914* (Detroit, 1978), 168–69.

7 Williams, *Marxism and Literature*, 55.

8 See Terry Eagleton, *Ideology: An Introduction* (London and New York, 1991), 1–2.

9 Nikolai Bukharin, *Historical Materialism: A System of Sociology* (Ann Arbor, 1976 [1969]), 208.

10 "Upon the different forms of property, upon the social conditions of existence, rises an entire superstructure of distinct and peculiarly formed sentiments, illusions, modes of thought and views of life"; Karl Marx, *The Eighteenth Brumaire of Louis Bonaparte*, in Karl Marx and Frederick Engels, *Selected Works* (London, 1968), 116. Vološinov, *Marxism*, 19.

11 G. V. Plekhanov, *Fundamental Problems of Marxism*, trans. Julius Katzer (London, 1969), 78.

12 Ibid., 80. This idea can be recognized as early as 1897 in Plekhanov's article "The Materialist Conception of History" (ibid., 103–38, esp. 115).

13 Ibid., 138.

14 Antonio Labriola, *Essays on the Materialistic Conception of History*, trans. Charles H. Kerr (New York and London, 1966 [1896]).

15 Ibid., 111, 219–20, 156.

16 On the appropriations of these aspects of Plekhanov's thought in the literary debates of the 1920s, see Herman Ermolaev, *Soviet Literary Theories, 1917–1934: The Genesis of Socialist Realism* (Berkeley, 1963), 61–65.

17 See, for instance, the criticisms in O. Voitinskaya, "Plekhanov–Pereverzev–Shchukin," *Marksistko–Leninskoe Iskusstvoznanie*, No. 4 (1932): 105.

18 Bukharin, *Historical Materialism*, 208. That ideology proper (art, science, etc.) should be viewed as an organized form of the disorganized "living experience of the collective," and hence as different by virtue of its structure from that experience, can also be inferred from Aleksandr Bogdanov's works on proletarian culture, especially On the Artistic Legacy (1918) and The Paths of Proletarian Creativity (1920); see also A. Bogdanov, *O Proletarskoi kul'ture, 1904–1924* (Leningrad and Moscow, 1924), 148 and 197–99.

19 Bukharin, *Historical Materialism*, 208, 209, 215.

20 V. N. Vološinov, *Freudianism: A Critical Sketch*, trans. and ed. I. R. Titunik, in collaboration with Neal H. Bruss (Bloomington, 1987 [1976]), 87.

21 I shall therefore use "life-ideology" rather than "behavioral ideology" here. Vološinov's consistent use of "zhiznennaia ideologia" in *Marxism and the Philosophy of Language* can likewise be traced back to his book on Freud, where he terms it "zhiteiskaia ideologia"; see V. N. Vološinov, *Freidizm* (Moscow, 1993 [1927]), 87 and 88; cf. *Freudianism*, 88 ("behavioral ideology").

22 Vološinov, *Marxism*, 91. See also *Marksizm i filosofiia iazyka* (Moscow, 1993 [1929]): "Zhiznennaia ideologia—stikhia neuporyadochennoi i nezafiksirovannoi vnutrennei i vneshnei rechi, osmyslivaiushchei kazhdyi nash postupok, deistvie i kazhdoe nashe 'soznatel'noe' sostoianie" (100).

23 Bukharin, *Historical Materialism*, 216.

24 Vološinov, *Marxism*, 90, 91.

25 See Vološinov, *Freudianism*, 87–89.

26 See Bukharin, *Historical Materialism*, 203.

27 Ibid., 205.

28 Vološinov, *Marxism*, 96.

29 Ibid., 14, 15.

30 Vološinov, *Marksizm*, 19.

31 Vološinov, *Marxism*, 15. For a precursor of this contention, see his *Freudianism*, 88.

32 Vološinov, *Marxism*, 11, 12. The same term, again used disapprovingly, also frequently appears in the first chapter of Medvedev and Bakhtin's *Formal Method in Literary Scholarship* (e.g., 4).

33 Vološinov, *Marxism*, 10.

34 Georg Simmel, "Vom Wesen der Kultur," in *Georg Simmel Gesamtausgabe*, Vol. 8 (Frankfurt a.M., 1993), 363–73; see esp. 370–71.

35 Georg Simmel, *Fragmente und Aufsätze aus dem Nachlass und Veröffentlichungen der letzen Jahre* (Hildesheim, 1967 [1923]), 24.

36 See *The Sociology of Georg Simmel*, ed. and trans. Kurt H. Wolff (Glencoe, IL, 1950 [1908]), where Simmel describes this process in a still fairly dispassionate manner (more as a sociologist striving for objectivity than a philosopher of culture facing the inevitability of its "tragedy"), speaking of the "complete turnover from the determination of the forms by the materials of life to the determination of its materials by forms that have become supreme values" (42). By 1918, however, with his essay on "The Conflict in Modern Culture," Simmel has clearly recognized the tragic inevitability of the life/form

opposition: "Life can express itself and realize its freedom only through forms; yet forms must also necessarily suffocate life and obstruct freedom"; Georg Simmel, *On Individuality and Social Forms: Selected Writings*, ed. Donald N. Levine (Chicago, 1971), 375.

37 Vološinov, *Marxism*, 10.

38 Ibid., 9. Again, see Medvedev and Bakhtin, *The Formal Method in Literary Scholarship*, 3, where no unfavorable distinctions are made between religion and the other elements of ideology proper and where "ideological creativity" is likewise used throughout the first chapter. See also, incidentally, M. M. Bakhtin, *Problemy tvorchestva Dostoevskogo* (Moscow, 1994 [1929]), 56 et passim.

39 Bukharin, *Historical Materialism*, 270.

40 Vološinov, *Marxism*, 91. Cf. Bukharin, for whom social psychology, as part of the superstructure, is likewise an intermediate element between it and the base: "The ideology is the outgrowth of a specific psychology; the psychology of a specific economy; the economy of a specific stage of the productive forces" (*Historical Materialism*, 230).

41 Vološinov, *Marxism*, 90, 91.

42 Vološinov's examples of such dead objects are the cognitive idea, when it is disconnected from the process of a living, evaluative perception, and, under the same conditions, the "finished literary work [*zakonchennoe literaturnoe proizvedenie*]" (*Marksizm*, 100). I quote from—and translate—the Russian text here because "zakonchennoe literaturnoe proizvedenie" is inadequately rendered as "any literary work" in *Marxism* (91). This translation misses the subtle (and exemplarily neo-Kantian) distinction implied in Vološinov's choice of "zakonchennoe" over "zavershennoe" between the physical process of finishing and the social process of accomplishing a literary work, the latter being possible only through the work's reception and appropriation by society.

43 Vološinov, *Marxism*, 91.

44 Ibid., 98.

45 See Vološinov's personal file published by Nikolai Pan'kov in *Dialog, Karnaval, Khronotop*, No. 2 (1995): 70–99, esp. 75, where it becomes evident that Vološinov translated two portions of Cassirer's work; see also his explicit references to Cassirer in *Marxism*, 11 and 47.

46 Ernst Cassirer, *Die Sprache*, Part 1 of *Philosophie der symbolischen Formen* (Berlin, 1923), 121; my translation. Cassirer's use of "energy" reveals the continuity between his and Humboldt's views of language. For Vološinov's discussion of Humboldt's ideas and for his criticism of Croce and Vossler (which follows Cassirer's), see *Marxism*, 48–49 and 50–52, respectively.

47 See Medvedev and Bakhtin, *The Formal Method in Literary Scholarship*, 16.

48 See Vološinov, *Marxism*, 15.

49 See Medvedev and Bakhtin, *The Formal Method in Literary Scholarship*, 16.

50 Ibid., 24.

51 See Vološinov, *Freudianism*, 88: "An exclamation of joy or grief is a primitive lyric composition [*proizvedenie*]."

52 Ibid., 89; ". . . chtoby v nei oformit'sya, uiasnit'sya i okrepnut' " (*Freidizm*, 89).

53 Vološinov, *Freudianism*, 90.

54 In the first Russian book-length study of the development of psychoanalysis in Russia, Vološinov's *Freidizm* is discussed (against all existing evidence) as Bakhtin's work, in

which is seen, rather one-sidedly and without sufficient arguments, the grim ideal of a totalitarian state that does not allow for any difference between official ideology and life-ideology and promotes the complete transparency of the unconscious; see Alexander Etkind, *Eros nevozmozhnogo: Istoriia psikhoanaliza v Rossii* (Moscow, 1994), 317. This account should not be surprising, given the lack of serious interpretations of *Freudianism.* Two notable exceptions are G. Pirog, "The Bakhtin Circle's Freud: From Positivism to Hermeneutics," *Poetics Today* 8 (1987): 591–610; and C. Emerson, "Freud and Bakhtin's Dostoevsky: Is There a Bakhtinian Freud without Voloshinov?," *Wiener Slawistischer Almanach* 27 (1991): 33–44, neither of which, however, foregrounds or investigates the aspects of interest to us here.

55 Vološinov, *Freudianism*, 88.

56 The way Vološinov suggests explaining the transformations of ideology is rather indicative of Simmel's impact on him. In the latter half of his career Simmel himself believed that the ubiquitous principle of struggle between life-contents and forms could indeed be translated into Marxist diction and employed to elucidate the regularities behind changes in the relations of production. For a comment on this idea, see Guy Oakes's introduction to Georg Simmel, *Essays on Interpretation in Social Science*, ed. and trans. Guy Oakes (Manchester, 1980), 34–35.

57 See Vološinov, *Freudianism*, 90.

58 Labriola, *Essays on the Materialistic Conception of History*, 152.

59 The failure to recognize this aspect of the continuity of Bakhtin's work is particularly palpable in the otherwise brilliant analysis of his early texts in N. K. Bonetskaya's essay on Bakhtin's "aesthetic as a logic of form" (in Isupov, ed., *Bakhtinologia*, 51–60). The trouble seems to lie in Bonetskaya's attempt to accommodate *Rabelais* in her observations. First, she is reluctant to admit that in the late 1920s the Bakhtin Circle produced work that was different in some respects and similar in others to the Dostoevsky book and the essays on the philosophy of the act, the author and hero, and form, material, and content. Second, she is equally disinclined to pay attention to the 1930s texts on the theory of the novel, despite the fact that it was precisely in those texts from the 1920s and 1930s that Bakhtin's ideas underwent a transformation, radically changing direction (but not losing their continuity with his earlier work). Bonetskaya posits a direct transition from *Dostoevsky* to *Rabelais* only to suggest that the latter is a less worthy book. Like many commentators on Bakhtin, she sees *Rabelais* and its concept of carnival as indicative of "deteriorated dialogue" (51) and betrayed humanist harmony, hence her struggle to find a place for *Rabelais* in Bakhtin's corpus without denting his otherwise decorous image. The dilemma of the two Bakhtins (the pre-1930s Bakhtin and the Bakhtin of *Rabelais*) is a false one, and perhaps it is high time to abandon it, especially if we are to understand Bakhtin's ideas in all their complexity and contradictory continuity. Bonetskaya's approach to *Rabelais* is even more surprising given her significant contribution to our knowledge of Bakhtin's great indebtedness to neo-Kantianism. In many respects *Rabelais* is no exception to this prevailing philosophical orientation of Bakhtin's. Bonetskaya simplifies things from the very outset of her article by claiming that with *Rabelais* Marxism supplanted an orientation toward neo-Kantianism in Bakhtin's work. But Marxism neither supplanted nor abolished Bakhtin's neo-Kantianism, but

only refigured it as a palimpsest which remains legible and active beneath the surface of his texts. With this in mind, we should try to reformulate the relationship of *Rabelais* to the rest of Bakhtin's oeuvre in new and different terms. His work has a unity, but it is not, as Bonetskaya is inclined to believe, a system; it is, rather, a flowing continuum with an underlying stability (but not fixedness) of philosophical assumptions.

For another well-supported critique of Bonetskaya's essay, along with an astute overview of recent Russian work on *Rabelais* and carnival, see David Shepherd, "'Communicating with Other Worlds': Contrasting Views of Carnival in Recent Russian and Western Work on Bakhtin," *Le Bulletin Bakhtine/The Bakhtin Newsletter* 5 (1996): 143–60, esp. 146–47.

60 M. M. Bakhtin, *Author and Hero in Aesthetic Activity*, in *Art and Answerability: Early Philosophical Essays*, ed. Michael Holquist and Vadim Liapunov, trans. Vadim Liapunov (Austin, 1990), 4–256; quotation from 203.

Robert F. Barsky

Bakhtin as Anarchist? Language, Law, and Creative Impulses in the Work of Mikhail Bakhtin and Rudolf Rocker

The various directions toward which Bakhtin studies are presently moving suggests that whatever the differences from one scholar to another, there remains a nagging question in much Bakhtinian work: What *else* can be done with Bakhtin? This is not, or should not be, a purely academic concern; indeed, it may be because Bakhtin's work is so obviously applicable to concerns beyond tenure-article production that it is so frequently asked. My suggestion would be to take him at his radical word and bring his ideas to bear upon this crucial moment in the inglorious history of the twentieth century. Whatever claims made to the contrary by increasingly self-satisfied corporate elites whose wealth has been growing by leaps and bounds even as the well-being of the majority throughout the world continues to decline, we are in desperate need of useful political alternatives and the ways of thinking thereabout that Bakhtin could offer. This is not to say that we ought to straitjacket theoretical works with undue political responsibilities; but Bakhtin's corpus, read in a properly historical perspective, contains political ideals whose impact could reach far beyond the histori-

The *South Atlantic Quarterly* 97:3/4, Summer/Fall 1998.

cal circumstances under which his works were written. "Ideals" should not be taken to suggest that Bakhtin's work is "utopian," if by this we mean politically irrelevant because unrealizable in the real world; indeed, I find in most of his work a rather consistent "political" theme which is very close to the pragmatic approach to society espoused by Pierre-Joseph Proudhon and, moreover, by Rudolf Rocker. A number of notable Bakhtin scholars see Bakhtin's interest in Rabelais and his sometimes utopian approach to language and society as an exception to be explained away. In *Mikhail Bakhtin: Creation of a Prosaics*, for example, Gary Saul Morson and Caryl Emerson categorically express their cynicism about that "professed utopianism, which is so much at odds with the anti-utopianism of Bakhtin's other writings. Bakhtin's lifelong dislike of systems, his distrust of final answers, and his preference for the messy facts of everyday life made him deeply suspicious of all utopian visions."[1] Among the "utopian visions" that Morson and Emerson expressly reject is his anarchism, which they associate with the work of Mikhail Bakunin.

A serious examination of Bakhtin's work with regard to questions of anarchism will, I think, show that Morson and Emerson are right as far as the definition of utopianism they employ and the utopian thinkers to whom they refer can bring them. The problem is that Bakunin is not a "utopianist," in my sense, nor is he the best comparative figure for understanding Bakhtin's anarchism (even though such aspects of Bakunin's theory as revolution's festival character are critical precursors). Bakhtin never cites (in terms of the available archive) any anarchist other than Rabelais, "who"—as noted by Rocker—"in his description of the happy Abbey of Thélème (*Gargantua*) presented a picture of life freed from all authoritative restraints."[2] So why do Morson and Emerson favor Bakunin over William Godwin, Peter Kropotkin, Pierre Proudhon, or Rudolf Rocker? The problem is compounded by the fact that their portrayal of Bakunin's work, and indeed their view of anarchism as a whole, is at best too narrow (often seeming to reduce Bakunin's corpus to his declaration that "the will to destroy is a creative will!"[3]), at worst simply incorrect. As a result, they take up many negative stereotypes of anarchy that have been promulgated in our society by self-interested elites who recognize a far more significant threat therein than could ever be found in totalitarian "challenges" such as Bolshevism or Maoism (both of which are discussed all the time). Consequently, anarchism, which could help explain the relationship between those facets of Bakhtin's works that are sometimes deemed incompatible, remains obscure.

Here, the problem of reading Bakhtin as an anarchist is approached in two ways: first, in order to situate Bakhtin's work in its appropriate political context, it is examined alongside that of Rocker rather than Bakunin (although there are important points of overlap); and second, Rocker's views on law are applied to Bakhtin's work and shown to help explain some of its apparent contradictions, especially where Bakhtin appears to favor a clearly determined sense of responsibility that seems (but is not) incompatible with anarchism, properly defined. The critical link between Rocker and Bakhtin—indeed, between anarchism in general and Bakhtin's approach—is the belief, explicit and implicit in the corpus of both men, that maximal freedom of interaction, movement, and intermingling is a vital and invigorating element for human development, that any attempt to limit human diversity and freedom is an impediment to this development, and that attempts to maintain them through the upholding of, say, natural law are essential. As Rocker puts it: "In every field authority leads to ossification and sterility, while the free unfolding of ideas is always creative."[4]

Morson and Emerson's viewpoint hinges upon the idea that the type of freewheeling "philosophic" anarchy found by some Westerners in Bakhtin's work is inappropriate because it makes him an apostle of such Bakuninian-anarchist "solutions." They suggest that the West has often treated Bakhtin as a "Bakunin of our times" and that "initial critical reception of Bakhtin in the West focused primarily on those passages in Bakhtin that do sound a great deal like Bakunin. His admirers described libertarian Bakhtin, an apostle of pure freedom and carnival license, who rejoices in the undoing of rules, in centrifugal energy for its own sake, in clowning, and the rejection of all authority and 'official culture.'"[5] To the degree that this is true (they and others also having described his appropriation early on by structuralists, Marxists, and Formalists), it nevertheless reflects an erroneous grasp of Bakunin's view and, more seriously, of anarchism as a historical reality. Murray Bookchin offers sufficient grounds for questioning Morson and Emerson's approach in a single passage:

> Beneath the surface of Bakunin's theories lies the more basic revolt of the community principle against the state principle, of the social principle against the political principle. Bakuninism, in this respect, can be traced back to those subterranean currents in humanity that have tried at all times to restore community as the structural unit of social life. Bakunin deeply admired the traditional collectivistic aspects of the Russian village, not out of any atavistic illusions about the past, but because he wished to see industrial society pervaded by its atmosphere of mutual aid and solidarity. Like virtually all the intellectuals of his day, he acknowledged the importance of science as a means of promoting eventual human betterment; hence the embattled atheism and anticlericalism that pervades all his writings. By the same token, he demanded that the scientific and technological resources of society be mobilized in support of social cooperation, freedom, and community, instead of being abused for profit, competitive advantage, and war. In this respect, Mikhail Bakunin was not behind his times, but a century or more ahead of them.[6]

In *Anarchism and Anarcho-Syndicalism* Rocker adds to this a description of Bakunin's economic approach when he writes that Bakunin "based his ideas upon the teachings of Proudhon, but extended them on the economic side when he, along with the federalist wing of the First International, advocated collective ownership of the land and all other means of production, and wished to restrict the right of private property only to the product of individual labour."[7] Both visions are more accurate portrayals of the (Bakunin) approach than the joyful rule breaking to which he is reduced in the Morson and Emerson text. It is true that Bakunin and Rocker (like most anarchists) are against the arbitrary or self-serving use of power; but Rocker is particularly interesting because he devoted much of his writing to the relationship between culture and structures of authority. The most powerful articulation of his views on culture is to be found in *Nationalism and Culture*, which is virtually contemporaneous with Bakhtin's "Discourse in the Novel." Here, Rocker relates the dangers of power to the suppression of cultural production, the parallel arising from the simple reason that "power is never creative. It uses the creative force of a given culture to clothe its nakedness and to increase its dignity. Power is always a negative element in history."[8] But even though anarchy in almost all of its forms is against power and authority, it does not follow that it "rejoices in the undoing of rules, in centrifugal energy for its own sake," or even "in clowning," as Morson and Emerson suggest.

To examine but one concrete historical example—the anarchy that existed in mountain pueblos in Spain after the 1870s—is to glimpse the degree to which being anti-authoritarian can also imply a need for forming social units on the basis of clearly defined values and goals. Bookchin's *Spanish Anarchists* provides an important glimpse into anarchist existence:

> [The] solidarity, reinforced by a harsh environment of sparse means and a common destiny of hard work, produces a fierce egalitarianism. The preferred form of transaction between peasants and laborers is *aperceria*, or partnership, rather than wages. Although they own the land and work as hard as the laborers, the peasants may give as much as half the crop to their temporary "partners." This type of relationship is preferred not only because it is wiser to share what one has in hand rather than to speculate on monetary returns, but also owing to a rich sense of fraternity and a disdain for possessive values. In the life of the *pueblo*, poverty confers absolutely no inferiority; wealth, unless it is spent in behalf of the community, confers absolutely no prestige. The rich who own property in or near the *pueblo* are generally regarded as a wicked breed whose power and ambitions corrupt society. Not only is the *pueblo* immune to their influence, but in reaction, tends to organize its values around the dignity of work and the importance of moral and spiritual goals.[9]

As this last statement indicates, the key relation was between being anti-authoritarian and "adopting all the personal standards of the Anarchists in the cities," standards which in some cases were consistently libertarian but not necessarily random, violent, or uncontrolled. "A man did not smoke, drink, or go to prostitutes, but lived a sober, exemplary life in a stable free union with a *companera*. The church and state were anathema, to be shunned completely. Children were to be raised and educated by libertarian standards and dealt with respectfully as sovereign human beings."[10] The key to this form of anarchism, which eventually gave way to a more anarcho-syndicalist approach as proletarian anarchism drifted increasingly toward syndicalism (particularly in the cities), was not this kind of chaotic breaking of rules for its own sake, but living "in a stable free union with a *companera*."

When read in this light, Morson and Emerson's conclusion reads like an argument for, rather than against, considering Bakhtin in a properly anarchistic framework: "It must be admitted that there are indeed elements of antinomianism, theoretical anarchism, and holy foolishness in his thought about carnival. But on the whole Bakhtin insulates himself against that sort of thinking better than it might at first appear. Judged by the entirety of his work, Bakhtin is, if anything, an apostle of constraints. For without constraints of the right sort, he believed, neither freedom nor creativity, neither unfinalizability nor responsibility, can be real."[11] This last observation speaks to the issue of what Rocker calls "natural law," to which we will return. Suffice to say that a strong current of Enlightenment and classical liberal thinking runs through certain strains of anarchism and that it shows up most clearly in the important place allocated to rationality and the role of law in anarchist society as described by Rocker. So once again, Morson and Emerson's view of "a dominant critical image of an anarchistic Bakhtin," in which "he is described as an antinomian rejoicing, Bakunin-like, in joyful destruction, carnival clowning, and novels-as-loopholes," hinges upon a misunderstanding of concepts of anarchy, as in their concluding sentence of this paragraph: "Bakhtin, who never gave up his commitment to ethical responsibility, is presented as playfully and anarchically irresponsible."[12] It is simply wrong to consider anarchy as necessarily irresponsible or ludic—wrong on both philosophical and historical grounds. "Anarchists," declares Rocker, "desire a federation of free communities which shall be bound to one another by their common economic and social interests and shall arrange their affairs by mutual agreement and free contract."[13] This description directly contradicts the view of anarchy projected by Morson and Emerson when they write that "generally speaking, Bakhtin was much less concerned with millenarian fantasies and holy foolishness than with the constraints and responsibilities of everyday living. Carnival, while offering a provocative insight into much of Rabelais and some of Dostoevsky, ultimately proved a dead end. In his last period, laughter but not the idealization of carnival anarchy remained—and the functions of laughter were more closely specified."[14]

It is not enough to suggest that Morson and Emerson simply misrepresent Bakunin and most of the anarchist tradition in *Mikhail Bakhtin*.

Indeed, I only mention this work because, even though otherwise carefully and rigorously argued and researched, it (like so many other texts) reduces "anarchy" to something analogous with "indeterminate chaos," thereby draining the political significance from a truly revolutionary corpus. Rather than harping on this text, we can go considerably further by turning to the work of Rocker. The description of anarchy in *Nationalism and Culture* helps explain not only the importance of carnival in Bakhtin's work, its relationship to ethical concerns, and Bakhtin's continued importance for anarchist politics, but also the crucial links between Rocker and Bakhtin in terms of their basic portrayals of language and social formations. I will quote more from Rocker's works (taking a relatively greater knowledge of Bakhtin for granted). It is interesting to consider how readily available works by Lenin, Mao, Stalin, and Trotsky are in any language, whereas Rocker, Proudhon, and even contemporary anarchists like Murray Bookchin and George Woodcock remain largely unknown.

We can begin our comparison between Bakhtin and Rocker in the unlikely area of language studies. Consistent with what Noam Chomsky has called a "Cartesian" approach to language,[15] Rocker claims that language itself does not have a national origin. Rather, human beings are endowed with the ability to "articulate language which permits of concepts and so enables man's thoughts to achieve higher results, which distinguish man in this respect from other species."[16] Rocker's objective in discussing language is to undermine notions of racial purity, upheld by the Nazis at the time when he was writing his book. More important, though, is his sense that discourse is like a living entity inasmuch as it constantly evolves and adapts, taking in new expressions and terms from various strata of society or from different cultures or groups. This dynamic, never-fixed status of language threatens authority and is therefore itself subject to various attempts on the part of authoritarian institutions like governments to control its functioning, according to both Rocker and Bakhtin. In a passage describing the regimentation of French life in the seventeenth century, Rocker gives the example of the establishment of the Académie in 1629, commenting that its institution was intended "to subordinate language and poetry to the authoritarian ambitions of absolutism." In effect, the authorities were aiming for a unitary French language by imposing upon it "a strict guardian that endeavoured with all its power to eliminate from it popular expressions and figures of speech. This was called 'refining the language.' In reality it deprived it of originality and bent it under the yoke of an unnatural despotism from which it was later obliged forcibly to free itself."[17] Bakhtin's approach questions attempts to repress heteroglossia, while also taking for granted (particularly in his discussions of the revitalization of languages and communities through the infusion of new genres and perspectives) not only the danger posed by efforts to establish uniform language practices but the very impossibility of doing so. For both Bakhtin and Rocker, the *vital*, living aspects of language must be protected from authoritarian suppression or oppression just as people must be. Says Bakhtin: "Language—like the living concrete environment in which the consciousness of the verbal artist lives—is never unitary. It is unitary only as an abstract grammatical system of normative forms, taken in isolation from the concrete, ideological conceptualizations that fill it, and in isolation from the uninterrupted process of historical becoming that is a characteristic of all living language."[18] And Rocker: "Every higher form of culture, if it is not too greatly hindered in its natural development by political obstructions, strives constantly to renew its creative urge to construct." And the sense that people, left to their own devices, will lazily let the sand of time slip between their inactive fingers is, for Rocker, but a poor scare tactic: "Always and everywhere the same creative urge is hungry for action; only the mode of expression differs and is adapted to the environment."[19]

Dialogism for Bakhtin is natural, but to the degree that it is suppressed by societal constraints (such as official or authoritative discourse), it is also an ideal which is only fully articulated in certain limited genres (such as the dialogic novel). Rocker emphasizes the degree to which authority threatens this ideal and should therefore be dismantled. Both uphold attempts to protect the community from those who would isolate it or provide it with a straitjacket of national character. This effort was particularly urgent for Rocker, who witnessed the rise of Nazi nationalism in his native Germany along with the various attempts to justify it or give it a historical basis. These relations nourish language's natural propensity to evolve, just like "an organism" which lives in a state of "constant flux": "Not only does it make the most diversified borrowings from other languages, a phenomenon due to the countless influences and points of contact in cultural life, but it also possesses a stock of words that is continually changing. Quite gradually and unnoticeably the shadings and gradations of the concepts which find their expression in words alter, so that it often happens that a word means today exactly the opposite of what men originally expressed by it."[20] Any effort to separate the utterance from its context is for Rocker a political act, for Bakhtin a senseless one, and for both a threat to the life of the language itself. Bakhtin argues that "discourse lives, as it were, beyond itself, in a living impulse . . . toward the object; if we detach ourselves completely from this impulse all we have left is the naked corpse of the word, from which we can learn nothing at all about the social situation or the fate of a given word in life. *To study the word as such, ignoring the impulse that reaches out beyond it, is just as senseless as to study psychological experience outside the context of that real life toward which it was directed and by which it is determined.*"[21]

To study language is therefore to recognize its contextual richness, including the infusion of other languages into a single language, for, as Rocker points out, "there exists no cultural language which does not contain a great mass of foreign material, and the attempt to free it from these foreign intruders would lead to a complete dissolution of the language—that is, if such a purification could be achieved at all. Every European language contains a mass of foreign elements with which, often, whole dictionaries could be filled."[22] This tendency is what Bakhtin's "polyglossia" means, as defined by Emerson and Holquist: "the simultaneous presence of two or more national languages interacting within a single cultural system."[23] His description of heteroglossia goes even further, into the various strata of languages which occur through the numerous points of contact between different types of language practice even within a given national language. For Bakhtin, "at any given moment of its historical existence, language is heteroglot from top to bottom: it represents the co-existence of socio-ideological contradictions between the present and the past, between differing epochs of the past, between different socio-ideological groups in the present, between tendencies, schools, circles and so forth, all given a bodily form. These 'languages' of heteroglossia intersect each other in a variety of ways, forming new socially typifying 'languages.'"[24] Again, as described by Bakhtin, this is a natural phenomenon which demands of language researchers a methodology appropriate to the task of discerning the different threads of discursive practice in a given utterance. To Rocker, this same phenomenon can be threatened and thereby endanger the very essence of society:

> For the development of every language the acceptance of foreign elements is essential. No people lives for itself. Every enduring intercourse with other peoples results in the borrowing of words from their language; this is quite indispensable to reciprocal cultural fecundation. The countless points of contact which culture daily creates between people leave their traces in language. New objects, ideas, concepts—religious, political, and generally social—lead to new expressions and word formations. In this, the older and more highly developed cultures naturally have a strong influence on less developed folk-groups and furnish these with new ideas which find their expression in language.[25]

Rocker goes on to note that in some cases the foreign expression for a particular idea is not adopted even when the idea is (or what he calls "loan-translation"). Then,

> we translate the newly acquired concept into our own language by creating from the material at hand a word structure not previously used. Here the stranger confronts us, so to speak, in the mask of our own language . . . [*Halbinsel* from peninsula, *Halbwelt* from demi-monde, etc.]. . . . These have an actually revolutionary effect on the course of development of the language, and show us most of all the unreality of the view which maintains that in every language the spirit of a particular people lives and works. In reality every loan-translation is but a proof of the continuous penetration of foreign cultural elements within our own cultural circle—in so far as a people can speak of "its own culture."[26]

What makes Bakhtin's work useful for immigration or refugee studies is its insistence upon the urgency of maintaining maximum openness between speech communities, lest the language and the community of speakers become frozen in a debilitating inbreeding of existing ideas and speech genres. This tendency, which is generally the product of efforts by some authoritarian structure like the State,

> will occur only when a national culture loses its sealed-off and self-sufficient character, when it becomes conscious of itself as only one among *other* cultures and languages. It is this knowledge that will sap the roots of a mythological feeling for language, based as it is on an absolute fusion of ideological meaning with language; there will arise an acute feeling for language boundaries (social, national and semantic), and only then will language reveal its essential *human* character; from behind its words, forms, styles, nationally characteristic and socially typical faces begin to emerge, the images of speaking human beings. . . . Language, no longer conceived as a sacrosanct and solitary embodiment of meaning and truth, becomes merely one of many possible ways to hypothesize meaning.[27]

So, the heteroglossia of language is nourished in situations in which people interact, and the recognition of this heteroglossia allows us to better understand how language actually functions. Again, this implies that structures of authority which attempt to seal off cultures from one another or to impose a standardized version of culture according to (say) nationalist ambitions are, for Bakhtin and Rocker, repressive forces. Rocker's views on how culture is stimulated are clear: "Cultural reconstructions and social stimulation always occur when different peoples and races come into closer union. Every new culture is begun by such a fusion of different folk elements and takes its special shape from this." Notice that he refers to both foreign elements (polyglossia) and to different strata of culture (heteroglossia). And notice as well that attempts to seal off cultures lead to a retrograde "inbreeding," nicely described by Rocker (and equally true for Bakhtin): "All experience indicates rather that . . . inbreeding would lead inevitably to a general stunting, to a slow extinction of culture. In this respect it is with peoples as it is with persons. How poorly that man would fare who in his cultural development had to rely on the creations of his own people!" Communities, like relationships, must be nourished and continually revitalized with diverse influences. Says Rocker, in one of his more purple passages: "New life arises only from the union of man with woman. Just so a culture is born or fertilized only by the circulation of fresh blood in the veins of its representatives. Just as the child results from the mating so new culture forms arise from the mutual fertilization of different peoples and their spiritual sympathy with foreign achievements and capacities."[28]

It is in this light that any notion of "originality" in Bakhtin's world is based upon fallacious assumptions, and any attempt to trace origins for political reasons (nationalism, e.g.) is for Rocker equally dangerous because it implies that purity is sought where there are interrelations and knowledge to be learned therefrom:

> We are always dependent upon our predecessors, and for this reason the notion of a "national culture" is misleading and inconsistent. We are never in a position to draw a line between what we have acquired by our own powers and what we have received from others. Every idea, whether it be of a religious, an ethical, a philosophic, a scientific or an artistic nature, had its forerunners and pioneers, without which it would be inconceivable; and it is usually quite impossible to go back to its first beginnings. Almost invariably thinkers of all countries and peoples have contributed to its development.[29]

This is an argument for the promotion of unfettered associations of peoples across all cultural and linguistic lines. And—yet another point of intersection between Bakhtin and Rocker—it is an argument for the study, and the fostering, of intertextuality:

> The inner culture of a man grows just in the measure that he develops an ability to appropriate the achievements of other peoples and enrich his mind with them. The more easily he is able to do this the better it is for his mental culture, the greater right he has to the title, man of culture. He immerses himself in the gentle wisdom of Lao-tse and rejoices in the beauty of the Vedic poems. Before his mind unfold the wonder-tales of the *Thousand and One Nights*, and with inner rapture he drinks in the sayings of the wine-loving Omar Khayyam or the majestic strophes of Firdusi. . . . In one word, he is everywhere at home, and therefore knows better how to value the charm of his own homeland. With unprejudiced eye he searches the cultural possessions of all peoples and so perceives more clearly the strong unity of all mental

> processes. And of these possessions no one can rob him; they are outside the jurisdiction of the government and are not subject to the will of the mighty ones of the earth. The legislator may be in a position to close the gates of his country to the stranger, but he cannot keep him from making his demands upon the treasure of the people, its mental culture, with the same assurance as any native.[30]

According to this scenario, the artist is of special interest since s/he is the one who promulgates the "mental culture" of a given place and time by setting down in a unique fashion the currents of existing heteroglossia, not by inventing something that stands outside of contemporary experience. Both Bakhtin and Rocker are clear about this idea that the originality of an artistic work is its form, the way in which it ties together already existing strands. Morson and Emerson describe Bakhtin's views of the artist as follows:

> Bakhtin's most cherished artists are those who enrich humanity's ways of visualizing the world by creating new form-shaping ideologies. The greatness of Goethe lies in his contribution to the sense of time conveyed by narrative genres; Rabelais played a decisive role in the novel's ability to sense conventions and assess popular social forms. Bakhtin also believed that the most valuable contribution of Western thought in the humanities was its diversity of genres. In this context, we can understand his impatience with literary histories stressing either the conflict of local schools, or the psychology of individual authors, or the "reflection" of social conflicts. By finding better ways to explore the wisdom of genres, criticism has much more important contributions to make.[31]

The creation of forms situates the author on the same plane as the world that he is describing; if anything, s/he is all the more deeply embedded in the prevailing chronotope. This is, yet again, consistent with Rocker's approach:

> Of course, the artist does not stand outside of space and time; he, too, is but a man, like the least of his contemporaries. His ego is no abstract image, but a living entity, in which every side of his social being is mirrored and action and reaction are at work. He, too, is bound to the men of his time by a thousand ties; in their sorrows and their joys

> he has his personal share; and in his heart their ambitions, hopes and wishes find an echo. As a social being he is endowed with the same social instinct; in his person is reflected the whole environment in which he lives and works and which, of necessity, finds expression in his productions. But how this expression will manifest itself, in what particular manner the soul of the artist will react to the impressions that he receives from his surroundings, is in the final outcome decided by his own temperament, his special endowment of character—in a word, his personality.[32]

But no matter how in tune the author is to the general "social discourse" of a society, s/he is also subjected to the limitations imposed by the ruling classes and the form of social organization. One of the constraints to which authors, like all others, are subject is the law; since this is a point of considerable interest for Bakhtin, and considerable confusion for those who conflate "anarchy" with "chaos," it is worth comparing Rocker and Bakhtin on law and laws.

Bakhtin does discuss specifically legal matters, such as legal discourse, hermeneutics, legal interpretation, power relations in the court, confession, professional discourses, and judicial matters. "The enormous significance of the motif of the speaking person is obvious in the realm of ethical and legal thought and discourse"; indeed, "the speaking person and his discourse is, in these areas, the major topic of thought and speech."[33] I would argue that Bakhtin's work is everywhere concerned with issues which could be usefully related to the study of law, including his discussions of alterity, the representation of the self, power in discourse, answerability, authoring, norms, responsibility, ethics, outsiderness, and authenticity—to name but a few.[34] Here I want to emphasize the degree to which responsibility, a fundamental concern for Bakhtin, is ingrained within the major tendencies of anarchist thought like Rocker's, as evinced by the important relationship established between anarchy and what Rocker calls "natural law." This emphasis raises further questions about the equivalence frequently posited between anarchy and chaos, as well as opening a discussion on responsibility and ethics in the works of Bakhtin and Rocker.

It is not surprising that, in their respective discussions of law and responsibility, both make frequent reference to the domain of cultural activity. One of the reasons why the "dialogized" space is idealized in Bakhtin's work is that it undermines attempts by official authoritative discourse to close down or limit the (natural) dialogism of human culture. Dialogic novels, public squares, or carnival spaces are of interest to Bakhtin precisely because they are places which cultivate dialogism and thereby nourish and revitalize the social domain. Rocker devotes considerable attention to the "cultural forces" in society as well because they

> involuntarily rebel against the coercion of institutions of political power on whose sharp corners they bark their shins. Consciously or unconsciously they try to break the rigid forms which obstruct their natural development, constantly erecting new bars before it. The possessors of power, however, must always be on the watch, lest the intellectual culture of the times stray into forbidden paths, and so perhaps disturb or even totally inhibit their political activities. From this continued struggle of two antagonistic aims, the one always representing the caste interests of the privileged minority, the other the interests of the community, a certain legal relationship gradually arises, on the basis of which the limits of influence between state and society, politics and economics—in short, between power and culture—are periodically readjusted and confirmed by constitutions.[35]

Here enters the domain of law which for Bakhtin and Rocker (an area I'd like to explore in future work) is legitimate to the degree that it promotes freedom. Rocker makes this claim overtly in the distinction he draws between natural law and positive law:

> In law it is primarily necessary to distinguish two forms: "natural law" and so-called "positive law." A natural law exists where society has not yet been politically organized—before the state with its caste and class system has made its appearance. In this instance, law is the result of mutual agreements between men confronting one another as free and equal, motivated by the same interests and enjoying equal dignity as human beings. Positive law first develops within the political framework of the state and concerns men who are separated from one another by reason of different economic interests and who, on the basis of social inequality, belong to various castes and classes.[36]

This "positive law" hands power over to the State, which, as Rocker goes on to say, "has its roots in brute force, conquest and enslavement of the conquered," and which is thereby given "a legal character." In other words, it is quite possible to promote legal resolutions to conflict, and indeed to found communities upon legal grounds, even from an anarchistic standpoint. But even more important, in terms of reading Bakhtin, it is also possible to argue that the Rabelais book (even from a legal perspective) is consistent with the rest of the Bakhtin corpus (Morson and Emerson's claim to the contrary notwithstanding).

I would suggest that what is being upheld in *Rabelais and His World* is a carnival of the folk that is specifically directed against the power of the rulers. Throughout the book, Bakhtin advocates laughter as a means of unsettling official dogma, of festivals as occasions to subvert official State gatherings, of riotous behavior to question authorized demeanor. "Unfinalizability" is most certainly one of the lessons we learn from this book, but it comes, in terms of its politics, from an anti-authoritarian and not a pro-chaos perspective. Morson and Emerson interpret the Bakhtin of *Rabelais and His World* as one who believes that "everything completed, fixed, or defined is declared to be dogmatic and repressive."[37] In fact, the book questions arbitrary State or official authority just as carnival does. In contrast to official society, "carnival does not know footlights, in the sense that it does not acknowledge any distinction between actors and spectators. Footlights would destroy a carnival, as the absence of footlights would destroy a theatrical performance."[38] This doesn't suggest eternal unruliness as the new norm, but rather an inclusive politics that knows no separation between rulers and ruled, a place where people are freed from the oppression of the other and are inside their own spaces, which they control and for which they are responsible. Morson and Emerson find in Bakhtin's writings about carnival that "only the destruction of all extant or conceivable norms has value," when it seems clear that he is simply questioning the ruler-enforced norms, as another *Rabelais* passage quoted by Morson and Emerson also suggests: "The principle of laughter . . . destroys . . . all pretense of an extratemporal meaning and unconditional value of necessity. It frees human consciousness, thought, and imagination for new potentialities."[39] The fact is (and here is the link to Rocker and his conception of the anarchist society) that freedom also creates the responsibilities which come naturally in train with liberation:

> Only in freedom does there arise in man the consciousness of responsibility for his acts and regard for the rights of others; only in freedom can there unfold in its full strength that most precious social instinct: man's sympathy for the joys and sorrows of his fellow men and the resultant impulse toward mutual aid in which are rooted all social ethics, all ideas of social justice. Thus Godwin's work became at the same time the epilogue of that great intellectual movement which had inscribed on its banner the greatest possible limitation of the power of the state, and the starting point for the development of the ideas of libertarian socialism.[40]

Reason and responsibility become the bases for individual decision making, not authority and power. And for this conception of law, Rocker draws upon various sources, including Richard Hooker, who "maintained that it is unworthy of a man to submit blindly, like a beast, to the compulsion of any kind of authority without consulting his own reason"; and John Locke, who opined "that common and binding relationships existed between primitive men, emanating from their social disposition and from considerations of reason." Others, who "aimed to set limits to hereditary power and to widen the individual's sphere of independence," included "Lord Shaftesbury, Bernard de Mandeville, William Temple, Montesquieu, John Bolingbroke, Voltaire, Buffon, David Hume, Mably, Henry Linguet, A. Ferguson, Adam Smith." Most of them, "inspired by biological and related science, had abandoned the concept of an original social contract" and "recognized the state as the political instrument of privileged minorities in society for the rulership of the great masses."[41]

What is most interesting here in the Rocker–Bakhtin relationship is the emphasis placed upon individuality and creativity, both of which will flourish in the anti-authoritarian societies described. But so too will a higher conception of responsibility and ethics, for, says Rocker, "all schemes having their roots in natural rights are based on the desire to free man from bondage to social institutions of compulsion in order that he may attain to consciousness of his humanity and no longer bow before any authority which would deprive him of the right to his own thoughts and actions." When we consider this kind of society to be the goal to which both aspire, the Rabelais book takes on a different glow, it seems to me, for, like Bakhtin's later work and that of Rocker, it is animated by a sense that great popular movements should look to overthrow institutions of power and authority in favor of free associations in which the seeds of freedom (and everything that grows along with them) will germinate vigorously. This is not simply a political objective, but a personal one as well, for, as Rocker (like Godwin, Warren, Proudhon, and Bakunin) recognized, "one cannot be free either politically or personally so long as one is in the economic servitude of another and cannot escape from this condition."[42]

Finally, both Bakhtin and Rocker emphasize the individual over the community, despite their stated views on the importance of considering the entire social domain when trying to account for the individual. This is one more point of overlap between Bakhtin's conception of what society is and should be like and society as envisaged by Rocker. The anarchist conception does not accept any compulsion to act, even for desirable ends; compulsion, regardless of the ends, is a power relation which will ultimately separate people, according to Rocker:

> It lacks the inner drive of all social unions—the understanding which recognizes the facts and the sympathy which comprehends the feeling of the fellow man because it feels itself related to him. By subjecting men to a common compulsion one does not bring them closer to one another, rather one creates estrangements between them and breeds impulses of selfishness and separation. Social ties have permanence and completely fulfil their purpose only when they are based on good will and spring from the needs of men. Only under such conditions is a relationship possible where social union and the freedom of the individual are so closely intergrown that they can no longer be recognized as separate entities.[43]

We have here the very basis of the kinds of relationships—confession, laying bare, dialogue—that are upheld by Bakhtin as desirable throughout his entire corpus. Laughter, carnival, dialogue, and excess are means of breaking through the many walls erected by those who would use compulsion to enforce their will; what lies beyond them in the anarchist conception, as described here, is the freedom to act, to create, and to enter into relationships of love, compassion, and responsibility based upon shared concerns.

Notes

1 Gary Saul Morson and Caryl Emerson, *Mikhail Bakhtin: Creation of a Prosaics* (Stanford, 1990), 94.

2 Rudolf Rocker, *Anarchism and Anarcho-Syndicalism* (London, 1990 [1938]), 17. In *Nationalism and Culture* (trans. Ray E. Chase [Montreal, 1998 {1937}], 131), Rocker, recalling a passage from *Gargantua* that informed a significant area of his anarchist approach to society, says, "A great advance was made by the French Humanist, François Rabelais, who in his novel, *Gargantua*, describes a small community, the famous Abbey of Thélème, of wholly free men who had abolished all compulsion and regulated their lives simply by the principle, 'Do what thou wilt' ":

> . . . because free men, well born, well educated, associating with decent company, have a natural instinct that impels them to virtuous conduct and restrains them from vice which instinct they call honour. Such people when repressed and enslaved by base subjection and constraint forget the noble inclination to virtue that they have felt while free and seek merely to throw off and break the yoke of servitude; for we always try to do what has been forbidden and long for what has been denied.

3 Morson and Emerson, *Mikhail Bakhtin*, 92.

4 Rocker, *Nationalism and Culture*, 467.

5 Morson and Emerson, *Mikhail Bakhtin*, 42, 43.

6 Murray Bookchin, *The Spanish Anarchists: The Heroic Years 1868–1936* (New York, 1977), 29–30.

7 Rocker, *Anarchism and Anarcho-Syndicalism*, 20.

8 Rocker, *Nationalism and Culture*, 83.

9 Bookchin, *Spanish Anarchists*, 90–91.

10 Ibid., 91.

11 Morson and Emerson, *Mikhail Bakhtin*, 43.

12 Ibid., 67.

13 Rocker, *Anarchism and Anarcho-Syndicalism*, 7.

14 Morson and Emerson, *Mikhail Bakhtin*, 67.

15 Noam Chomsky, *Cartesian Linguistics: A Chapter in the History of Rationalist Thought* (New York and London, 1966).

16 Rocker, *Nationalism and Culture*, 284.

17 Ibid., 429, 287.

18 M. M. Bakhtin, "Discourse in the Novel" (1934–35), in *The Dialogic Imagination: Four Essays*, ed. Michael Holquist, trans. Caryl Emerson and Michael Holquist (Austin, 1981), 259–422; quotation from 288.

19 Rocker, *Nationalism and Culture*, 83, 346.

20 Ibid., 277.

21 Bakhtin, "Discourse in the Novel," 292.

22 Rocker, *Nationalism and Culture*, 277.

23 See their glossary in Holquist, ed., *Dialogic Imagination*, 431.
24 Bakhtin, "Discourse in the Novel," 291.
25 Rocker, *Nationalism and Culture*, 278.
26 Ibid., 282.
27 Bakhtin, "Discourse in the Novel," 370.
28 Rocker, *Nationalism and Culture*, 346.
29 Ibid., 453.
30 Ibid., 347.
31 Morson and Emerson, *Mikhail Bakhtin*, 284.
32 Rocker, *Nationalism and Culture*, 474.
33 Bakhtin, "Discourse in the Novel," 349.
34 I have discussed legal matters from a Bakhtinian perspective on numerous occasions; see, e.g., Robert F. Barsky, *Constructing A Productive Other: Discourse Theory and the Convention Refugee Hearing* (Amsterdam, 1994); "The Discourse(s) of Literature and the Law," in *Face to Face: Bakhtin in Russia and the West*, ed. Carol Adlam, Rachel Falconer, Vitalii Makhlin, and Alastair Renfrew (Sheffield, UK, 1997), 372–85; "La problématologie dialogique: Quel rôle joue le questionnement dans le domaine de la littérature et du droit?," in *Mikhail Bakhtine et la pensée dialogique (Colloque de Cerisy)*, ed. Clive Thomson (London, ONT, forthcoming); and "Outsider Law in Literature: Construction and Representation in *Death and the Maiden*," *SubStance* 84 (Winter 1997): 66–89.
35 Rocker, *Nationalism and Culture*, 86.
36 Ibid.
37 Morson and Emerson, *Mikhail Bakhtin*, 92.
38 Mikhail Bakhtin, *Rabelais and His World*, trans. Hélène Iswolsky (Bloomington, 1984 [1968]), 7.
39 Morson and Emerson, *Mikhail Bakhtin*, 92, 93.
40 Rocker, *Nationalism and Culture*, 148.
41 Ibid., 140, 142.
42 Ibid., 143, 167.
43 Ibid., 246.

Maroussia Hajdukowski-Ahmed

Bakhtin without Borders: Participatory Action Research in the Social Sciences

A subject as such cannot be perceived and studied as a thing, for as a subject it cannot, while remaining a subject, become voiceless, and, consequently, cognition of it can only be *dialogic*.
—Mikhail Bakhtin, "Toward a Methodology for the Human Sciences"

Dialogue is not separate from action, but it is concomitant to it.
—Paulo Freire, *Pedagogy of the Oppressed*

The oppressed are victims of social injustice; their significance, however, does not reside in the fact of their victimization but in the possibility that their agency will transform their lived relations.
—Peter Hitchcock, *Dialogics of the Oppressed*

In examining the dialogic relationship between theory and action here within the framework of a health-promotion project currently under way with immigrant women in Hamilton, Canada, I describe a sociological approach known as Participatory Action Research (PAR). For reasons of space, the relationship between Bakhtin and the critical theory on which PAR is grounded must remain implicit, while the bridges that can be built between theory and action, on the one hand, and between Bakhtin and the social sci-

The *South Atlantic Quarterly* 97:3/4, Summer/Fall 1998.

ences, on the other, are allowed to come to the fore.[1] Bakhtin's theories are congruent with PAR in the following ways: (1) the rejection of a dichotomous mode of thinking and of the human subject's reification in knowledge production; (2) the adoption of an exotopic and an empathic position in the act of understanding; and (3) the work's grounding on dialogic communication and the validation of popular knowledge and cultural diversity. The dialogics of PAR produce an epistemology and an ethics geared toward a politics of recognition and a praxis of participatory democracy.

All research acts are, in both a self-reflexive and a social way, attempts to understand and justify "Being-as-event." My own research is now taking place at a point when my intellectual development is dialogically linked to my historical being in the world. Those members of my generation who were in France as adolescents during the Algerian War of Independence and as students during the events of May 1968 became particularly sensitized to the intense dialogic questioning of reflection/action inspired by the works of Althusser, Sartre, Benjamin, Foucault, and ultimately Bakhtin.

Bakhtin's works can be considered a dialogue between his existence as event and the historical context in which it is inscribed. According to him, our unique presence in history forces us not only to assume a position of answerability, but also to account for it. Why? Because to actualize oneself in life is to act and not remain indifferent to this totality, which happens only once. At the same time that we are implicated by our historical being and our language in social interaction, we answer to the world for this active presence. Answerability links theory with action, art with life, and forecloses the possibility of a chiasmus or a dichotomous relationship between them.[2] Answerability is inescapable, and no alibi is possible: "It is only my non-alibi in Being that transforms an empty possibility into an actual answerable act or deed."[3] Values are what give theory its validity within the unity of the answerable Being-as-event, which is not a given but an experience in process. Responsibility is what links "the world as experienced in actions and the world as represented in discourse."[4]

Bakhtin clearly distances himself from a phenomenological approach he deems individualistic and that fails to account for the dialogical experience with the other. He does not pull back from the concept of action, since for him an utterance is already a form of action, but recoils from commitment as too close to a dangerous monologism—one with the totalitarian effects that he knew only too well.[5] This reminds us of the importance of the historical context in which Bakhtin constructed his work and his own passionate plea for dialogism, for which he paid the price of internal exile. In a democratic context dialogism takes on a more philosophico-aesthetic shade, but during the Stalinist repression Bakhtin's work undoubtedly constituted both a political act and a political horizon.[6]

In our own contemporary context, the way the academy functions makes it difficult to assume historical answerability. As an institution based on a dichotomous relationship to the agora, it is isolated by the political geography of the campus and by the academic/political legitimation of discipline-based knowledge. In the realm of the social sciences in particular, the politics of research legitimizes and promotes "pure" research while hiding its epistemological and ideological bases behind a screen of empirical objectivity.[7] Academia's legitimizing processes are grounded on a dichotomous worldview; consequently, more strictly disciplinary/vertical research is rewarded than the interdisciplinary/lateral research that connects fields. Esoteric language is similarly favored over popular idioms, individual intellectual property rights over interactive collaboration (e.g., in the criteria for professional assessment), and the quantitative over the qualitative. This political agenda is implemented within a subsidizing system that rewards intensive technologized production, thereby further distancing the academic researcher from the community. As noted by Anthony Wall, to participate in this dichotomized mode of knowledge is to reproduce power structures based on domination and to exclude any possibility for productive dialogic exchange.[8] This political/epistemological bias has been rejected and denounced as much in feminist criticism, particularly by ecofeminists such as Maria Mies and Vandana Shiva, as in postcolonial criticism (e.g., Gayatri Chakravorty Spivak, Homi Bhabha), both of which critiques inform this study.[9] My own reflections have been formulated through (not above and beyond) experience, as those of an "organic intellectual" (Gramsci, Freire)—also known as a "reflective practitioner" or an "action researcher"—with Bakhtin's concepts of answerability and participatory thought providing the initial impetus to my PAR practice.

Against the pursuit of an abstract, specialized philosophy, Bakhtin defends the practice of "participatory thought," in which the active process and the product are not separated, but rather linked as an indivisible unit in the contextual integrity of life. According to Bakhtin, we naturally assume the standpoint of involved participants insofar as we are socialized human beings contributing de facto to history. Participative thinking is oriented toward "what-is-to-*be*-attained."[10] This practice prevents the reification of theory, as "our world as answerable deed 'must not oppose itself to theory and thought, but must incorporate them into itself as necessary moments that are wholly answerable.'"[11] The reification of dialogism in particular, which academic commodification has fossilized, isolated, and emptied of its dynamic tension and its ethico-political orientation, can also be countered by participative thinking.[12] Such thinking breaks the closed circle of knowledge shared only among initiates that feeds the academic political economy more than it informs social change. The dialogism that links theory to practice also prevents the reification of action when it is cut off from critical thought and helps to keep both in a state of tension and reciprocal interruption. This dialogism also reduces the power relation that typically holds between the academic researcher and the community participant/research subject (in my case, the immigrant woman), who is often reduced to a mute example. Thus any operational use of Bakhtin's dialogical concepts in social research (e.g., "Being-as-event," the unity of theory and action, participatory thinking, the exotopic position of the empathic researcher, an ethics of responsibility) will give that research the same theoretical ground as PAR.

Dialogism, which is neither dialogue nor dialectics, is a philosophy of communication that maps the discursive territory of difference. Bakhtinian dialogism conceptualizes the self as constructed through language so as to be and to transform social interaction; any self can thus become an agent of historical change. Language, which is beyond systematization, does not have an independent existence, but is shaped by the sociohistorical context in which it is grounded. Our utterances are unique (nonrepeatable) and heterogeneous; they are saturated with voices, accents, values, intentionality, and worldviews in dialogue within the self (inner speech) or with others. Language is characterized by heteroglossia, or speech diversity, and this diversity is not only linguistic or cultural but socio-ideological. Dialogism acknowledges and validates (as opposed to concealing, subsuming, or transcending) the heterogeneity of utterances and the worldviews they entail: "every utterance . . . partakes of social and historical heteroglossia."[13] The discursive space is one of struggle not between individual wills or logical contradictions, but among sociolinguistic points of view. In dialogism, as Wall notes, understanding means that "instead of trying to transcend the otherness of the object of knowledge in a desperate move to rise above it, . . . the participant in dialogue lets the other of the present pursuit of knowledge enter into the very words and thoughts with which understanding is to be achieved."[14] The act of understanding is not reductionist, but rather leaves the markers of difference intact. Dialogism is thus the heart of PAR.

Participatory Action Research is a sociological qualitative theory that developed out of critical theory and was formulated in the 1970s.[15] Its history spans the political struggles of various groups and movements, including students, feminists, antiracists, gays and lesbians, and ecologists. Participatory Action Research is critical theory applied to concrete situations of need, where it is deployed as an active reflection (or reflexive action) by both an intellectual/practitioner and a social group confronted with significant issues. As both a counterdiscourse to any form of hegemony and a multivoiced dialogic practice, PAR is doubly dialogical.[16] Focused on the coming to consciousness of an exploited or marginalized social group, it deals with the contradiction at work between a power-maintaining ideology (a patriarchal culture, e.g., or an immigration policy) and a social reality with emancipatory possibilities. The goal of PAR is always to improve the life of such a social group on its own terms. In acknowledging and validating popular knowledge and collective decision making (against the tendency of both Marxist grand narratives and postmodern disoriented fragmentation), PAR puts life and legitimacy back into the knowledge exchanged in the public square. The academic who practices PAR from an exotopic standpoint is motivated by empathy, so can let go of power while exchanging knowledge and sharing experience with a community group. S/he functions at once as an intellectual/practitioner and a facilitator/participant in this process.

There are several important features which combine to distinguish PAR from other approaches in social science research. Although dialogism is the driving force of PAR,[17] it is also community-determined, with the researcher deferring to a community's sense of the issues to be researched and resolved within its specific historical and spatial context. The community or social group then braids its own knowledge with that of the researcher/facilitator to orient and target that shared knowledge toward the well-being of the group. The knowledge, experiences, and practices of all participants can thus be interactively connected and legitimized. There is no attempt to divide the process from the product, the production of dialogue from its effect; instead, these are unified in the coming to consciousness (and empowering) of the participants, who maintain control over the process. Their foregrounding as speaking subjects gives participants, particularly women, a voice, and all participatory action revolves around the right to speak in an ethico-political sense. (Quoting bell hooks, Budd Hall stresses our collective and individual responsibility to distinguish between speaking for the sake of self-promotion while exploiting "the 'exotic' other" and gaining the ability to speak as "a gesture of resistance, an affirmation of struggle."[18])

While its ethic emanates from the abolition of the subject-researcher/object-informer dichotomy, as a qualitative method PAR systematically keeps individuals and their urgent needs from being obscured by jargon and numbers, including statistics. Participatory Action Research is thus paradigmatic of sociological research that adheres to an ethics of answerability.[19] Such an ethical position is essential to ensuring that the participants and their utterances do not become "disposable" and that the results of the research generate recommendations which can positively affect their lives. The researcher is primarily accountable to the community and only secondarily to his/her institution or granting agency, a dual accountability that is itself a source of dialogic tension between two research paradigms.

In accordance with its qualitative approach, PAR privileges all forms of dialogue, such as focus groups, personal interviews, storytelling, and popular theater, as means of access to knowledge and the gathering of data. This methodology helps the researcher catch nuances, contradictions, and fluctuations in the process of knowledge creation and dissemination. It goes without saying that such a methodology requires a considerable temporal and emotional investment, as well as a willingness to ignore the deadlines and demands for quantification of productivity imposed by granting agencies and institutions. At the stage of data analysis, it is the emergence of a pattern through reiteration that constitutes the truth-value of the analysis, which is made with the participants. Furthermore, the instrumental validity of the knowledge generated does not depend on either extrinsic criteria, such as verification by a control group or random selection of participants, or its perfectability according to its own inner law, but rather on its usefulness in transforming the situation relative to the participants' experiential input.[20] As in a Bakhtinian approach, such qualitative research requires the researcher/practitioner to recognize the subject status of the participants and to valorize the "everydayness" and cultural specificity of the knowledge that surfaces in their utterances. This research thereby creates a holistic knowledge that can account for the individual's historical uniqueness, including his/her body and personal past, and for the collective memory of his/her community.

Following a national competition in 1993, four academic researchers received a grant from the Health Ministry of Canada and the Social Sciences and Humanities Research Council to undertake research projects on the promotion of health (physical, mental, emotional, and spiritual) in relation to work (remunerated or nonremunerated and in or outside the home). I chose to work with groups of immigrant women and to analyze the effects of ethnocultural factors and immigration on work and health.

The following six groups, of approximately eight women each and composed on the basis of distinct ethnocultural profiles, participated in various PAR projects:

1. The "De Mujer a Mujer Group" addressed the question of Latin American women's mental health. Community facilitators were trained (in participant-organized workshops) to enhance the self-esteem of Latin American women in their new sociocultural context. The group decided to communicate exclusively in Spanish.
2. The "Work Action Group," composed of women of different origins who work in a food-processing factory where immigrant women comprise the majority among the workers, has identified such health problems as repetitive-strain disorders and (as they became aware of their rights) such exploitative conditions as overtime paid at the regular rate at the factory. Working in collaboration with a legal aid office, participants have conducted targeted research, composed and distributed information aimed at raising the consciousness of the factory workers, and implemented an action plan.
3. This group, also composed of women of different origins, has worked toward the formation of a support group for refugee women who entered Canada as torture victims.

4. This group, composed of South Asian high school students, has organized focus groups to identify mental health problems related to self-esteem, racism, and intergenerational or intercultural conflicts. The students organized a cultural show at their school to increase public awareness of their culture and to improve their own self-esteem.
5. The "Accreditation Group," composed mainly of foreign-educated/trained female physicians who have been unable to practice medicine in Canada, has addressed questions to do with professional accreditation and integration.
6. This group served as an advisory committee for the other five, creating a network of communication and community partnerships between the groups and immigrant organizations.

These six action/research groups have used various PAR methods, such as focus groups, interviews, questionnaires, and culturally informed modes of communication, to gather information from immigrant women in their own words. The data collected was then analyzed and used to prepare an action plan. A project report reflecting the voices of the participants was edited and approved by them. Over 100 immigrant women have participated in the projects to date.

At the first meeting of the advisory committee (in October 1994), the following statements were made and questions raised: "We want neither forms nor questionnaires, neither numbers nor statistics. . . . We have been researched to death. . . . What has happened to all those reports? Who benefited from them? What do reports tell us that we don't already know? . . . We know our own needs and we know what has to be done: let's take action now." Such comments by immigrant women, which have been repeatedly voiced since then, indicate their doubts not only about the academic institution but also about the methodologies that reify them, contrary to their own experience, and that do not hold the researcher directly accountable to the community. These women opted for the more "radical" form of PAR, in which research merges with action in the dialogical process/product. After gathering data needed to address the identified issues, they prepared action plans and continued to organize activities aimed at resolving these issues until they considered the project to have been completed. They also controlled their own action/research budgets.

Their experience led them to apply and practice Bakhtinian critical theory in the form of a constructive politics of doubt. Over the course of the project, these women identified different worldviews and the interests each represented in their own everyday lives, and they practiced action/research as an empowering, health-promoting counterdiscourse to traditional research. For example, the "Accreditation Group" viewed the regulatory barriers to their professional accreditation as a political discourse on immigrants and of corporate medicine, which wanted to maintain and reserve its privileges. As one woman remarked during a July 1996 focus group meeting, "They [immigration officials] said there are no openings for doctors in Canada, but they gave us many points for our education; it's because they want educated nannies and taxi drivers. . . . The *Spectator* [a local newspaper] claims Hamilton is short of doctors, so why do they create so many obstacles for us? Because doctors want to keep their control and their big salaries." As they moved beyond data collection on this issue, they worked (in a support group and during information workshops) toward the removal of obstacles in their personal lives as well as drafting policy changes. They overcame the sense of inadequacy and fatalistic helplessness that those regulatory barriers had engendered, and several participants subsequently gained admission to graduate programs in the health sciences.

Practicing PAR with immigrant women not only forces the researcher to deconstruct any theory that sanctions dichotomy, but PAR itself challenges the very notion of theory. Bakhtin rejected any separation between "elite" and "popular" culture, particularly in his study of Rabelais. In the same spirit, and like Vandana Shiva, participatory action researchers understand culture not as a superstructure but as integral to a way of life and a way of perceiving work, health, and basic survival needs.[21] The circumstances under which immigrant women in Canada work do not readily lend themselves to consideration within the web of dichotomizing influences that have traditionally opposed the private and the public sphere; immigrant women tend to do more work at home than native Canadian women do, and they often assume more unpaid caregiving obligations in response to cultural expectations (e.g., South Asian women in an extended family).[22] Moreover, distinctions on the basis of education can become irrelevant when many women who hold degrees from universities in their countries of origin work in Canadian factories or take night courses to improve their condition. Their status has also usually entailed a degree of socioeconomic and geographic mobility that is difficult to capture through a quantitative approach (i.e., statistics based on a standard questionnaire), which tends to freeze an immanent or dynamic reality into a fixed image. Women's (particularly immigrant women's) work and knowledge are marked by diversity and fluidity. (No one was more sensitive to the mobility of existence than Bakhtin.[23]) This situation has effects on the health of immigrant women. (The definition of health has been considerably expanded by Health Canada and the World Health Organization to cover mental, emotional, and spiritual, as well as physical, health.) Some women's health issues are specific to women, such as reproductive health, or are experienced differently by women, such as cardiovascular health, and are treated as distinctive. Immigrant women experience other specific health problems as well, particularly in the area of mental health (e.g., stress of family separation or of adaptation), which are often resolved in different contexts and ways.[24] They also perceive and experience their life stages and their health in accordance with specific ethnocultural factors. Finally, the transformation of the present health-care system from one geared to costly clinical/medical care into one with a home-care structure will affect all women, but particularly immigrant women.[25] While women in general will continue to bear a greater responsibility for the care of the sick and the elderly population (and no doubt at even lower wages), many immigrant women also assume a large share of the caregiving in their extended families and already comprise a large percentage of waged home-care workers.

Using a dialogical approach in analyzing and acting on the sociocultural determinants of immigrant women's health means listening to and understanding the intense dialogism of their utterances; it means hearing and accounting for gendered differences of worldview (e.g., Latin American "machismo") or for generational worldview differences (e.g., South Asian parents and teenagers on the issue of dating) within a particular culture. It means listening to the dialogical interaction between the traditions of the incoming culture and the norms of the host culture (e.g., on spanking children) or between women from different cultures who comprise a single ethnic group or community (e.g., Latin American women, who may represent the considerable cultural differences between Argentina and Guatemala or Chile).[26] Sometimes a dialogic tension polarizes gendered and ethnocultural representation in one culture that comes into contact with another. In the process, women may, for instance, take an exotopic position vis-à-vis both cultures and compare them. If they then perceive femininity as a sociocultural construct, it can transform their beliefs and practices. The PAR methodology is simply a friendly host in the social sciences to dialogical criticism, a means of reporting such utterances and the transformative process they undergo, a way of making sense of them, of validating and operationalizing them in our research/action. Both PAR and Bakhtinian dialogism operate from a position of "empathic exotopy" which allows for culture's validation and critical understanding.

How does exotopy create a space for critical understanding? Bakhtin describes the process as follows:

> In the realm of culture, outsideness is a most powerful factor in understanding. It is only in the eyes of *another* culture that foreign culture reveals itself fully and profoundly. . . . A meaning only reveals its depths once it has encountered and come into contact with another, foreign meaning: they engage in a kind of dialogue, which surmounts the closedness and one-sidedness of these particular meanings, these cultures. We raise new questions for a foreign culture, ones that it did not raise itself; we seek answers to our own questions in it. . . . Such a dialogic encounter of two cultures does not result in merging or mixing. Each retains its own unity and *open* totality, but they are mutually enriched.[27]

As is the case with both Bahktin and PAR, empathy is what moves me as a researcher/practitioner toward the project participants and into them as myself, only to return to my unique position outside the other, from which I can see that other in her totality and thus understand her experience from the inside/outside. In that understanding, my acts of empathizing and objectifying are not dichotomized; they interpenetrate each other.[28] This position is reflected in the virtually direct reporting by the PAR researcher of utterances, since "the more dogmatic an utterance, the less leeway permitted between truth and falsehood or good and bad in its reception by those who comprehend and evaluate, the greater will be the depersonalization that the forms of reported speech will undergo."[29] Tzvetan Todorov remarks that "Bakhtin denounces the generalizing effect of reported speech at the expense of speech for which the speaking subject is fully responsible."[30] The direct reporting of an utterance is not a stylistic but an ethical and political choice that enables a relatively muted voice to be heard and that recognizes the contribution of every subject to cultural production and to history. The immigrant is a particularly complex subject.

It is difficult to agree on a definition of the immigrant, which may be legalistic, such as the one to which Statistics Canada subscribes (any person born outside of Canada), or self-defining (any person who perceives him/herself as such). Setting aside the immigrant defined as an economic and sociopolitical construct, which would take us down a different discussion path, the one I employ here is the second (self-identification), which has been approved by Health Canada.[31] This definition is compatible with the feminist dialogical action/research approach that enables participants' perceptions to be expressed. Self-perception integrates social perception, better expresses the fluidity and complexity of immigrant identity, and is a sound basis on which to position oneself in a given community.[32] From this perspective, a third-generation person of color could still be considered an immigrant, if that accorded with her self-perception and way of life.

Individual and cultural identity is always in the process of being formed and transformed, constantly nourished by new sources and currents, but this process is intensified for the immigrant, whose identity formation is plurivocal and accelerated, as Georges Vignaux remarks: "To enter into a different culture is necessarily to step into another universe of significations, to change codes, to displace one's own reference points, and this is generally done through the mediation of transposing concrete experiences into discourse."[33] Identity then becomes exploded, mixed, transitional, unstable, and always under construction. For immigrant women, especially, the process occurs in a space of struggle and power relationships where position becomes agency. In the course of emigration, these women often lose their original professional status and identity, and those who are sponsored by a spouse often find that their access to language training and educational opportunities is more limited than his. When a new language must be learned and their children acquire it more rapidly, some degree of parental authority may be lost by these women as well. Here is how one of the members of the "Accreditation Group" described the experience during a January 1996 meeting:

> I was respected as a legal administrator in my country and by my children when I joined my husband in Canada after he found a job. He is the one who wanted to emigrate because he hated the regime

> in our country. I had to follow if I wanted to keep my marriage. I have cleaned houses, looked after children, cared for mentally challenged adults. It was very hard. This is why I have decided to study in Canada. . . . Often, because of my accent, people don't believe me when I tell them I finished law school in my country; they think I barely passed third grade. My children also tease me and correct me.

The process of identity recognition, if it is to be conducive to well-being and transform subjecthood into agency, must first be *voiced*.

"But I hear *voices* in everything and dialogic relations among them," said Bakhtin,[34] for whom voice endowed dialogism with profound significance by its representation of the concreteness of individuals. Intonation, a corporeal anchor and bearer of social value and meaning, also disrupts the body/mind dichotomy.[35] Feminist critique has reinforced this point of view by calling attention to women's (and immigrant women's) having been dispossessed of their voices, along with their knowledge and their past.[36] When minorities become invisible and inaudible in health research,[37] it can have deleterious effects on their physical and mental health. The following comments by participants in PAR projects eloquently attest to such dispossession and its effects:

> I had to give an oral presentation on immigrants to my class of twenty-seven students. Only five were interested, and they were all women of color. The others did not even want to hear me, they don't even want to know.
>
> . . . .
>
> Because I spoke bad English, I had no credibility. Her [an administrator's] jaw dropped when she heard I had finished law school in Poland.
>
> . . . .
>
> When I had to open an account in a bank, I could not speak English well, but I filled out a form and wrote "doctor" as my profession. The teller looked at me, and I looked back; I had no makeup on. "Doctor?" she said. She scratched out "doctor" and wrote "student."
>
> . . . .
>
> I come from an English-speaking country, but I am Black. When we arrived in Canada, my two sisters and I were sent to school. I was

> immediately put in an ESL [English as a Second Language] class and my two sisters were put one grade below their level. No questions asked. . . . The authorities spoke of me among themselves in front of me, as if I were invisible; they would say, "She. . . ."
>
> . . . .
>
> I may speak with an accent, but I don't think with an accent.
>
> . . . .
>
> My head is going to explode one of these days. Four years in Canada. I have so much knowledge of medicine, and I read so much. I am going crazy learning and not participating. I have attempted suicide in my mind many times. I have anxiety disorders and sleep disorders. I still read a lot in my field—it is a defense mechanism for not being able to practice.
>
> . . . .
>
> I look strong, but nobody knows what I am inside. But my body knows. My jaws are locked, I grind my teeth.

In my action/research, it is not only the voices of immigrant women that become central to the process, but also the culturally informed language of their bodies—their mannerisms—which are transcribed as accurately as possible, since these are also bearers of knowledge, value, and meaning. Vocal modulations, laughter, hesitations, and silences, as well as postures and gestures, are noted and interpreted by the facilitator and participants. All precautions are taken to avoid cultural anthropophagy and knowledge monopoly on the part of the researcher. It is important for the researcher to be conversant with the culture of the participants in order to understand the signification of their communications, along with whatever values these might embody.

Many immigrant women, including those who do not yet speak English (or French) when they arrive in Canada, are polyglots, so they are doubly silenced in this regard, apart from their oppression as subjected women in patriarchal cultures. Much is therefore at stake when we enable their "voicing." To listen to these voices is to acknowledge and affirm their hybridity. A hybrid construction "contains mixed within it two utterances, two speech manners, two styles, two 'languages,' two semantic and axiological belief systems."[38] Cultural hybridity can create mental stress, sometimes with tragic consequences. The immigrant woman walks a tightrope between two cultures, two value systems, sometimes two penal codes (customary and legal). In Canada, she could be legally charged for spanking her child. Many immigrant women must also cope with professional hybridity, such as the parking attendant who was a physician in Burundi or the housekeeper who was a sculptor in Argentina. Their utterances emerge from layers of experiences and speech genres. The physician from Burundi described her own marked hybridity in these terms during a February 1996 meeting: "As an immigrant, I am treated like an amnesiac. I have a Canadian present but also a past from somewhere else. I feel better when it is acknowledged." As for the hybridity or heteroglossia in the women's speech, it reflects tensions between the present and the past, as well as those between or among different socio-ideological groups, and a flawed translation can have serious consequences. One misunderstanding that took several sessions to clear up, for example, involved the nature of "nursing homes" (private clinics in India vs. retirement establishments in Canada). Another misunderstanding came to light when several South Asian adolescents answered "yes" to the question "Do you drink?" and could have unwittingly generated data making them out to be alcoholics.

It is also important to understand corporeal and gestural hybridity. For example, a lowered gaze in a South Asian woman signifies deference. For those who come from countries with dictatorial regimes, demeanor can be traumatically loaded, with the noise of a car or a doorbell's unexpected ring provoking strong reactions that may be misinterpreted. A reference to writing a "report" made one member of the "De Mujer a Mujer Group" go red with anger, recalling as it did the Spanish term *raportar*, which had connotations of police surveillance for her.

How could any one questionnaire, passive observation, or meeting possibly account for all these hybridities and their shifting? How could any meaningful health promotion be undertaken on the basis of erroneous interpretations? The immigrant woman's utterance is at least a double-voiced one, heavy with its own history and space, with a layered identity, with emotions and values. An Indian woman from Rajasthan describes snow as like the cool sand of the Thar Desert at dusk. How are the value, the subversive function, the pain and pride evoked by the "popular kitchens" of Chile or Guatemala to be translated? No "scientific" discourse could render the semantic, emotive, cultural, and political prism of such an expression. Numerous sessions are necessary to get from silence to speech, then to translate and interpret so as to minimize the risk of betrayal. This "betrayal" is also a sign of resistance to translation; it creates a gap—the space of the immigrant's irreducible subjecthood and agency—thus putting the authority of the translator and of representation itself into question. As Peter Hitchcock rightly observes, "Bakhtin's thoughts on hybridity, interference, and plurivocality may prove fruitful in destabilizing the operative logic of translation as control. . . . Bakhtin's notion of co-authoring and answerability, while not removing the will-to-monologism of translation, attempts to pick away at the seams of the unitary author. . . . If the subaltern subject speaks at all, it is through this decentering process, not in an objectified individual voice of ontological and ideological being."[39]

The dialogical hybridity of identity entailed by immigration is a potential source of enrichment in social interaction, knowledge creation, and health promotion, but if it is not heeded, understood, or validated, the immigrant woman becomes a silenced, subaltern subject, which can have serious consequences for her mental health. Let us join forces here with postcolonial critics and subaltern theorists, who address diversity and mobility, situating—and validating—them within a historical context of power relations.[40] "Can the Subaltern Speak?" Spivak answers her own question with an emphatic "no": the subaltern cannot speak either because she is silenced as a colonized subject or because aspects of her identity, such as race and gender, disappear from the frame (as in an ossified Marxism) or her subjecthood becomes an aporia (as in poststructuralism). Potentially emancipatory narratives are thus thwarted. Even when her voice is foregrounded, the conditions of knowledge dissemination in a hegemonic, first-world language (such as English) can lead to its misframing or misrepresentation. The subaltern remains a construct to be "spoken," an ever-represented other.

In the PAR context, the immigrant woman is considered a subaltern subject whose agency articulates with her relocation and reinscription in a new context. She does not function within the domains of legitimized language, knowledge, and power, often belonging to an economically disadvantaged group which is likely to have emigrated from a formerly colonized country. She may have internalized both a cultural silencing of women and a silencing imposed by her ethnocultural community, intent on protecting its reputation. The woman of color is triply subaltern, as Spivak remarks: "Clearly, if you are poor, black and female, you get it in three ways."[41] The situation of the subaltern is shared by that 24 percent (a little over half of whom are women) of the Hamilton population who have emigrated in the past decade from either developing countries or those in conflict. As confirmed by local reports, immigrant women tend to occupy low-level positions (often in more than one job), are badly paid, and suffer from various health problems related to their condition as immigrants.[42] In such situations of unrecognized need, the counterdiscursive effects of PAR can be useful, especially to women who are facing various forms of conflict and struggle. If religious or ethnic tensions were experienced in the immigrant's country of origin, these can have spillover effects in the host country. A nearly universal distrust of academia among the participants in the PAR projects was sometimes compounded by a lingering political distrust among those who came from countries under a repressive regime. Immigrants are not "blank slates"; they embody a personal past and the history of their country of origin, which, together with cultural and emigrational conditions, shape their present lives and affect their well-being. The dialogical approach of participatory action research can capture and engage the complexity of their identity and encourage context-specific emancipatory action through which subaltern subjects may transform themselves and each other into participating agents in their communities.[43]

While Bakhtin never emigrated, he did experience internal exile and the inability to express himself freely, which informed an insightful account of his own forced hybridity. Emigration always partakes of the larger temporality and is both paradigmatic and historically specific.[44] The generic and the specific, in dialogue, feed one another. Immigration is accomplished through "the intrinsic connectedness of temporal and spatial relationships" specific to the chronotope.[45] Since emigration is chronotopic, it engenders the subject, organizing or even fashioning events and experiences. A qualitative approach such as PAR is particularly suited to this chronotopic situation, permitting the researcher and participants to grasp spatiotemporal synchrony and diachrony, to extract patterns, variations, and changes, and to explicate cultural nuances of meaning that inform the desired change. The PAR approach requires a high degree of personification in social research.

Bakhtin recognized the limits between reification and personification in theory in the human sciences, and the philosophy he articulated in "Toward a Methodology of the Human Sciences" is embedded in PAR:

> The exact sciences constitute a monologic form of knowledge: the intellect contemplates a *thing* and expounds upon it. There is only one subject here—cognizing (contemplating) and speaking (expounding). In opposition to the subject there is only a *voiceless thing*. Any object of knowledge (including man [and woman]) can be perceived and cognized as a thing. But a subject as such cannot be perceived and studied as a thing, for as a subject it cannot, while remaining a subject, become voiceless, and, consequently, cognition of it can only be *dialogic*. . . . The dialogic activity of the acknowledged subject, and the degrees of this activity. The thing and the personality (subject) as *limits* of cognition. . . . The event-potential of dialogic cognition. Meeting. . . .
>
> Understanding as correlation with other texts and reinterpretation, in a new context. . . .
>
> Complete maximum reification would inevitably lead to the disappearance of the infinitude and bottomlessness of meaning. . . .
>
> . . . .
>
> In the human sciences precision is surmounting the otherness of the other without transforming him [or her] into purely one's own.[46]

The need for accuracy and for an ethics of difference in knowledge creation on (and with) immigrant women compel us to move toward personification and away from a reifying theorization, especially since the quantitative methods of social science research (polls, statistics, etc.) may be unfamiliar in their own cultural contexts.[47] (Anthony Wall goes so far as to suggest that such methods are typical of Western epistemology, while Alan Bishop sees Western mathematics in particular as an instrument of colonial oppression.[48]) The cultures of immigrant women have their own ways of creating knowledge, such as the popular theater, or *arpilleras*, of Latin Americans or the reggae of various Caribbean cultures. We must seek—and validate—knowledge where it is to be found in order to restore its original efficacy and integrate it dialogically into our collective knowledge, which can only be enriched by it. The process of creating and validating knowledge itself contributes to the mental health of immigrant women as well as constituting an epistemological approach with an implicit ethics and politics of research, in contrast to traditional approaches, which transform participants into disposable objects while appropriating their voices and their knowledge. Numbers, formulas, and jargon often mask the urgency of these women's needs.[49] When separated from action, quantitative research is accountable mainly to an institution. Qualitative research such as PAR, on the other hand, is concerned with efficacy and must answer to the participants, whose current welfare is at stake. Participatory Action Research is inscribed within the temporality of a life and its immediate needs, lending this research an urgency, particularly when at-risk populations are involved and during periods of economic crisis or political change, with all their attendant feelings of insecurity. Instead of paying an expert for sophisticated computerized data analysis, for example, we paid immigrant women to transcribe the focus-group discussions and then taught them how to code the data manually, thereby empowering them with skills and remuneration while gaining perhaps more accurate results.

These considerations raise questions about the politics of research disconnected from action. One might even wonder if research, in the social sciences at least, is not at times a way of creating the illusion of action, perhaps to delay or prevent it. At the academic/institutional level, my own particular epistemology amounts to a political counterdiscourse that has charted a rather thorny path between the distrustful skepticism of immigrant women, on the one hand, and the incredulity of peers and granting agencies who are still reluctant to recognize the scientific legitimacy of PAR, on the other.

A methodology such as PAR brings in its wake a different politics of multiculturalism for Canada, one that would not look to the government to subsidize the reductionist folklorization of ethnocultural groups, but would instead enable political control by those groups themselves. On this point, I subscribe to the politics of recognition advocated by Charles Taylor, who invokes Bakhtin in the course of arguing against the politics of rights advocated by one brand of liberalism. Taylor perceives "rights liberalism" as a hegemonic monologic discourse: "The claim is that the supposedly neutral set of difference-blind principles of the politics of equal dignity is in fact a reflection of one hegemonic culture."[50] Contemporary feminism, race relations, and multiculturalism are all premised on the idea that the withholding of recognition is a form of oppression.[51] Since identity is shaped dialogically, however, cultural dialogism implicitly grants such recognition. For Taylor, withholding recognition amounts to an ethico-political violation.

On the international level, the PAR methodology subscribes to a politics of alternative development that functions counter-discursively to such hegemonic, ethnocentric development strategies as the globalization implemented by the IMF or the World Bank. Alternative development works toward "the indigenization of development concepts and practices."[52] This accords with the diversification advocated by Mies and Shiva, who show that monocultures (literally and figuratively) endanger the cultural interdependence that is essential to the survival of the planet. Monocultures are the deeds (or rather misdeeds) of a hegemonic capitalist and colonial imperialism that resists biodiversity as an obstacle to (mono-)technological progress. Mies and Shiva consider women privileged historical agents for a desirable biodiversity. But the myth of a value-free, ideology-neutral research must yield to research that is consciously oriented by an acknowledged ideological position.[53] There is no paradox in the statement that objectivity and accuracy depend on the empathic inclusion of subjectivities.

Let us not, however, end on a note of complacent panegyric, but rather with a few words of caution. The ethnocultural factor must not be isolated or privileged at the expense of other important conditions in the formation of identity or the affirmation of diversity because, in doing so, the PAR methodology would risk sanctioning certain practices harmful to women (such as genital mutilation). This makes it necessary to bring a feminist critical perspective to bear on our analysis. The dialogical combination of gender, ethnocultural, and race factors permits their mutual disruption and correction, thus precluding the hegemony of any one type of factor. This methodology is also most useful at the microlevel, as PAR based on voicing could become difficult, costly, and less relevant in a project involving a large number of people. At the microlevel, however, PAR becomes a catalyst and a tool for a politics of recognition, entailing both an emancipatory practice and an experience in participatory democracy, ultimately offering the best epistemological, ethical, and political means of enhancing the well-being of immigrant women.

It may be unfair to reduce Bakhtin to "a very bad example, though one with some very good arguments," because he whiled away the 1917 Revolution "reading in the library."[54] Not only did he pay the price of exile for his writings, but these included some of the most compelling pages ever written on the meaning and value of dialogism and on the non-alibi of every being in historical agency—both notions of great relevance to the contemporary intellectual and the practitioner of Participatory Action Research.

Bakhtin's thought is indeed without borders and defies any unifying appropriation.

—Translated by Anne Malena

Notes

This article was written with the assistance of a Social Science and Humanities Research Council and Health Canada grant, which is gratefully acknowledged. I would also like to gratefully acknowledge the collaboration of Myrna Pond, a research assistant with the project who facilitated two PAR groups; Minoo Farragheh, Nazilla Khanlou, and Barbara Chudyk, cofacilitators of other PAR groups; Isik Urla Zeytinoglu, who acted as a consultant and partly funded the article's translation; and all the immigrant women who have participated in the PAR project.

1 Critical theorists, who are mainly to be found in the social sciences, behave like distant neighbors with the literary critics and philosophers who predominate among Bakhtinians (and vice versa). Separated by an illusory fence, each group cultivates its own patch, using the same tools and, from time to time, exchanging a few polite words over that fence. Sometimes they echo each other, practicing a fortuitous or unacknowledged intertextuality. For example, the title of Michael Holquist's 1981 collection of Bakhtin's essays *The Dialogic Imagination* echoes, without referencing, Martin Jay's 1973 title *The Dialectical Imagination*. Similarly, Peter Hitchcock's 1993 *Dialogics of the Oppressed* echoes the title of Paulo Freire's 1970 *Pedagogy of the Oppressed*. The term *dialogism* frequently appears in critical theory texts, typically without reference to Bakhtin, although one notable exception is Michael Gardiner's meaningful dialogue between Bakhtin and critical theory in his 1992 *Dialogics of Critique*. If critical theory started out with dialectics, it has gradually become dialogical as it has gained some distance from its Marxist origins. The emergence of social activism based on criteria other than class, such as gender (feminism, gay and lesbian activism) or race (antiracist movements, postcolonial criticism), has also contributed to a rapprochement between critical theory and Bakhtinian thought.

2 See Michael Holquist, Foreword to M. M. Bakhtin, *Toward a Philosophy of the Act*, ed. Michael Holquist and Vadim Liapunov, trans. Vadim Liapunov (Austin, 1993), vii–xv, esp. xi–xv; and M. M. Bakhtin, "Art and Answerability" (1919), and *Author and Hero in Aesthetic Activity* (c. 1920–23), in *Art and Answerability: Early Philosophical Essays*, ed. Michael Holquist and Vadim Liapunov, trans. Vadim Liapunov (Austin, 1990), 1–3, esp. 2, and 4–256, esp. 5.

3 Bakhtin, *Philosophy of the Act*, 42.

4 Holquist, Foreword to *Philosophy of the Act*, ix.

5 Holquist notes that Bakhtin, Heidegger, and Sartre, all three of whom witnessed historical horrors, avoided the philosophical abstraction that had until then characterized Western thought, which is somewhat detached from the reality of the world. He even recognizes that Bakhtin's work, prior to and more so than Sartre's, opens onto collective action; see his "Introduction: The Architectonics of Answerability," in *Art and Answerability*, ix–xlix, esp. xxix–xxx.

6 Bakhtin's words on aesthetic activity in *Author and Hero* receive an added weight when read in terms of their historical context, since, for him, aesthetic activity is a unique way of being/acting in the world and of contributing to it. He analyzed Rabelais's work not as an inert aesthetic object, but rather as a text/act pointing toward the horizon of a democratic utopia. "The great man in Rabelais is profoundly democratic," as Bakhtin puts it in "Forms of Time and of the Chronotope in the Novel: Notes toward a Historical Poetics" (1937–38), in *The Dialogic Imagination: Four Essays*, ed. Michael Holquist, trans. Caryl Emerson and Michael Holquist (Austin, 1981), 84–258; quotation from 241. In *The Dialogics of Critique* (London and New York, 1992), 181–84, Michael Gardiner also recognizes that Bakhtin traced the horizon of an unalienated, egalitarian society, though without defining the means to create such a society. Dialogism was to be the driving force of this truly democratic society, as well as a source of energy for numerous cultural practices. In the historical context of Stalinism, such a literary standpoint or any declaration of religious faith constituted a seditious act.

7 See Budd Hall, Introduction to *Voices of Change: Participatory Research in the United States and Canada*, ed. Peter Park, Mary Brydon-Miller, Budd Hall, and Ted Jackson (Westport, CT, and London, 1993), xiii–xxii, esp. xviii–xix. According to Susan Silverman, granting agencies determine the orientation of research. The neutrality of money is an illusion. Even when a researcher wants only to publish a study, the granting agency puts pressure on him or her to orient the research in the preferred direction; see her "Practical Relevance of Qualitative Research," in *Interpreting Qualitative Data* (Halifax, 1993), 172–82, esp. 173. See also Alan Beattie, "Knowledge and Control in Health Promotion: A Test Case for Social Policy and Social Theory," in *The Sociology of the Health Service*, ed. Jonathan Gabe, Michael Calnan, and Michael Bury (London and New York, 1991), 162–202.

8 See Anthony Wall, "Levels of Discourse and Levels of Dialogue," in *Dialogism and Cultural Criticism*, ed. Clive Thomson and Hans Raj Dua (London, ONT, 1995), 65–82, esp. 65.

9 See Nancy Jay, "Gender and Dichotomy," in *A Reader in Feminist Knowledge*, ed. Sneja Gunew (London and New York, 1991 [1990]), 89–105; Maria Mies and Vandana Shiva, *Ecofeminism* (London and Atlantic Highlands, NJ, 1993); Gayatri Chakravorty Spivak, "Can the Subaltern Speak?," in *Colonial Discourse and Post-Colonial Theory: A Reader*, ed. R. J. Patrick Williams and Laura Chrisman (New York, 1994), 66–111; and "The Post-Colonial Critic" (interview), in *The Post-Colonial Critic*, ed. Sarah Harasym (New York, 1990), 67–75; Homi K. Bhabha, "Cultural Diversity and Cultural Differences," in *The Post-Colonial Studies Reader*, ed. Bill Ashcroft, Gareth Griffiths, and Helen Tiffin (New York, 1995), 206–13; and "Postcolonial Authority and Postmodern Guilt," in *Cultural Studies*, ed. Lawrence Grossberg, Cary Nelson, and Paula Treichler (New York, 1992), 56–69; *Third World Women and the Politics of Feminism*, ed. Chandra Talpade Mohanty, Ann Russo, and Lourdes Torres (Bloomington, 1991); and Sara Suleri, "Woman Skin Deep: Feminism and the Post-Colonial Condition," in Ashcroft et al., eds., *Post-Colonial Studies Reader*, 273–83.

10 Bakhtin, *Philosophy of the Act*, 11.

11 Holquist, Foreword to *Philosophy of the Act*, xiv. See also Bakhtin's remarks here (19n and 86 n. 29).

12 See M. M. Bakhtin, "Discourse in the Novel" (1934–35), in Holquist, ed., *Dialogic Imagination*, 259–422, esp. 273. See also Peter Hitchcock, *Dialogics of the Oppressed* (Minneapolis, 1993), xi–xxi and 192. The same concerns are expressed by Ken Hirschkop, "Introduction: Bakhtin and Cultural Theory," in *Bakhtin and Cultural Theory*, ed. Ken Hirschkop and David Shepherd (Manchester, 1989), 1–38; and by Clive Thomson, "Dialogue, Culture and the Dialogic: bell hooks and Gayatri Chakravorty Spivak," in Thomson and Dua, eds., *Dialogism and Cultural Criticism*, 47–65.

13 Bakhtin, "Discourse in the Novel," 272.

14 Wall, "Levels of Discourse," 69.

15 See Philip Wexler, *Critical Theory Now* (London, 1991), 55; see also Gardiner's excellent account in *Dialogics of Critique*, 82. For a feminist approach to critical theory, see Elisabeth Meese and Alice Parker, *The Difference Within: Feminism and Critical Theory* (Amsterdam, 1988); and B. Marshall, "Feminist Theory and Critical Theory," *Canadian Review of Sociology and Anthropology* 25 (1988): 208–30.

If Bakhtin often occulted sexual and ethnocultural difference, so too have some critical and PAR theorists. Against these tendencies, Patricia Maguire's work on feminist PAR has focused on women's needs as voiced by women and has followed an action plan accountable to women. She stresses women's diversity on the basis of class, race, and sexual identity, and, like other PAR researchers, she works from an empathic-outsider position that could be called exotopic. My own PAR projects, as research conducted by women, on women, and for women, is of course informed by feminism. See Maroussia Hajdukowski-Ahmed, "Bakhtin and Feminism: Two Solitudes?," in *Mikhail Bakhtin and the Epistemology of Discourse*, ed. Clive Thomson (Amsterdam and Atlanta, 1990), 153–63; Dale Bauer, *Feminism, Bakhtin and the Dialogic* (Albany, 1991); Patricia Maguire, *Doing Participatory Research: A Feminist Approach* (Amherst, 1987), esp. 105; and Margaret Denton, Maroussia Hajdukowski-Ahmed, Mary O'Connor, Karen Williams, and Isik Urla Zeytinoglu, "A Theoretical and Methodological Framework for Research on Women, Work and Health," McMaster Research Centre for the Promotion of Women's Health, McMaster University Working Papers Series 1 (1994).

16 See Donald E. Comstock and Russell Fox, "Participatory Research as Critical Theory: The North Bonneville, USA, Experience," in Park et al., eds., *Voices of Change*, 103–24, esp. 120 and 122; and see Hall's Introduction. See also L. David Brown and Rajesh Tandon, "Ideology and Political Economy in Inquiry: Action Research and Participatory Research," *Journal of Applied Behavioral Science* 19 (1983): 277–94.

17 See Peter Park, "What Is Participatory Research? A Theoretical and Methodological Perspective," in Park et al., eds., *Voices of Change*, 1–19, esp. 12–13; Gardiner, *Dialogics of Critique*, 166; Paulo Freire, *The Politics of Education: Culture, Power, and Liberation*, trans. Donaldo Macedo (London, 1985), 54; and *Pedagogy of the Oppressed*, trans. Myra Bergman Ramos (New York, 1970), 132; and Hitchcock, *Dialogics of the Oppressed*, 4–5.

18 Hall, Introduction to Park et al., eds., *Voices of Change*, xvii.

19 Silverman ("Practical Relevance of Qualitative Research," 173) outlines three research

paradigms that characterize the three main types of researchers found in the social sciences: the liberal, who seeks knowledge for its own sake; the bureaucrat, a consultant who must answer a specific question; and the activist, who puts his/her research at the service of a particular worldview. We could add a fourth, the PAR dialogician.

20 In quantitative research, the recourse to random selection or a control group is based on a hypothesized universalism and equality which in effect levels or conceals differences.

21 See Mies and Shiva, *Ecofeminism*, 16.

22 On immigrant women and work, see Donald Tomaskovic-Devey, *Gender and Racial Inequality at Work* (Ithaca, 1993); and the bibliography (which includes reports, position papers, and community studies) compiled by R. Ng and A. Estable, "Immigrant Women in the Labour Force: An Overview of Present Knowledge and Research," *Resources for Feminist Research* 16 (1987): 29–33.

23 As Holquist notes in his Introduction (xvi) to *Art and Answerability*, Bakhtin agreed with Hermann Cohen on the importance of the concept of process to the opening and the energy charge of experience, to the "ungiven," the unachieved.

24 On immigrant women and health, see especially B. Singh Bolaria and Rosemary Bolaria, *Racial Minorities, Medicine and Health* (Halifax, 1994); B. Singh Bolaria and Harley D. Dickinson, *Health, Illness, and Health Care in Canada*, 2d ed. (Toronto, 1994 [1988 ed.: *Sociology of Health Care in Canada*]); Canadian Task Force on Mental Health Issues Affecting Immigrants and Refugees, *After the Door Has Been Opened: Mental Health Issues Affecting Immigrants and Refugees in Canada* (Ottawa, 1988); and *Healthsharing* 12:3 (1991), a special issue on "Immigrant and Refugee Women's Health."

25 Three members of the "Accreditation Group" who had practiced medicine in their own country were employed as home-care providers in Canada prior to seeking accreditation as physicians.

26 See my "Manushi: Conversion or Conversation," in *Critical Studies*, ed. Clive Thomson (Amsterdam, 1995), 85–109, esp. 89 (on inter- and intracultural dialogism in an Indian feminist journal).

27 M. M. Bakhtin, "Response to a Question from the *Novy Mir* Editorial Staff," in *Speech Genres and Other Late Essays*, ed. Caryl Emerson and Michael Holquist, trans. Vern W. McGee (Austin, 1986), 1–9; quotation from 7.

28 See Bakhtin, *Philosophy of the Act*, 15.

29 V. N. Vološinov, *Marxism and the Philosophy of Language*, trans. Ladislav Matejka and I. R. Titunik (Cambridge, MA, 1986 [1973]), 120.

30 Tzvetan Todorov, *Mikhail Bakhtine: Le principe dialogique* (Paris, 1981), 157. Wall stresses the same point in "Levels of Discourse" (78).

31 See Nadia Klimko and Ted Richmond, "Ethno-Racial Data Collection: Results of a Pilot Project," *Health and Canadian Society/Santé et societé canadienne* 2 (1993): 119–32, esp. 119. On the definition of immigrant women as a political construct, see *Health, Race and Ethnicity*, ed. Thomas Rathwell and David Phillips (London, 1993), 4; and Roxana Ng, "The Social Construction of Immigrant Women in Canada," in *The Politics of Diversity*, ed. Roberta Hamilton and Michele Barrett (Montreal, 1987), 269–82. For a definition based on self-identification, see Vivienne Walters, Rhonda L. Lenton, and Marie McKeary, *Women's Health in the Context of Women's Lives: A Report* (Ottawa, 1995), 6.

32 See *Ethnic Groups and Boundaries: The Social Organization of Cultural Differences*, ed. Fredrik Barth (Boston, 1969); cited in *Immigrants and Refugees in Canada: A National Perspective on Ethnicity, Multiculturalism and Cross-Cultural Adjustment*, ed. Satya P. Sharma, Alexander M. Ervin, and Deirdre Meintel (Saskatoon and Montreal, 1991), 78.

33 Georges Vignaux, "Problématiques et analyses inter-culturelles: Mutations européennes et nouvelles perspectives," in *Mots, représentations: Enjeux dans les contacts interethniques et interculturels*, ed. Khadiyatoulah Fall, Daniel Simeoni, and Georges Vignaux (Ottawa, 1994), 5–33; quotation from 22. See also Hitchcock, *Dialogics of the Oppressed*, 10–11; Jocelyn Létourneau, *La question identitaire au Canada francophone* (Quebec, 1994), ix; and Amina Jamal, "Identity, Community and the Post-Colonial Experience of Migrancy," in *Resources for Feminist Research/Documentation pour la recherche féministe* 23–24 (1994–95): 35–41.

34 M. M. Bakhtin, "Toward a Methodology for the Human Sciences," in Emerson and Holquist, eds., *Speech Genres*, 159–72; quotation from 169.

35 See M. M. Bakhtin, "The Problem of Speech Genres," in ibid., 60–102, esp. 79. See also Bakhtin, "Discourse in the Novel," 264; and Todorov, *Mikhail Bakhtine*, 194–95.

36 See Maria Lugones and Elisabeth Spelman, "Have We Got a Theory for You?," *Women's Studies International Forum* 6 (1983): 573–81, esp. 573.

37 See Walters et al., *Women's Health in the Context of Women's Lives*, 16.

38 Bakhtin, "Discourse in the Novel," 304.

39 Hitchcock, *Dialogics of the Oppressed*, 188–89.

40 See Paul Gilroy, "Urban Social Movements, 'Race' and Community"; and Stuart Hall, "Cultural Identity and Diaspora," in Williams and Chrisman, eds., *Colonial Discourse and Post-Colonial Theory*, 404–21, esp. 412; and 392–403, esp. 393. See also James Clifford, "Traveling Cultures," in Grossberg et al., eds., *Cultural Studies*, 96–117.

41 Spivak, "Can the Subaltern Speak?," 90.

42 See Minoo Farragheh and Maroussia Hajdukowski-Ahmed, "Immigrant Women, Work and Health: A Literature Review," McMaster Research Centre for the Promotion of Women's Health, McMaster University Working Papers Series (forthcoming).

43 In response to the issue raised by Hitchcock (*Dialogics of the Oppressed*, 13), who wonders whether any current theorization of the subject encompasses the questioning and politicization that characterizes the dialogism of the oppressed, I would point to the theorization occurring for the past two decades in the social sciences (e.g., in anthropology); see, for example, Francis Affergan, *Exotisme et altérité* (Paris, 1987). Another example would be PAR itself. In titles of works featuring only such qualifiers as "subaltern" or "oppressed" (e.g., Spivak's "Can the Subaltern Speak?" or Hitchcock's book), the "victim image" is reinforced and the *constructive agency* of those groups overlooked (although the latter may be emphasized in the text itself, as it is in Spivak's and Hitchcock's).

44 See Paul Carter, "Spatial History," in Ashcroft et al., eds., *Post-Colonial Studies Reader*, 375–78, esp. 377.

45 Bakhtin, "Forms of Time and of the Chronotope in the Novel," 84.

46 Bakhtin, "Methodology for the Human Sciences," 161–62, 169.

47 On the importance of ethics in research on human subjects and, in particular, the effects of women's silencing, see my "Framing of the Shrew: Discourses on Hysteria

and Its Resisting Voices," in *Bakhtin: Carnival and Other Subjects*, ed. David G. Shepherd (Amsterdam, 1993), 177–96.

48 Wall, "Levels of Discourse"; and Alan Bishop, "Western Mathematics: The Secret Weapon of Cultural Imperialism," in Ashcroft et al., eds., *Post-Colonial Studies Reader*, 71–76, esp. 71.

49 See Huguette Dagenais, "Quand la réalité fait éclater les concepts: Réflexion méthodologique sur les femmes et le développement dans la région caraibe," in *Women, Feminism and Development/Femmes, féminisme et développement*, ed. Huguette Dagenais and Denise Piché (Montreal and Kingston, 1994), 111–51, esp. 113.

50 Charles Taylor, "The Politics of Recognition," in *Multiculturalism: A Critical Reader*, ed. David Theo Goldberg (Oxford and Cambridge, MA, 1994), 75–107; quotation from 85.

51 Ibid., 81.

52 Huguette Dagenais and Denise Piché, "Concepts and Practices of Development: Feminist Contributions and Future Perspectives," in Dagenais and Piché, eds., *Women, Feminism and Development*, 49–73; quotation from 55.

53 See Mies and Shiva, *Ecofeminism*, 38.

54 See the last paragraph of Hirschkop's "Bakhtin Myths, or, Why We All Need Alibis," in this issue of *SAQ*. His judgment on Bakhtin is somewhat less harsh in "Bakhtin, Philosopher and Sociologist," in *Face to Face: Bakhtin in Russia and the West*, ed. Carol Adlam, Rachel Falconer, Vitalii Makhlin, and Alastair Renfrew (Sheffield, UK, 1997), 54–67.

Anthony Wall

A Broken Thinker

Or again, what harm would it have done us to have remained uncreated?
—Lucretius, *On the Nature of the Universe*

Bakhtin is a broken thinker and the pieces of his thought are strewn in virtually every direction. It is ironic that as the early writings are becoming more widely known—texts that are, without exception, fragments of varying scope and length—interpretations are being proposed that purport to give the *entire* picture of Bakhtin or to read these fragments through the prism of his later works. Although his oeuvre begins in fragments rather than wholes, readers are often tempted to read such fragments in a Romantic framework, as if each one were a tiny mirror, a miniature reproduction, of a greater and mysterious whole. "To show that the totality is present as such in every part, and that the whole is not simply the sum but the co-presence of all the parts in terms of the co-presence of the whole in itself (since the whole *is* also the detachment or the closing off of the part)—this is the essential necessity that flows from the individuality of the fragment."[1]

The *South Atlantic Quarterly* 97:3/4, Summer/Fall 1998.

What is fascinating, but no less problematic, when dealing with Bakhtin as a thinker and as a writer is that in his case there never is a whole, only broken pieces. For us, then, the whole is not a set, an eternally subsisting totality, of potentially replaceable parts. Many modern thinkers who address the problem of the fragmented life of the modern individual (e.g., Popper debating Lukács) seem to revert to this desire for a totality, which assumes various guises.[2] In terms of the part/whole relationship in Bakhtin's writing, I would not advocate a logic of stockpiling and accrual nor plead for the postmodern Western subject's right to pick and choose, wherever he likes, amongst the fragmentary spoils he has forcefully "acquired" in accordance with an illogical and "indifferent" set of consumer needs.[3] I would warn, rather, against the logic of "replacement parts,"[4] which, far from upholding the value of the fragment as a possible site of resistance to centripetal discursive forces, denies that fragment's worth by making it subordinate to something more important and—of course—more lasting. Contrary to these schemes of thought, Bakhtin's fragmentary thinking is not about replaceable parts. "To affirm definitively the fact of my unique and irreplaceable participation in Being is to enter Being precisely where it does not coincide with itself: to enter the ongoing event of Being."[5]

In speaking of the fundamentally fragmentary nature of Bakhtin's thinking, however, let us not fall into the simplistic trap of opposing fragments as an image of relativism to notions of unity, but rather take to heart Michael Gardiner's warning against too enthusiastically adopting an overly individualistic "ethics of dialogism."[6] The fragment should be read not as a textual equivalent to the autonomous social individual ("as a self-enclosed and impervious fragment"[7]) but as a figure for the difficult relationships that exist on the edges of any human individuality. The question of the fragment's polyvalent edges is integral to Bakhtin's prosaics, which seeks to apprehend the varied means of the individual's entering into relationships of all sorts with concrete and abstract others.

Beginning with the early incomplete, fragmentary essays that led Bakhtin's "career" into several "false starts," one is tempted to read beyond the surface content/sense of his thoughts to their unspoken but implicit fascination with the problematic relationship between parts and wholes. That these fragmentary essays, which are irreducibly incomplete, should evince a noticeable fascination with wholeness may be no accident on the part of a thinker whose writing so often contradicted itself and was wont to retell in a different light that which had already been told. While it is all too easy to write off the fragmentary nature of many early works as mere accidents in an otherwise carefully thought out philosophical program, the fact remains that Bakhtin completed few of his works and that the essays we are now reading from early in his career—those keen on wholeness and unity—are, significantly, the ones most hopelessly bereft of the very characteristics of which they dream. "This act is truly real (it participates in once-occurrent Being-as-event) only *in its entirety*. Only this *whole* act is alive, exists fully and inescapably—comes to be, is accomplished."[8]

The difficulties associated with finding the appropriate mode for reading Bakhtin, the best tack for dealing with his fragmentary beginnings, are complicated by the incredible history of his works' editing. Not only can we discern numerous reading strategies whose principal aim is to create wholeness where there are fragments, but Bakhtin's editors have been especially guilty of "creating" seemingly unified texts out of a long series of notes or several disjointed papers. The essay entitled "Toward a Philosophy of the Act" is not the only example of such an editorial feat, as can be witnessed by the fact that what was published in Russian in 1986 as a single essay has been divided by Vadim Liapunov and Michael Holquist between two different books, the small volume of the same title and the "Supplementary Section" appended to *Author and Hero in Aesthetic Activity* in *Art and Answerability*,[9] although, according to the essay's Russian editor, S. G. Bocharov, it actually formed part of a now lost *preceding* section of this essay. *Art and Answerability* is itself an example of a tentatively reconstituted whole, given Holquist's insistence on the essays therein as "part of a great untitled work Bakhtin never finished, a project we have called 'The Architectonics of Answerability' for reasons internal to the remaining fragments."[10] As always with Bakhtin, there are apparently many other fragments that his editors do not permit us to see or that have simply disappeared. Yet another, more interesting example is a work whose wholeness was not questioned until very recently; according to some oral accounts, the chronotope essay only became one when Bakhtin's editors began to work on it.

There are some obvious problems, therefore, in Gary Saul Morson and Caryl Emerson's summary of "Toward a Philosophy of the Act" in their introduction to *Rethinking Bakhtin*, where the "third part" of the fragment (i.e., the "Supplementary Section" in *Art and Answerability*) is read as belonging to one and the same work, albeit with some skeptical questioning of the essay's treatment by "Soviet editors" such as Bocharov.[11] Furthermore, as Morson and Emerson go on to say, they do not see the sense of the "moments" in "Toward a Philosophy of the Act," for on their reading the constituent moment becomes a mere "aspect" and the inherently chronotopic nature of the young Bakhtin's essay, which purports to think abstractly through the utterly individual nature of the singular event, loses its dynamic and contradictory dimension. In their reading of the "two-faced Janus," they explicitly seek to eliminate everything theoretical, thereby eliminating one fundamental side of the "head," claiming that all such doubling splits are inherently "dangerous."[12] What Bakhtin means to show throughout his fragment, however, is the necessity of preserving at least *two* realms:

> It is only the once-occurrent event of Being in the process of actualization that can constitute this unique unity; all that which is theoretical or aesthetic must be determined as a constituent moment in the once-occurrent event of Being, although no longer, of course, in theoretical or aesthetic terms. An act must acquire a single unitary plane to be able to reflect itself in both directions—in its sense or meaning and in its being; it must acquire the unity of two-sided answerability—both for its content (special answerability) and for its Being (moral answerability).[13]

My own approach to this text here will be to consider it part of Bakhtin's irreducibly fragmented "beginnings." That he should have begun with fragments raises a question about the very conceiving of new and fresh beginnings within and beyond the discursive realm of cultural acts (a problem that would be explored by Michel Foucault[14]). But the undeniable presence of fragments from the very start also raises a question about the advisability of drawing any conclusions as to where Bakhtin was actually headed when he began to write in his early twenties. These initial fragments point to a curious *indirectedness* in his thinking, a term we can use to stress the impossibility of predicting on the basis of any given fragment where the thoughts expressed within it would actually lead. It is important to develop an anti-essentialist stance toward Bakhtin's work, in my view, in order to counter attempts to treat one or another of his early texts as if it contained all the parts that were missing when we previously read Bakhtin's later works. Such attempts yield, at best, reductive and stagnating readings, for they posit a fixed and immutable essence in Bakhtin's early thought that could only have developed with maturity. At their worst, they partake of a dehumanizing tendency to deny a given thinker the right to change, even to contradict himself, and they thus construe individuality in such a way as to claim an understanding of the whole from a single part. As Alfred Arteaga clearly shows, the basis of any such attitude toward another human being is the objectifying use of antithesis and synecdoche: "The rhetoric of antithesis restricts heterogeneity to the dominant Self, and the synecdoche acts to disallow individuation to the Other. To know one is to know all."[15]

Instead of papering over Bakhtin's fragmentary beginnings, it is perhaps time to think of what they might mean for us, his readers, to be faced with so many unfinished pieces, with what the young Bakhtin refers to as Janus-like signs: "An act of our activity, of our actual experiencing, is like a two-faced Janus."[16] The fragment can be seen as either a curious piece of something else or as part of a nonexistent whole. The indirectedness of Bakhtin's thinking seems to indicate the necessity of imagining, from any given piece, several simultaneously possible routes: "It is as if rays of light radiate from my uniqueness and, passing through time, they confirm historical mankind, they permeate with the light of value all possible time and temporality itself as such, for I myself actually partake in temporality."[17] The fragment seems to come from several different paths at once and to lead simultaneously in several different directions. The parts and pieces of Bakhtin's thinking are not simply details of a larger but temporarily indiscernible whole. There is no encyclopedic vision within his framework that would simulate totality in an incredible proliferation of detail or a systemic attachment to everything that seems peripheral.[18] If Bakhtin's thought processes are to be examined along their edges, then these must be recognized as the edges of fragments, not of global concepts. If we are to respect the idea of "becoming" so crucial to Bakhtin's thought, if we are to understand meaning as stratified and multilinear, and, finally, if we are to construe his vision in terms of a prosaics of the world and its inhabitants, we need to consider most carefully the role that fragmentary texts play in Bakhtin's understanding of interpersonal behavior.

Speaking of "indirectedness" enables us to avoid the temptation to construe Bakhtin's fragmentary thinking in terms of staunchly opposed reflections on the difficulty of the social individual, on the one hand, and the impossibility of abstractions, on the other. Unfortunately, such an opposition seems to predominate in the commentary on "Toward a Philosophy of the Act," as in this statement, for example: "Hostility to all forms of 'theoretism' . . . was one constant in Bakhtin's long career."[19] This is surely misleading in relation to a text which explicitly states that "an indifferent or hostile reaction is always a reaction that impoverishes and decomposes its object."[20] My own reading of "Toward a Philosophy of the Act" here proposes neither that it "consists of a long attack on a style of thought Bakhtin calls 'theoretism' " nor that it exhibits a "fundamental dislike of systems,"[21] stressing instead the dynamic but complicated relationship between parts and wholes and the powerful forces of edges.

Just imagine that the Epicurean philosopher Lucretius had spoken in *De rerum natura* not about the atoms and celestial bodies of the universe, but instead about social bodies and the meanings they constitute by virtue of their place in the universe. Such an imaginary reading might yield someone rather like Mikhail Bakhtin, a materially minded philosopher who began, as did Lucretius, by concentrating upon bits and pieces and wondering about their relation to a hypothesized whole. Rather than reading a full-scale history of the fragment into Bakhtin's writings, therefore, it might be better to read his thoughts *as* fragments. For however we choose to explain Bakhtin's fragmentary beginnings—whether as indicating that he never wished to bring his early works to completion or perhaps that he just outgrew them—when we look at Bakhtin as a thinker, his thought looks back at us in broken pieces with varying degrees of similarity and disagreement. We come into contact with what David Lloyd attributes to hybridization: "an unevenness of incorporation within a developmental structure rather than an oscillation between or among identities."[22]

Fragmentary beginnings are not something that must be overcome. Broken pieces—an amputated limb, unfinished manuscripts, rotting pages, copious but disjointed notes, lost books, frequent moves and exile—provide no reason to be appalled by Bakhtin's unconventional intellectual career. Neither his unwillingness to forge an ultimate, overarching synthesis nor his willingness to speak about his own incompleteness is an aspect of his thought that should be cause for alarm. And why should we feel "shock" over a reference to Bakhtin's "incomplete" body or to the stump left after his leg's amputation?[23]

Reading Bakhtin has often consisted in efforts to compensate for the fragmentary nature of his works, although there has been very little talk about fragments as such.[24] In all fairness, however, it must be acknowledged that the fragmentary nature of Bakhtin's work is something that *shows* rather than being explicitly discussed by him. It can be seen in the shifting pieces of his oeuvre as they proceed from note to essay form—and from collected volumes in Russian to different configurations in English, French, or German. The essays appear in forms and lengths that vary according to the whims of their editors, while very few finished monographs appear at all. We have just the Dostoevsky book, which he revised only after considerable nudging from his followers, and the Rabelais book, which must have left a bitter taste on Bakhtin's palate after its rejection as a doctoral thesis. And significantly, as a counterpart to the fragment "Toward a Philosophy of the Act," which speaks at great length about wholeness, the Rabelais book—one of his few "whole" texts—speaks quite explicitly about *membra disiecta*.[25]

Like the child who has virtually infinite possibilities in the future, the fragmentary beginning also speaks to an abstract possibility which must acquire "flesh and blood." The child's future lies entirely in front of the presently lived moment, but which direction will that life take in the future? As a series of beginning moments in Bakhtin's intellectual career, his fragments prod us to think carefully about the question of how "progress" could ever occur in his work. And when we read the young Bakhtin's fragments after having read his later works, we encounter a curiously reversed temporal "progress" in his thought, sometimes with surprising or even grotesque effects. ("Even if the restitution of the past is a plus for our knowledge of a foregone era, it is above all a promise for the future in the eyes of creative persons."[26]) We must be careful to retain a certain sense of open-endedness with respect to these fragments, given the strong possibility that our reading of the young Bakhtin "back" from our own future and in terms of his may well cut away the open-ended nature of the fragment itself.

Just try to explain to a child crying over a recently broken toy that you, the complete adult, are unable to reassemble the broken pieces simply by pressing them together. The broken toy leads to the child's realization that time moves forward and, in so doing, often eliminates many possibilities during its passage. The broken toy will no longer be able to do all the interesting things it once could do, if only because its immortal status has been lost and its ultimate vulnerability exposed. It is material proof that accidents can happen which take on the form of "disastrous events," or, in Lucretian terms: "So you may see that events cannot be said to *be* by themselves like matter or in the same sense as space. Rather, you should describe them as accidents of matter, or of the place in which things happen."[27]

So, too, do new configurations of matter and space remind us that it is forever impossible to restore broken pieces to the form in which they once belonged or to ever re-member them and reestablish the wholeness they once upheld. (As Nancy Miller writes, reading, for a woman, is often a reminder that "her identity is also re-membered in the stories of the body."[28]) In light of this context, it is not surprising to find the body at the center of the part/whole problematic in Bakhtin's thought. Moreover, a sort of symbiotic relationship between tone and body can be identified, with "tone" and "intonation" two other terms for a body that provides the link between individuality and the social world: "Everything that is actually experienced is experienced as something given and as something-yet-to-be-determined, is intonated, has an emotional-volitional tone, and enters into an effective relationship to me within the unity of the ongoing event encompassing us."[29] The whole's ability to be broken down, the fact that it cannot remain intact forever, is a basic requirement of becoming. As Lucretius noted, "Partless objects cannot have the essential properties of generative matter—those varieties of attachment, weight, impetus, impact and movement on which everything depends."[30] Or, in Bakhtin's terms, "An object that is absolutely indifferent, totally finished, cannot be something one becomes actually conscious of, something one experiences actually."[31]

The times and places *issuing forth* from Bakhtin's scattered texts convey a temporal movement other than linear progression. His various pieces—books, jottings, fragments, notes, and essays—do not appear to be cumulative. Contradictions are always possible where memory does not seem to store or stockpile information for future use. Bakhtin was apparently always able and prepared to start again from another point of view, similar to Roland Barthes's self-described method: "Liking to find, to write *beginnings*, he tends to multiply this pleasure: that is why he writes fragments: so many fragments, so many pleasures."[32] The young Bakhtin's metaphorics of light can serve as a metaphor in turn for the indirectedness of his thought: multiple rays which "fan out" from multiple sources,[33] with each ray another fragmentary beginning. If the Bakhtinian fragment is seen in terms of advancing multiple lines, we can better understand why it is impossible to read Bakhtin's corpus backwards, that is, to read back innocently, even though he may have (as is often claimed) later revisited the questions left undeveloped in his early work. It is likewise impossible to patch up broken or amputated limbs and reattach them to the central body of Bakhtin's thought. His having "returned" to rethink what he had previously said, and often to contradict his earlier pronouncements, should not be viewed as intentional efforts to (re)establish a new and improved whole out of the imperfect parts of the past. It seems far more probable that these were actually fresh starts. When the older Bakhtin would revisit the younger, it was not simply to correct himself, to fill in the gaps or to be more precise, but more a matter of showing the infinite possibilities entailed by starting off in another direction from where you once stood. Like M.-Pierrette Malcuzynski, I have little use for readings based on positing two distinct intellectual personalities, the "young" and the "old" Bakhtin,[34] reminiscent of the manner in which Althusser cast his questions about Lukács's Marxism. The function of fragments in Bakhtin's thinking points most urgently toward the need to understand how the edges of any piece in a body of work make their multiple contacts with the other edges.

Let us not mistake Mikhail Bakhtin for a kind of philosophical Humpty-Dumpty whom we might somehow put back together if we could recruit enough king's horses and enough king's men to the task. Just as we could never be certain that what we had managed to reconstruct even resembled what it was before it fell to pieces, neither can we undo what the passage of time, the movement of matter and place, has done to what was subject to its forces. Those readings of Bakhtin which seek to reconstruct his lost thought from the scattered pieces of his work represent an unworkable enterprise that overestimates, or rather misconstrues, what cultural memory is all about. At the core of every memory operation lies a profound unpredictability, and this is the basis of the indirectedness of Bakhtin's thought as it unfolds over time. It is the same as the indirectedness that grounds semantics and the philosophical impossibility of expressing the irreducibly particular in a language built on generalizations. The workings of memory, both individual and collective, always strive to "embody" disparate elements from a given abstract system and to turn them into the event of their expression. Speaking, writing, and communicating in general are all modes for the embodiment of meaning—that which constitutes the eventness at the heart of every dialogic exchange. Among the countless examples of this image of incarnated meaning in "Toward a Philosophy of the Act," consider the following pair:

> Mathematical time and space guarantee the possible sense-unity of possible judgments (an actual judgment requires actual emotional-volitional interestedness), whereas my actual participation in time and space from my unique place in Being guarantees their inescapably compellent actuality and their valuative uniqueness—invests them, as it were, with flesh and blood.
>
> . . . .
>
> Only the value of mortal man provides the standards for measuring the spatial and the temporal orders: space gains body as the possible horizon of mortal man and as his possible environment, and time possesses valuative weight and heaviness as the progression of mortal man's life.[35]

The body of meaning and exchange is precisely that which escapes the predictability of any preestablished system. The body is always the event that interrupts the smooth unfolding of an abstract idea, a three-dimensional synchronicity appearing in a semantic space which is often inadequate for coping with it.[36] This is also the point of view taken by Michel de Certeau, who, in his work on everyday practices, discusses how people "cheat" the system not maliciously or dishonestly, but because in merely moving through space the body will always find shortcuts and will always adapt its surroundings to its own particular needs and habits.[37] As the site where unexpected encounters outwit predictions and where multiple bumps and openings outmaneuver any attempt to close off the outside world, the body as incarnated meaning enables Bakhtin to counteract, while thinking of the irreducible individuality of any act, any process that would render us "determined, predetermined, bygone, and finished, that is, essentially not living," creatures.[38] The fragment, as the interruptive body, is based not on an overarching principle of wholeness but on an economy of regions where it operates (to borrow from Drew Leder) "according to indigenous principles" and where it incorporates "different parts of the world into its space."[39]

"Toward a Philosophy of the Act" is a profound statement on chronotopicity. In numerous passages, time and space are bundled together as essential components in the process of "embodying" meaning, that is, the transformation of abstract possibility into concrete, lived reality. "I exist in the world of inescapable actuality, and not in that of contingent possibility."[40] With Bakhtin, open possibilities, understood as possibilities for comparison and juxtaposition, become a matter of asking how a given fragment links up with what precedes and follows it. Here, we can ask how, as a fragment, "Toward a Philosophy of the Act" compares with other fragments.

There is, no doubt, a certain usefulness to comparing, on the one hand, the way chronotopicity is expressed or manifested in terms of both an event and its irreducible indirectedness in this particular fragment with, on the other, its treatment elsewhere in Bakhtin's work. Given that in the early fragments the uniqueness of the event is described in almost desperate terms, it would be appropriate to see how space and time are woven together in Bakhtin's work during, say, the "sociological" period of the 1930s. There are, however, certain controversial aspects that such a comparison would have to take into account, not the least of which is the tendency to transform the fragmentary early writings into integral parts of a larger whole. For our own purposes here, such a comparison (its usefulness to understanding Bakhtin's intellectual career notwithstanding) should not be the means of attaining a global picture of his thought, which would be to treat it "as a whole." Moreover, we should pay very careful attention to two nasty methodological traps that such comparisons can readily set even for a reading aimed at respecting the indirectedness of these early fragments from Bakhtin's oeuvre.

The first trap to be avoided is that of projecting a sort of 1990s Western-style fascination with ethics, through whatever insidious means, onto these most vaguely termed and furtively expressed ideas from Bakhtin's intellectual youth. Let us admit, as a starting point, that the things we say and feel about ethics at the end of the twentieth century are too often tainted by being steeped in individualistically centered or pragmatically oriented perspectives that are not necessarily consonant with the neo-Kantian enterprise pursued in the 1920s by the young Bakhtin. In other words, the question of ethics and its place in his early work is strongly suggestive of an impossible dream—explaining Bakhtin entirely on the basis of a single issue. A further problem is the fact that "Toward a Philosophy of the Act" contains a number of loosely expressed notions that Bakhtin may or may not have intended to explore later on. Any such movement toward a whole from a small piece would oblige us to employ a number of tools inappropriate to the task of reading a fragment; these tools, forged for the specific ideological needs of the late twentieth century, give us very little by way of any new means for grasping the complexities of Russia at the beginning of the century, where and when this fragmentary essay was written.

The second—and related—methodological trap would follow from a decision to read "Toward a Philosophy of the Act" primarily as a text stressing ethical questions and considerations contextualized by a set of ethical principles peculiar to the neo-Kantian project as Bakhtin saw it at the time. Such ethical questions are not universally expressible norms valid for any and every context. Here, the trap would consist in taking this particular ethical point of view (if that were indeed what must be read as primary in the fragment) and projecting it onto later or other (i.e., not neo-Kantian) theoretical frameworks developed by Bakhtin. The ethical framework in "Toward a Philosophy of the Act," to the extent that it can be deciphered, is in some ways radically different from the types of considerations developed in his essay on speech genres, for example, or in his readings of Rabelais and Gogol. Bakhtin's thinking would become quite different from what it was in the early fragments, and, even in those instances where he seems to have returned to some of the issues he explored earlier, how can we be certain that he was returning to precisely the same issues as before?

The profound indirectedness of the original fragments means that it is hazardous to draw from the discussions in any given early piece a set of irreversible vectors that will inevitably lead to some conclusions at the expense of others. When we consider how intensely interested this young prosaist would become in such diverse writers and thinkers as Shakespeare, Saussure, Bergson, Kant, Freud, Buber, Dostoevsky, Gogol, Goethe, and Rabelais (diverse, that is, except in gender), then what becomes obvious is that a certain madness lies in believing it possible to envisage from Bakhtin's very first fragments all the twists and turns of his future work on dialogic thinking, as if the contours of this project had already been precisely delineated even before the project itself existed.

The important reasons why Bakhtin's thought is from the very start, or rather from each of its several starts, steeped in indirectedness all have to do with chronotopicity, the peculiar temporality and spatiality of any site which must make way for time and matter. We can imagine Bakhtin's career as constituted by a loose set of reflections that move back and forth across a number of theoretical fields but without appearing to lead in one particular direction. Niklas Luhmann's concept of communication is useful for understanding Bakhtin's movement from one idea to another, from one fragment to another.[41] Luhmann sees communication as the permanently mobile process of achieving appropriate forms for a given medium of expression which functions within an always larger cultural environment. Like the early Bakhtin, he is concerned with the relationship between a larger whole and the smaller units within it. His conceptualization offers a useful way of seeing the process of giving form to communication as a transformation especially of time and space, each of which is applied to an originally formless meaning intention. This effectively chronotopic metamorphosis of thought into speech certainly describes what the young Bakhtin construed according to the parameters of a struggle between the tendency toward a fixed or systematized expression (what he would later call centripetal forces), on the one hand, and the need to account for the utterance or the event of meaning (what would later be termed the centrifugal forces of speech), on the other. In "Toward a Philosophy of the Act" these are presented concurrently not in a binary opposition, but as a framework for understanding the difficult relationship in which any given part is engaged with the larger parts to which it may or may not be well integrated. Luhmann expresses this problem by recourse to the term *Anschlussfähigkeit*: the ability of a given unit to enter into relations with other units, or, more literally, "the ability to make connections." (Indeed, this view of the way signs can forge links with the extraverbal world of everyday practice is consonant with Vološinov's concept of the relationship between an utterance and the larger context, which he explains with reference to the notion of "enthymeme."[42]) Applied to Bakhtin's career, this "ability" of a given item "to make connections" is not so much a semiotic question of the individual sign's linking up with the next and that one with the third, and so on (i.e., the concatenation of otherwise independent signs), as it is a question of understanding how his various fragments, of different stature and scope, link up with one another. This question is undoubtedly linked to the fundamental problem of how we arrive at social structures starting from individual beings, themselves fractured in a world that makes multiple demands on them. For our purposes here, the question is what we can do with such pieces as "Toward a Philosophy of the Act"—or, more pertinently, what Bakhtin did with them.

In understanding Bakhtin not as a whole but as a variously disjointed and juxtaposed set of fragments, each engaged in heterogeneous relations with any and many others, we can retain the necessary element of risk embodied at the edges of any Bakhtinian fragment: "It is precisely doubt that forms the basis of our life as effective deed-performing, and it does so without coming into contradiction with theoretical cognition."[43] (This doubt is precisely what is potentially closed off by readings of Bakhtin that seem proud to be proceeding "retrospectively."[44]) Risk is the fundamental element that Mary Russo develops with such elegance in her study of the "female grotesque." She shows the necessity of allowing for chance, uncertainty, in any adequate understanding of how even the strangest social bits are assigned a place in their world: "Unlike the models of progress, rationality, and liberation which dissociate themselves from their 'mistakes'—noise, dissonance, or monstrosity—this 'room for chance' emerges within the very constrained spaces of normalization."[45] We know that, for Bakhtin, it was essential to keep possibilities open rather than closing them off—the same issue that would arise at different moments of his thinking in relation to prose read in silence.

Relative to the embodiment of meaning and to the event of expression as intimately linked to Bakhtin's chronotopic thinking, *The Formal Method in Literary Scholarship* gives us a tool for conceptualizing his notion of "becoming." There we find the "body-sign [*telo-znak*],"[46] a useful way of seeing "becoming" as bodily meaning-making within the linguistic systems available to us. In short, the body-sign is the incarnated communicational event. This problem is also broached, albeit from a different angle, in Michael Holquist's *Dialogism*. Holquist is intent on showing that we can best understand the chronotope in terms of an event, the material event of implicit meaning's taking on the precise contours of time and space in a given situation and in relation to a particular speech partner. Holquist's view is supported by the fact that for Dostoevsky (Bakhtin's favorite author) the greatest issues approached by philosophers, the ultimate questions of life, could never be understood as pure abstractions, but rather had to take on material contours in a particularized event of meaning. They had to be embodied in order to be adequately understood. This is precisely, according to Holquist, the role of the chronotope in Bakhtin's thinking. Any shared fable (*fabula*) in our culture is grasped only in the concrete forms with which a particular version (*syuzhet*) of the story endows it; in other words, it must be chronotopically transformed. The abstract fable cannot directly penetrate our consciousness, so it must be grasped indirectly through the "flesh and blood" situation provided by the event of its recasting in a particular form. "Stated in its most basic terms, a particular chronotope will be defined by the specific way in which the sequentiality of events is 'deformed' (always involving a segmentation, a spatialization) in any given account of those events. It is this necessary simultaneity of figure (in this case, plot) and ground (or story) that constitutes the dialogic element in the chronotope."[47] Whether Holquist's Formalist-fable story of the chronotope is entirely consonant with Bakhtin's thinking in general is not the issue. What is important in our context is the connection between abstraction as never immediately available to consciousness and indirectedness as a basic necessity of human meaning-making in general. This indirectedness must always proceed through the real-life situation expressed by the chronotope.

However, one unfortunate consequence of Holquist's conception of the chronotope's "dialogism" is that his fable seems to confine it to narrative, whereas it may be more useful to step beyond the realm of artistic (literary) expression and see the act in the broader context of real-life situations. As Bakhtin notes, "Aesthetic activity is a participation of a special, *objectified* kind; from within an aesthetic architectonic there *is* no way out into the world of the performer of deeds, for he is located outside the field of objectified aesthetic seeing."[48] Here we see the contours of a semiotic thinking which, not being limited to artistic expression per se, can use certain aesthetic forms to get a better handle on the complex, real-life situatedness of human beings interacting with one another. Bakhtin's fragmentary project calls for a radical rethinking of "prosaics," which must not be understood in opposition to any theoretical construing of human eventness any more than it can be opposed to the poetic-aesthetic understanding of human situatedness. A study of how fragments interact with one another shows enormous differences in their respective degrees of autonomy. It is not always advisable to treat a fragmentary piece as "coherent" in itself, but often better to consider its inherent incompleteness as a call for help from the outside. In Judith Butler's words: "It is important to resist that theoretical gesture of pathos in which exclusions are simply affirmed as sad necessities of signification. The task is to refigure this necessary 'outside' as a future horizon, one in which the violence of exclusion is perpetually in the process of being overcome."[49] The relationship between any two given fragments is not necessarily dialogical but one that can be termed (borrowing from Lloyd) an example of "intercontamination."[50] An interesting case in point is the relationship between the "Supplementary Section" appended to *Author and Hero* in *Art and Answerability* and the title essay in *Toward a Philosophy of the Act,* two texts offering significant variants on similar ideas and analyses of the same poem. If we view an act as a sort of behavioral fragment, we can see how such "intercontamination" works, insofar as that act does not constitute an absolute contrast to all that is different from it. "An answerable deed," says Bakhtin, "must not oppose itself to theory and thought, but must incorporate them into itself as necessary moments that are wholly answerable."[51]

If Bakhtin's thinking from fragments does in fact point to the need to rethink the way we understand a prosaic vision of the world, there would also be a need to incorporate within that vision certain ideas on the *prose du monde* of Maurice Merleau-Ponty and Michel Foucault. Of course, we must first agree on what we mean by "prosaic" and "prose" even if, as a preliminary move, we might say that the very terminological imprecision surrounding these notions is part and parcel of the indirectedness of communication we associate with Bakhtin's earliest fragments. It remains to be shown, nevertheless, that the most provocative questions touched on in "Toward a Philosophy of the Act" are less entrenched in classical ethics (as an autonomous philosophical discipline) than couched in terms of the problem of how a given part or fragment engages in potential relationships with other parts or larger wholes along its edges. It is from the angles of Luhmann's *Anschlussfähigkeit* and Bakhtin's fragments that we can attain the bases for understanding the energy of a prosaic world.

For our purposes, the prosaic must be characterized over and against its etymological definition as *oratio prosa* (discourse which proceeds straight ahead), if for no other reason than that we are dealing with writers whose prose is capable of proceeding in a number of directions rather than merely straightforwardly.[52] Prose, as the embodied expression of indirectedness, would therefore also need to be distinguished from the related ideal of the *pro-position*, with its similar etymology of "that which has been placed in front, that which has been set forth." The indirectedness that lies at the heart of prosaic expression is intimately linked with the problem of smaller parts which must (or perhaps must never) fit into larger ones. In other words, this is the same problem as the disrupting influence of the time of utterance into the smooth space of what is being said or of apparitions of past history or even glimpses of the future within the time and space of an utterance act in the present. It is the unsettling arrival of social reality in the seemingly private realm of an individual's thinking. Thus prosaics, the study of any expression that takes form in prose, must be concerned with memory, both individual and cultural, as it too is steeped in the difficult arrivals of foreign times and places within the present unfolding of the utterance seeking to frame them. Intimately linked, prose and memory are two ways of approaching the problem of how any event of expression occurring between different persons and respecting all their differences in history and origin can ever come to be seen as a single whole.

From the very start, prosaics can be placed in a position where the directions in which it is headed are never steadfastly set out in advance. Prose is seen, even in Bakhtin's early fragments, in relation to double-faced phenomena, or the "two-faced Janus," which cannot be reduced without irrecuperable loss to a single dimensionality. "If the 'face' of the event is determined from the unique place of a participative self, then there are as many different 'faces' as there are different unique places."[53] Given that one of the distinguishing features of prose for Bakhtin, especially that of the novel, is its ability to carry more than one voice—indeed, a multiplicity of visions, moments, perspectives, and points of view—then the only way of getting at the heart of prose is through such multiplicity. Just as blood vessels branch out from the heart in every imaginable direction to feed every cell of the body, so too does prose, the vessel of *le multiple*,[54] redefine the space and time in which it evolves. Or, as Lucretius puts it, "Now, we see that water flows out in all directions from a broken vessel and the moisture is dissipated, and mist and smoke vanish into thin air."[55] Time will no longer be adequately represented by the traditional image of a river flowing along a single riverbed or without twists and turns. The only river of time by which we could image the movement of prose would now have to be that of a delta, splitting into thousands of branches, changing direction according to the season, even backing up completely with tidal waters at unpredictable intervals.

From the very beginning, Bakhtin's prosaics would exhibit a similar pattern of branching out and changing direction in accordance with the strange logic of the multiple. It seems reasonable to assume that he himself did not know in which direction he was proceeding and into which intellectual quarters he was headed. When Bakhtin began writing those texts he never finished, he would have been hard put to say where everything was going to lead. How can we then claim that there was an implicitly coherent project in those fragments? And if Bakhtin truly believed (as Morson and Emerson seem to think) that the most important notions covered in "Toward a Philosophy of the Act" were those of ethical responsibility relating to the individual's engaged obligations, can we not say now, for more than one reason, that he was perhaps speaking about something very different? This would be consistent with prosaic indirectedness as leading in several directions at once, thus never proceeding as a straightforward proposition. Similarly, we could say in accordance with this fundamental indirectedness that Bakhtin's many projects are all *disoriented*: his many beginnings, in many fragments and under several names, were continually being launched without a particularly well-defined goal having been spelled out. Contrary to those who have claimed to see a clearly defined project in Bakhtin's early texts and those who have claimed that his fragments contain *in nuce* what he would develop in detail when he matured, the early fragments and certainly "Toward a Philosophy of the Act" leave us with a much more scattered impression. In what is supposed to be the start of a dialogic method in the human sciences, for example, there is a sense of profound insecurity, one that corresponds to the difficulty of thinking through the event of theoretical thought in the course of its very constitution *as an event*.

If by the bodily delivery of the word we necessarily understand the fundamental characteristics of a disruptive event—a rupture within an abstractly conceived life continuum—then the utterance is indeed an interruption that allows for the entry of everyday existence into the realm of potentially inert meaning. We are in the realm of the accident or rupture that we ourselves, as social and biological beings, bring into play in the otherwise smooth flow of abstract time. In the event of human meaning-making, there is always much stir and movement even when that movement is an undirected or misguided one.

Readings that stress the unbridled energy exuded by Bakhtin's broken thinking often convey some worry to do with its disquieting potential. "Because meaning can only be acquired by recourse to a global whole, one that is impossible to grasp within the magma of social discourses, it is undermined by doubts that are increasingly difficult to bear."[56] We can accept these doubts as productive and see in them the sign of our necessary participation in, as opposed to our passive observation of, the unfolding of social discourses. "In this view, we are capable of knowing what is around us not because we are separated from it, subjects facing objects, but because we are part of it, order amid disorder."[57] The reading of Bakhtin that I have been pursuing here finds it less worrisome than stimulating that his prosaic vision would contribute to seeing words alone as never adequate to expressing the eventful character of meaning in the making. Aided only by the philosophical vocabulary he knew, Bakhtin had great difficulty in dealing with the disruptive forces of the event; if the event seems disquieting, it is precisely because it never lets things be. The event of meaning-making interrupts the continuous illusion that wholeness seeks to maintain; it disrupts the even flow of words striving for a deceptively calm rhythm by its forceful insistence on meanings that move in every direction at once. Disorientation may ensue from this lack of direction, but this very indirectedness may itself be the trace of a broken thought in motion. If the aim is to speak to this thought, it would seem much less appropriate to try to capture it—while undoing its multiple facets—than to ask multiple questions of it as it moves.

Rather than discounting it as mess or counting it out of any serious theoretical discussion, we should set ourselves toward understanding this indirectedness in terms of its basic refusal to remain still. In his thinking, Bakhtin jumps from fragment to fragment and from topic to topic. It is doubtful that he ever had any master game plan in mind as he proceeded in this way. "Toward a Philosophy of the Act" conveys a sense of continually stirred ideas which come back, over and over again, to the linkages between wholes and parts and between time and space. Those who insist on reading it in terms of the texts Bakhtin would write later on—as if this one were already leading in a well-defined direction—can point to a number of similarities, superficial or profound, between what the young Bakhtin says here and what the more mature Bakhtin would later say. Such readings can point to his Baron Münchhausen figure who tries to raise himself up by his own hair,[58] the heavy stress on tones and intonation informing Bakhtin's understanding of meaning as embodied utterances and responsibilities. This emphasis, furthermore, points toward obvious parallels between Bakhtin and Vološinov (which Morson and Emerson, for obvious reasons, fail to underscore). Then there is the idea of the rough draft, which would reappear in Bakhtin's writing as scaffolding that is no longer visible, but still significant, once the building has been completed.[59] In de Certeau's terms, this stressing of similarities over time is based on a reading of *strategies*, while Bakhtin proceeded more on the basis of *tactics*:

> What I call a *strategy* is the calculation (or the manipulation) of power relationships which becomes possible once a site for the will or a capability (a private enterprise, an army, a municipality, a scientific institution) can be isolated. A strategy presupposes a particular site which can be described as *separate* and which forms the basis from which relationships with an *outside*, expressed in terms of goals and threats, can be managed. . . . I call a *tactic* an action calculated with reference to the absence of any *separate site*. In this case, there is no *outside* which delimits its scope or conditions its automony.[60]

It should be clear, therefore, why the possibilities in Bakhtin's cursus are necessary, given the absence of any overarching set of superconcepts capable of anticipating all future possibilities even before they have arisen, such as a military strategist would deploy from the very start in accordance with whatever outcome he was planning every step of the way. In Bakhtin's case, his moves from one fragment to the next, from one piece to another, can best be conceptualized as "risk-taking tactics."[61] For every striking similarity we find between the young and the older Bakhtin, there is surely an even more important dissimilarity: think of his language of light, of fullness, unity, and truth. This plethora of likenesses and differences between the Bakhtin we already know and the younger one whom we are only now discovering should lead us to resist any temptation to select only those elements from the work of the young Bakhtin that parallel what he wrote later (thereby disregarding his basic thesis that an utterance as such is unrepeatable). By accepting the fragmentary nature of the greater part of Bakhtin's writing, however, we come to see every textual utterance as a highly significant threshold, an in-between zone marking off the *here* of a given text from the *theres* of prior texts and those to come. Such a liminal space, surrounding the fragment on all sides, allows us to appreciate the productive nature of the fragmentation at the heart of Bakhtin's events.

Of course, an emphasis on the undirected fragment is not incompatible with seeing ethics as an important component of "Toward a Philosophy of the Act." It *does* seem ill-advised, however, to project anything Bakhtin said about ethics in an early fragment onto all his later writings. It would be more fruitful, at the very least, to incorporate his ethics of the individual act into a framework which can accommodate the productivity of those thresholds or cracks that lie between the various fragments. This mode of reading is certainly preferable to attempts to paper over the profound differences among Bakhtin's various pieces, moves that make the cracks invisible. These cracks between the texts in Bakhtin's corpus are possibly seen as the sites where the marks of his individuality can be identified. In them we witness the strange temporality of a present that would be repeatedly and variously reactivated and thereby constituting an excellent illustration of the in-between. As both the here and the now of an event at the heart of the early Bakhtin's thinking, this in-between starkly contrasts with the purely taxonomic and literary chronotopes, lying outside the personal purview of the writer himself, that dominate the later fragmentary essay on the chronotope.

In "Toward a Philosophy of the Act," Bakhtin does not use the terms "chronotope" and "threshold," but he nevertheless formulates his descriptions of eventness in terms of a time and a space that are inextricably linked. Among the numerous examples here of this entanglement, I shall limit myself for now to two. In the first, Bakhtin speaks of the unique place (space) and of a beginning (time) in such a manner as to indicate that time is certainly no more powerful than space, but rather that both are mixed in a sort of solution: "It is only the acknowledgment of my unique participation in Being from my own unique place in Being that provides an actual center from which my act or deed can issue and renders a beginning non-fortuitous." The second example is perhaps more obvious: "This actual participating from a concretely unique point in Being engenders the real heaviness of time and the intuitable-palpable value of space, makes all boundaries heavy, non-fortuitous." Without one or the other ingredient, the character of becoming would be lost for Bakhtin. It is also instructive to note where they are treated separately, particularly in the early sections of this fragment, where the emphasis is on space: "In relation to everything, whatever it might be and in whatever circumstances it might be given to me, I must act from my own unique place, even if I do so only inwardly"; "for, after all, my performed act (and my feeling—as a performed act) orients itself precisely with reference to that which is conditioned by the uniqueness and unrepeatability of my own place."[62] Such pronouncements surely do not bode well for interpretations of Bakhtin's chronotope as inherently more temporal than spatial. The chronotopicity of "Toward a Philosophy of the Act" certainly takes space as well as time to be an indispensable component of its dynamism.

Regardless of the validity of this last observation, Bakhtin seems to have been intent on strewing his methodological path with contradictions; his efforts to use the impossible tools of general philosophical abstractions to address irreducible individuality rendered the fragment, in and of itself, part of the eventness about which he could speak only with great difficulty. The problem is the essential "impossibility of positing novelty and of conceptualizing it."[63] Bakhtin's attempts to do so within his abstract language in statements such as the following one seem hopelessly inadequate, perhaps grotesque: "The moment of what is absolutely new, what has never existed before and can never be repeated, is in the foreground here and constitutes an answerable continuation in the spirit of that whole which was acknowledged at one time."[64] The impossibility of speaking of eventness can only be *comprehended* (Kierkegaard's term referring to the existential paradoxes that are exacerbated by language[65]), that is, this impossibility can only be approximated by oblique reference to particular aporiatic or inexplicable situations. In Bakhtin's case, the paradox consists in dreaming about totality within a fragment. A contradiction appears in the eventful clash between his tools and his explicit aims, a situation reminiscent of a paradox with which the ancient Greeks were most fascinated: the paradox of movement. As we remember, they understood something that moved to be simultaneously here and not here, sensing as they did the impossibility of separating time and space analytically in order to explain an intrinsically chronotopic phenomenon. When we abstractly dissect movement, we see an infinite sequence of tiny thresholds, each a fragment of the larger whole and each recasting the problem of a present time and a present space that repeatedly renew themselves and allow for further division. "In one perceptible instant of time, that is, the time required to utter a single syllable, there are many unperceived units of time whose existence is recognized by reason."[66] Each fragment of movement is caught between the space of its past and the space of its future, with its contradictory directedness assembled from out of the conflicting elements present in both.

"Toward a Philosophy of the Act" provides certain indispensable tools for understanding the indelibly chronotopic energy on the edges of any fragment. As we move between Bakhtin's fragments, we cannot predict with any degree of reliability whether we are beginning something new or continuing on with something old, whether we are setting off in a new direction or doubling back in our tracks. From the very start, a possible trajectory is conceivable in virtually any direction, and this virtuality is itself inhabited by the infinite configurations of the times and spaces which constitute possible events. The complicated and convoluted relationships between the parts and the dreamt-of whole in Bakhtin's fragment reproduce the difficulties of understanding how the autonomous individual is related to the larger social group of which he is a member (or in terms of which he is an outsider). "One should remember that to live from within myself, from my own unique place in Being, does not yet mean at all that I live only for my own sake." Let us not be fooled by the fact that Bakhtin uses spatializing metaphorics to speak of individuality, nor assume on the basis of such imagery that we are dealing with an impregnable fortress: "I occupy a place in once-occurrent Being that . . . cannot be taken by anyone else and is impenetrable for anyone else."[67] In certain passages of his early writing, this utopic realm of wholeness is given the name of "aesthetics": "The mere fact that a cognitive-ethical determination relates to the *whole* human being, that it encompasses all of him, already constitutes a moment that is aesthetic"; or it is approached from the angle of architectonics: "the intuitionally necessary, nonfortuitous disposition and integration of concrete, unique parts and moments into a consummated whole."[68] In all instances, we see in Bakhtin's thought a tense relationship between the nonexistent wholeness of his philosophical aspirations and the hard reality of his fragmentary thought, as in this statement: "My active unique place is not just an abstract geometrical center, but constitutes an answerable, emotional-volitional, concrete center of the concrete manifoldness of the world, in which the spatial and temporal moment—

the actual unique place and the actual, once-occurrent, historical day and hour of accomplishment—is a necessary but not exhaustive moment of my actual centrality—my centrality for myself."[69]

These times and spaces are anything but inert and immutable, and they can be grasped as dynamic components of events endowed with energy and significance by the endless flux of social interaction. Social times and spaces allow us to come to grips with the eventful nature of extra-aesthetic human life in general. In those instances where he speaks of their possible combinations, Bakhtin provides tools for rethinking the rules of such combinations, social and material. Every event is actually a false start of the sort we have already seen here, particularly due to the impossibility of fitting it neatly in with everything that precedes and follows it. Stuck between preceding and succeeding, while proposing infinitely varied inroads into both, the fragment is an event which partakes of the indirectedness of every temporal and spatial configuration of what is becoming. When Bakhtin speaks in his early texts of the movement inherent in every authentic act, therefore, he does not hesitate to work toward an activity that, as we have noted, "is like a two-faced Janus." In this particular instance, it would seem promising to understand his reference to the Roman god quite literally.

It is possible, then, to read Bakhtin's own work according to his proposals for reading the prose of the world. We can, for example, read Bakhtin as a writer of "artistic prose"—to take a term intelligently exploited by Emily Schultz[70]—accordingly reading his intellectual life as a prosaic one full of indirected and disoriented fragments. In striving to make room for a boundless supply of surprises, we would resist predictable series. "Having acknowledged once the value of scientific truth in all the deeds or achievements of scientific thinking, I am henceforth subjected to its immanent law: the one who says *a* must also say *b* and *c*, and thus all the way to the end of the alphabet. The one who said *one*, must say *two*: he is drawn by the immanent necessity of a series (the law of series)."[71] When dealing with Bakhtin's career of fragments, it is not long before we discover his Freud, who might have described the problem of Bakhtin's fragmentary life trajectory as that of someone who did not know where to find his beginnings or his ends. Freud and Bakhtin had a shared fascination with the idea that it is pragmatically impossible for us to know our beginning or our end (i.e., our birth or our death). This irremediable lack of acquaintance with the two most important "events" of our lives is what makes the idea of orienting life in relation to them a hazardous operation. The problematic presence/absence of birth and death within conscious life preoccupied Bakhtin throughout his career and was undoubtedly related to his profound belief in the fundamental unfinalizability of the human being. In Elisheva Rosen's terms: "The attractive elements of fantastic depiction, one expressed through incompletion and by broken pieces, wins out against those of coherent representation, something which conforms and is expected."[72] Curiously, in another early fragment, this impossibility of knowing is construed by Bakhtin in terms of an indispensable knowledge: "The only important thing is that a life and its horizon have terminal limits—birth and death."[73] (This is surely an instance of Kierkegaard's way of approaching a paradox by "comprehending its incomprehensibility."[74]) The contemporary thinker Peter Sloterdijk, in describing our own period as suffering from an inability to speak of its origins and its end, refers provocatively to a "poetics of the beginning [*Poetik des Anfangens*]."[75] When everything we do and say is oriented in relation to events we cannot know, we are likely to encounter existential difficulties, which is all the more reason to recognize that, whatever the young Bakhtin might have said in his early fragments, he did not necessarily know what he would say later on the very same topic.

It is as if we were trapped in the unenviable situation of having totally lost our defense mechanisms—as if some frightful virus had destroyed our sense of orientation. Talk of viruses is an interesting component of medieval historian Aaron Gurjewitsch's reading of Bakhtin's carnival. Gurjewitsch says, for example, that our modern viruses play essentially the same ideological role in our lives as evil spirits and demons played during the Middle Ages. Not coincidentally for the indirectedness presumed to be at the heart of Bakhtin's prosaic world, one of the most striking characteristics of the devil is precisely his ability to trick us by forever giving us the impression that he is moving forward when in reality he is moving backwards: "When the devil has taken on human form, it is impossible to view him from behind, since evil spirits have no back and they always move in a way similar to crustaceans."[76]

The indirectedness of an incomplete body is the same as that of a fragment pointing simultaneously toward a thousand other pieces; any one of these may be the one toward which it will eventually head. There is an inherent multiplicity, since any given element can indeed be represented as belonging to several possible directions at the same time. In this respect, it is very different from the sort of bilingualism described by Tzvetan Todorov, who cannot imagine the simultaneous action of two cultural identities appearing together.[77] In the dynamic chronotopicity by which Bakhtin's pieces together construct provisionary new wholes, we begin to perceive a basic mechanism of human memory, perhaps the best of models for studying the prose of the world. Memory, like a changing configuration of fragments, always operates on the basis of reconstitutions that can never be totally successful. It is the process, without beginning or end, by which heterogeneous elements from every imaginable time and place are rearranged in a new, temporary whole and are thereby given a new temporality and a new spatiality—that of uttering a memory. Like myths of social harmony and cohesion, memory gives the illusion that the profound differences among all the heterogeneous elements it has recently appropriated have disappeared in the process ("hegemony envisions so contiguous a discourse that the troping collapses from consciousness and the power of discursive representation is rewritten as the power of literal presentation"[78]). Something inside us, our need to believe in a greater whole, pushes us to reject the validity of fragmentary meaning. To "re-member" pieces or broken bodies—the verb's derivation from the Latin *rememorare* notwithstanding—suggests to readers of Bakhtin the folly of trying to put lost members back in place. If memories are etymologically lost in too many members, everything seems to point toward a problematic reconstitution of the members that have been strewn in every which direction. In the prose of the world, any one of these members or fragments of an apparently lost, coherent body can be seen as its back or front, as its tail or head. With the loss of any functional distinction between before and behind in a world without head or tail, we begin to appreciate the untenability of a nostalgic yearning for a return to that wholeness in time and in space prior to this bewildering dismemberment. Nostalgia, according to Jean-Luc Nancy, is the impossible desire to return to one's beginning by erasing all traces of the passage of time and the transformations of space. Appearing when any reader or interpreter of the world's prose hoists himself into the position of a universal and eternal reader capable of transcending both moving time and changing place, it is "nostalgia for the universal position occupied by the intellectual in the narrative of representation."[79]

Interrupting these desired smooth junctures as a pimple interrupts the smooth texture of our skin, the body's members represent an inexhaustible source of unexpected semantic–somatic events: bodies without backs, bodies with two faces, bodies with too many tails. Likely to break off at any time in any and every direction, the fragments of the dismemberable body provide the basic ingredients of the prose of the world. The price of meaning is insecurity or risk: when fragments are re-membered, when meaning is "embodied," the reverse operation of dismemberment is always just as easily accomplished, since no glue can ever put the pieces back together again just as they were. Any re-memberment of the various fragments is no more and no less permanent than the members who constitute a given social group. Re-memberment is played out in a drama where authority and illusions are the principal actors. Every utterance is an attempted re-memberment, which always proceeds through the desire to master its pieces. Re-memberment and dismemberment are two names for the to-and-fro movement that underscores the impossibility of knowing what direction a fragment will take. In the very attempt to control the prose of this world we are taken in by its indirectedness.

It would seem that Merleau-Ponty's *prose du monde* and Bakhtin's *intonation* both speak to how we put our world together by re-membering its broken-off pieces. If, in Merleau-Ponty's philosophy, our body, as the site of gesticulation, is that which allows us to participate in the world's unfolding,[80] then the indirectedness of this world's prose gives us to understand the price of any such participation. The fragments that we re-member, the pieces we string together, can, by virtue of their ambivalent nature as back and front, turn against us. In Merleau-Ponty's view, we should understand ourselves philosophically as the objects of our own questions: "Philosophy is the entire set of questions by which the person who asks these questions is himself put into question by what he asks."[81]

In the conceptual framework provided by Bakhtin's early fragments, where meaning is manifested in the chronotopically dynamic incarnation of multiple possibilities, the significant links between re-membering and fragmentation cannot be ignored. Since every fragment can potentially turn in any direction on its way to the next or the prior one, what is attained is a prosaic world in which "the living word, the full word, does not know an object as something totally given." The world of prose is inhabited by indirectedness, and all those who participate do so without any permanent knowledge of the line to be followed or of the birth they prolong. The prose of this world must ultimately be understood as the domain of Bakhtin's two-faced Janus, the god of indirectedness who, living in a zone between a beginning and an end, makes of us, its pieces, not insignificant pieces "washed on all sides by the waves of empty possibility,"[82] but living and re-membering palimpsests whose fragmented meanings remain to be discovered in an onslaught from many sides.

Notes

This essay takes several ideas from a paper presented at the August 1995 international conference "Bakhtine: La pensée dialogique" held in Cerisy-la-Salle, France. Those ideas, which at the time seemed quite reasonably expressed, are developed beyond recognition here.

All translations are my own unless otherwise indicated.

1 Philippe Lacoue-Labarthe and Jean-Luc Nancy, *L'Absolu littéraire* (Paris, 1978), 64.

2 See Hans-Robert Jauss, *Ästhetische Erfahrung und literarische Hermeneutik* (Frankfurt a.M., 1982), 677–78.

3 David Lloyd, "Adulteration and the Nation: Monologic Nationalism and the Colonial Hybrid," in *An Other Tongue: Nation and Ethnicity in the Linguistic Borderlands*, ed. Alfred Arteaga (Durham, 1994), 53–92; quotations from 77.

4 See Cecil Helman, *Body Myths* (London, 1991).

5 M. M. Bakhtin, *Toward a Philosophy of the Act*, ed. Michael Holquist and Vadim Liapunov, trans. Vadim Liapunov (Austin, 1993 [1986]), 42.

6 Michael Gardiner, *The Dialogics of Critique* (New York, 1992), 75.

7 Bakhtin, *Philosophy of the Act*, 33.

8 Ibid., 2.

9 See M. M. Bakhtin, *Art and Answerability: Early Philosophical Essays*, ed. Michael Holquist and Vadim Liapunov, trans. Vadim Liapunov (Austin, 1990), 208–31.

10 Michael Holquist, "Introduction: The Architectonics of Answerability," in ibid., xix.

11 *Rethinking Bakhtin: Extensions and Challenges*, ed. Gary Saul Morson and Caryl Emerson (Evanston, 1989), 264–65 n. 25.

12 Ibid., 13.

13 Bakhtin, *Philosophy of the Act*, 2–3.

14 "Instead of beginning to speak, I should have preferred to surround myself in speech, and to travel well beyond any possible beginning"; Michel Foucault, *L'Ordre du discours* (Paris, 1971), 7.

15 Alfred Arteaga, "An Other Tongue," in Arteaga, ed., *An Other Tongue*, 9–33; quotation from 19.

16 Bakhtin, *Philosophy of the Act*, 2.

17 Ibid., 60.

18 See Georges Benrekassa, *Le Langage des Lumières: Concepts et savoir de la langue* (Paris, 1995), 11.

19 Morson and Emerson, eds., *Rethinking Bakhtin*, 29.

20 Bakhtin, *Philosophy of the Act*, 64.

21 Morson and Emerson, eds., *Rethinking Bakhtin*, 7, 14.

22 Lloyd, "Adulteration and the Nation," 91.

23 See Gary Saul Morson and Caryl Emerson, "Imputations and Amputations: Reply to Wall and Thomson," *diacritics* 23 (1993): 93–99.

24 See, for example, Gary Saul Morson and Caryl Emerson, *Mikhail Bakhtin: Creation of a Prosaics* (Stanford, 1990), where reference is made only to "Dostoevsky's deliberate fragment," *The Brothers Karamazov* (253).

25 Renate Lachmann's recent work on Russian modernism takes an insightful look at the issue of broken and dispersed bodies relative to Bakhtin's carnival and in Jan Kott's *Eating of the Gods*; see, especially, her discussion of *sparagmos* in *Memory and Literature: Intertextuality in Russian Modernism*, trans. Roy Sellars and Anthony Wall (Minneapolis, 1997 [1990]), 155, 309.

26 Elisheva Rosen, *Sur le grotesque: L'ancien et le nouveau dans la réflexion esthétique* (Paris, 1991), 12.

27 Lucretius, *On the Nature of the Universe*, trans. R. E. Latham (London, 1951), 41.

28 Nancy K. Miller, *French Dressing: Women, Men and Ancien Régime Fiction* (New York, 1995), 47.

29 Bakhtin, *Philosophy of the Act*, 33.

30 Lucretius, *Nature of the Universe*, 45.

31 Bakhtin, *Philosophy of the Act*, 32.

32 Roland Barthes, *Roland Barthes by Roland Barthes*, trans. Richard Howard (New York, 1977 [1975]), 94.

33 Cf. Morson and Emerson's useful translation "fan out" (*Rethinking Bakhtin*, 24) and Liapunov's "radiate" (*Philosophy of the Act*, 60).

34 See M.-Pierrette Malcuzynski, *Entre-dialogues avec Bakhtin: Ou, Sociocritique de la (dé)-raison polyphonique* (Amsterdam, 1992), 73.

35 Bakhtin, *Philosophy of the Act*, 59, 65.

36 See Anne Deneys-Tunney, *Ecritures du corps* (Paris, 1992), 7.

37 Michel de Certeau, *L'Invention du quotidien* (Paris, 1990), 48.

38 Bakhtin, *Philosophy of the Act*, 9.

39 Drew Leder, *The Absent Body* (Chicago, 1990), 2.

40 Bakhtin, *Philosophy of the Act*, 44.

41 See Niklas Luhmann and Peter Fuchs, *Reden und Schweigen* (Frankfurt a.M., 1989).

42 See Antonio Gómez-Moriana, *Discourse Analysis as Sociocriticism: The Spanish Golden Age* (Minneapolis, 1993): "Since any statement presupposes more than it says, Voloshinov calls the use of language an enthymeme" (138).

43 Bakhtin, *Philosophy of the Act*, 45.

44 Morson and Emerson, eds., *Rethinking Bakhtin*, 23; see also "in hindsight" (22) and "keeping in mind Bakhtin's other writings in his first and second periods" (26).

45 Mary Russo, *The Female Grotesque* (New York, 1995), 11.

46 P. N. Medvedev and M. M. Bakhtin, *The Formal Method in Literary Scholarship: A Critical Introduction to Sociological Poetics*, trans. Albert J. Wehrle (Cambridge, MA, 1985 [1928]), 12.

47 Michael Holquist, *Dialogism: Bakhtin and His World* (London and New York, 1990), 114.
48 Bakhtin, *Philosophy of the Act*, 73.
49 Judith Butler, *Bodies that Matter: On the Discursive Limits of "Sex"* (New York, 1993), 53.
50 Lloyd, "Adulteration and the Nation," 74.
51 Bakhtin, *Philosophy of the Act*, 56.
52 "Etymologies of the modern term begin with the Latin *prosa*, from *prorsus*, 'straightforward,' 'direct,' making *prorsa oratio* or *prosa oratio* or *prosa*, which means 'a straightforward speaking without diversion or interruption, right through to the end of the period' "; Jeffrey Kittay and Wlad Godzich, *The Emergence of Prose: An Essay in Prosaics* (Minneapolis, 1987), 193.
53 Bakhtin, *Philosophy of the Act*, 45.
54 See André Belleau, *Notre Rabelais* (Montreal, 1990).
55 Lucretius, *Nature of the Universe*, 109.
56 Jean-François Chassay, *L'Ambiguïté américaine* (Montreal, 1995), 60.
57 William Paulson, *The Noise of Culture* (Ithaca, 1988), 49.
58 Bakhtin, *Philosophy of the Act*, 7.
59 Ibid., 44.
60 De Certeau, *L'Invention du quotidien*, 59–60.
61 Russo, *Female Grotesque*, 189.
62 Bakhtin, *Philosophy of the Act*, 43, 57–58, 41–42, 46.
63 Rosen, *Sur le grotesque*, 14.
64 Bakhtin, *Philosophy of the Act*, 40.
65 See Peter Fenves, *"Chatter": Language and History in Kierkegaard* (Stanford, 1993), 153.
66 Lucretius, *Nature of the Universe*, 155.
67 Bakhtin, *Philosophy of the Act*, 48, 40.
68 Bakhtin, *Art and Answerability*, 226, 209.
69 Bakhtin, *Philosophy of the Act*, 57.
70 Emily Schultz, *Dialogue at the Margins: Whorf, Bakhtin and Linguistic Relativity* (Madison, 1990).
71 Bakhtin, *Philosophy of the Act*, 35.
72 Rosen, *Sur le grotesque*, 21.
73 Bakhtin, *Art and Answerability*, 209.
74 As quoted in Fenves, *"Chatter,"* 153.
75 Peter Sloterdijk, *Zur Welt kommen—Zur Sprache kommen: Frankfurter Vorlesungen* (Frankfurt a.M., 1988), 31–59.
76 Aaron J. Gurjewitsch, "Höhen und Tiefen: Die mittelalterliche Grotesque," in *Mittelalterliche Volkskultur*, trans. Mathias Springer (Munich, 1987), 277, 280.
77 Tzvetan Todorov, "Dialogism and Schizophrenia," in Arteaga, ed., *An Other Tongue*, 203–14, esp. 211.
78 Arteaga, "An Other Tongue," 20.
79 Lloyd, "Adulteration and the Nation," 92.
80 Maurice Merleau-Ponty, *La Prose du monde* (Paris, 1969), 193.
81 Maurice Merleau-Ponty, *Le Visible et l'invisible* (Paris, 1964), 47.
82 Bakhtin, *Philosophy of the Act*, 32, 50.

Rachel Falconer

Bakhtin's Chronotope and the Contemporary Short Story

In "The Flash of Fireflics," Nadine Gordimer writes of a recent "general and recurrent dissatisfaction with the novel as the means of netting ultimate reality—another term for the quality of human life." She claims that "the novel is dead," while "the short story is alive" because its method and approach are more suited to "netting" this "ultimate reality"—"where contact is more like the flash of fireflies, in and out, now here, now there, in darkness."[1] Gordimer's privileging of the short story is polemical, of course, but the increasing number of collections now being published does support her view that the genre has some special resonance for today's reading public.[2] Shot through with postmodern skepticism about the concept of chronological, historical time, the contemporary short story is particularly well placed to "net" our culture's apocalyptic sense of impending crisis, of time foreshortened, or already run out, before the end of the millennium. But this is not simply a matter of capturing Western millennial angst in writing, for, once net, that protean cultural angst turns and wreaks a fascinating havoc on narrative forms.[3]

According to Bakhtin, all genres and generic

The *South Atlantic Quarterly* 97:3/4, Summer/Fall 1998.

distinctions may be defined by their "*chronotope* (literally, 'time space') . . . the intrinsic connectedness of temporal and spatial relationships that are artistically expressed in literature."[4] Or, in Gary Saul Morson's paraphrase, "Each narrative genre implicitly manifests a specific model of temporality."[5] As we know, Bakhtin argued polemically for the preeminence of the novel among literary genres, and one important reason for his preference was that the novel's unique temporal aspect seemed to grant the fictional human subject greater autonomy and freedom. In other genres, Bakhtin argued, the future of the hero is predetermined simply by virtue of being prestructured in narrative. But in its most "developed" manifestation, that is, in the Russian realist tradition, the novel preserves the appearance of autonomy by creating an unfinalized present and future for the protagonist that approximates the open-ended temporality experienced by a living human being. If Tolstoy created a sense of historically contingent time, with its asymmetrical structure of closed past and open future, Dostoevsky's achievement was to create a sense of time as genuinely "free" by locating "author, characters, and readers all together on the *very edge of the historical present*." As Morson goes on to explain, however, "In order to render palpable the act of choosing, Dostoevsky focused everything on the moment in which choice is made."[6] And if this focused chronotope gave his protagonists maximal freedom of choice in the *present*, it also seemed to reduce their "fundamentally historical nature" by cutting them off from any sense of past or future.[7]

Disagreeing with Bakhtin, Morson argues that the Russian realists retained both historicity and presentness by their narrative practice of what he terms "sideshadowing," suggesting that historical events, though incontrovertibly real, "might just as well not have happened."[8] This technique of sideshadowing encapsulates a time concept that Morson himself wishes "to explore and recommend," one in which the individual acts both freely and meaningfully within a coherent historical continuum.[9] But he then criticizes the "disease of presentness" he finds in contemporary literature, much as Bakhtin is said to have later criticized Dostoevsky. Morson identifies four major manifestations of the "diseased" way in which contemporary narrative represents time as (1) *desiccated present tense* (the present experienced as prologue or epilogue to another time); (2) *isolated present tense* (Dostoevsky's time concept, according to Bakhtin: the present deprived of historical connectivity); (3) *hypothetical present* (real time experienced as "elsewhere," as if in some parallel universe); and (4) *multiple time* (the present experienced as multiple versions of "reality," as in Borges's story "The Garden of Forking Paths").[10] In each case, the "infected" narrative fails to provide the human subject with a fully fleshed chronotope (a sense of past, present, and future), which is necessary for his/her meaningful intervention in the world.

To Morson's diagnosis of "presentness" as a "disease," we might add that of late capitalism as a "now culture." Notably close to Morson's concern with lack of agency is Fredric Jameson's argument that postmodernist culture's lack of historical sense deprives it of the foundation for political praxis.[11] In *Chronoschisms*, Ursula Heise considers the influence of science and technology on the postmodernist conception of time. In addition to "the shortening of temporal horizons in the late twentieth century," she argues, "the co-existence of radically different time scales from the nanoseconds of the computer to the billions of years in which contemporary cosmology calculates the age of the earth and the universe" has led contemporary novelists to question conventional models of narrative and teleological causation.[12] For Heise, postmodernism's emphasis on "presentness" may be construed positively or negatively, as her analyses of richly experimental texts by Samuel Beckett, Christine Brooke-Rose, and others demonstrate. Her examples are drawn mainly from texts of the 1960s, however. For J. G. Ballard, the experimentation of the 1960s was based on an open-ended time sense that has changed for the worse:

> The sixties were a time of endlessly multiplying possibilities, . . . a huge network of connections between Viet Nam and the space race, psychedelia and pop music, linked together in every conceivable way by the media landscape. We were all living inside an enormous novel, an electronic novel, governed by instantaneity. In many ways, time didn't exist in the sixties, just a set of endlessly proliferating presents. Time returned in the seventies, but not a sense of the future. The hands of the clock now go nowhere. . . . It's possible that my children and yours will live in an eventless world, and that the faculty of imagination will die, or express itself solely in the realm of psychopathology.[13]

Whether contemporary narrative suggests the infinite possibilities of present time or only its futility, there are distinct problems with Morson's anatomy of it as a "disease." Although he identifies three stages in Bakhtin's thinking about Dostoevsky and the chronotope of "presentness," Morson enters into debate with Bakhtin only at the third and most critical stage. Even if we agree on Bakhtin's *eventual* disillusionment with Dostoevsky's time sense, the question is (as always with this critic) with which Bakhtin—early, middle, or late—we are to engage. Furthermore, in *Narrative and Freedom* Morson applies realist criteria to nonrealistic texts in at least two ways. First, he expects fictional characters to demonstrate agency by exercising choice within a narrative sequence. As Heise points out, however, "Postmodernist characters are not conceived mimetically as 'realist,' self-possessed individuals with the ability to intend and act in the first place; frequently they appear as partly human and partly linguistic constructs."[14] Second, Morson assumes that the fictional representation of a protagonist exercising choice in an unfinalized temporality can somehow translate itself through the reader to the world, that a mimetic relation exists between the world and the text. But if a contemporary text were to "sideshadow" its events with alternative ones, that narrative device would not be enough to restore a skeptical reader's faith in historical process. Suggesting that an *alternative* sequence of events might have taken place does not address postmodernism's more fundamental point that it may be false to conceive of time as *sequence* at all.

Neither Morson nor Heise considers generic differences in discussing contemporary fiction, but the oversight is especially serious in the case of a Bakhtinian. As Morson himself observes, the time sense of a text is inextricably linked to its genre. Certainly, the high degree of generic hybridization in contemporary narrative makes it more difficult to identify the boundaries between one kind of text and another. All the same, in many cases such distinctions are drawn, if only to make us aware of their transgression. Two seminal short fictions discussed by Heise and Morson are Barth's "Lost in the Funhouse" and Borges's "Garden of Forking Paths," the representation of time in both of which is fashioned on the "grid" of a short story chronotope. In his essay "A New Refutation of Time," Borges declares, "Time does not exist outside the present moment," implying that there is no such thing as sequence, whether as "the succession of terms in a series" or "the synchronism of terms in two series."[15] But why should Borges so often choose to explore the ramifications of this theory in short story form? The question requires that we understand something of the generic chronotope of short fiction before examining how this inherited time–space gets fashioned by contemporary temporal perspectives.

To my knowledge, no one has yet attempted a history of the short story chronotope. But a survey of recent genre criticism reveals that untheorized *assumptions* about the short story chronotope differ significantly depending on whether examples are drawn from modern or postmodern texts.[16] Thus, even in the absence of a complete history, we can see that a distinctly modernist chronotope takes shape in the genre and then gets "handed down" to short fiction of later eras, which in turn acts within and reacts against these inherited confines. Certain elements of the modernist chronotope are retained, others rejected or transformed. It was Poe's prescription for the story of "a unity or totality *of effect*" that proved most influential among the genre theorists of the 1960s.[17] Frank O'Connor, in *The Lonely Voice: A Study of the Short Story* (1963), B. M. Eikhenbaum, in *O. Henry and the Theory of the Short Story* (translated in 1968), and Mary Rohrberger, in *Hawthorne and the Modern Short Story: A Study in Genre* (1966), all interpreted the short story's brevity as a sign of a generic interest in unity, whether a formal completeness or a thematic singularity encompassing a moment of vision—knowledge as revelation (complete, static) as opposed to knowledge acquired through time and experience.[18] Broadly speaking, these definitions intersect with "period" definitions of modernism, and the texts used to support such definitions (by James, Chekhov, Mansfield, Woolf, Joyce) are mainly modernist ones.[19]

Many readers of today, specialists and nonspecialists alike, still retain modernist expectations of the short story chronotope. If modernist writing challenges the notion of objective or "public" time with juxtaposed, conflicting individual temporalities, it is because, as some theorists argue, this privileging of private over public is characteristic of short fiction. According to May, for example, "the novel is primarily a social and public form," while "the short story is mythic and spiritual." "Mythic," for May, apparently connotes "individual": "In the short story, we are presented with characters in their essential aloneness, not in their taken-for-granted social world."[20] Elsewhere, he argues that the short story focuses "on eternal values rather than temporal ones and sacred/unconscious reality rather than profane/everyday reality and reminds us of Poe's dictum that the story tends toward the universal, having an affinity for the formalistic, the epitome, the essential truth or idea or image that rises above time and negates chronological progression."[21] Such glimpses of "universal truth" are hard-won and transient in the short story, but the same could be said about the modernist experience of time. Quoting C. S. Lewis, May theorizes that the short story narrative aims to capture "something else, something other than a process and much more like a state or quality."[22] This "state or quality" that "rises above" the temporality of narrative looks very much like modernist epiphany to me.[23]

One inherited modernist expectation of the genre, then, apparently has to do with knowledge as revelation rather than what is acquired through experience. Another is that the short story tends to be more self-consciously artificial than the novel. Resisting the reader's desire to "get inside" it, the story strives to maintain an ironic distance between reader and text. Near the end of "Forms of Time and of the Chronotope in the Novel," Bakhtin argues that the encounter between a reader and a text is itself a meeting of chronotopes: "In the completely real-life time–space where the work resonates, where we find the inscription or the book, we find as well . . . real people who are hearing and reading the text. . . . The work and the world represented in it enter the real world and enrich it, and the real world enters the work and its world as part of the process of its creation. . . . This process of exchange is itself chronotopic."[24] As we shall see, the chronotopic encounter between reader and text is particularly characteristic of the modernist short story, and its heightened temporal self-consciousness a crucial feature of contemporary practice.

How much of this inherited, "modernist-inflected" chronotope gets retained in postmodernist and other contemporary short fiction? The modernist concept of epiphanic time no longer seems appropriate for contemporary practitioners or theorists of the genre. As Miriam Clark notes in a recent overview of American science fiction, "If the modern story is situated at the fringes of society—the locale of human loneliness, as Frank O'Connor puts it—the stories of our time are founded not on the margins but in the ruined public sphere."[25] Norman Friedman calls most of the genre's inherited modernist features into question when he defines the short story as simply "short fictional narrative in prose," although he admits to problems with the relativity of the term "short." But at least his definition highlights one point of critical consensus; all the genre theorists agree on its brevity, and most concede another, related characteristic: the short story's structuring around a sense of imminent closure. Thus Friedman argues, "It is the *imminence* of the end," that is, "its relative closeness to the beginning," which differentiates the "effects" of short fiction from those of "longer works."[26] If "imminent closure" can be substituted for "epiphanic time" as the dominant chronotope in contemporary definitions of the short story, Susan Lohafer further refines the genre's "contemporary," as opposed to "early" and "modern," forms of closure. She argues that the "stagings of closure" in early short stories involved the reader's "cognitive adjustment from wonder to wisdom," while modernist closure moved the reader from "a naive world-view to a skeptical one"; contemporary short fiction, in contrast, tends to close by drawing the reader out of a position of knowledge or strength and leaving her/him "at risk—but adjusting in a strange world."[27] Thus not only are we more conscious of the ending's imminence, but endings in today's stories clarify less than they did in earlier fiction.

If Lohafer's cognitive studies apply to the genre as a whole rather than to American short fiction exclusively, then the short story has clearly crystallized some important contemporary views on time. As Frank Kermode argued over thirty years ago in *The Sense of an Ending*: "Apocalyptic thinking . . . governs contemporary thinking, which is characterised by a sense of crisis, rather than an identifiable temporal end. . . . Although for us the End has perhaps lost its naive *imminence*, its shadow still lies on the crises of our fictions; we may speak of it as *immanent*."[28] But rather than imagining a fixed point at which time will end, clarifying human history hitherto (the traditional function of Judgment Day), contemporary notions of imminent/immanent disaster hold no such promise of revelation. If we seem to be suspended in time and anticipating destruction, we also feel, contrarily, that we are *already* living in the aftermath of time, according to Katherine Hayles:

> Since the 1960s, the consensus that there is a fixed end point has been eroded by our growing sense that the future is already used up before it arrives. . . . The rhythm of our century seemed predictable. World War I at the second decade; World War II at the fourth decade; World War III at the sixth decade, during which the world as we know it comes to an end. But somehow it did not happen when it was supposed to. By the ninth decade, we cannot help suspecting that maybe it happened after all and we failed to notice.[29]

This failure of the apocalypse to materialize, to reveal and clarify, has had strange effects on the contemporary consciousness of time. Hayles goes on to argue that time now seems split "into a false future in which we all live and a true future that by virtue of being true does not have us in it."[30] Either way, we have reached a dead end with temporal duration.

This sense of temporal *impasse* also informs the genre of short fiction today. In "Some Aspects of the Short Story," Julio Cortázar comments, "The short story writer knows that he can't proceed cumulatively, that time is not his ally. . . . The story's time and space must be condemned entities."[31] For Gordimer, "the short story is a fragmented and restless form, a matter of hit or miss," and for that reason it suits contemporary consciousness, which is best "expressed as flashes of fearful insight alternating with near-hypnotic states of indifference."[32] V. S. Pritchett saw a similar correspondence between the short story, which he called "the glancing form of fiction," and "the nervousness and restlessness of contemporary life."[33] The comments of these practitioners lend weight to Clark's argument that "generic qualities of brevity, compression and ephemerality along with the story's minimal temporality make it a logical vehicle for the displacement of postmodernist loss and the thematization of diminished, even failing historicity."[34] Therefore, generic chronotope and contemporary Western time sense converge upon a shared premise that "time and space are condemned entities."

At this point we may ask whether short fiction has simply absorbed the pessimistic implications of postmodernism's "diminished, even failing historicity," or if it offers any resistance to the widespread sense of displacement and loss of agency. As a way of *opening up* this question to debate, I want to consider two British texts that have arresting ways of representing time, Martin Amis's collection of stories *Einstein's Monsters* and Duncan McLean's edited volume of new Scottish writing *ahead of its time*. The former thematizes the lack of agency entailed by a doomed sense of time on the scientific and technological level, where our cosmological timescales dwarf the human life span, and our ability to destroy the planet reduces all time to present crisis; the latter offers more of a sociopolitical lens on the same theme, with the reluctant members of a late-capitalist, Thatcher-infected "society" shown stagnating in various temporal backwaters of apathy, poverty, and violence. These two different collections together raise a range of issues to do with the short fiction chronotope.

In *Einstein's Monsters* the short story form enables Amis to focus on a single theme, the threat of nuclear holocaust, while presenting a range of different responses to it so that no one perspective dominates and the exercise of agency rests finally with the reader. In *ahead of its time* short fiction is interspersed with poetry and excerpts from longer works, so the story operates within the context of a broader generic "cultural intervention," as McLean describes it.[35] The singularity of this collection resides in the unique *time and place* of its intervention, with contemporary Scottish voices emerging from and against an inherited (English) culture of apathy and violence. Agency again straddles the text/reader border, insofar as these writings engage the current mood and desire for political change in Scotland. Both collections explore situations in which "time and space are condemned entities" by means of a genre of which "time is not [an] ally"; yet each works within its own cultural and generic limitations to discover space and time for individual praxis.

In Amis's introductory essay, "Thinkability," he describes a generational divide between writers who deal with the world that existed before nuclear weapons and those who, like himself, write "on the other side of the firebreak." For the latter, the apocalyptic point of no return has already been reached; there is no such thing as a post-nuclear "future." But Amis also intends to show that there is no "present" now either: "As yet undetonated, the world's arsenals are already waging psychological warfare," that is, the nuclear holocaust is "already happening inside our heads." For Amis, this helps "to explain why something seems to have gone wrong with time—with modern time; the past and the future, equally threatened, equally cheapened, now huddle in the present. The present feels narrower, the present feels straitened, discrepant, as the planet lives from day to day."[36]

While *crisis* may be *imminent* throughout this collection, it is never specifically *present*. The imprecision as to the onset of the "firebreak" in these stories underlines the difficulty of establishing a sense of chronology from within crisis time. "Holocaust," one might argue, refers only and always to the eradication of the Jews under Nazism. To many, this is the moment when history "empties itself" of value. But history did not end, since we are still *here* and time still *passes*. The term thus gets reapplied to successive points of no return, "firebreaks" that remind us we are living outside history. In *Einstein's Monsters*, these points range from the "evolutionary firebreak of 1945" at Hiroshima and 29 August 1949 (when the Russians successfully tested their first atom bomb) to "the year 2045 AD . . . Tokyo," Amis's imagined end point and site for the last "firebreak." In one sense, this imprecision allows us some room to maneuver (it is not too late; we are not dead *yet*); but in another sense, such maneuvering is just a form of alibi-hunting. Some writers, especially those who write science fiction (e.g., J. G. Ballard), find it consoling or even exciting to imagine "life" after nuclear holocaust; it provides scope for baroque descriptions of genetic and temporal inversions.[37] But Amis insists that "the correct attitude to nuclear war is one of suicidal defeatism. Let no one think that it is thinkable. Dispel any interest in surviving, in lasting. Have no part in it."[38] Avoiding the temptation to respond to the time we are (not) in by manufacturing alibis, as it were, in time, Amis *places* the subject (theme, speaker) of *Einstein's Monsters* in the unthinkably destroyed present. The individual stories effect various compromises between thinkability and unthinkability, insofar as (like Ballard's) they do imagine life afterward. But they are meant to be thought through and then, if possible, *unthought*. Their chronotopes are "condemned" in Cortázar's sense, since the temporal spaces they explore must ultimately remain unactualized for—*unthinkable* to—the reader. Each of the five stories in this collection imagines a different "unthinkable" post-nuclear future as a potential present. The choice of genre is essential to the preservation of each imagined future's "unthinkability." Together, they effect a Borgesian bifurcation of possibilities, with each projected scenario helping to cancel out the others in the sequence. Three of the five entail futuristic, post-nuclear disaster settings ("The Time Disease," "The Little Puppy That Could," and "The Immortals"), while two have "realistic" settings in a suspended present, with the holocaust psychologically imminent but the actual explosion yet to come ("Bujak and the Strong Force, or God's Dice" and "Insight at Flame Lake"). Thus the lack of any sequential linkage between one story and the next contributes to the weakened sense of temporal progress as we move out of an extended present ("Bujak" and "Insight") and from an immediate future ("The Time Disease") to a relatively distant one ("Little Puppy," "Immortals"). Regardless of the point where it falls along the temporal continuum, each story takes place within a cross section of time that is both "already present" and "unthinkably" possible in the future. Two stories end relatively optimistically ("Bujak" and "Little Puppy"), while the other three invite the reader to reject their imagined futures. The sequence as a whole is not geared toward a more thinkable and potentially more acceptable post-nuclear future, but neither is the implied reader expected to become increasingly "wiser" or "better prepared" as s/he turns from one story to the next. The sequential disconnectedness between each story and the next allows us to reject each possible future as it unfolds, yet the cumulative effect is of a present that branches into numerous possible futures. In this sense, the short story appears better able than the novel to accommodate a proliferation of potential futures while maintaining a basic narrative logic.

The possibility of an Einsteinian reversal of time occurring at the point of the "firebreak" is explored in "Bujak and the Strong Force, or God's Dice." Here the notion of "holocaust" is applied to an individual's experience of time. Tragedy (if that is the word) occurs out of the blue; it has no motive, no teleology, and no apparent sequentiality until events are later retraced in the court scene. Bujak returns home to find wife, mother, and daughter raped and murdered, then discovers their killers asleep in the house. Instead of taking revenge, he drags them off to the police station and thereby fails to fulfill the reader's (and the narrator's) expectation; for some reason, Bujak chooses disarmament. When the narrator asks Bujak about this years later, he simply says, "One must make a start." For Bujak, this (non)act constitutes a *temporal* reversal, marking a break between one "life" and the next, in which various aspects of himself are reversed (becoming physically weak where once he was strong, e.g., and verbal where once he was forceful). Curiously, the reversal of time in Bujak's case is made possible by unthinkability. Why does Bujak not kill the two sleeping men? (As the narrator reminds him, "No court on earth would have sent you down.") Bujak does not kill them because they have become unthinkable to him—untouchable: "Really the hardest thing was to touch them at all. You know the wet tails of rats? Snakes? Because I saw they weren't human beings at all. They had no idea what human life was. No idea! Terrible mutations, a disgrace to their human moulding."[39] The narrative becomes highly paradoxical here, with the "unthinkable" attaining a regenerative power by virtue of remaining beyond touch. In order to bring the reader to that paradoxical point, the narrator must himself think through the "unthinkable." If that unthinkable act is the detonation of a nuclear bomb by one of the superpowers, it is addressed indirectly by means of this "untouchability." Amis himself says only, "My impression is that the subject resists frontal assault. For myself, I feel it as a background which then insidiously foregrounds itself."[40] In allegorically reducing the superpower mentality to Bujak's mindset, Amis reduces the decision-making *scale* to the individual level. The point of unthinkability is further distanced by being deflected from the narrator, the speaking voice, to another character. The narrator himself fails to imagine his own family destroyed and concludes: "But in fact you cannot think it, you cannot go near it. The thought is fire."[41] Moreover, Bujak's reaction to the murderers is described and analyzed only retrospectively rather than by "frontal assault" at the time he discovers them. By such narrative indirection, Amis keeps the event of nuclear holocaust remote, both temporally and spatially, while establishing correspondences between our present situation and the imagined future. If this story is "only" about ordinary human criminality, it is also about the damage that humanity as a whole will do and suffer from in the event of nuclear war. The Glasgow youths who murder Bujak's family already represent, allegorically, the genetic mutations of a post-nuclear future ("I saw they weren't human beings at all. . . . Terrible mutations, a disgrace to their human moulding").

The possibility that the "apocalypse," whenever it occurs, might throw time into reverse (as Einstein theorized happened at the beginning of the universe) is one that Amis explores at novelistic length in *Time's Arrow* and in short form in "The Time Disease" (the third story in *Einstein's Monsters*). "The Time Disease," set on the other side of the "firebreak," describes a world turned upside down by the effects of nuclear fallout, including distortions of the "normal" temporal patterns.[42] Survival here depends on doing nothing, so no one expends much emotional, physical, or mental energy. The ironic twist is that the "time disease," a form of radiation sickness, does not accelerate the ageing process but the reverse; "coming down" with "time" here means dying of *youth*. Amis thus deploys the concept of time reversal to defamiliarize and satirize aspects of our present culture that reflect a time "gone wrong" (fear of ageing, inability to distinguish real events from media fictions, etc.).

The concept of time reversal receives its perhaps most lyrical and terrifying expression at the end of "Bujak and the Strong Force," however. The narrator concludes Bujak's story by observing, "Now that Bujak has laid down his arms, I don't know why, but I am minutely stronger," adding, "I don't know why—I can't tell you why."[43] But if the reasons for disarmament cannot be explained, their effects can be described. The narrator's resurgence of hope is expressed as an altered understanding of time, with "minutely stronger" meaning both "a little" and (stronger) "by the minute." At this point he relates Bujak's Einsteinian understanding of the cosmos:

> The universe would expand only until unanimous gravity called it back to start again. At that moment, with the cosmos turning on its hinges, light would begin to travel backward, received by the stars and pouring from our human eyes. If, and I can't believe it, time would also be reversed, . . . then this moment as I shake his hand shall be the start of my story, his story, our story, and we will slip downtime of each other's lives, when, out of the fiercest grief, Bujak's lost women will reappear, born in blood . . . until Boguslawa folds into Leokadia, and Leokadia folds into Monika, and Monika is there to be enfolded by Bujak until it is her turn to recede, kissing her fingertips, backing away over the fields to the distant girl with no time for him (will that be any easier to bear than the other way around?) and then big Bujak shrinks, becoming the weakest thing there is, helpless, indefensible, naked, weeping, blind and tiny, and folding into Roza.[44]

This apocalyptic vision includes what might be considered a characteristically postmodern conception of time: the narrative present is foreshortened by the cosmic scale of the image, and the subject loses its individual agency within this collapsing perspective. Nevertheless, time seems to reacquire value here, for even on this cosmic scale the passage of time becomes rehumanized, measured by a succession of generations. And the universe, while temporally vast, is seen to shrink spatially until all its unmanageable energy (Bujak and the superpowers) is reduced to a harmless singularity (Roza, the narrator's child, named after Bujak's murdered mother).

Time reversal works particularly well in the short story structure of "Bujak," in contrast to its novelistic exploration in *Time's Arrow*, the overdetermined plot of which casts narrator and reader into a mechanistic game of reversed everyday actions and emotions.[45] When treated at novelistic length, the Big Bang theory leaves us in a bleak universe where events can only be played out in a forward or backward direction; they can never be *different*. (Such a universe would render Morson's sideshadowing impossible to conceive, since open-ended, undetermined time could not exist in the past, the present, or the future.) "Bujak" merely touches upon these implications in a parenthetical question: "Will that be any easier to bear than the other way around?" But since the theory is not played out on a temporal axis, the dominant impression conveyed by the story is of an opening out, a release from future-blind crisis time, a narrative present instinct with other temporalities. To my mind, this is the thrust of the tense shift from conditional to future midway through the final paragraph (quoted above), with the "linchpin" phrase "if, and I can't believe it." In *Time's Arrow*, on the other hand, a single sequence of events is played out in two directions (forward and back). In "Bujak" that doubled sequence (implied by "if") is doubly negated ("and I can't believe"), such that the time reversal is felt as a sudden potential rather than a *re*determined sequence. Moreover, it is Bujak's active intervention that brings the reversal about, while the protagonist of *Time's Arrow* simply suffers it blindly. "Bujak" also invites the reader to intervene in this process at the end of the story, which, we are told, "shall be the start of my story, his story, our story," a story thus made dependent on reader memory. One cognitive consequence of the short story's brevity is our later remembering much of it at the level of linguistic detail (which is less often the case with longer works). Thus a reader's own time reversal might entail reading the detail of Bujak's "folding into Roza" (the elder) back into the earlier image of Bujak's taking "possession" of "the folded child" (Roza the younger) "with his arms."[46]

In "Insight at Flame Lake" and "The Little Puppy That Could," Einsteinian time, conceived as a concentration of energy rather than a simple reversal of chronology, offers still greater scope for human agency. While "Bujak" draws implicit analogies between the escalation of the arms race and the expansion of the temporal and spatial distortion of the universe, "Insight" and "Little Puppy" link the nuclear warhead itself to a moment when the universe will contract into such density that it must explode.

"Insight at Flame Lake" explores how the very existence of nuclear arms exerts an insidious psychological pressure on contemporary Western society.[47] Here, then, the "future" holocaust is projected onto present-day ordinary experience rather than vice versa. The narrative consists of a series of entries in Dan's notebook and Ned's diary during the course of a summer. From these sources, we piece together a "sequence" in which Ned invites his nephew Dan to share a family holiday with his wife and child at their lakeside cottage. Dan, still recovering from the trauma of his father's suicide, has just been diagnosed with schizophrenia. He is determined to cure himself without the prescribed drugs, and his condition begins to worsen. This process goes unnoticed by his uncle, who continues to encourage the boy to play with the baby, Harriet, as a form of natural therapy. The double first-person narrative allows Amis to explore his notion of a pervasive cultural anxiety operating here upon two very different mindsets. Dan's imagination operates on both macro- and microcosmic scales. As the son of a nuclear physicist, he has a heightened awareness of "subatomic" and "superlunary" forces. Ned's concerns, by contrast, are all on a resolutely ordinary scale: daily newspapers, slightly paranoiac relations with a neighbor over his jeep, the growth of his baby. And yet both characters feel an "exponential violence" building up in their world. Ned measures an increasing violence by reported instances of child abuse; Dan feels it in the "bigger picture," the "distortions and malformations" of nuclear power. For Dan, the lake *is* some kind of nuclear missile being fueled daily by the sun's heat pouring into the water.

Jameson has compared the postmodern subject's loss of temporal sense, "its capacity actively to extend its pro-tensions and re-tensions across the temporal manifold and to organize its past and future into coherent experience," to the pathological condition of schizophrenia, and Dan's heightened perception is not unlike the state that Jameson attributes to the postmodern subject: "This present of the world or material signifier comes before the subject with heightened intensity, bearing a mysterious charge of affect, here described in the negative terms of anxiety and loss of reality, but which one could just as well imagine in the positive terms of euphoria, a high, an intoxicatory or hallucinogenic intensity."[48]

Dan's schizophrenic consciousness is manifested in a lack of connectives between his thoughts, passivity (Ned's diary records the way Dan sits for hours in one spot), and a heightened sensitivity both to physical pain (mosquito bites are "exquisite" but also "torture") and to communicative signals (Fran's glances are misread as sexual invitations, the baby's stare as an existential challenge). Temporal and spatial scales are schizophrenically skewed in Dan's imagination, as he himself is aware. He recognizes, for example, that when he perceives Harriet as growing to cosmically huge proportions, he is experiencing a routine symptom, "*size-constancy breakdown*."[49] Tensions imperceptible to Ned mount up in Dan until he decides to "foreclose the great suspense." Ned records finding the boy's room in chaos the next morning: "The bedclothes and curtains had been torn to pieces, torn to rags. As I stood there and stared I had the sense of great violence, violence compressed and controlled—everything was scrunched up, squeezed, strangled, impacted, imploded." Up to this point, Amis has held the reader, as well as Ned, in suspense about the effects of Dan's illness. But a sense of foreboding has been instilled in the reader, who, unlike Ned, is made aware of Dan's worsening condition. The silent debates Dan holds with Harriet, together with a number of references to "dead baby" stories in Dan's notebook and Ned's pervasive but unfocused anxiety about child abuse, all contribute to the reader's anticipation of Dan's killing Harriet. At this point, however, the reader discovers that Dan has killed "only" himself. And the *actual* image of his frail body, seen through Ned's eyes, immediately cancels out the reader's *imagined* sense of the boy as threatening and dangerous: "At once I saw his thin body, face down in the shallows." Just before finding the body, Ned thinks to himself, "So the lake was a dud, a fizzle—; it never quite went off."[50] At a symbolic level, then, Amis represents Dan's death as another act of disarmament, like Bujak's. Because the immanence of nuclear power is greater in this story, a more violent response is required from Dan to cancel out the threat of imminent explosion. In both stories, though, the fulfillment of expectation is blocked by an exercise of *choice* in an apparently determined sequence of events.

Again, the textual chronotope is open-ended and invites active, "writerly" reading. The text, consisting of fragmentary, nonconcurrent diary and notebook entries, must be assembled and interpreted. An overtly rationalistic reading is one possible way of interpreting Dan's death, for example, as suicide associated with schizophrenia and having nothing to do with Ned's family. This is clearly Dr. Slizard's interpretation. Read "paranoically," however, the story might seem to suggest that, since there is more bufotenine in the boy's blood than is normal and his father's blood showed the same high levels, an inherited form of nuclear-aggravated schizophrenia led to Dan's death. While we might privilege the "sane" voice of Ned's diary (reflections of a narrator expecting to return to his text and to a self coexistent with the person who wrote it) over the tentative and self-questioning voice of Dan's notebook, a *schizophrenic* reading yields a pattern of correspondences among different types of violence (child abuse, social violence, expansion of nuclear industry, the heat of the lake, mosquitoes biting, infantile growth, and female fat). It is after all this same notebook, written in the midst of Dan's illness, that gives us the clearest "insight" into a possible connection between his own pathological condition and nuclear energy:

> Dad was one of the fathers of the nuclear age. Then, when the thing was born, he became its son, along with everybody else. So Dad really threw an odd curve on that whole deal about fathers and sons. First he was the thing's father, then he was the thing's son. Great distortions and malformations should clearly be expected to follow on from such a reversal.[51]

This escalation of hostile energy may be insidiously related to a national increase in violence (i.e., more cases of child abuse and murder). If Ned remains perplexed, stating numbly, "I don't know what is wrong,"[52] the reader is nevertheless able to make connections, perhaps rational, perhaps schizophrenic, among the different types of actual and immanent violence.

"The Little Puppy That Could" takes place at some point following a nuclear holocaust, when, "after its decades of inimical quiet, the planet earth was once again an hospitable, even a fashionable address." Beyond this temporal–spatial "firebreak," Amis's Earth seems to operate according to the laws of a contracting universe. Thus not only is chronology reversed, but our whole conception of time hangs in the balance between chronology and randomness. At first it would appear that the holocaust has unleashed countless genetic possibilities on the world, the current chaos of which also constitutes an opportunity for the surviving "low-level" life-forms. "In the deserts the lower forms flourished in their chaos: you could hardly turn your head without seeing some multipedal hyena or double-decker superworm pulsing toward you over the mottled sands."[53] Such scenes are common in science fiction and reflect the influence of contemporary scientific thinking on the popular imagination. In Ilya Prigogine's branch of chaos theory, as Heise explains, when a system is no longer in a state of equilibrium or near equilibrium, "its evolution can become haphazard and unpredictable. . . . At these moments of disequilibrium, . . . entropy may not increase but decrease, and new forms of order and complexity may emerge."[54] As Amis explores the implications of this world of seemingly endless potential, his style acquires a demotically liberating energy, as in this passage: "Natural selection had given way to a kind of reverse discrimination—or tokenism. Any bloody fool of an amphibious parrot or disgraceful three-winged stoat had as much chance of survival, of success, as the slickest, the niftiest, the most single-minded dreck-eating ratlet or invincibly carapaced predator."[55] The linguistic inventiveness of this description, with its neologisms and internal rhymes, is proof enough that the narrator, despite his expressed disapproval, can be as exhilarated as any *Star Wars* fan by the idea of genetic mutability.

But more problematically, the survivors lack agency; even the survival-of-the-race instinct has become muted and ineffectual: "Down the soft decades they had lost the old get up and go—the know-how, the can-do. Predation and all its paraphernalia had quite petered out of their gene cams and pulse codes." Communal decisions (e.g., whether or not to "move out and go nomad for a while") are made by genetic instinct rather than conscious thought: "Site-tenacity was, alas, pretty well the only stable element in the local DNA transcription. How could you run when, in your head, this was the only place?"[56] Thus, rather than fight off the giant, ravenous dog that comes to prey on the village, they offer it a weekly human sacrifice. At the level of macrocosmic analogy, the dog signifies the last contraction of the universe to a crushing density of matter, for the animal has gravitas in its own right; heavy with the weight of its diseases and not so much evil as an instrument of the end, it inspires the reluctant respect of the villagers. ("Everyone was secretly impressed by the dog's asceticism in restricting himself to one human per week."[57])

The regular appearances of this new "Natural Selector"[58] help to establish a rhythmic, ritualized form of temporality. This scenario gives a sinister slant to Elizabeth Ermarth's celebratory concept of postmodernist "rhythmic time," in which "neither large-scale narrative sequence nor, indeed, coherent individual identities can be envisioned."[59] Here the incoherence of individual identity opens the way for fascist-style ritual and religiosity: "Although the village was godless, the crater was agreed to be at least semi-sacred, and the people felt its codes, sensed its secrets with reluctant awe." While the present and future of the villagers may be described as overdetermined, their sense of the past is comparatively open-ended. Revival of memory functions as a kind of future, such as when, toward the end of the story, Andromeda's name is drawn for sacrifice in the weekly lottery. Andromeda (for never explained reasons) still acts as an individual; she has named herself, for example, and has adopted a puppy that appeared (again, with no explanation) out of nowhere. Although the others want the puppy destroyed, Andromeda gets her way because of her exceptional status in the village. Even here, the narrator reflects, "everyone has time for beauty, for art, for pattern and plan. We all come round to beauty in the end."[60] Thus to the villagers, she clearly embodies some lost but remembered humanity—its art, beauty, youth, and agency. The prospect of her loss awakens a somnolent capacity for resistance in the villagers: "On this night of sacrifice, of new nausea and defeat, the shouldered heads would not bow to receive their blows. . . . Now you could feel the low rumble of hot temper, of petulant mutiny." Andromeda's puppy, the "antimatter or Antichrist" of the dog, acts spontaneously where its counterpart does so by habit. But "spontaneity" is associated here with instinct or genetic memory (i.e., as what "puppies do"). The puppy's temporal universe retains its openness because it looks back, and here only the past provides any possibility of what we would recognize as a future. Thus the puppy wins its first victory over the dog when its memory is aroused, and, its "inner templates shuffling and dealing," the dog searches "for stalled memories, messages, codes."[61]

The story's conclusion plays out an Einsteinian scenario where matter (the dog) and antimatter (the puppy) spiral toward a central gravitational point: "For a time the puppy seemed freer than air, whimsically lithe, subatomic, superluminary, all spin and charm, while the dog moved on rails like a bull, pure momentum and mass, and forever subject to their laws." Following up the nuclear analogy, the puppy tricks the dog into self-detonation, which leads to the destruction of both canines: "With a howl of terror and triumph he hurled himself high into the flames—and the dog, like a blind missile, heat-seeking, like a weapon of spittle and blood, could only follow."[62]

Again, it is the genre that makes this juxtaposition of temporalities work. Generically speaking, the clash of values between puppy and dog is manifested as a contest between realism and romance, each with its own distinct chronotope. While the dog's weekly appearance imposes sequentiality on the villagers' lives, the puppy simply appears out of the blue and then stays, as is characteristic of events in the romance, where, as Bakhtin tells us, "'suddenly' is normalized; . . . it becomes something generally applicable, in fact, almost ordinary. The whole world becomes miraculous. . . . The entire world is subject to 'suddenly,' to the category of miraculous and unexpected chance."[63] According to the narrator, "It had happened the night before the night before."[64] Elsewhere, using the puppy as focalizer, the narrator refers to time as a "wave, or packet." The place is likewise nonspecific, with the puppy running across "fallow fields" (but where?). In the romance chronotope, actions are not motivated or caused by preceding events but occur symbolically, allegorically. "Where had the little puppy come from? Where was the little puppy heading?" asks the narrator. "Of course, the little puppy had no idea where he had come from or where he was heading."[65] From the romance perspective, the dog, with its calculating nature, its miasmic hide sporting a squad of post-Darwinian life-forms, its "doggedness," is nothing but a freak, a monstrous anachronism; the puppy's concluding metamorphosis as a boy (and a prince at that), however, is as unbelievable and symbolically apt as a romance ending should be (as well as suggestive of time's renewal with Adam and Eve's return to Eden). Many short story theorists have explored the genre's flexible allegiance to the traditions of fantasy and romance, on the one hand, and to those of realism, on the other.[66] Here the choice of romance over realism opens up a greater range of possible futures than those available to "Bujak."

The last story of the collection, "The Immortals," dramatizes a significant problem for the author/narrator: how to articulate the end of time.[67] Strictly speaking, you cannot locate yourself within either a place or a time if both have become meaningless, while human history's value can only be assessed with critical distance, the very perspective that is then lost. Jean-François Lyotard has claimed that history's organization into "grand narratives" is no longer possible for the Western postmodern consciousness.[68] Here, Amis invents a narrator who believes he is immortal and thus possesses that now impossible panoramic perspective on historical process. From this perspective, the narrator can induce a sense of pride in the implied reader over humanity's historical accomplishments. The "immortal" is impressed by "our" efforts in the Renaissance, for example: "You really came through. To tell you the truth, you astonished me." He has to hurry to get there in time to witness it, though, before the whole thing is over. He can see patterns of destruction emerging in what seem to him just a few minutes of eternity: "What was the matter? Was it too *nice* for you or something? Jesus Christ, you were only here for about ten minutes. And look what you did."[69] Although the narrator's position outside history enables him to discern its larger patterns, his macrocosmic perspective actually achieves the opposite result from the human perspective, reducing history to a few transient moments in the eternal existence of the universe.

The narrator thinks he is exempt from the general fate of humanity, including the apocalypse that is said to have happened in 2045, but, as the reader understands by the end of the story, he is one of the last human survivors of the nuclear holocaust: "I have a delusion also, sometimes. Sometimes I have this weird idea that I am just a second-rate New Zealand schoolmaster who never did anything or went anywhere and is now painfully and noisily dying of solar radiation along with everybody else." The immortal also stands for the contemporary postmodern observer, who, though perhaps possessed of an *abstract* knowledge of space, time, and history, lacks any sense of *personal* addressivity in time. The immortal catches glimpses of his own "eventness," but dismisses them as delusory: "It's strange how palpable it is, this fake past, and how human: I feel I can almost reach out and touch it. . . . There was a woman, and a child. One woman. One child. . . . But I soon snap out of it."[70] Ironically, even with all the time in the world at his disposal, the immortal is the only protagonist in *Einstein's Monsters* who lacks any agency whatsoever. Not only does he fail to acknowledge his real world (if it can be called "real"), but even in the world of his imagination he is an observer, someone who cannot afford to get too involved. Set in a post-apocalypse future, "The Immortals" is the darkest story of the collection, not least because its chronotope is one in which agency seems to have been lost, and time to have been utterly foreclosed.

Here again, however, we find resistance to closure at the level of reader–text chronotope. As Amis remarks in the introduction to *Einstein's Monsters*, "If we could look at ourselves from anything approaching the vantage of cosmic time, if we had any sense of cosmic power, cosmic delicacy, then every indicator would point the same way: *down*." This vantage point *is* achieved by the "immortal" narrator, although he himself necessarily remains unaware of his pre–nuclear holocaust readership; his chronotope may be wrong for him while still working for us, including Amis, for whom "the pessimistic view would seem . . . to be the natural one."[71] As we have seen, the representation of contemporary culture in *Einstein's Monsters* is often a negative one. Most of the characters are victims who, lacking agency to various degrees, conform to Jameson's anatomy of postmodern culture as a whole. At the same time, however, Amis suggests various ways in which value, weight, and space for individual agency may be acquired in the present, as is reflected by his own exercise of agency at the narrative level. Applying a puppyish "spin and charm" to his plot development, Amis plants a surprise twist in each story: Bujak does not kill the murderers, Dan does not kill Harriet, the "time disease" is youth, the puppy becomes a human being, the immortal is not so. This narrative "lightness" of touch (in Italo Calvino's sense[72]) is in itself a deliberate gesture of defiance against the temporal determinism that spawned the nuclear arms race.

If this is so, there is still space, and a *need*, for the reader's agency in the reception of this collection of (post)holocaust "postcards." When these stories are read in order, an increasing "unbelievability" becomes apparent at the level of technique. "Bujak" opens the collection with an assured, third-person commentary on another's tragedy, and the suspense is manipulated with perfect control. The slippage in tone from satire to sentimentality becomes more ragged in "Time Disease" with a more noticeable narrative strategy. The saccharine tone of "Little Puppy" is difficult to take seriously, seeming strained, even gooey, while the suspense in "The Immortals" falls a little flat, compared to its execution in "Bujak": we know from the beginning that the speaker is deluded, since he calls himself the immortal (in the singular), while the plural title indicates otherwise. Although these may be technical lapses on Amis's part, as narratorial lapses of *insight* they paradoxically contribute to the effectiveness of *Einstein's Monsters* as a whole. An increasingly improbable narrative style corresponds to an increasingly improbable world. As is typical of contemporary short fiction, the collection unravels in its telling, then leaves it up to the reader to think through and discard each "unthinkable" text.

Amis's 1980s obsession with *the bomb* can still provide us with a timely image of the chronotope in contemporary short fiction. However much the genre may condemn time and space, all narrative must express meaning through time. Cortázar resolves this paradox by describing short story time as a kind of explosion; like a photograph, the story presents itself as a statement of its own incompleteness, its partiality relative to the whole picture, and thereby "acts like an explosion which fully opens a much more ample reality."[73] Recalling the chronotope of the reader–text interface, Cortázar's "more ample reality" is an explosion of meaning that only comes into being through a fusion of both chronotopes, the text's and the reader's.[74]

The editor of *ahead of its time* conceives of his collection as a similarly explosive force that "detonates" on contact with a contemporary readership.

Clocktower Press, explains McLean, began as a publishing initiative to circulate stories "written in the language of the day, about the ideas and problems that confronted us here and now," and, most importantly, to circulate "when the ink [was] still wet." This series of publications was "not a commercial, money-making venture, but a cultural intervention. The booklets were intended to be literary time-bombs. At first glance they looked slight and inoffensive, even lightweight, but once they were out in the world, once the stories and poems they contained lodged in readers' minds, they'd start a chain reaction that would have disproportionately large effects."[75] Whether these Scottish stories, now published in London by Jonathan Cape and marketed throughout Britain, retain the same cultural immediacy (and purity of purpose) is a problem that relates to the changing chronotope of reader reception. *Ahead of its time* contains both reprinted material from the Clocktower booklet and new material acquired for the Cape edition. Which part reads more explosively? Perhaps the main point is that the volume's title can now be interpreted in terms of Scottish writing that *was* "ahead of its time" and with which we have now caught up or of Scottish writing that still *is* ahead of its time and with which we have yet to catch up. In this way, the breadth of material in the Cape edition offers hope for an extended temporality, a present which recuperates, and projects into, the recent past and the immediate future. But if the tone of the introduction is optimistic ("it's a good time to be alive and reading"[76]), the actual short stories often address "downbeat" issues: violence, poverty, social apathy.

Time does indeed seem to have run out for many of the characters in these stories. Some suffer from pathological disorders or the effects of economic depression; others have violent accidents or are brutally attacked. Such conditions prevail in chronotopes where preventative or recuperative action seems impossible, reinforcing Jameson's notion of the impossibility of individual praxis in postmodern cultural time–space. How, then, does such writing transform into a literary time bomb in which agency once again becomes thinkable and practicable?

"Sally the Birthday Girl" by Brent Hodgson represents life on an ordinary suburban street where the residents have become anaesthetized to public violence. The protagonist, Sally, witnesses a succession of "ghastly sights"—brutal acts—on the afternoon of her fourteenth birthday. While she is the text's main focalizer "at the scene of the crime," her observations are filtered through the bland voice of a third-person narrator, who also supplements his/her reportage with direct quotations from the police, issued as official comment after each "event." What this narrative device immediately demonstrates is the divide between privately witnessed event and publically articulated interpretation. Not only does the "official" voice of the police commentator misrepresent what happens, but Chief Constable George Kimberly also refuses to accept any police accountability with respect to crime, whether as implicated in its *causes* or as responsible for its *effects*. For example, one man in the street is shot by police because they mistake a cucumber in his hand for a pistol; they then offer a glaringly inadequate alibi: "The officers of the response vehicle fired their weapons because they feared for the lives of members of the public." But still more disturbingly, even at the private level there appears to be no sense of connection to or among the violent acts that appear to the street's inhabitants to be merely "ghastly sights." As Sally's mother comments, "What a day your birthday is turning out to be. You hear about things like this all the time on the TV, but when it is happening on your own doorstep, it is a real shock."[77] Although she draws a distinction between real events and those experienced only vicariously through the media, her experience of an actual event is likewise vicarious, and her use of cliche and of the impersonal "you" indicates an abstracting or generalizing of the present moment as if it were media reported.

If the time–space coordinates of this story's chronotope are meticulously registered, it is to emphasize their meaninglessness, since no causal or other connection is made between events, nor is any explanation given for the increased frequency and scale of the violence. The occurrence of each event is precisely recorded in terms of both time and place. Sally's birthday party, for example, "was in her own home at number 20, Westwood Road and it began at 3.15." The first crime occurs at 3:16 at number 25, the second at 3:17 at number 27, and so on. Here temporal and spatial markers have become alibis for the *absence* of any meaningful understanding of time or space. Hodgson represents a world in which the public response to personal disaster is distorted to the same extent as time and space are. Such distortions, as registered in the characters' speech, indicate a cultural failure to "address" (in Bakhtin's sense) criminality. Hodgson distances himself (and the reader) from this empty chronotope (and suggests alternatives to it) by means of parodic repetition, dialogization, and disruption of narrative structure. The official voice of Chief Constable Kimberly gets dialogized through repetition *ad absurdum* of his inadequate responses and, ultimately, his confusing of police and criminal activity. The sixth and last crime is unwittingly caused by the police, as Kimberly authorizes "the release of 22 prisoners [to assist] . . . in the cleaning up operation."[78] The prisoners pillage the street and rape all the surviving women. But this confusion between criminal and police activity is also registered as a temporal reversal, with police commentary *after* the event revealing its *prior* context.

A rupture in the plot sequence occurs at this point as well. The narrative has developed along a twofold structure of action, or "ghastly sight," and police reaction thus far, but with the final crime this pattern gets disrupted. A man "with an overpowering smell" walks into Sally's house and toward her mother. The temporal and spatial markers are again carefully noted: "Sally was on the floor clutching the dead shoulder of her friend Mandy Brown, when the eyes of her mother greeted the man who came into the room."[79] At this point, the narrator switches levels to report Kimberly's official reaction to the "event." Several ruptures are noticeable here. For the first time in this story we are given a glimpse into the inner perspective, if not the inner voice, of a protagonist when Sally's mother makes eye contact with her assailant. Moreover, this event remains "unfinalized" as the narrator switches to reported speech before telling us what happened next. Given Kimberly's reaction and the end of the story, there can be little doubt that Sally's mother is raped along with the rest of the women. But, as a result of the narrator's truncated description, the reader senses the possibility of different outcomes *within* an actualized sequence. Clearly, this is a good example of Morson's "sideshadowing," but Hodgson also makes the reader aware of her/his own collusion in this event as the textual silences lure us into mistaking a prior sequence for present and future inevitability. Finally, we may take into our readerly chronotope the double awareness of two "time zones," one inevitably closed and the other still unfinalized.

The opening paragraphs of Alan Warner's "Car Hung, Upside Down" similarly cast the protagonists as powerless with respect to their environment.[80] Donald John and Spunkhead are described as hanging upside down in a sycamore tree after their car has swerved off the road. The clock on the dashboard of the likewise suspended car has stopped at 10:33, with the time graphically rendered upside down in the text. This typographic anomaly signifies the chronotope of the entire story. Following Bakhtin, we might say that the narrative begins at the scene of wreckage characteristic of the adventure novel's "road chronotope"; the two protagonists, having been pitched off the road, go off the chronologically and biologically forward-driven axis of experience as well and, landing in a tree, end up in a position where going "forward" is to be pitched into emptiness.[81] (Donald John and Spunkhead are thus driven into the "condemned" vertical literary space which Cortázar claims is the only one possible in contemporary short fiction.) Also relevant here is Bakhtin's description of Dante's "form-generating impulse" (in comparison with Dostoevsky) to "'synchronize diachrony,' . . . which is defined by an image of the world structured according to pure verticality." In going on to describe the tension between synchronic and diachronic impulses in Dante, Bakhtin elaborates on "the images and desires that fill this vertical world," which are in turn "filled with a powerful desire to escape this world, to set out along the historically productive horizontal."[82] Warner's two protagonists, on the contrary, display no eagerness to "escape this world." They even appear to enjoy their spatial and temporal suspension and frequently pause in their desultory progress down the tree for conversation, tree-carving, and horizon-scanning. In relation to the Dantean/Dostoevskian verticalized chronotope, the inversion of traditional values assigned to height/depth axes is virtually parodic in "Car Hung." Here, anabasis means certain death, while katabasis means survival and escape.

As the narrative progresses and the characters are forced downward by warning explosions from the car above, time begins to acquire greater "weight" or value, as is evident from Warner's imagery. The two men are surrounded by detritus (cigarette butts, spliffs, empty bottles, pornographic magazines), while in the tree's topmost branches "gatherings of naked winter twigs were violently twisted, shoved up against the still-intact windscreen."[83] But there is also evidence of "deepening" psychological processes: when Donald John tells a story about a stag caught in a frozen lake, Spunkhead's "light" and literal interpretation ("You never shagged it then?") is overridden by Donald John's weightier, metaphorical reading ("I'm thinking if a big hoor of a stag can go through this ice so can I").[84] Finally, the image that transfixes them both is of a beached whale, whose split flesh Donald John "tastes" in the back of his throat when he himself is wounded. Fascinated at the outset with insubstantial, manifold, infinitely recyclable bodily images, Donald John momentarily feels the singularity and weight of "real" flesh.

If the protagonists learn a new way of seeing, suspended thus at an inverted space–time of 10:33, their experience (and their relation to time) must be distinguished from the suspensions of modernist epiphany. At their most philosophical (which isn't very), neither character experiences any sort of transcendence to a state outside their situation. Their responses are resolutely "ordinary" and low-key, as is underlined by the contrast between their colloquial Scots dialect and the narrator's "RP British." Thus once Donald John has his feet on the ground, he finds himself regretting his inability to take time seriously and "unbelieving that his last minutes should only have had ridiculous concerns in his mind . . . his mind where he'd prepared so long, only to have this humiliating trash, jumble and mess up there. Unbelievable." While this may be read as an authorial condemnation of postmodernist consciousness, it should also be noted as one that is expressed from within that very mindset and chronotope. In direct contrast to modernist transcendence, here the character's "weighted" sense of addressivity is registered in the present: "He'd fallen. Eyes close to the grass were dead. Maybe. Splendid morning reflected in the black pupils. Maybe not. The day only just started and dead!"[85]

These last few lines, apart from describing with extraordinary power the final seconds of life, gesture toward the issue of fiction's ability to represent the "image of man" (as Bakhtin puts it) in "real" time. Brought to the surface not so much in any particular reading of the text itself as in the way the text forces the reader to reflect on the reading process, this ending provides a good example of McLean's literary time bomb "lodging" in the reader's mind and setting off a chain reaction well beyond the apparently "lightweight" text. Does Donald John die in the end? "Maybe. . . . Maybe not." As these lines remind us, first-person narrators do not die. And the possibility of an onlooker who might have come away and written this story as if narrated by Donald John is specifically ruled out: no one saw the crash or could have seen the wreckage from the road.

In "The Immortals," Amis explores the mentality of a character who wants to die and thinks he can't; his delusion notwithstanding, "the immortal" is right about that—as a first-person narrator he *cannot* die. In Amis's hands, this condition becomes an important signifier of what is "wrong" with postmodernist consciousness: the inability to think oneself out of a fictional state or status. From this I-for-myself perspective, we cannot think ourselves dead either. So if Bakhtin's (and Morson's) concern is how the novel could represent a human being's encounter with time in its fully open-ended aspect, perhaps we have arrived (with the short story?) on the other side of the same question: How can I, or rather "I," die?

Describing the death of a protagonist from that character's point of view and in the first-person voice, but without any narrative framing device (no obviously "faked closure," as Kermode would put it), is relatively rare. If Warner's conclusion works without seeming gimmicky, I think it does so by virtue of the genre. As a short story, "Car Hung" can balance itself on the edge between conflicting fictional modes (here, e.g., fantasy and realism). However fantastical, even comically impossible, Donald John's exclamation "The day only just started and dead!" might seem, it is in a sense realistic, too. The very last line of the story directs our gaze, through that of the dying focalizer, to Donald John's "other": "Spunkhead was running, screaming, first in this direction, then in that." Blank space then follows, as would the blankness of unconsciousness—or "maybe not." This ending leaves the reader suspended between the resisting openness of Donald John's consciousness and the imminence of textual/temporal closure.

"Bonny Boat Speed" by James Meek also defamiliarizes and distorts the road chronotope of the everyday-adventure novel, in this case collapsing and "condemning" it temporally rather than spatially. Con accepts a late-night lift to the ferry from a friend, Arnold, whose daughter, it turns out, Con has unwittingly gotten pregnant. Arnold uses the speed of his driving to terrify Con into an admission of guilt, and the car skids out of control, plunging into the firth a hundred yards from the departing ferry. Con, the main focalizer, is a man who sees life as a network of freak occurrences, statistical improbabilities, an attitude accompanied by a feeling of personal nonaccountability. When a stranger with whom he has just spoken gets killed in a car crash seconds later, his main reaction is: "I didn't summon up the juggernaut, did I." His lack of emotional response derives from an intricate but abstracted temporal sense; to Con, the chance crossing of his life with those of others represents nothing but randomness, sometimes freakish but invariably disconnected from his own emotional/volitional being. This sense of inviolability also affects his relationships, such as those with Arnold and (we gather) Arnold's sixteen-year-old daughter. Images of car accidents recur in this story, and Con's inability to imagine the point of impact functions as a sign of his inability to occupy time as *present*: "Straight away you imagine it happening in slow motion but it doesn't of course, you don't see it like that any more than you see the flight of a shell from a gun. There's a loud noise and in an instant, like a badly edited film, it jumps, it's all arranged across the road, perfectly, peacefully, the broken cars, the glass, the bodies and the wheels spinning slowly."[86] The temporal skid from before to after in this description, like the fictionalizing of reality as "badly edited film," reveals the characteristically postmodernist difficulty Con has in conceptualizing the "real," once-occurrent present.

For Arnold, whose dangerous driving has already killed his wife, the moment of collision can be imagined as actual and finalizing. But in a sense, since he alone survives the accident, he continues to suffer the trauma of his apparent inviolability. His repeated speeding after the crash can be interpreted as an attempt to exorcise this survivor's guilt as well as, perhaps, an attempt to achieve physically what he may perceive mentally: time "cheapened, foreshortened." If this is so, each new speeding episode that he survives only increases the traumatic feeling of invulnerability and of temporal emptiness. His other notable trait, inventing and selling apocryphal facts/statistics, suggests that for him the past comprises a storehouse of images to be plundered, decontextualized, and circulated for immediate consumption. Both Con and Arnold are trapped within a present that is felt as a void.

When Arnold has Con trapped in the speeding car, the latter is forced to face his addressivity in time in the most literal way. He maps his chances of survival against the distance remaining between the car and the ferry berth: "As things stood the rest of my life was being measured out in red cat's eyes beaded along the A90, and the vision of the long cat of after dark expired at the water's edge, if not sooner." Con at first attempts to "transcend" this space and the guilt Arnold is pressing him to accept: "I was working up an anger because I could see we were going to make it to the terminal and up the ramp no bother. 'She was old enough to be living by herself. It's not like I was the first.'"[87] But Con's attempts to alibi himself only prompt Arnold to increase his speed. Throughout the journey, Con also tries to slow things down by pointing out the clocks they pass, hoping to "neutralize" time—and the need for haste. But again Con is defeated because he keeps discovering that these clocks aren't synchronized. Deprived of an objectified, public time, Con's private time is now wholly determined by Arnold, who can stretch out, foreshorten, or terminate his life at will.

With less than a minute between the ferry's scheduled departure and their possible collision, Con does exert agency in this radically foreshortened chronotope: he pulls on the handbrake. The car skids, and plunges into the water. And at this point Arnold intervenes to save the drowning Con, a traumatic repetition with a difference since here he *is* able to save his passenger. Con also, finally, experiences a car crash as real (i.e., as pertaining to him), and in this moment his temporal sense (as it were) shifts gear:

> For a certain time, memory, the present and apocrypha became the same thing, like the Father, the Son and the Holy Ghost. I remembered the car flying off the end of the pier before it actually happened, and I felt it skim three times across the waves like a stone as if it really did, though I knew I was feeling, with every bone in my muscle, the apocryphal version of what truly took place, and the vague, imaginary sense of hitting the water once and going down was what was real.[88]

The gathering of impressions into a single, transient but visionary moment reads at first like the experience of epiphanic time. But Con is not experiencing a transcendental reality here. He actually *feels* the apocryphal, the false version of what happens; whatever he "learns," it is still within the limits (if that is the word) of a postmodern, fictionalizing consciousness. The "real" event, though simultaneous, registers in his mind as secondary and anticlimactic. (This is also true for the reader, who must read the alternatives sequentially.) The last thing he does is to attempt an escape from addressivity and reality's closure: "I got free just as a part of me I never knew I had started to try to rationalise the death experience into something negotiable but only making it worse."[89] If he "gets free," it is because Arnold saves him. In this case it is not individual but interpersonal agency that interrupts the certainty of time's being definitely up.

Today, as I write, Scotland has voted for a devolved Parliament with tax-raising powers. Whether reflected or in part created by collections such as this one, there is no doubt that individual and collective agency is still possible, and perceived to be so, in the contemporary political–historical context of that country today. Technologically speaking, we have advanced from the Cold War years in which Amis's futuristic scenarios seemed not just conceivable but probable. Perhaps it is through the imaginative intervention of texts like his that we have discovered ways to invert time, to back away from nuclear singularity. In any case, the brevity, provisionality, and exploratory openness of these short fictions have surely led them to resonate in readers' minds, with the "disproportionately large effects" that accrue from a powerful fusion of different chronotopes: the diachronically inherited chronotope of the short story genre, the synchronic chronotopes of postmodern cultural discourse, and the chronotope of the individual reader's confrontation with an individual text. In their disclosure of space and time for agency, I believe, these short fictions restore some sense of "limitless possibility" to contemporary thinking about time.

Notes

1 Nadine Gordimer, "The Flash of Fireflies," in *The New Short Story Theories*, ed. Charles E. May (Athens, OH, 1994), 263–67; quotations from 263, 264.

2 In his Introduction to *New Short Story Theories* (xi–xxvi), May, for example, identifies a "renaissance" of interest in the short form, at the level of practice and theory (xi).

3 See, for example, John Barth's short story "Menelaiad," in *Lost in the Funhouse* (New York, 1969), 130–67. Proteus, the shape-shifter, caught by Menelaus, eventually turns himself into an image of Menelaus. "Proteus becomes the figure for the multiple temporalities in which Menelaus loses himself," according to Ursula K. Heise, in *Chronoschisms: Time, Narrative, and Postmodernism* (Cambridge and New York, 1997), 71.

4 M. M. Bakhtin, "Forms of Time and of the Chronotope in the Novel: Notes toward a Historical Poetics" (1937–38), in *The Dialogic Imagination: Four Essays*, ed. Michael Holquist, trans. Caryl Emerson and Michael Holquist (Austin, 1981), 84–258; quotation from 84.

5 Gary Saul Morson, *Narrative and Freedom: The Shadows of Time* (New Haven and London, 1994), 5.

6 Ibid., 105. See also Bakhtin, "Forms of Time and of the Chronotope in the Novel," 249.

7 Morson, *Narrative and Freedom*, 106.

8 Ibid., 118.

9 Ibid., 5.

10 Ibid., 173–233 (chap. 5, "Paralude: Presentness and Its Diseases").

11 See Miriam M. Clark, "Contemporary Science Fiction and the Postmodern Condition," *Studies in Short Fiction* 32 (1995): 147–59, esp. 152.

12 Heise, *Chronoschisms*, 6–7; see also 47–77.

13 Quoted in a 1984 interview by Thomas Frick excerpted in *Short Story Criticism* 1 (1988): 81–83; quotation from 82–83.

14 Heise, *Chronoschisms*, 65–66. She also makes the point that "even if we assumed with Morson that metafictional novels relied on rationally and realistically conceived characters who find themselves in a deterministic universe, the question remains whether the text as such could be considered determinist if it juxtaposes several universes that take the same events to different outcomes, and gives none of them ontological priority over the others. It is precisely this kind of juxtaposition that opens up interpretative possibilities for the reader and manifold layers of textual self-referentiality that cannot appropriately be called determinist" (66).

15 Jorge Luis Borges, "A New Refutation of Time," in *Jorge Luis Borges: A Personal Anthology*, ed. Anthony Kerrigan (London, 1968), 44–64; quotations from 60–61.

16 For good overviews of generic criticism, see *Short Story Theory at a Crossroads*, ed. Susan

Lohafer and Jo Ellyn Clarey (Baton Rouge and London, 1989); and May, ed., *New Short Story Theories*, especially his annotated bibliography. Although little use has been made of Bakhtin in short story criticism, one notable exception is Dominic Head's *Modernist Short Story: A Study in Theory and Practice* (Cambridge, 1992 [1991]). Head reasons that Bakhtin would probably class the short story ("*as it is usually defined*"), along with poetry, as monologic, since the two genres have analogous "formal properties": "The frame story, the single action, [and] the simple plot reversal . . . in the well-plotted, unified story . . . tend to invite a monologic governing narrative discourse, conscious of the controlling structure and so more clearly directed than the discourse of the novel" (96). Head counters this conjectured position with a "dialogic approach" to the modernist short story, the "disunifying devices" of "which are seminal features of the literary effects produced in the genre" (x); for Head's discussion of other heteroglossic effects, see also 31, 68–69, and 72.

17 Edgar Allan Poe, "Review of *Barnaby Rudge* by Charles Dickens," *Graham's Magazine* (February 1842), in May, ed., *New Short Story Theories*, 66.

18 For a historical overview of short story criticism, including these seminal works, see Susan Lohafer, "The State of the Art: Introduction to Part 1"; and Norman Friedman, "Recent Short Story Theories: Problems in Definition," in Lohafer and Clarey, eds., *Short Story Theory*, 3–12 and 13–31, respectively.

19 See Heise, *Chronoschisms*, on distinctions between modernist and postmodernist time concepts.

20 Charles E. May, "The Nature of Knowledge in Short Fiction," *Studies in Short Fiction* 21 (1984): 329, 333.

21 May, Introduction to *New Short Story Theories*, xviii, xxiii; see also "Poe on Short Fiction," in ibid., 59–72.

22 May, Introduction to *New Short Story Theories*, xix.

23 See Morris Beja, *Epiphany in the Modern Novel* (London, 1971).

24 Bakhtin, "Forms of Time and of the Chronotope in the Novel," 253, 254.

25 Clark, "Contemporary Science Fiction and the Postmodern Condition," 150. The image of the ruined public space frequently appears as a local chronotope in much British short fiction as well; see, for example, the decaying and neglected back rooms, basements, and pawn shops of Shena McKay's fiction in her *Collected Short Stories* (London, 1994 [1974]).

26 Friedman, "Recent Short Story Theories," 29, 26.

27 Susan Lohafer, "A Cognitive Approach to Storyness," in May, ed., *New Short Story Theories*, 301–11; quotations from 308. See also John C. Gerlach, *Toward the End: Closure and Structure in the American Short Story* (University, AL, 1985); Gerlach cites Robert Adams, Frank Kermode, David Richter, and Barbara Herrnstein Smith.

28 Quoted in Head, *Modernist Short Story*, 196.

29 N. Katherine Hayles, *Chaos Bound: Orderly Disorder in Contemporary Literature and Science* (Ithaca, 1990), 279–80.

30 Ibid., 280.

31 Julio Cortázar, "Some Aspects of the Short Story," in May, ed., *New Short Story Theories*, 245–55; quotation from 247.

32 Gordimer, "Flash of Fireflies," 265.

33 Quoted in Head, *Modernist Short Story*, 190.

34 Clark, "Contemporary Science Fiction and the Postmodern Condition," 153. Similarly, Clare Hanson notes that "the contemporary interest in the short form is . . . very much part of the postmodernist tendency. As in the modernist period, the short form is in the vanguard of experimental writing"; *Short Stories and Short Fictions, 1880–1980* (London, 1985), 172.

35 Duncan McLean, Introduction, *ahead of its time*, ed. Duncan McLean (London, 1997), xi.

36 Martin Amis, "Introduction: Thinkability," in *Einstein's Monsters* (London, 1987), 1–24; quotations from 18 and 17.

37 For an excellent example, see the title story in J. G. Ballard's *Myths of the Near Future* (London, 1982), 7–43.

38 Amis, "Thinkability," 13.

39 Amis, "Bujak and the Strong Force, or God's Dice," in *Einstein's Monsters*, 25–48; quotations from 46 and 47.

40 Amis, "Thinkability," 19.

41 Amis, "Bujak and the Strong Force," 46.

42 Amis, "The Time Disease," in *Einstein's Monsters*, 69–86.

43 Amis, "Bujak and the Strong Force," 47.

44 Ibid., 47–48.

45 Maya Slater makes the useful point that *Time's Arrow* does turn us into careful, scrutinizing readers, since we actively look for inconsistencies and mistakes in the backward description of events; see her "Problems When Time Moves Backwards: Martin Amis's *Time's Arrow*," *English: The Journal of the English Association* 42 (1993): 141–52. But to my mind, the activation of the reader in "Bujak" is more inventive; in the novel we are really only involved in catching the narrator out in a game where the rules are intricately circumscribed.

46 Amis, "Bujak and the Strong Force," 46.

47 Amis, "Insight at Flame Lake," in *Einstein's Monsters*, 49–68.

48 Fredric Jameson, *Postmodernism, or, The Cultural Logic of Late Capitalism* (Durham, 1991), 25, 27–28.

49 Amis, "Flame Lake," 57.

50 Ibid., 66.

51 Ibid., 57.

52 Ibid., 67.

53 Amis, "The Little Puppy That Could," in *Einstein's Monsters*, 87–118; quotations from 98.

54 Heise, *Chronoschisms*, 259.

55 Amis, "Little Puppy," 98.

56 Ibid., 105, 108.

57 Ibid., 108–9.

58 Ibid., 98.

59 Elizabeth Deeds Ermarth, *Sequel to History: Postmodernism and the Crisis of Representational Time* (Princeton, 1992), 20.

60 Amis, "Little Puppy," 106.

61 Ibid., 112, 114.

62 Ibid., 115–16, 116.
63 Bakhtin, "Forms of Time and of the Chronotope in the Novel," 152.
64 Amis, "Little Puppy," 92.
65 Ibid., 89.
66 Critics who have traced romance roots in short fiction include Propp, Bettleheim, Bierce, Canby, Marcus, May, and Rohrberger, while those who have identified the genre's realist affinities include Baldwin, Barzini, and Fitzgerald; see the annotated bibliography in May, ed., *New Short Story Theories.*
67 Amis, "The Immortals," in *Einstein's Monsters*, 119–32.
68 Jean-François Lyotard, *The Postmodern Condition: A Report on Knowledge*, trans. Geoff Bennington and Brian Massumi (Manchester, 1979), 135. See also Heise's discussion of Lyotard in the context of postmodern temporality (*Chronoschisms*, 16–17).
69 Amis, "The Immortals," 126, 130–31.
70 Ibid., 131.
71 Amis, "Thinkability," 20, 16.
72 See Italo Calvino, "Lightness," in *Six Memos for the Next Millennium* (London, 1996 [1988]), 3–29.
73 Cortázar, "Some Aspects of the Short Story," 246.
74 Of course, this meeting of text and reader chronotopes occurs in every act of reading, so is not a function of contemporary narrative technique. But the potency here is that the text and the reader, as far as possible, inhabit simultaneous chronotopes. The text both reflects and defamiliarizes the reader's exact sense of the present.
75 McLean, Introduction to *ahead of its time*, x, xi.
76 Ibid., xvii.
77 Brent Hodgson, "Sally the Birthday Girl," in McLean, ed., *ahead of its time*, 143–47; quotations from 143, 146.
78 Ibid., 147.
79 Ibid., 146.
80 Alan Warner, "Car Hung, Upside Down," in McLean, ed., *ahead of its time*, 231–41.
81 For the chronotope of the road in the novel of everyday adventure, see Bakhtin, "Forms of Time and of the Chronotope in the Novel," 165.
82 Ibid., 157.
83 Warner, "Car Hung," 231.
84 Ibid., 240.
85 Ibid., 241.
86 James Meek, "Bonny Boat Speed," in McLean, ed., *ahead of its time*, 101–18; quotations from 102, 106.
87 Ibid., 114, 115.
88 Ibid., 117–18.
89 Ibid., 118.

Nikolai Pan'kov

Archive Material on Bakhtin's Nevel Period

As we know from his conversations with Viktor Duvakin, Bakhtin gives the date of his arrival in Nevel as 1918. It was Lev Pumpianskii, then on military service in this small town, who persuaded him to move there, according to Bakhtin; Petrograd went hungry, while in Nevel "it was possible to make a living, and there was as much food as you could wish, and so forth."[1] Although Bakhtin was a little inclined toward autobiographical mythmaking, which was conditioned by a whole series of circumstances and is far from rare among eminent individuals,[2] in this case his claim easily bears archival verification. The materials of the Velikie Luki branch of the Pskov Region State Archive (where the documentary records relating to Nevel from 1910 to the early 1920s are currently held) not only enable our verification of the dates of Bakhtin's Nevel period, but also generally enhance our knowledge of this period. In fact, the sections devoted to Nevel in both published biographies of Bakhtin are extremely sparing in any kind of

The *South Atlantic Quarterly* 97:3/4, Summer/Fall 1998.
"Arkhivnyje materialy o nevel'skom periode biografii M. M. Bakhtina" by Nikolai Pan'kov, in *Nevel'skij sbornik*, Vol. 3 (St. Petersburg: Acropol')

detail. Katerina Clark and Michael Holquist rely in their well-known book on only one version of Bakhtin's "curriculum vitae" and a few archival publications.[3] Larisa Konkina and Semen Konkin also restricted themselves, for some reason, to a reference to an archival statement sent from Velikie Luki and confessed that "no concrete information regarding Mikhail Bakhtin's employment in educational establishments in Nevel between 1918 and 1920" is available.[4] But any information relating to Bakhtin's life and activities is valuable for an adequate understanding of his spiritual evolution, all the more so if it reveals important facets of an actually experienced historical epoch or relates to scientific, political, or other aspects of the personal and social lives of the people of the time.

It is unfortunately true, however, that the materials of the Velikie Luki archive either were incomplete from the very beginning or a significant part has since been lost, so any reconstructed picture will inevitably be marked by substantial lacunae. Even the date of Bakhtin's arrival in Nevel remains for the moment insufficiently precise: the year 1918 is beyond doubt, but pinpointing the exact date still poses certain difficulties. The curriculum vitae cited by Clark and Holquist shows that Bakhtin began work as a schoolteacher in Nevel on the first of January 1918 and joined the staff of the local *gimnaziia* (high school) in August of that year. Clark and Holquist consider it most likely that Bakhtin was first in Nevel for a brief visit while completing his education at Petrograd University and then moved there as early as that spring.[5] Pumpianskii, however, mentions in his autobiographical notes that "it was already summer when Mikhail Mikhailovich arrived" in Nevel.[6] The name Bakhtin appears in currently available archive material for the first time only in October 1918. His attendance at meetings of the school council in Nevel is recorded in minutes dated 29 October, while minutes from 26 October record that Bakhtin's candidacy was balloted by the members of one of the school committees, although it is unclear whether he was actually present on that day; yet another document attests that Bakhtin began teaching in the Nevel Unified Labor School on the first of October 1918.[7]

A clearer sense of Bakhtin's domestic circumstances and employment [*budnichnaia rabota*] may be gained from an overview of the general situation in the education system in post-Revolutionary Nevel.[8] The following schools were operational in Nevel at the beginning of 1918: the private Muliarchik *gimnaziia* for girls (opened in 1906); the Sventsiany *gimnaziia* for boys (transferred to Nevel at the request of its local government following the school's evacuation from Sventsiany); the Novaia Vileika teacher training college (also evacuated to Nevel in September 1915); the upper primary school, the Jewish primary school, and a few other minor schools.[9] The teacher training college was transferred in September 1919 to the town of Lebedian in the Tambov region,[10] and the Nevel Unified Labor School (First and Second Levels) arose on the basis of the remaining establishments in the summer of 1918.

This variety of educational institutions was a product of the radical school reforms undertaken by the Bolshevik People's Commissariat for Education headed by Anatolii Lunacharskii. These reforms abolished all examinations (entry, exit, and progressive), the grading system for the evaluation of knowledge and conduct, compulsory homework, and the awarding of diplomas (these were to be replaced by certificates which would not, according to the PCE, bestow "any rights or privileges" on their recipients). The division of schools into primary or upper primary and *gimnaziia* or into "modern" trade, technical, or commercial schools was also abolished. All schools in the Russian Federation were given the same designation, which was defined in the Statute on Unified Labor Schools of the Russian Federation as follows: "What does it mean for a school to be unified? It means that the entire system of ordinary schools, from kindergarten up to university, should consist of a single school, one continuous ladder. It means that all children should enter one and the same type of school and begin their education equally, and that they should all have the right to climb to the highest rungs of the ladder." A little further on, however, it is stated that "the concept of a unified school does not necessarily imply uniformity," and a pledge is made both "to offer a wide-ranging independence to the various sectors of national education" and not to restrict "the educational creativity of pedagogical councils" or even "private initiative." As regards the "labor" component of the new schools, the Statute continues: "The new schools should be labor schools. This is of course far more of a necessity for the schools of a Soviet state in the process of transition from a capitalist to a socialist regime than it is for the schools of progressive capitalist countries, although such a necessity has also been recognized there and, to a certain degree, realized."[11] Labor is said to be not simply a subject but a "fundamental teaching" aimed, first, at instilling "an active, lively, and creative knowledge of the world" in students and, second, at fully preparing them for practical life, and for the acquisition of "any specialism," any methods and forms of work in agriculture and industry. Of course, the usual range of traditional subjects (in accordance with the various types of schools) found a place in the program: "Russian language, mathematics, geography, history, the branches of biology, physics and chemistry, and modern languages." The only subjects to be dropped entirely were "dead" languages and divinity. (The schools were to be secular.)

As we shall see, the project described in the Statute would be enthusiastically endorsed by the "school workers" [*shkraby*] of Nevel, and the young Bakhtin would actively participate in both discussion of the problems which arose in the process of realizing that project and, indeed, in the realization itself. The schools were democratized and became completely free of charge, open to all, and even compulsory. That enthusiasm for a shift toward concrete reality was congenial to Bakhtin and would be embodied a few years later in philosophical work opposed to the dominance of "theoretism." Both personalistic and "dialogic" overtones can be discerned in the PCE Statute and, it would seem, in the initial pedagogical practice of the Unified Labor Schools: "The personality remains of the highest value in socialist culture. But this personality can fulfill its potential only in a harmonic and united society of equals."[12] Later, alas, different tendencies would prevail, such as featured, for example, in the Introductory Philosophy Program of 1918: "Every philosophical system must be viewed not in itself [but] as a philosophically constructed, relatively finalized, and complete expression of the system of thought of a recognized broad collective—of a social grouping or class of a given epoch."[13]

The unified school was divided into two levels, the first for children aged eight to twelve (a five-year course) and the second for children aged thirteen to sixteen (a four-year course). Compared to the boys' *gimnaziia*, the two-level system divided the first three years (including a preparatory year) from the fourth to seventh years and abolished the eighth year.[14] It would seem that there was nothing coincidental in this correspondence between the structure of the new schools outlined in the Statute and that of the boys' *gimnaziia*, which was at once a point of orientation for the reformers and the very model of education their innovations were designed to overcome. All things considered, the Sventsiany boys' *gimnaziia* served as the main constructive element of the Nevel Unified Labor School.

In conversation with Duvakin, Bakhtin refers to the Novosventsiansk boys' *gimnaziia*, recalling that "when the war began, Novosventsiansk was very soon occupied by the Germans," and the school was transferred to Nevel.[15] But prior to the First World War the *gimnaziia* had been located in Sventsiany (in the Vilna Province), not at the nearby Novosventsiansk station on the North–West Railway. The *gimnaziia*, which had opened in 1913 on Kaznacheiskaia Street in the same building as the town council, had only the first and second years to begin with. When a third grade was added in the 1914–15 academic year, the number of pupils reached eighty-nine. The school received 17,548 roubles and 25 kopecks in State funding and charged a fee of 50 roubles.[16]

At the beginning of September 1915, German troops under the command of Field Marshal Von Hindenburg and General Ludendorf mounted what has since come to be known as the "Vilna operation" (or "Sventsiany incursion"), which led to the retreat of Russian military divisions along the Western Dvina River line to the towns of Dvinsk (now Daugavpils), Vileika, Baranovichi, and Pinsk.[17] The school was hurriedly evacuated—so hurriedly, in fact, that there is contradictory evidence as to where it was transferred and even when it resumed its activities.[18] But one document, "Short List of Institutions and Establishments in the Vilna Educational District [*okrug*] for 1916," issued that year by the district's Education Authority in Mogilev (where it had been evacuated following the "Sventsiany incursion"), however, indicates that the Sventsiany boys' *gimnaziia* was "not functional," but that "its office, headed by its director, State Councillor P. A. Iankovich, was currently located at 19 Oranzhereinaia Street in the town of Tsarskoe Selo."[19] In any case, during the 1917–18 academic year, the Sventsiany boys' *gimnaziia* was operating "with five principal and three parallel years, and with a total of 260 pupils."[20] The premises of the local upper primary and Jewish primary schools were used for lessons.[21] According to the PCE list of evacuated educational establishments within the Vilna Educational District for 1918, the property, textbooks, and other teaching materials of the boys' *gimnaziia* were not transferred;[22] it is clear, however, from documents in the Velikie Luki archive that some school property had been saved during its evacuation (e.g., a samovar, a typewriter, a few ikons, a pair of brass candlesticks, and various musical instruments). An inventory of July 1918 listed items acquired after the evacuation (desk lamps, inkwells, and clothes- and shoe-brushes, among other things). The school's main library holdings consisted of 210 titles in 349 volumes, while the pupils' library held 245 titles in 258 volumes (including those which had survived from the time at Sventsiany). Assorted tables, compasses, maps, and models are also listed among the school's equipment.[23]

As for the staff, apart from the head, Pavel Adamovich Iankovich (whom

Bakhtin already knew from his own school years at the Vilna boys' *gimnaziia*, where Iankovich had taught mathematics prior to his move to Sventsiany), only Aleksei Gusarevich, who taught natural history and geography, remained from the pre-evacuation period.[24] All the other teachers were new; the minutes of the summer 1918 teaching committee meetings (not long before all the intermediate educational establishments in Nevel merged into one unified school) mention, among others, V. O. Verzhbolovich, N. I. Zorin, P. V. Skvortsov, T. V. Fedorov, K. A. Kirshevskaia, and E. M. Iurgenson.[25] During that same summer, the parents' committee also met and firmly opposed the transfer of the school; after a brief period as the renamed Nevel Boys' *Gimnaziia*, the school was merged with others as the V. I. Lenin Soviet Unified Labor School (Second Level). A request for the transfer of all property of the *gimnaziia* was sent to Moscow and, most likely, approved, although no such authorization has survived among the other documents. Its library holdings were transferred to the new school, as recorded at one of the school council meetings.[26]

The life of the school during the years immediately following the Revolution was full of the energy and dynamism which gripped many people at that time. People welcomed the transformations then taking place; they hoped that life would get better and believed in "the bright future." The young Bakhtin, too, as he appears in the Velikie Luki archive material, seems to have been caught up in the daring Sturm und Drang of the time. This extremely strong-willed, active teacher and practical "man of action" seems so unlike the Bakhtin of the later years, famed not just for his academic works but also for his silence, his reserve, and his aloofness from the everyday realities of that time! Let us leaf through some documents from the archives in order to get a sense of this inspiring atmosphere in which Bakhtin spent two years, when Nevel was living through a brilliant era.

The most detailed information is contained in minutes from 1918 meetings of the Unified Labor School Council and in assorted other documents from 1920. On 26 October 1918 (when, as already noted, Bakhtin's name first crops up), a general meeting occurred and was attended by 27 school workers, 4 representatives of the executive of the Education Department, 10 representatives of the working population, and 10 pupils.[27] The question of school council organization was discussed, as was the committee structure and election of a presidium within each council. The "creation of several school councils," which "would be more effective than one or two councils with many members," was proposed in the course of a brief discussion. However, the Education Department resolution was adopted, which entailed "the creation of only two school councils for the Nevel Soviet Unified Labor School (First and Second Levels)," with the aim of "unifying the activity of all school workers in Nevel." The Department representatives had refused to consider any other alternative, although it later became necessary to divide up the councils. In addition to the pair of school councils (one for each level), an overall regulatory committee, a library committee, and two (separate) resource committees were created. "By a majority of the votes" in the election of the seven-member library committee, from the school workers were elected Gusarevich, Bakhtin, and Gorbatskii. Although we have no attendance list for this meeting, we may assume that Bakhtin's candidacy would hardly have been balloted in his absence. Elections for the presidium of each council were held the same day. The Second Level Council elected a three-member presidium, to be headed by Marin Dimitriev. There are no extant minutes of the other council meeting, but it is likely that this was when Bakhtin was elected chair of the First Level Council, in which capacity his name appears in documents from the following months.

The question of the number of councils and the size of their membership soon developed into a controversy in its own right (which we can only touch upon in passing here). The matter came up again only three days later, at the meeting on 29 October, when it was suggested that the Presidium of the Second Level Council, "the jurisdiction of which covers the former Sventsiany boys' *gimnaziia*, the former upper primary school, and the upper years of the Muliarchik girls' *gimnaziia*," could not "manage such a number of component parts given its current resources."[28] It was necessary in addition to elect Aleksei Gusarevich and Matvei Kagan (who, later declining to serve on the Presidium "for personal and family reasons," was replaced on 29 December by G. V. Gorbatskii).[29] The intransigence and tendency toward centralization of the regional authorities (who were guided by PCE directives, but seem to have taken the "unified" in the school's name too literally) created further problems; a protest made at this same meeting concerned "the paperwork produced by the reformed school councils," which was said to be "several times greater than when . . . each establishment served only its own limited area."[30] It also became necessary, therefore, to attend to the need for increased administration of both councils.

Along with the purely administrative matters taken up at this meeting, some curricular issues were also resolved. The curriculum was confirmed, including the allocation of hours among the following subjects: Russian language, mathematics, drawing, history of art, manual labor and the history of labor, natural science (including physics), geography, history, sociology, German, French, singing and music, introductory philosophy and psychology, hygiene, and gymnastics. (Two versions of the curriculum had been proposed, and the one selected was improved by the addition of gymnastics and hygiene, and by the merger of physics with chemistry and manual labor with the history of labor.) The Education Department representative, "comrade Shiriakov," proposed the introduction of a new subject, "socialism studies," to which "comrade Bakhtin" responded, "It will be necessary to examine the history of socialism in detail while studying sociology, and there is therefore no need to separate the study of socialism off as a special subject." The meeting supported Bakhtin. Kagan then proposed adding English language to the curriculum, and Gorbatskii spoke in favor of Latin, fencing, and boxing; all these subjects were approved as electives.

On the whole, these first few meetings of the Second Level Council involved sharp and partisan discussion, with decisions by no means always going the way the local authorities advocated. In such cases, definite digressions from the official line can be observed. Despite the difficult and intense times, a relative freedom of expression prevailed and was used to advantage by Bakhtin on a number of occasions.[31] More generally, the minutes of these meetings add up to an archival "pedagogical chronicle" of Bakhtin's Nevel period. The meeting on 12 November 1918, for example, began with the election of a chairman from a slate of four candidates: "comrades Dimitriev, Kagan, Novik, and Bakhtin. Comrade Dimitriev was elected on a majority vote."[32] Bakhtin aspired to a leading role, it would seem, then yielded to a more powerful leader. Dimitriev had been the chairman of the upper primary school teaching committee for the first half of 1918,[33] and, upon the formation of the Unified Labor School, had forced the head of the Sventsiany boys' *gimnaziia*, Pavel Iankovich, into the background. (Iankovich was soon, for some reason, to disappear completely.) With Dimitriev now occupying the key position of Presidium chair on the Second Level Council, the parallel position on the less prestigious First Level Council opened up for Bakhtin. It is possible that there was for a time a secret rivalry between Bakhtin and Dimitriev: the attendance records of meetings typically list Dimitriev first, and only once, on 17 November, did the secretary write: "Comrades present: Bakhtin, Dimitriev, Kagan, Iurgenson, Shul'ts, Amosov."[34] The 17 November meeting, incidentally, was chaired by Dimitriev (from a slate of which and how many other candidates he was elected is not clear), and this would always be the case from then on. Bakhtin had to be content with a secondary role, despite the fact that, as far as we can tell, his implicit authority among his colleagues was quite strong: in all subsequent elections (such as for various committees), his candidacy would receive unanimous support, while the other candidates provoked conflicting opinions.

The main issue on 12 November was undoubtedly the coordination of labor with the other subjects (here we see the distinguishing characteristic of the Unified Labor School!). We will allow the participants in the discussion to speak for themselves, their monologues and remarks having been concisely recorded in the minutes:

> Comrade Kuznetsov spoke on this issue, declaring that it was necessary to increase the number of lessons on manual labor.
>
> Comrade Kagan said that lessons in all subjects (mathematics, history, etc.) are in some way connected with labor.
>
> Comrade Shul'man [argued that] it was necessary to link all subjects to labor. The school should produce people who are accustomed to labor, who are capable of working. He requested responses, in order somehow to approach this painful issue. In addition, [he argued that] it was necessary to organize a committee, in order to work out a plan for the coordination of labor with the other subjects.
>
> Comrade Kagan proposed that the debate be closed, and that a committee composed of school workers/subject specialists, two pupils, and one representative of the working population be elected.
>
> Comrade Shul'man proposed that this matter should be discussed by all sides, so that everyone might become familiar with the opinion of the school workers.
>
> . . . .
>
> Comrade Kuznetsov requested that all teachers report on the measures they have taken to coordinate labor with other subjects.
>
> Comrade Bakhtin proposed that the debate be closed. The issue was put to a vote. The proposal to close the debate was passed by a majority of votes, and the meeting proceeded to the election of a committee.[35]

While this fragment from the minutes can help clarify the political and psychological background to events, including the actions of such notable figures for us as Bakhtin and Kagan, given that so much remains unknown —and errors are therefore unavoidable—restricting ourselves merely to the exposition of facts would be too simplistic. We shall, therefore, attempt to convey a relatively likely version of events. It seems reasonable to infer from this fragment that here, as in the minutes of the October meetings discussed earlier, a certain restrained opposition toward the authorities with regard to the implementation of school reforms is apparent. The same Kuznetsov and Shul'man (representatives of the Education Department) who in October imposed their will with regard to the number of school councils in November attempted to introduce lessons on labor into the educational process to a maximal degree so as to be able to report back on the implementation of prescribed measures. Although the teachers were not opposed to bringing education more in line with practical life, they did resist the imposition of unreasonable extremes from above. To this end they tried to create, as quickly as possible, a committee composed of specialists, pupils, and representatives of the working population in order to ensure that problems were addressed competently—and without pressure from the authorities.

Kuznetsov and Shul'man insisted on participating in and, moreover, directing this process of committee creation as well. Their strategy was to let all the teachers speak and report on what they had done, which would make it clear who should be part of the committee. It went without saying, of course, that the Party lobby would be included. Everything nevertheless got out of hand, and the meeting unexpectedly closed after a discussion of the committee's composition: "The representatives from the Education Department and from the working population and the pupils were obliged to leave for an extraordinary Party meeting."[36] Even in 1918, exactly which "Party" was meant is not specified; therefore, everything is quite clear: among the teachers, as far as we can tell, there were no Party members.

A few days later, at the meeting on 17 November, discussion about this labor committee resumed. It seems likely that the regional establishment had modified its tactics in the meantime, for Kuznetsov was absent, and Shul'man and the other Education Department representatives did not participate in the discussion, the tenor of which changed as a result. Kagan, who had earlier fought for an immediate vote without any further debate, now proposed "the organization of a general meeting for the presentation of several reports" regarding the coordination of labor and learning. The liking of this Marburg school adherent for theoretical studies had its effect, no doubt, so that once free of the need to lead the struggle against the "excesses of labor," Kagan gave in to his own inclinations. Dimitriev, however, set the meeting on a more practical course by declaring that "the committee itself would present several reports on this question" and then proposing "that the meeting consider how the committee should be organized." Novik favored passing the formation of the committee on to the Presidium, but Kagan convinced everyone that the committee should enjoy the trust of the entire council. The results of the democratic (and open) vote were as follows: "Bakhtin—unanimous; Kagan—unanimous; Zorin—unanimous; Iankovich—20 in favor, 13 abstentions; Novik—unanimous; Barshchevskaia—21 in favor, 4 abstentions; . . . Dimitriev—unanimous; Verzhbolovich—27 in favor, 10 abstentions."[37] (Representatives of the pupils and the working population would be elected by those groups.)

Attention then turned to another crucial question of the time, namely, that of "discipline." Discussion revolved around a resolution on self-discipline proposed by the Council of Pupils' Deputies and read out by one of them. Shul'man, intervening only at the request of the chair, reported that the Education Department had ratified this resolution with only a few amendments and that, in the Department's opinion, these rules applied to both pupils and staff. It is difficult for us to assess the logic of such a turn of events, but it is curious that the authorities, even while once again imposing their will (otherwise, why put the question in this way?), did so fairly delicately, by means of a somewhat circuitous maneuver. But a champion [*fronda*] soon appeared, mounted on his charger, the eternal disturber of the peace: "In the opinion of comrade Bakhtin, the Council of Pupils' Deputies cannot take it upon itself to issue rules concerning discipline for both pupils and staff; there is no doubt that these rules were issued for pupils only, otherwise this would not be *self*-discipline. He requested that the pupils' representatives speak to this matter." Conflicting opinions were expressed, making it necessary to resort to the invariable means of overcoming conflict then—the formation of a committee. Bakhtin's proposals on the number of committee members and the procedures for their election were put to a vote, along with those of several others, and carried the meeting: "comrade Bakhtin—unanimous; Kagan—23 in favor,

9 abstentions; Gorbatskii—22 in favor, 9 abstentions; Gusarevich—10 in favor, 21 abstentions; Dimitriev—25 in favor, 8 abstentions."[38]

Along with the minutes of the school council meetings, incidentally, one set of minutes from a Council of Pupils' Deputies meeting of 11 April 1919 has also survived.[39] The second item on the agenda, listed as "First Level School Council," was a proposal "to refer the incident with comrade Bakhtin to the School Board." The nature of this incident remains unknown, but we cannot exclude the possibility that a conflict of opinion (perhaps even related to the issue of subjecting teachers to Council of Pupils' Deputies rules) had become something more serious. Two other notable items on the meeting agenda were the request for 3,000 roubles from the Education Department to fund "cultural-enlightenment activity" and that "remedial classes" be instituted.

Another document from the year 1919 in the Velikie Luki archive contains the "minutes of a meeting of Nevel school workers (First and Second Levels) on 29 May."[40] Two of the matters taken up at this meeting were "the allocation of summer work" and "the organization of a central library." The nature of "summer work" remains unknown, but proposals relating to it refer to the appointment of supervisors—teachers with various specializations: natural science, geography, literature, archaeology, history, and so on. "Comrades Pumpianskii, Bakhtin, Zorin, Verzhbolovich, Sokolovskii, and Rutkevich" were appointed supervisors in literature, and "comrades Gorbatskii, Bakhtin, Slonimskii, Pumpianskii, and Gorbatskaia" in archaeology and history. The name Pumpianskii appears only in this document, which also includes that of Mariia Iudina's elder sister, Anna (named a "supervisor of children at camp").[41] As for the central library, a committee formed to oversee its organization and operation included Bakhtin, Gorbatskii, Nikol'skii, Zorin, Slonimskii, and others.

The various and sundry Velikie Luki archive documents from 1920 include minutes of Second Level School Council meetings and those of First and Second Level School Council Presidium meetings, as well as personnel forms and records of teachers. The spectrum of issues addressed at meetings was extremely broad. There is no doubt that various everyday matters were a continual preoccupation: teachers' wages and "additional allowances," the receipt and distribution of bread rations for staff and pupils, the establishment of queues for the baths, and so on.[42] The inadequacy of the school premises was one source of anxiety. Attempts were made to expand these premises beyond the buildings of the former Muliarchik girls' *gimnaziia* and the upper primary school as early as 1918, but these first few years were marked by conditions of extreme overcrowding, necessitating two and sometimes even three shifts, nonetheless. Then there were other difficulties relating specifically to the situation during the Civil War. For example, in June 1920 the upper primary school building was occupied by the Supply and Engineering Divisions of the Fourth Army, which meant dividing school property up between the other premises.[43]

Matters directly related to the educational process were also considered, of course. By 1920 it had become clear that the school could not, after all, manage without any systematic evaluation of learning, and proposals concerning "improvement in pupils' progress," "assessment of learning in each year of study," and "tests" were adopted. The number of hours allotted to various subjects was altered, for example, those for Russian language and mathematics were increased. Chemistry was dropped, and political economy added, due to the lack of chemicals and other materials. Several items on the agenda pertained to labor classes, such as "lessons in carpentry and bookbinding for the purpose of repairing classroom furniture and textbooks" and "finding premises for the establishment of a tailoring workshop."[44]

Much attention was paid to the pupils' personal development and the broadening of their horizons. As early as 1918, the Second Level School Council was considering biweekly "symphony concerts for pupils." Eight societies were formed at the same time: sociology, philosophy, literature, history, physics and chemistry, natural science and geography, and art (including drama and the history of art).[45] In 1920 premises were sought not only for the tailoring workshop but also "for the establishment of a permanent town museum," and attempts were made to "organize excursions for the pupils of Nevel." The activities of school societies continued, although the number of different ones may have declined, since some minutes mention only natural science and geography, history and philology, and history and archaeology societies. At the beginning of September 1920, a cultural-enlightenment committee was formed (with Kagan, Pigulevskii, and Bakhtin representing the teachers), and lectures were read in the town's communal reading rooms. Pupils were required to enroll in summer classes, which, in view of their manual nature, were probably part of the "summer work," as had been the case in 1919. (There is a reference in one set of minutes to "summer lessons" in the kitchen gardens and the workshops, as well as on excursions.) On 26 May Bakhtin made a report on summer lessons in the human sciences and subsequently joined the corresponding committee, along with his sister, Mariia Bakhtina, Dimitriev, and others. Kagan was a member of the committee on physics and mathematics.[46]

The issue of the number of school councils surfaced once again in August 1920. Having suffered the incoherence and ineffectiveness of extreme centralization, the school collective finally decided to remedy the situation. On 31 August it was proposed that (1) three independent but linked Second Level School Councils be created, one for each component school, and (2) the First Level School Council be subdivided into four independent councils," with two additional resource committees, one for each of the school's levels.[47]

As has already been noted, from the end of 1918 until the middle of 1920 Bakhtin served as Presidium chairman of the First Level School Council, the jurisdiction of which covered "eight schools with a significant number of pupils."[48] Minutes of these council meetings have either been lost or were not taken at the time. (As we know, Bakhtin would become notable for his particular dislike of writing letters and other documents.[49]) Only the minutes from a meeting on 4 February 1920, signed by Bakhtin and relating to the "Committee on Secondment of Town School Workers to the Provinces," have survived.[50] In response to an Education Department directive to send someone to the provinces (where there were many vacancies), Bakhtin refused, citing illness, military call-ups, and the teachers' extremely heavy workloads. The following documents have also survived: Information on School Workers for the Education Department (from 1919 or 1920), which Bakhtin did not sign; a "list of newly elected school workers at the Soviet Unified Labor School (First Level)" (September 1919); Information on Probationary Teachers at the Unified Labor School (First Level) in Nevel, "in accordance with an Order of the Revolutionary Military Council for the Western front, 2 June 1920 (No. 1070)"; and a note to the Statistics Section of the Education Department on the number of teachers in the various school departments (signed by Bakhtin). Regarding Bakhtin himself, the first (unsigned) document records his age as twenty-three and that he was unmarried, of Russian nationality, with a "higher education," had been a teacher since January 1916 and at the Nevel school since 1 October 1918. In the information provided by order of the Revolutionary

Military Council, Bakhtin's age is given for some reason as twenty-six, but the other details are consistent ("completed higher education," "worked in profession for four years"); in addition, Bakhtin's specialization ("teacher of philology"), his military service status ("exempt [*belobiletnik*]"), and his current mobilization as a lecturer by the Political Section are all recorded.[51]

Bakhtin and Dimitriev, as chairmen of the First and Second Level School Councils, carried a reduced teaching load (an average of 15 hours per week vs. an ordinary teacher's load of 24). In 1918 Bakhtin taught seven classes on history and sociology at the Second Level, and eight on Russian language at the First, while Dimitriev taught fifteen classes on history, sociology, and natural science at the Second Level.[52] By January 1920, the average teaching load for council chairmen had been reduced to two classes per week (as opposed to eighteen for ordinary teachers), but both Bakhtin and Dimitriev taught an additional twenty-one per week.[53]

School documents handwritten by Bakhtin are of particular interest, allowing us to "reconstruct" distinct moments and details of his educational activity. In one such document, he wrote: "I, the undersigned school worker in my fourth year in the Second Level of Collective No. 3, hereby certify that Khasia Mendelevna Ianovitskaia, a pupil in the Fourth Year of the Second Level, has passed Russian language fully satisfactorily, and may be discharged from the Unified Labor School, Second Level. 5.VII.1920. M. Bakhtin." Another scrap of paper filled out in Bakhtin's own hand (typed forms were of course still unavailable at the time) records: "In accordance with a proposal of the staff of School No. 3, Second Level of 5.VII.1920, Khasia Ianovitskaia may receive her certificate of completion of the Second Level. Chairman of staff of School No. 3, M. Bakhtin."[54] A 1920 form filled out in Bakhtin's own hand has also survived:

1. Surname, name, patronymic—Bakhtin, Mikhail Mikhailovich.
2. Age—25 years.
3. Profession—
4. Current occupation—School worker.
5. Name of institution—Nevel Unified Labor School, First Level.
6. Party affiliation—Non-Party.
7. Pre-Revolution service—Teacher.
8. Post-Revolution service—Teacher.

Signed M. Bakhtin.[55]

Other records provide details on the lives of certain colleagues of Bakhtin during his years in Nevel: Anna Veniaminovna Iudina (23, fourth-year student in Physics–Mathematics, Petrograd University, Second Level school worker, non-Party, did not work prior to the Revolution); Mariia Mikhailovna Bakhtina (21, First Level school worker, non-Party, completed education pre-Revolution, worked in Dept. No. 1 of the People's Bank in Petrograd post-Revolution); Grigorii Nikiforovich Muliarchik (57, non-Party, pre-Revolution teacher in state, regional, and local schools, inspector of the upper primary and State schools); Pavel Ignat'evich Sokolovskii (55, non-Party, pre-Revolution teacher); Georgii Aleksandrovich Koliubakin (27, bacteriologist, Second Level school worker, called up for military service pre-Revolution, regional Military Commissar for Nevel and aide to the Education Department post-Revolution).[56]

Matvei Isaevich Kagan, one of Bakhtin's closest friends, has already been mentioned several times here and is, of course, well-known, but his details are worth noting nonetheless. He was born in 1888, a Second Level school worker, non-Party, and a teacher both pre- and post-Revolution. Two other friends of Bakhtin's, Valentin Nikolaevich Vološinov and Boris Mikhailovich Zubakin, also worked in education, though not in Nevel but in Rykshino and Chuprovo, respectively. In 1920, however, Vološinov taught Russian language and history in Nevel Schools No. 2 and No. 3, Second Level.[57]

Bakhtin was scheduled to teach Russian language (4 classes in School No. 2 and 8 in School No. 3) in September 1920 (i.e., following the division of the Unified School), but he did not do so, for he left Nevel around that time. Bakhtin's tenure on the Cultural Enlightenment Committee expired on 14 September, and on 25 September "P. I. Sokolovskii was elected to this same committee in place of the departed . . . Bakhtin."[58] On 23 September our hero received confirmation of his appointment to the post of lecturer in Western European literature from the Council of the Vitebsk Institute of People's Education.[59] Bakhtin's path now led to the provincial capital, where a new chapter in his biography was about to begin.

Notes

The following abbreviations of transliterated Russian documentary identification terms are used in all references to archival material: f. = *fond* (stock); op. = *opis* (catalogue); d. = *delo* (matter); l[l]. = *list*[*y*] (page[s]); ob. = *oborot* (reverse); k. = *karton* (box).

1 V. D. Duvakin, *Besedy V. D. Duvakina s M. M. Bakhtinym* (Moscow, 1996), 228, 134.

Nevel was at that time part of the Vitebsk Province [*guberniia*] and is currently part of the Pskov Administrative Region [*oblast*].

2 For example, in a holograph autobiographical note of 1920, Bakhtin records that "from 1910 until 1912 I was in Germany, where I attended four semesters at Marburg University and one semester in Berlin" (Vitebsk Region State Archive, f. 204, op. 13, d. 8, l. 44). In fact, Bakhtin never travelled abroad; his friend Matvei Kagan, however, studied in Germany. See Aleksandr Lisov and Elena Trusova, "Replika po povodu avtobiograficheskogo mifotvorchestva M. M. Bakhtina" (A Remark on Bakhtin's Autobiographical Mythmaking), *Dialog, Karnaval, Khronotop*, No. 3 (1996): 161–66; and Nikolai Pan'kov, "Zagadki rannego perioda (eshche neskol'ko shtrikhov k 'biografii' M. M. Bakhtina)" (Mysteries of the Early Period [A Few More Details toward a "Biography" of M. M. Bakhtin]), *Dialog, Karnaval, Khronotop*, No. 1 (1993): 74–89.

3 See Katerina Clark and Michael Holquist, *Mikhail Bakhtin* (Cambridge, MA, and London, 1984), 35–62, 361–65.

4 S. S. Konkin and L. S. Konkina, *Mikhail Bakhtin (Stranitsy zhizni i tvorchestva)* (Pages from His Life and Art) (Saransk, 1993), 53.

5 Clark and Holquist, *Mikhail Bakhtin*, 361–62 n. 6. I have been able, thanks to the kindness of the executors of Bakhtin's personal archive, to familiarize myself with another version of Bakhtin's CV, which varies somewhat from the one cited by Clark and Holquist. Here it says that Bakhtin "was a schoolteacher in the First and Second Levels in Nevel and chair of the Presidium of the School Council of the Unified Schools of the First Level" from 15 August 1918 until 1 October 1920. This CV was probably compiled during Bakhtin's exile in Kustanai (i.e., with the benefit of hindsight), but the information in it is confirmed by a "Certificate of the Nevel Unified Labor School" of 9 August 1920 (N449). No mention is made of the *gimnaziia* in the CV cited by Clark and Holquist.

6 Quoted in Duvakin, *Besedy*, 320 (comments).

7 Velikie Luki archive, f. R-608, op. 1, d. 4, l. 73; f. R-608, op. 1, d. 4, ll. 53–55; and f. R-608, op. 2, d. 16, l. 89ob.

8 Regarding the post-Revolutionary situation in Nevel beyond the educational sphere, see Liudmila Maksimovskaia, "Muzei v provintsii" (The Provincial Museum), in *Muzei Rossii: Poiski, Issledovaniia, opyt raboty* (The Museums of Russia: Searches, Research, and Experiences) (St. Petersburg, 1995), 61–69.

9 See *Nevel'skii uezd Pskovskoi gubernii: Istoriko-ekonomicheskii ocherk* (The Nevel *uezd* of the Pskov Province: A Historico-Economic Sketch) (Nevel, 1925), 15–16.

10 Ibid., 16.

11 *Edinaia trudovaia shkola: Polozhenie o edinoi trudovoi shkole RSFSR* (Moscow, 1918), 3, 4.

12 Ibid., 10.

13 "Proekt programmy filosofskoi propedevtiki, 2-ia polovina 4-go goda vtoroi stupeni novoi shkoly: Predvaritel'nye zamechaniia" (Introductory Philosophy Program, Second Level, Fourth Year, Part 2 of the New School: Preliminary Remarks), State Archive of the Russian Federation, f. 2306, op. 4, d. 123, l. 12.

14 See *Edinaia trudovaia shkola*, 18.

15 Duvakin, *Besedy*, 26.

16 See *Pamiatnaia knizhka Vilenskogo uchebnogo okruga na 1915 god* (Records of the Vilna

Educational District for 1915) (Vilna, 1915), 70. Cf. the first Vilna boys' *gimnaziia* (founded in 1803), where there were 673 pupils in 1915 and the fee was 80 roubles (10). It is possible, however, that there were attempts to found a *gimnaziia* in Sventsiany even before 1913. I found a document in the Latvian State Historical Archive (f. 567, op. 23, d. 909, l. 10b.) in which mention is made of a Sventsiany *gimnaziia* as early as 1867; apart from an "executive director" (identified as Konstantin Strokov, teacher of Russian language), all other posts were for some reason vacant.

17 See Nikolai Evseev, *Sventsianskii proryv: Voennye deistviia na vostochnom fronte mirovoi voiny v sentiabre–oktiabre 1915 goda* (The Sventsiany Incursion: Military Activity on the Eastern Front in the World War during September–October 1915) (Moscow, 1936), 54–83 and 197.

18 Some evidence indicates that the *gimnaziia* reopened in Nevel in 1915; Velikie Luki archive, f. R-608, op. 1, d. 4, l. 33.

19 "Kratkii spisok uchrezhdenii i uchebnykh zavedenii Vilenskogo uchebnogo okruga na 1916 god" (Short List of Institutions and Establishments in the Vilna Educational District for 1916) (Mogilev, 1916), 3. It is typical that the date of the evacuation of the Sventsiany boys' *gimnaziia* is not shown in the 1918 PCE "Information on Evacuated Educational Establishments in Belorussia" (in contrast to instances relating to other educational establishments); see State Archive of the Russian Federation, f. 2306, op. 4, d. 237, l. 22.

20 Velikie Luki archive, f. R-608, op. 1, d. 4, ll. 33, 46. According to information given to the PCE, 246 pupils were taught at the Sventsiany boys' *gimnaziia* in 1917; see State Archive of the Russian Federation, f. 2306, op. 4, d. 237, l. 22.

21 Velikie Luki archive, f. R-608, op. 1, d. 4, l. 14.

22 State Archive of the Russian Federation, f. 2306, op. 4, d. 237, l. 22.

23 Velikie Luki archive, f. R-608, op. 1, d. 4, ll. 23–24.

24 In the *Pamiatnaia knizhka Vilenskogo uchebnogo okruga na 1911–12 gg.* (Records of the Vilna Educational District for 1911–12) (Vilna, 1912), Iankovich is still listed among the teachers of the first Vilna boys' *gimnaziia* (8). In the records for 1914 (70) and 1915 (70), it is noted that Iankovich, a graduate of the Physics–Mathematics Faculty of Petrograd University, had been head of the Sventsiany boys' *gimnaziia* since 1 July 1913. For Bakhtin's recollections of Iankovich, see Duvakin (*Besedy*, 26), where Bakhtin says that Iankovich was liked by himself and by all the other *gimnaziia* staff because he was "logical and precise" and "was able somehow to explain everything, to make everything clear."

Aleksei Petrovich Gusarevich, a graduate in natural sciences of Iur'ev (Tartu) University, worked at the Sventsiany boys' *gimnaziia* from 23 October 1913, according to the records for 1915 (71). See also his personal record and information about him in documents from the Nevel Unified Labor School (note his age, 46, in particular); Velikie Luki archive, f. R-608, op. 2, d. 16, ll. 9, 105; and op. 1, d. 4, l. 80ob.

25 Information on the personnel of the Nevel Unified Labor School is mainly concentrated in Velikie Luki archive, f. R-608, op. 2, d. 16.

26 Velikie Luki archive, f. R-608, op. 1, d. 4, ll. 73, 75ob.

27 Ibid., f. R-608, op. 1, d. 4, ll. 53–55.

28 Ibid., f. R-608, op. 1, d. 4, ll. 73–77 (for the fall 1920 curriculum, see also d. 4, l. 43).

29 Ibid., f. R-608, op. 1, d. 4, l. 92.

30 Ibid., l. 76.

31 The numerous disputes in which Bakhtin played an active part are examples of this free exchange of the most varied opinions ("many-voicedness," so to speak). See the selection of material published in Nevel newspapers compiled by Liudmila Maksimovskaia, "*Molot* 1918–20," *Nevel'skii sbornik* 1 (1996): 147–58; and "K ustnym rasskazam M. M. Bakhtina o Nevele (kommentariia kraeveda)" (On Bakhtin's Oral Accounts of Nevel [A Local Historian's Commentary]), in ibid., 100–101.

32 Velikie Luki archive, f. R-608, op. 1, d. 4, ll. 51–52.

33 Ibid., f. R-608, op. 1, d. 4, ll. 82–86.

34 Ibid., f. R-608, op. 1, d. 4, ll. 56–58.

35 Ibid., l. 51.

36 Ibid., l. 52.

37 Ibid., l. 56 ob.

38 Ibid., l. 57 ob.

39 Ibid., f. R-608, op. 1, d. 4, l. 98.

40 Ibid., f. R-608, op. 1, d. 4, l. 50.

41 In addition to Anna Iudina, the Velikie Luki archive documents mention her father, V. G. Iudin, a local doctor and chairman of the Sventsiany boys' *gimnaziia* parents' committee, who often took part in discussions of the many questions that were important for the collective; see ibid., f. R-608, op. 1, d. 4, ll. 14, 32, 53. On Mariia Iudina, see *M. V. Iudina: Stat'i, Vospominaniia, Materialy* (Articles, Reminiscences, Materials) (Moscow, 1978); Anatolii Kuznetsov, "'Kovsh dushevnoi glubi' (Nevel' v zhizni M. V. Iudinoi)" ("From the depths of the soul" [Nevel in the life of M. V. Iudina]), in *Nevel'skii sbornik* 2 (1997): 10–21; and Duvakin, *Besedy*, 227–61.

42 Velikie Luki archive, f. R-608, op. 1, d. 41, ll. 1, 2, 4–5; and d. 4, ll. 88–89ff.

43 Ibid., f. R-608, op. 1, d. 4, ll. 46–47, 94; and d. 41, ll. 3–3ob., 8–8ob., 11, 20, 41, 32–32ob. The "presence" of war is also felt in materials other than the reports on the army occupation of school premises. For example, a "Front week" (7–14 November) was held in the school, with a gathering-concert, a collection, and contributions from wages to the "Red Front" (ibid., f. R-608, op. 1, d. 41, l. 7).

44 Ibid., f. R-608, op. 1, d. 41, ll. 4ob., 16ob., 18, 15, 6ob., 1.

45 Ibid., f. R-608, op. 1, d. 4, ll. 94ob., 90ob. See also the oral reminiscences of E. L. Linetskaia: "The Petersburg intelligentsia had gathered in Nevel, so for all its provincial character, the town was actually not very provincial. Because of the symphonic concerts, because of the fact that we had outstanding pedagogues in the school," in Liudmila Maksimovskaia, "Peterburgskie vstrechi (razgovory s E. L. Linetskoi)" (Petersburg Encounters [Conversations with E. L. Linetskaia]), *Nevel'skii sbornik* 1 (1996): 141.

46 Velikie Luki archive, f. R-608, op. 1, d. 41, ll. 1, 1ob., 5ob., 49, 53, 40ob., 24, 22–23ob.

47 Ibid., f. R-608, op. 1, d. 41, l. 43ob.

48 Ibid., f. R-608, op. 1, d. 4, l. 76.

49 For example, in his correspondence with Mariia Iudina in the 1940s, I. I. Kanaev continually remarks, "Wherever M. M. [Bakhtin] is, I write to him, but he has never replied" and asks what "the *Mikhi*" (as he called Bakhtin and his wife, Elena Aleksandrovna)

were up to, adding, "I've written to them constantly, but no reply"; and "I will wait for news from you of the fate of Rabelais [i.e., Bakhtin's dissertation], because *Mikh* is hardly likely to send me anything himself"; Manuscript Department of the Russian State Library, f. 527, k. 14, d. 13, ll. 1, 4, 6.

50 Velikie Luki archive, f. R-608, op. 1, d. 4, ll. 48–49.

51 Ibid., f. R-608, op. 2, d. 16, ll. 89–90; op. 2, d. 2, ll. 3–4; and op. 2, d. 16, ll. 106–7. As is clear from the "list of schools and school workers of the Nevel *uezd* for June–September 1919," Bakhtin worked at that time with Mariia Bakhtina, Z. V. Shul'ts, K. N. Borisovets, and others in the fourth department of the First Level School (with 5 sets of pupils), in two shifts, and in a building on Karl Marx Square. A total of 10 departments are named in this document, along with their current locations (ibid., f. R-608, op. 2, d. 2, ll. 3–4).

52 Ibid., f. R-608, op. 1, d. 4, l. 87ob.

53 Ibid., f. R-608, op. 1, d. 41, l. 13.

54 Ibid., f. R-608, op. 1, d. 41, ll. 30, 30ob. Khasia Ianovitskaia was one of a number of pupils who, having already transferred to the one-year teacher training course, often missed classes. At the beginning of June 1920, the Teaching Council of School No. 3 resolved to award them certificates of completion on the basis of exams (ll. 27, 28). Kagan certified in a handwritten statement on the same page (l. 30) as Bakhtin's that Ianovitskaia had passed mathematics and physics.

55 Ibid., f. R-608, op. 2, d. 16, l. 20.

56 Ibid., f. R-608, op. 2, d. 16, ll. 16, 20, 74, 1, 21, 41, 43, 73. In conversation with Duvakin (*Besedy*, 136), Bakhtin recalled Koliubakin as one of the most active participants in the Nevel scholarly society, to which Bakhtin himself, Pumpianskii, and Kagan, among others, also belonged. On this scholarly society, see also Maksimovskaia, "K ustnym rasskazam M. M. Bakhtina o Nevele," 98–102.

57 Velikie Luki archive, f. R-608, op. 2, d. 16, l. 75; op. 12, d. 5, l. 17; d. 6, ll. 20ob., 72, 124, 127, 198, 199ff.; d. 7, ll. 4, 157ob., 159ob., 194; and op. 1, d. 41, ll. 54–55ob., 61. It is interesting that Vološinov was apparently not noted for punctuality at work. On 23 October 1920, a joint meeting of the Council Presidiums of Schools No. 1, 2, and 3 adopted the following special resolution: "To request formally that school workers Vološinov, Kazakevich, and Koliubakin appear on time for classes, and, in the event of a negative response, to offer their classes to other teachers" (op. 1, d. 41, l. 68ob.).

58 Ibid., f. R-608, op. 1, d. 41, ll. 47ob., 49, 53, 57ob., 69.

59 Vitebsk Region State Archive, f. 204, op. 1, d. 40, l. 29.

Peter Hitchcock

The Bakhtin Centre and the State of the Archive: An Interview with David Shepherd

The idea for this interview emerged not long after the Bakhtin Centre came into existence in 1994 and was discussed further in Sheffield, England, in 1995. Given David Shepherd's interest in coordinating an electronic edition of the works of Bakhtin, we optimistically thought that the best way to conduct this interview was on-line: I would submit questions and David would see what he could do with them. Our enthusiasm for this electronic conversation, however, was opposed by the nature of e-mail itself. It wasn't just that the questions required more reflection than most people attempt on-line (answers could also be uploaded at a later date, if necessary), nor that e-mail couldn't indeed provide a conversational mode for the piece (clearly, it could), but that for the interview to become a dialogue (dialogic or otherwise) in the end we needed a slightly less ethereal context for our exchange. What we needed was a concrete context recognized by both of us to condition the immediacy of the utterance. In short, we needed a fleshly counterpart for our sympathetic co-experiencing; or, to borrow the title of a recent Bakhtin collection, we needed to be "face to face."[1] We also, of

The *South Atlantic Quarterly* 97:3/4, Summer/Fall 1998.

course, needed more time! Now, in the age of the emoticon, it might seem scandalous to suppose that we could still have a use for conversations of this kind, but it does suggest that we haven't quite excised the body from the communicative act. Bakhtin, I believe, would be as fascinated by this necessity as he would be intrigued by the electronic vistas before us. While he would respect the fact that the forms of answerability must be in flux, he might also wonder whether a "disjected" subjectivity is becoming the norm of social interaction.

This interview was conducted (in-person) at the University of Calgary, Alberta, Canada, on 25 June 1997, the last day of the Eighth International Bakhtin Conference.

PETER HITCHCOCK: Could you say something about the evolution of the Bakhtin Centre at the University of Sheffield and what role you envisage it playing in Bakhtin studies today?

DAVID SHEPHERD: The idea initially was just for the Centre to provide a focus within the institution for the study of Bakhtin, and indeed theory generally. The institutional aspect at Sheffield hasn't worked out too badly. It does coordinate a certain amount of material on theory, but the other side of it was really the international profile, including the database, which I always saw as only the first step. What I wanted to do from the start was really move toward the electronic edition. Setting up the Centre within an institutional context was a way to attract funding for that project. Start-up funding came from the University of Sheffield, and for that of course I am eternally grateful. Their efforts made it possible to get funding from the Humanities Research Board (HRB) of the British Academy. And that has allowed us to move ahead with the electronic publication project. In that sense, the future of the Centre is relatively secure. The basic infrastructural support is from the University, in particular from my own (Russian) department. I really saw the Centre as a way to gather information about what people were doing elsewhere and then to disseminate it—but also, of course, shaping the agenda of Bakhtin studies, which I've tried over the years to just let happen. Things roll along and certain issues inevitably come to the surface.

PETER HITCHCOCK: Making information available in the first place is going to change or shape agendas. . . .

DAVID SHEPHERD: Exactly, you can't predict what's going to happen until you start doing these things. What kind of information are you going to get? For instance, we have visiting speakers come along to the Centre and give papers, and they vary enormously in their range; depending on how much we can get out of them in terms of text, we can make their papers available on the Website. But that is in no sense a specific agenda. I know that sounds pragmatically British and liberal, but that's just the way it is. The Centre has been in existence for three years now. I think that what it is going to be increasingly associated with is the redefinition of Bakhtin in fairly traditional scholarly terms. There are certain traditional philological things that need to be done with Bakhtin, especially in the (Russian) Collected Works, that aren't necessarily being done the way I'd like to see them done. I hope to bring together that traditional, scholarly, good practice in working with Bakhtin's texts—but, in doing it through the electronic media, I hope to move that forward and redefine not just Bakhtin but also the very editorial and scholarly processes brought to bear on that. So, in that sense, in my more ambitious moments, I see this as going beyond Bakhtin studies, as offering a kind of model for dealing with certain types of thinkers.

PETER HITCHCOCK: And it would have to be a model, one model among others, since not everyone has the infrastructure to handle that form of information.

DAVID SHEPHERD: Yes, that's right. But it's a practical model in the sense that much of our communication about these things goes on this way right now, so much of the information we need to carry on discussions is available electronically. If we continue to have this tension, this distance between the traditional outputs and traditional modes of discussion and the new forms in which a lot of information is now coming to us, we're not going to move forward. So, it will happen anyway—I don't want to overstate the ambition or the pioneering nature of what we're doing—but I think that Bakhtin is a particularly good case to do it with because he is so undefined, elusive, and because so much has been done with him so far.

PETER HITCHCOCK: In addition, the Centre has basically taken over the function of the *Bakhtin Newsletter*.

DAVID SHEPHERD: Yes, we now try to keep people updated on what's going on in Bakhtin studies. Basically, we offer our Webpages for people to advertise their own work, to advertise forthcoming conferences and so on. They can add things on-line to the Analytical Database of Work by and about the Bakhtin Circle.[2] To date, an important principle in the compilation of this bibliography has been that people should not add entries relating to their own work; however, that is under review, and the next stage is to make the database more of a freestanding system to which material is sent and undergoes just a light editorial process in Sheffield. And, given the sheer volume of material that we face, we have had to give up our ultimate goal of exhaustiveness. One reason for this development is that we'll only have funding for a research assistant to handle this kind of work for another year, and I don't envisage being able to get any other funding for such a position. So, I'll have to take on some of that work myself or give it to graduate students, but, now that the Centre is fairly well-known, I think it can probably support itself and grow on its own.

PETER HITCHCOCK: Well, the more widely known the Centre is, the better its reputation and the better the chance for more funding.

Let's shift gears a little here. Some years ago, Michael Holquist suggested that "the Bakhtin who is most able to assume the role of being one of the major thinkers of the twentieth century is the Bakhtin who remains to be discovered."[3] As we approach the end of the century, do you think we are any closer to the discovery Holquist evokes? What evidence do you believe supports such a discovery, or has the ebullience that marks Holquist's desire waned as more work has been done on Bakhtin?

DAVID SHEPHERD: I'm not sure that we're any closer. I've had a very strong sense of déjà vu at this conference. I think we've heard an awful lot of these papers before. I've been very surprised at the reinvention of the wheel. I don't want to sound offensive to colleagues at all, and it's partly a sign of the health of Bakhtin studies that a lot of new people are coming in who haven't been to one of these things before. But those of us who have been to a lot of them, and have spent a lot of time looking at things about Bakhtin, don't need to be told certain things that we're being told about Bakhtin at this conference. And so I think a lot of Bakhtin studies is sort of running on the spot or going round in circles.

Certainly, the Bakhtin who is going to emerge in the next ten years is going to be a rather different Bakhtin. He is going to be, I hope, less mythologized, more introspective—this is where the kind of work that Brian Poole is doing is so important. The Bakhtin who is seen to belong, rather than being somebody in relation to whom everybody else can belong. I'm not sure that I want Bakhtin to be a first among equals or unequals. I think we desperately need a sense of perspective on him, and we need to roll back on that sense of Bakhtin as having always already been there, done that, and given us all the answers. It really is all there: we just need to look at Bakhtin and compare him with thinkers *X, Y,* and *Z,* and we'll realize the extent to which Bakhtin depended on others rather than anticipated them. Then we can move on to a more sober assessment of where Bakhtin might belong in the twentieth century. But it's still far too early to know how important Bakhtin was.

My own position on Bakhtin has always been that if I do not allow for the possibility that the man was a charlatan, then I can't be interested in him. I have to have in mind the possibility that at the end of the day, whenever I stop working on him—and I hope I will stop working on him—I may just realize that he was actually not worth it. What comes out at the end may not be some grand synthesis, some set of answers, some figure to whom one can bow down, but just the discovery that we have more to learn from how Bakhtin was treated than from what he actually signified. His ideas may just turn out to be other people's. And that doesn't worry me. I have to allow for that possibility. I think that it is unlikely. I don't approach Bakhtin with the wish to knock him down from his pedestal, but if I don't have in mind the idea that he might have been a bit of a charlatan, then I can't work with him.

PETER HITCHCOCK: This reminds me of Anthony Wall's point that Bakhtin is a "broken thinker," but that that doesn't necessarily make him a bad thinker. You just have to humanize him a little bit more.

DAVID SHEPHERD: Of course, the move you would usually make after that is to say Bakhtin was so special that he gives us a new model of what it means to be a major thinker. Maybe, maybe not. He may just have been this provincial guy who wasn't able to say everything he wanted to say, but, had he had those possibilities, what would have come out of them? I don't know. He may turn out to be comparatively minor, and that doesn't worry me in the slightest. And in order to find that out you've got to do a lot of work.

PETER HITCHCOCK: The 100th anniversary of Bakhtin's birth was marked in a variety of ways, not the least of which was the Seventh International Bakhtin Conference, held in Moscow (26–30 June 1995). This landmark conference gave many Bakhtin scholars from around the world their first opportunity to meet their Russian counterparts. The results were mixed. I, for instance, was greatly impressed with the range of original research being done on Bakhtin in Russia, but I also noticed a preponderance of papers and presentations on an ethical, moral, spiritual, and ultimately religious Bakhtin. Clearly, the archive supports such readings. But how much of this emphasis is defined by the current contexts of Russian intellectual life, and how much closer do you think the ethical Bakhtin is to a Bakhtin who is, in essence, Russian?

DAVID SHEPHERD: It's very rare that you can read certain effects off certain historical moments in any direct way. But you have been able to do that remarkably in Russia since about 1990, especially in relation to Bakhtin studies. It was identified fairly early on by Caryl Emerson, when she talked in a totally positive way about a liberal-humanist Bakhtin emerging in Russia—which is fine. These things are going to happen. The ethical Bakhtin, the Russian Orthodox Bakhtin, the Russian religious/mystical philosopher Bakhtin—these are all things that are bound to emerge. The problem is this primacy of all things Russian, which is all part of the idea that is supporting it—it's feeding on itself. It is the word "Russian" that's overloaded here because Bakhtin was Russian, and that fosters all sorts of a priori positions. But it is absolutely linked to the current historical situation precisely at that point where it claims to be free of it, where it claims to be a leap out of history, out of this long nightmare of history that they have had since 1917, and back to that quasi-ahistorical realm where they can just be Russian, be ethical, as if that itself were not connected to the rather fraught atmosphere of at least 1905, going back, arguably, to 1861 and even before then. There is a genuine attempt to lift Bakhtin out of history, to see him as an embodiment of that peculiarly Russian capacity to escape history, to transcend history, which is associated with other thinkers. And that is simply a historical gesture, of course. It is a product of the current historical moment. I think it is changing. I think there is now more of a proliferation of Bakhtins in Russia. I think that has emerged at this conference. There is still, however, that bottom line of "Well, we're Russian and he's Russian. He's our thinker. We understand him."

This is a position with which one of the people who knew Bakhtin very well—Vadim Kozhinov—is now associated. I haven't met him, but I've heard from those who have that Kozhinov says, "Oh, you're from the West, you can't understand him." He has an afterword in the volume of transcriptions of Bakhtin's conversations with Duvakin in 1973.[4] What he does very interestingly is pick out a moment in the conversation where Bakhtin says something like "I was always very interested in the Kantian tradition," and he says we must pay attention to the fact that Bakhtin used the past tense and that, as he got older, he actually became more concerned with Russian traditions. Kozhinov ends by drawing attention to the fact that, during Bakhtin's interviews with Duvakin, his cat kept walking in and that at various points he talked to the cat. Kozhinov's idea is that this capacity to empathize with the cat and talk to the cat somehow symbolizes Bakhtin's distancing himself from the Kantian position. He didn't actually call the article "From Kant to the Kitten," but that was what he wanted to call it: "Bakhtinskii dialog. Ot Kanta do kotenka" (Bakhtinian Dialogue: From Kant to Kitten). But, of course, by saying that, he gave it that title. This is quite symptomatic. What, in effect, do you come out with? A Bakhtin who is cut loose from any affiliation inimical to Russian tradition. It is a blatantly political move in the name of an apolitical, transhistorical Bakhtin.

PETER HITCHCOCK: Given that gesture toward a Russian Bakhtin, do you feel some hostility over the fact that the Bakhtin Centre is in Sheffield and not in Vitebsk or Orel?

DAVID SHEPHERD: No, I've never felt that. It may be there. I feel a certain unease with the very title of the Centre because one is not supposed to take the name of the great man in vain—putting his name on a door might not be seen as an appropriate thing. But no, I haven't. I'd have to say that people have been only positive about this, at least to my face! I would understand it, however, because there you're really talking about relative institutional privilege. From the perspective of a British academic I would like a lot more money for the Centre, but I know that in British terms we're extremely well-off, to be able to get a Centre which has a space, has computers, is more than headed notepaper—which is what you usually get. For the Russians. . . .

PETER HITCHCOCK: They wouldn't usually get even the headed notepaper. . . .

DAVID SHEPHERD: Yes, although apparently a Bakhtin Centre has just been set up at the European Humanities University at Minsk. That is going to be the institutional base for Nikolai Pan'kov's journal, *Dialog, Karnaval, Khronotop.*

PETER HITCHCOCK: And Vitebsk isn't far.

DAVID SHEPHERD: Anyway, I haven't felt animosity. I would understand such a reaction. I think once the Centre begins to improve its profile in trying to position Bakhtin and following through on some of the lines of argument that people like Poole are putting forward, then I think the sparks may begin to fly. Especially, again, since it might seem like a few smart-arsed Western intellectuals are barging in with technology that most Russians don't have access to, and so on and so forth. We'll see.

PETER HITCHCOCK: Perhaps we could compare this situation of the "Russian Bakhtin" to the differences in the Bakhtin registered in other national formations. Whether this is a margin within a margin or not, one notes a sharp distinction between, say, a Slavicist "prosaic" Bakhtin in the United States and a cultural-materialist Bakhtin in the United Kingdom. Are such distinctions useful in assessing the state of Bakhtin studies, or are more important distinctions to be made within national boundaries and, indeed, within and between the academic disciplines drawn by individual nation–states? I suppose what I am getting at in this line of argument is actually a commentary not just on the expertise required in Bakhtin studies (particularly with regard to untranslated texts), but also on the internal logic of Bakhtin's thinking, and whether this itself is a means to unlearn and reconceptualize the way maps of knowledge and knowledge dissemination get drawn. There is no unitary Bakhtin because this would itself betray the way he conceives knowledge (following somewhat the line of argument which says that Bakhtin the prestructuralist is a poststructuralist by virtue of his post-foundational thinking). In a sense, the more the lessons of Bakhtin get articulated, the more enigmatic or multiple Bakhtin must become. How would you assess the relationship of Bakhtin's writing to its interpretation?

DAVID SHEPHERD: There was a time when I thought that nothing but good could come of a multiple Bakhtin because I thought that that was in the spirit of Bakhtin's work. I think I still think that, but it is beginning to fossilize in the sense that even some of these Bakhtins are becoming entrenched. From the examples you've given, such as the "Slavicist 'prosaic' Bakhtin in the United States," there are very clear limits on what you can and can't do—outside of Bakhtin studies. If you're looking at Bakhtin in relation to Russian literature or Slavic literature, then that is very entrenched and he's been canonized in a certain way. (This is largely true of

English literature in England, where it's basically, with exceptions, post-Lodge analysis.) We've got a series of fossilized Bakhtins, and what is happening in a lot of these areas is that the work being done with Bakhtin is not retroactive on Bakhtin, the way it used to be. This is a pity because people need to rethink "the" set of concepts as they use them at a time when those concepts themselves are in question because of the archivists' work. I wouldn't propose an absolute opposition between the archivists and the interpreters. This is a necessary stage, as I've mentioned, where we've got to get back to those traditional approaches on the basis of what's in the archive simply in order to satisfy ourselves that we were right in the first place—that there is a multiple Bakhtin, that there is no single Bakhtin. Nobody's archive is going to provide a coherent picture.

PETER HITCHCOCK: Most non-Slavicists who come to Bakhtin and Bakhtinian analysis remain distinctly under- or uninformed about the state of the Bakhtin archive in Russia. Could you explain something of the secret aura that has built up around these manuscripts, and perhaps give some indication of what we might still expect to issue forth from the archive?

DAVID SHEPHERD: What has appeared in the first published volume of the Collected Works, volume 5, is most of the previously unpublished Bakhtin.[5] Everything else that appears, however, will be different from what we have already, in the sense that it will be textually more reliable. Some of the texts in the past were inaccurate because of the difficulty of reading Bakhtin's manuscripts, because of problems in dating, and because of censorship. So everything is going to be different, but, on the basis of what I know (as someone who doesn't have any direct access to the archive), what is slightly disappointing is that we're going to get the texts that were more or less prepared for publication and some others now deemed to be publishable. What we're not going to get are Bakhtin's notebooks. Now, maybe you wouldn't get that with any thinker. These are the books in which he made notes on the people whom he was reading, which are, by all accounts, immensely revealing. Some of that would come through in the editorial apparatus, but not all of it can. Ironically, this is precisely the area where the electronic edition would give you the scope for all of it: an enormous work but a work both of homage and of critical distance. The idea would be to take all these notebooks, transcribe them, and have that text available and searchable in relation to the primary texts—and also digitized so that people can actually look at the image of the notebooks; that's the homage side of things. But this is what is going to be absent from the Russian project. We're going to have a very, very selective view of what Bakhtin's sources were because not everybody in that collective is working in the same way. What one hears is that there are tensions within the group working on the archive. There are people working on their own particular volumes and apparently not always sharing information. There is not a single description of the contents of the archive in its entirety. There is no list. Nobody can point to a list and say this is what is in the archive.

PETER HITCHCOCK: No list? That's remarkable! And even though this will be assumed to be the complete works—a sort of unified Bakhtin based on a unified Collected Works—the editing process itself would actually seem to support a more fragmented or multiple Bakhtin.

DAVID SHEPHERD: Yes, with that tension between the intention and the effect. To be fair to the Russian editors, they intend this to be a collected rather than a complete works, but the implication is that this is to be the definitive edition; yet we really do need some of those basic techniques of reading texts for their absences.

PETER HITCHCOCK: Will there be a statement at some time about the editorial process used, the mode of selection for the Collected Works?

DAVID SHEPHERD: There's already been something along those lines in volume 5, which simply explains it as a question of revisiting the manuscripts of already published works and adding a few other unpublished works. But I don't think there's anything more explicit about the editorial policy adopted. Again, I think that is one of the silences we're dealing with; and again, different people will be coming to this with different agendas. Some of the editors, for instance, will privilege Russian sources over non-Russian sources. They will pass by in silence, say, Bakhtin's reliance on Cassirer. They won't deny it, but they won't give it due prominence. They will emphasize how Bakhtin connects to other contemporary Russian thinkers with whose work he might not have had such direct contact. Obviously, in a Bakhtinian spirit, that's fine; it would be even finer if you did that alongside more traditional, source-based scholarship. You've got to do that, surely. Theory requires that, and that requires theory. So the different editors are working in different ways.

PETER HITCHCOCK: And these various methods of editing would seem to preclude the possibility of there ever being a list.

DAVID SHEPHERD: It would seem so, because the thing about Bakhtin's archive is that it's not held in an *archive*. It is held in somebody's flat.

Another part of the agenda is to reinforce the idea that Bakhtin was the author of the disputed texts. These are going to be published within the edition as Bakhtin Circle texts, but it is quite clear that the majority of the editors believe that Bakhtin was the author. Bocharov has told me as much: "I am convinced he is the author."[6] Yet in what other case would we come across such statements as "Vološinov, whose authorship of *Marxism and the Philosophy of Language* has not yet been proved"? Why should it be "proved"? His name is beneath the title. His university records show that he was planning to write such a book. And yet, because of the mystique surrounding Bakhtin, we are asked to assume that Vološinov needs to be proved innocent or guilty, or whatever—or that Bakhtin needs to be proved innocent of the charge of not writing it!

PETER HITCHCOCK: Of course, Bakhtin himself fed that mystique.

DAVID SHEPHERD: He did, but Bakhtin simply said a lot of contradictory things. We can't privilege the word of Bakhtin because, for perfectly good reasons, his word was unreliable. It had to be at certain times—partly because he was old when he gave a lot of those interviews, partly because he had to steer a very delicate course. At certain times of his life he claimed aspects of the biography of his brother and the biography of his friend Matvei Kagan.

PETER HITCHCOCK: Including a university education!

DAVID SHEPHERD: Exactly. There's nothing terribly wrong with that in the circumstances of the time. It's absolutely understandable. The man was trying to carve out for himself a safe institutional position. It was a difficult period. But the sense that one has to hang on every word Bakhtin said—if he said at some point, "I wrote that"—is partly contradicted by the fact that other things he said were categorically untrue and also that he said the opposite as well. So you just can't tell.

PETER HITCHCOCK: Speaking of selective or impossible reaccentuation, do you, as a skilled translator of Russian texts, think that the retranslation and reediting of specific texts might alter the reception of Bakhtin outside Slavic studies? If so, in what ways? Does a particular example come to mind?

DAVID SHEPHERD: Well, the texts collected in *The Dialogic Imagination* are the ones that always strike me as those that most need reconsidering.[7] There's an awful lot of sloppiness in the translation. These are texts that were translated and published in 1981 at the height of the theory boom in the United States. Perhaps it was helpful that Bakhtin could be made to sound like somebody who was participating in that. And he does. He doesn't sound like a Russian thinker of the 1930s or 1940s. A retranslation should allow the philosophical side of those texts to emerge, not to mention the "borrowed" side of those texts. And, of course, Bakhtin himself said that he was more of a philosopher, describing the literary scholar as a sort of "in-between" figure. But I think that disparaging "in-between" is the moment of highest praise for him. I think this will emerge in retranslation—that Bakhtin is between literary theory and a more philosophically oriented project.

Maybe the other text to mention is the Rabelais book.[8] I myself have not worked with this text that much. But it is in need of retranslation. Some short sections have been omitted, and the sources are not fully indicated. Again, I can't separate out retranslation from editing (a rigorous examination of sources). And this will have a great effect on the terminology used. We're going to realize that a lot of what we've assumed to be original terminology isn't, in fact, and is therefore richer—because it's not just Bakhtin's terminology. I think the Rabelais book and the stuff on the novel will have the most effect. The early philosophical work, which is the most recently translated, is among the best of the translations. Thus what we might find is that the apparent distance Holquist identified in his introduction to *Art and Answerability* between the early and late works is not that great after all, terminologically. There is a progression there.

PETER HITCHCOCK: And Brian Poole is also suggesting that chronologically they are closer too.

DAVID SHEPHERD: Yes, for instance, that the work on philosophy and the Dostoevsky book was all going on in the second half of the 1920s and centered on the work of Max Scheler. But there is such a resistance to that. Poole's position on this topic will be laid out in greater detail in the second edition of *Bakhtin and Cultural Theory*.[9]

PETER HITCHCOCK: When you first coedited that collection with Ken Hirschkop, your own essay on reader-response theory and other essays within the volume suggested a whole array of possibilities for dialogic critique at or beyond the limits of competing critical apparatuses. Now that you're going to a second edition, perhaps this is a good time to reflect on what has happened since its original publication in 1989. Would you say those possibilities still lie before us, or have some avenues been closed off by subsequent investigations and analyses?

DAVID SHEPHERD: Well, look at the changes to the edition itself. Ken has cut down his introduction, based on the feeling that either he no longer believes some of what he said or that some of this no longer needs to be said. The two new papers we've got include Poole on the dating and sources of the early philosophical manuscripts and Pan'kov on the events surrounding Bakhtin's defense of his dissertation in 1947. This is proof of how Ken and I have shifted ground toward more rigorous philological approaches and away from more rarified theory in light of the material that has come into the public domain since then. And that will make the other work look rather different. There's also going to be a new bibliographical essay based on the material available to the Bakhtin Centre.

PETER HITCHCOCK: Will you be extending the glossary?

DAVID SHEPHERD: No, actually, the glossary is something we haven't done much work on, and we may get rid of it.

PETER HITCHCOCK: There was discussion at one point that Morson and Emerson would publish a "heteroglossary."[10]

DAVID SHEPHERD: Yes. . . . There is a glossary under preparation in Moscow, but I think that any such glossary should be done electronically on the basis of a fully cross-referenced and searchable text. You've got to look at frequency. You've got to look at context. You've got to look at various combinations of the terms available. I'm sure it could be done other ways, but one person really doesn't have enough time or resources.

PETER HITCHCOCK: We each have our explanations for the relevance of Bakhtin today, some of which are contained in the previous questions (and responses), but I wonder if you could speak to the role of Bakhtin in the reconfiguration of the English academy in particular. Is dialogism seen to promote disciplinary dialogue in any significant way, or has his impact been limited to questions of reforming knowledge within prescribed disciplinary borders? My question is piqued both by Bakhtin's ever-ambivalent relationship to institutions of knowledge (though the feeling was mutual for the most part!) and by the fact that higher education in England is in a period of rapid change. What would you say at this point?

DAVID SHEPHERD: This is where you come up against very real institutional configurations. At the risk of sounding parochial about it, an awful lot of the way research is done and received is determined these days by government funding. And this reinforces traditional boundaries. It claims to reward interdisciplinary activity, but everything has to be drawn back to a "unit of assessment" (to use the vocabulary of the Research Assessment Exercises we undergo every five years or so in the UK), which is more often than not coterminous with a traditional academic department. I think this is probably impeding genuine interdisciplinarity and collaboration. For example, you might be able to co-supervise a Bakhtin student doing research, but that student has always got to belong to one or the other department involved. The paradox, then, is that interdisciplinarity is what we're all talking about, and Bakhtin seems to fit absolutely in with that. (This is one of the pitches of the Bakhtin Centre—as a place for multidisciplinary and interdisciplinary research.) But at the end of the day everybody has to go back to their department. That's sad. The Centre doesn't have the kind of institutional existence that would allow it to be directly funded and therefore to introduce permanent changes in the way in which disciplinary boundaries are drawn. So you get a Bakhtin Centre that is run from a Russian department—which gets measured against other Russian departments in the country that have a rather more traditional profile and also cover a whole range of areas with which Bakhtin has very little to do. So, yes, Bakhtin does promote disciplinary dialogue and it does happen at conferences, etcetera, but, particularly in Britain, the institutional framework is slow in responding to that—for brute economic reasons. And you can bring Bakhtin to bear on that as much as you like, but it won't change anything!

PETER HITCHCOCK: Exactly. Once someone says, "It's the economy, stupid," then Bakhtin has to take a backseat. Just to return to the nature of the Bakhtin Centre for a moment: I daresay that the main function of the Centre will be to provide a Website more than a library in the conventional sense. This is a technological reality that must be embraced, however cautiously.

Will it be possible, for instance, to do textual analyses of some of Bakhtin's manuscripts? Will there be facsimiles of the original manuscripts on view? How close is the Centre to being a fully functional electronic research library?

DAVID SHEPHERD: I would love to be able to do this with the Centre. As far as the plans for an electronic edition go, at this stage, provided that all the negotiations with the parties who hold rights go well, I would envisage publishing—preferably on the Web but possibly on CD-ROM as well or instead—Russian texts accompanied by new English translations. One of the reasons I got a very frosty reception to the idea of an electronic edition when I broached it a few years back was that I'd made the mistake of running through what you could do with an electronic edition, including digitizing the manuscripts and so on. There was an instant "No!" That access is not going to be available, and I just have to respect that. I think it's a great pity. That would have made it a real research tool. So, it will be limited, but its great virtue is going to be in the editorial apparatus. This is bound to be different from the one employed in the printed edition. So it's not just that we want to do things differently—the electronic edition requires such a difference. But, of course, it's partly because the take of the Bakhtin Centre itself will be different from that of the editorial team in Moscow. We will not be pursuing the same agenda.

PETER HITCHCOCK: So we'd have to qualify "fully functional" somewhat?

DAVID SHEPHERD: Yes, and although we associate this kind of thing with rapid access and so on, it is going to be quite a number of years before everything that we would want to see in there is there. The reason I want to go for Web rather than CD-ROM publication is that it can be incremental. We can start to get texts up and running quite early. That will determine the future development of the Website because the editorial apparatus will evolve—it will develop in ways that I can't yet foresee.

PETER HITCHCOCK: In addition, you're still getting secondary material sent to you in the usual way.

DAVID SHEPHERD: Yes, all of which needs to be somehow assimilated both into the database and into the plans for the electronic edition.

PETER HITCHCOCK: So who is in charge of indexing?

DAVID SHEPHERD: Well, we have a research assistant who tries to put as much of this into the database as possible and to file things logically. But some things are just there. It's a bit like the Bakhtin archive—nobody actually knows how much is in there! It's not a huge amount. It's a reasonably useful resource of secondary material on Bakhtin. But we are developing it all the time. In the context of the new project we're buying a lot of new material, particularly Russian philosophy from the beginning of the twentieth century.

PETER HITCHCOCK: The bulk of the "visitors," let's say, will be electronic visitors.

DAVID SHEPHERD: Yes, as they are now. And obviously, I'll be taking care of things to make sure those visits are "pleasurable" ones—rewarding experiences and so forth. A lot of people are now familiar with the database. We try to make other kinds of material available, including links to other sites.

PETER HITCHCOCK: It appears that most of the defining book-length works on Bakhtin are English-language texts (with a few notable exceptions, like Todorov's[11]). What Russian texts do you believe would reshape this perception? How would they alter the field as a whole? (Of course, such questions are never far from the politics of translation.)

DAVID SHEPHERD: I can't think of any that would have that overall effect. It may be that I'm not close enough to this. But there aren't that many monographs on Bakhtin in Russian. And they don't have that synthetic overview of, say, Clark and Holquist's or Morson and Emerson's,[12] or even the early Todorov book. There are biographies of Bakhtin. There are approaches to Bakhtin in terms of the I and the Other (like Makhlin's monograph[13]), but as yet there isn't a work available that could be seen to offer a coherent alternative overview. Russian Bakhtin studies is extraordinarily fragmented. It's all going on in the journals, but there still isn't a group of articles that would radically alter perceptions in the West. Some of the Russian-language material is beginning to find its way through—the collections *Face to Face, The Contexts of Bakhtin* (which I edited and which contains five Russian papers),[14] and of course this issue of *SAQ*. All of this illustrates quite well the fragmented nature of the Russian scene, but in some ways this mirrors the situation in the West: analyses which range from Bakhtin-as-aesthetician to Bakhtin's intellectual affiliations in the early 1920s to Bakhtin as a way of reading Soviet literature.

PETER HITCHCOCK: Russia is in a period of tremendous change and it is too early to say what its new identity will be, but have these changes resulted in a reevaluation of Bakhtin vis-à-vis Russia's other major thinkers?

DAVID SHEPHERD: Certainly, I think one of the differences between Bakhtin and a number of other thinkers is that, after all the partiality with which he was published and appropriated before the collapse of the Soviet Union, at least he *was* published. There are others who had to wait until the early 1990s for this to happen (the philosopher Aleksei Losev, for example). Bakhtin is being seen, alongside them, as at least of equal caliber. He is being seen in Russia as one among a particular set of thinkers—perhaps even privileged as a good guy, while certain other thinkers associated with the Soviet period have fallen away. In some cases, Bakhtin is a pretext for bringing other thinkers out into the open. I don't know of another thinker who is currently receiving the kind of attention that Bakhtin is getting in Russia these days.

PETER HITCHCOCK: Of course, it still may be too early to say, given what's going on in the archive, and also given the Russian struggle to come to terms with a tumultuous twentieth century—seventy-four years of one thing and now something else. Interestingly, some people are saying that Russia now looks like the Russia in crisis before the Revolution.

DAVID SHEPHERD: But in many respects it still looks remarkably like the pre-1991 Russia. There's clearly a lot of institutional drag and inertia, and this definitely has an effect. I think one can detect traces of that in the range of appropriations of Bakhtin that have come out, including some papers at this conference. A lot of them are still couched in official rhetoric—the official structuring of a paper and the form of argumentation. And that comes back to the reinvention-of-the-wheel material that I mentioned earlier—going through the basics before you get to the point. So, with the institutions where they are, there is still a need to do a nod in this direction and that before you get down to the substance.

PETER HITCHCOCK: Just to push an assessment of cultural exchange a little more, what kinds of Bakhtinian analysis are getting translated into Russian? In general, does Russian Bakhtinian scholarship remain largely isolated from outside influences?

DAVID SHEPHERD: Less so now than it was. Pan'kov's *Dialog, Karnaval,*

Khronotop regularly publishes Russian translations from English, and some articles in English. I don't think any of the major monographs have been translated into Russian—chapters from them have. Probably the one Western commentator on Bakhtin who has been most translated is Caryl Emerson, perhaps because of a congeniality between her agenda and that of some of the Russians. In general, however, it is a piecemeal affair. Vitalii Makhlin has been very good about this; he has, for instance, translated a number of papers from *Bakhtin and Cultural Theory* that wouldn't necessarily support his view of Bakhtin but which he considers important for Russian readers. There have also been translations from Clive Thomson's special issue of the *Bakhtin Newsletter,* "Bakhtin around the World." Emerson's *First Hundred Years of Mikhail Bakhtin* is a good candidate to be the first monograph translated in its entirety.[15]

PETER HITCHCOCK: What would you like to have happen in order to enhance the position of the Bakhtin Centre over the next five years or so? Is the institutional support for the Centre relatively secure?

DAVID SHEPHERD: Technically, we're secure for the next seven years. Craig Brandist's position (as research fellow) is technically secure for seven years—four years HRB funding and three years University funding. What I'd like to do is attract more graduate students to the Centre. We usually have about half a dozen graduate students working at the Centre at any one time. And I want more and more of those students to be involved in the work on the electronic edition. In our recent communications we've identified three areas where we'd like to see graduate students working, to bring together and look at the work that's been done so far and to write a dissertation about that. But I'd also like them to make a contribution to the editorial apparatus of the electronic edition. I'd really like to develop that, plus find any other funding I can get to support another research fellow to work on the edition, since it is such a huge undertaking—bigger than I originally envisaged. That would give me the greatest pleasure and alleviate the most worries.

PETER HITCHCOCK: Just out of interest, do you have any Russian graduate students who use the facility?

DAVID SHEPHERD: There are a couple of them working there right now. One is researching in an area not directly associated with the electronic edition, but another Russian started working with us in January 1997 specifically on the Bakhtin Circle, Western linguistics, and the philosophy of language. She will be asked to do some work on part of the editorial mechanics of the text. One other very important project that I'd like to mention is, of course, *Dialogism*, the international journal of Bakhtin studies we have recently started at the Centre. This has been a difficult task so far, and it has come with the usual assortment of delays and setbacks, but I see this as a crucial component of our work because it represents a more traditional outlet for matters Bakhtinian. I hope it will provide a forum not just for the Centre's activities but for other people to channel their work via the Centre. We also intend to build into the work of the journal collaboration with *Dialog, Karnaval, Khronotop*, which will allow us to exchange articles and collectively keep abreast of research and articles that should be translated in a timely fashion. We'll also run book reviews, perhaps some bibliographic information, conference announcements, and an assortment of advertising. Eventually, we'd like to do some special issues. We have some possibilities in mind already, including one on queer studies/theory. We'll be publishing two issues a year once we get into the swing of things.

PETER HITCHCOCK: So, despite the hardships, there is some good news on the horizon. Thank you very much for your time.

DAVID SHEPHERD: Thank you.

Notes

1 *Face to Face: Bakhtin in Russia and the West*, ed. Carol Adlam, Rachel Falconer, Vitalii Makhlin, and Alastair Renfrew (Sheffield, UK, 1997).

2 http://www.shef.ac.uk/uni/academic/A-C/bakh/bakhtin.html.

3 Robert F. Barsky and Michael Holquist, "Dialogue: Conversation between Robert F. Barsky and Professor Michael Holquist," *Discours social/Social Discourse* 3 (1990): 1–22; quotation from 5.

4 V. V. Kozhinov, "Bakhtin v zhivom dialoge" (Bakhtin in Living Dialogue), in V. D. Duvakin, *Besedy V. D. Duvakina s M. M. Bakhtinym* (Moscow, 1996), 272–81.

5 M. M. Bakhtin, *Raboty 1940-kh–nachala 1960-kh godov* (Works from the 1940s to the Early 1960s), Vol. 5 of *Sobranie sochinenii v semi tomakh* (Collected Works in Seven Volumes), ed. S. G. Bocharov and L. A. Gogotishvili (Moscow, 1996).

6 Sergei Bocharov, of the Academy of Sciences Institute of World Literature in Moscow, is one of Bakhtin's literary executors (along with Vadim Kozhinov). Now a leading literary critic, he was one of the young scholars who rescued Bakhtin from provincial obscurity in the 1960s.

7 M. M. Bakhtin, *The Dialogic Imagination: Four Essays*, ed. Michael Holquist, trans. Caryl Emerson and Michael Holquist (Austin, 1981).

8 M. M. Bakhtin, *Rabelais and His World,* trans. Hélène Iswolsky (Cambridge, MA, 1968).

9 *Bakhtin and Cultural Theory,* ed. Ken Hirschkop and David Shepherd (Manchester, UK, 1989). The second edition is forthcoming in 1999.

10 See Gary Saul Morson, with Caryl Emerson, "Extracts from a *Heteroglossary,*" in *Dialogue and Critical Discourse: Language, Culture, Critical Theory,* ed. Michael Macovski (New York and Oxford, 1997), 256–72.

11 Tzvetan Todorov, *Mikhail Bakhtin: The Dialogical Principle,* trans. Wlad Godzich (Minneapolis, 1984 [1981]).

12 Katerina Clark and Michael Holquist, *Mikhail Bakhtin* (Cambridge, MA, and London, 1984); Gary Saul Morson and Caryl Emerson, *Mikhail Bakhtin: Creation of a Prosaics* (Stanford, 1990).

13 Vitalii Makhlin, *Ia i Drugoi: Istoki filosofii "dialoga" XX veka. Materialy k spetskursu* (St. Petersburg, 1995).

14 *The Contexts of Bakhtin: Philosophy, Authorship, Aesthetics,* ed. David Shepherd, Studies in Russian and European Literature 2 (Amsterdam, 1998).

15 Caryl Emerson, *The First Hundred Years of Mikhail Bakhtin* (Princeton, 1997).

Vitalii Makhlin

Questions and Answers: Bakhtin from the Beginning, at the End of the Century

The problem of authorship is not just the principal issue in Bakhtin's general theory of discursive creativity in a "speech-thinking act." One could argue that authorship is also a methodological question prior to anything else in Bakhtinian criticism. It has always been so, but the problem is more urgent than ever now because Bakhtin studies has entered a new crisis stage. We are on the verge of discovering a "third Bakhtin"—a new author—distinct from those of the 1960s and the 1980s. In locating this changing image, this new Bakhtin, we might start with the author of the Rabelais book, of whom it is high time to repeat what he himself said of Dostoevsky. For indeed, Bakhtin has not yet become Bakhtin; he "is still becoming him"[1]—becoming a productive other, that is, in the form of "thou art" or "you are."

Coming to terms with this double-bodied issue of issues means moving between Bakhtin's concept of authorship, on the one hand, and his own authorship as a principal condition of possibility for an integral or systematic judgment of *anything* in his writing, on the other. To that end the Rabelais book, or rather its idea of "grotesque realism," might be considered a new

The *South Atlantic Quarterly* 97:3/4, Summer/Fall 1998.

"form of vision," in a strictly Bakhtinian sense. It is not accidental that in many interpretations of Bakhtin's thought his authority disintegrates, with parts of the whole becoming opposed or at best quite alien to, or isolated from, one another. Interestingly enough, it is this very dissociation of sensibility (to borrow from T. S. Eliot) that Bakhtin articulates and accentuates in the history of the reception of both Dostoevsky and Rabelais. That is why, I believe, a new phase in Bakhtinian criticism must inevitably concentrate on a new integration (or perhaps reintegration) of Bakhtin's own authorial position. An adequate understanding and appropriate reception of the Rabelais book will become possible if we are able and willing to see it as a "specific authorial intent," the "speaker's plan or will to speak"[2]—something that is not so much "determined" as *motivated.* Bakhtin's own idea of "active understanding" implies even more, I think, namely, that what can and must be recognized and actively shared is not only motivation but the speaker's will or intent. It is dialogically shared even when (and particularly when) the other's own authorial position contains an element of self-negation and self-deconstruction (or, in Dostoevsky's formulation, "It's not you, Ivan, not you!").

Let me offer a provocative notion: the Rabelais book (like the Dostoevsky book) has yet to be "discovered." Nobody, to my knowledge, has dared to take its author seriously enough to reconstruct his sources and his "will to speak," both within and beyond his own historical context. No one has attempted to reflect on or explain the meaningful difference between Bakhtin's questions and our own motivational context of questions directed at his answers—or indeed at his questions.

This meaningful difference between Bakhtin and Bakhtin studies is itself a condition of possibility for any valid judgment or interpretation of either him or ourselves (i.e., of our interest, or uninterest, in his ideas). And this is precisely what Bakhtin meant by his statement at the beginning of his concise "history of laughter" from the sixteenth to the twentieth century, a statement that could serve as a hermeneutic starting point in any future attempt to reconstruct the "authorial intent" of the Rabelais book. Rabelais's contemporaries, Bakhtin remarks, understood his imagery at once—an understanding so immediate that the carnival imagery Rabelais used was clear and unambiguous—which is why, Bakhtin adds, "the understanding of those contemporaries is incapable of giving us any clue or answer to *our own questions about Rabelais,* since for them these questions did not exist."[3]

Let us try to suspend our will to answer our own questions within the postmodern horizon of understanding. Let us forget, for a moment, about Bakhtin's alleged Marxism or even Stalinism, about "discourse" and "deconstruction," about feminist studies and cultural studies. Let us even forget what Bakhtin himself said about "active understanding" and attempt to see what is actually meant or implied or intended here. By doing so, we can distinguish four points made by Bakhtin on the basis of this key hermeneutic statement—and thus take a first step toward reconstructing his authorial position in twentieth-century culture. In terms of our questions about Rabelais in particular, the first point concerns Bakhtin's idea of "open seriousness [*otkr'etaya ser'osnost*]"[4]—the central notion of the Rabelais book. The second point has to do with viewing modern or postmodern culture through the medium of systemic folk-laughter imagery (the subject matter, in fact, of Bakhtin's hermeneutics of carnival and the carnivalesque).

The issue of "open seriousness" in laughter interests me as a problem of logic: What does it mean? Why does Bakhtin use this formulation repeatedly throughout the Rabelais book and, in modified form, in the work on Dostoevsky, where it appears in connection with a nontragic or seriocomic characteristic of Dostoevsky's poetics (as a prosaic analogy to the "unfinalizability" of the world)?

Bakhtin's interest in folk laughter per se, however, seems to be as a specific, systemic "gesture of consciousness"—a communal point of view on communality. This communal viewpoint is a type of authorial position, a creative position the "object-hero" of which is creation itself. For Bakhtin, folk-laughter imagery thus becomes an answer to his question about authorship and its "crisis," particularly within the modern. The tone and meaning of laughter and of grotesque realism, Bakhtin insists, have gradually changed. The older structures have altered, despite their apparent unchangeability. They tend more and more to satirize man, the world, and creation at large, as if the author-satirist herself were wholly outside her "hero" (i.e., outside his object of criticism), as if her surplus of vision established a radically utopian—and not participatively interested—autonomy. In addition, Bakhtin insists on the importance of the systemic imagery of folk or popular culture, which he calls grotesque realism, and he stresses this significance for us—contemporaries of the twentieth century.

Second, the "dark language of folk laughter [*narodnaya smehhovaya kul'tura*]" is, according to Bakhtin's authorial intent, itself an authority (i.e., an authorial plan or intent). For, and in, Bakhtin any *vouloir dire*, any authorship that we take an interest in, implies not merely questions and answers in general, but also a characteristic *will to answer* (sometimes even with what is otherwise deemed a final answer). And this, from the point of view of an other (an interpreter, for instance), turns out to be a *question*.

Third, "our questions about Rabelais," Bakhtin asserts, were for Rabelais's contemporaries already *answers*. That is, they *knew* the answers immediately; what they did *not* know were the questions being answered. Their answers were something they lived through. They knew the original as something natural or naturalized and, for this very reason, as something *incomplete*.

Bakhtin's fourth point is this: What Rabelais's contemporaries possessed as answers amounted, in reality and in essence, to a specific kind of *experience* that we of the twentieth century are only able to possess as *questions* precisely because we lack those answers. In this sense, our words, "our questions about Rabelais," are not purely theoretical (not *die Produkte des Wissens*, "the products of knowledge" in both Bakhtin's and Konrad Burdech's evaluations of the Renaissance). Rather, theoretical and historical questions are themselves motivated and approbated by our lived experience—by us as Rabelais's noncontemporaries.

What I have identified here as Bakhtin's key hermeneutic statement in his Rabelais book implies that an ontologically eventful difference between the end of the Middle Ages, on the one hand, and the end of this "newer time," on the other, is itself a condition of possibility for cognition and recognition; it is a definite pattern of experience inscribed in a continuous history. This pattern, far from being a construct of the mind, is deeply rooted in an eventfulness of social or communal being; it constitutes a pattern of historicity in itself, namely, an experience of the permanent regeneration of the past as a concrete historical possibility for a communally productive and justified *future*. Thus the ontologically eventful noncoincidence of folk laughter with its own essence and truth—this split or nonepistemological rupture in the reception and understanding of its meaning—constitutes the motivational context that Bakhtin calls "our questions about Rabelais." What are these questions? And to what extent are they *ours*? In other words, to what extent do we share, and recognize productively, our own participation in the very pattern of absolute historicity that Bakhtin calls "carnival"?

We should not be too hasty in formulating answers to these questions; we had better "think twice." That is precisely what we did *not* do in the two previous periods of *rezeptions geschichte* (in the 1960s and, to some extent, in the 1980s). To be more precise, either "our questions about Rabelais" were ignored or Bakhtin's (easily explicable) elusive or hidden answers were taken for our own. Thus, the questions being unknown, the answers were appropriated by "revolutionary" (post)moderns, who, ironically, represent the very kind of thinking Bakhtin opposed. (It is noteworthy that the same thing happened with his concept of "dialogue.") What Bakhtin had in mind when he foregrounded "our questions about Rabelais" was, in fact, a *permanence-in-shift*, the ontological difference between the Rabelaisian imagery of laughter and its deformation in the history of modern art and modern thinking in general. One might conjecture that the appropriation since the 1960s of Bakhtin's idea of carnival is instead a seriocomic confirmation of his theory through a misunderstanding. The prevailing interpretations of the Bakhtinian carnivalesque—for or against—have very little to do with the author of the Rabelais book (or of the work on Dostoevsky, for that matter). They are, however, vivid examples of the crisis in creative attitude, in art and in life, in the historical "creature" itself, in man's very attitude to the creation and the creator. Bakhtin insists in his Rabelais book (and in the early manuscripts) that this crisis has actually deformed and distorted the nature of the author and authorship.

Bakhtin was interested not in laughter in general, but in a specifically formative experience of folk laughter, which he called "ambivalent." Ambivalent laughter is a kind of communal authority, an authority implying regeneration of the community, the world, and the individual by way of sharp criticism, even negation, of them all. This unity of "no" and "yes" in folk laughter and in grotesque realism more generally is counterposed in the Dostoevsky book to both "closed" laughter and the "closed" seriousness of the "whole ideological culture of modern times." It is therefore absolutely wrong to speak of "utopia" in Bakhtin because the utopian element in folk laughter cannot be understood against the background of speech-thinking acts in the modern and postmodern world. What Bakhtin implies here is that modern "man" (as well as the "pure satirist" in fiction) *excludes himself* from the object of his critical laughter: first, the author of such a speech-thinking act authors as if he has escaped his own critical attitude, finding in this negative act an excuse (or "alibi," as the early Bakhtin might have said); and second, the author as satirist fails to see that his chronotopic act of "utopian" negation ought to be all the more serious and ideal the less reality is serious and ideal. A "pure satirist" remains within an idealistic and ideological pattern of self-image that prevents us from seeing a "common ground of experience" and thus the "criminal state of the world" (as Bakhtin puts it, in the moralistic terms typical of the 1944 additions to the Rabelais book).[5] The "state of the world" is inevitably a *caricature* of our own best aspirations, while at the same time this caricature is *noncoincident with ourselves.*

It is naive to take Bakhtin as naive. Like Dostoevsky, he saw a human being as a creature without an alibi for her/himself, a caricature of her or his idealism, yet capable of becoming "better" by "dying" and being "revived"—by finding out that she or he is a fool, or a "criminal," looking in the mirror of his/her heavenly motherland. From this perspective, "open seriousness" signifies recognition of oneself as an object of laughter, both in oneself and in an other, as a condition of possibility—the discovery of the productive possibility of regeneration. Open seriousness of authorship as a speech-thinking act goes *beyond* the mirror image of the world and the self.

Finally, it is pertinent to go one step further and apply Bakhtin's answer to the problem of authorship as "open seriousness" to Bakhtinian criticism itself now, when it is approaching a critical point both within and outside of Russia. This self-reflexive moment consists, I believe, in the fact that what we have thought and written of Bakhtin up to the present has been more or less a "double" of our inspirations and fears, not a reflection of *his* authorial intent. The focus on "self-image" has not yet been overcome in Bakhtinian criticism. It is impossible to understand an answer to a question without understanding the question itself. To understand Bakhtin's questions, however, appears to imply, as a condition of this possibility, an experience "in the body" of something Bakhtin really meant or intended to say. In our epoch of self-image deconstruction, the time is ripe to take his hermeneutics of regeneration, as well as his theory of carnival laughter, quite seriously as a means of regenerating Bakhtin's authorial outsideness in our (post)modern world.

Notes

1 Mikhail Bakhtin, "Toward a Reworking of the Dostoevsky Book" (1961), in *Problems of Dostoevsky's Poetics*, ed. and trans. Caryl Emerson (Minneapolis, 1984), 283–302; quotation from 291.

2 M. M. Bakhtin, "The Problem of Speech Genres," in *Speech Genres and Other Late Essays,*

ed. Caryl Emerson and Michael Holquist, trans. Vern W. McGee (Austin, 1986), 60–102; quotation from 77–78.

3 M. M. Bakhtin, *Tvorchestvo Fransua Rable i narodnaia kul'tura srednevekov'ia Renessansa* (Moscow, 1990 [1965]), 70–71; my translation here and elsewhere unless otherwise indicated.

4 Ibid., 134.

5 M. M. Bakhtin, *Raboty 1940-kh–nachala 1960-kh godov* (Works from the 1940s to the Early 1960s), Vol. 5 of *Sobranie sochinenii v semi tomakh* (Collected Works in Seven Volumes), ed. S. G. Bocharov and L. A. Gogotishvili (Moscow, 1996), 89.

Michael Holquist

Afterword: A Two-Faced Hermes

The life which has no knowledge of the air it breathes is a naive life.
—Mikhail Bakhtin, *Author and Hero in Aesthetic Activity*

The title of this superbly edited special issue already betrays some of the anxiety that pervades it. As the high quality of these essays makes very clear, it is a creative anxiety, but there is an uneasiness nonetheless. In his self-conscious and wise introduction, Peter Hitchcock suggests that the basis for this anxiety may be explained in terms of Mikhail Bakhtin's own ideas as they are expressed in *Author and Hero*: "Will critics settle for a 'not yet' or 'not all' Bakhtin, or will they insist that 'their' Bakhtin is complete according to the excess of their seeing?" Anthony Wall addresses the same ambiguity in his essay ("A Broken Thinker") as he meditates "the fundamentally fragmentary nature of Bakhtin's thinking." Individual essay titles (like the issue as a whole) raise "questions" or employ "myth" as a euphemism for "untruth," while interrogatives abound (as in Robert Barsky's innovative "Bakhtin as Anarchist?"). Brian Poole says it very well in his contribution ("Bakhtin and Cassirer"): "We still do not know who Bakhtin was."

The *South Atlantic Quarterly* 97:3/4, Summer/Fall 1998.

It does not help that the effort to figure out who Bakhtin *is* finds contradictory evidence in Bakhtin's own accounts of who he *was*. But some of these essays also raise suspicions that even his heretofore undoubted erudition may be spurious. Those contributors whose work has brought them into contact with the so grandly named and frequently invoked "Bakhtin archive," having become familiar enough with the casualness, the clutter, and the lovable but vexing quirkiness of the whole operation, observe a proper humility in invoking its authority. It is therefore not surprising, perhaps, that a certain hesitation can be sensed in many of these essays.

That wariness finds an icon in the diacritical apparatus hovering nervously over the repetition of Bakhtin's name in the issue's title. If so undialogical an element as a single unifying theme were to have crept into this patently heteroglot collection, it might well be, as Hitchcock suggests, the repeated attempt to understand the slash that separates the first Bakhtin from the second, as well as the quotation marks adorning that posterior, *other* Bakhtin: "To be 'true' to Bakhtin's theorization means that one must decenter Bakhtin as an author, yet there is simply no way, politically or philosophically, to do so without acknowledging the incommensurability of Bakhtin with 'Bakhtin.'" But the titular slash cum quotation marks heraldically signify the scandal of authorship in the Bakhtinian canon, not merely the high theory involved in Bakhtin's early work *Author and Hero*. Indeed, the now emerging questions of sheer plagiarism in Bakhtin's writing are so rude that they bring us back to the term's origin in the Latin word for kidnapping. One of the ways this special issue of *SAQ* marks a new level of development in Bakhtin studies is in signaling the reversed direction that questions about the mysteries of authorship must now take: even as debate continues over the potential plagiarizing *of* Bakhtin by Medvedev and Vološinov, the publication here of Poole's essay means we must now consider the plagiarizing *by* Bakhtin of Ernst Cassirer. What kind of *hero* could Bakhtin be when, as *author*, he engaged in practices for which undergraduates are routinely punished? And yet, as Poole argues with appropriate subtlety, Bakhtin still *is* a kind of hero, able to authorize programmatic statements of the sort we find, among other places, throughout this special issue—a hero, though, of a very special, difficult to define type, one for whom Wall's thoughtful (but, I would repeat, anxious) characterization of "broken thinker" may be accurate. Wall's essay and Ken Hirschkop's "Bakhtin Myths" are particularly insightful attempts by two old Bakhtinian hands to solve a problem that all readers of Bakhtin must confront unless—as certain of his students have done—they avoid the problem by assuming it does not exist, thus winning the right to raise their own flag over a Bakhtinism of one kind or another (usually grounded in a vulgarized ethics). The problem of knowing who "Bakhtin" was, or is—an apparently temporal discrepancy that any version of Bakhtin must theoretically address—is not, of course, a dilemma peculiar to Bakhtin.

One of the great virtues of this collection is the new attention it brings to this quandary, which emerges not only as a problem in how to assimilate Bakhtin but also as a central *Problemstellung* in virtually all strands of post-Enlightenment thought. The specific problematic of Bakhtin/"Bakhtin" is, at a first level of abstraction, how to think in some systematic way about a thinker who took such pains to escape the potential fossilization of most systems. But, as Bakhtin's weird meditations in his early philosophical fragments suggest, at a higher level of abstraction, the problem is really one of—abstraction—that is, of "drawing away" (past participle *ab-trahere*) or, more specifically, the drawing away that all thought entails in its outsideness to "the open event of being." Thought is, in Bakhtin's peculiar sense of the word, "aesthetic," insofar as it enters into communion with, but is *not*, actual Being in process of becoming.[1]

The slash between Bakhtin and "Bakhtin" may thus be read as a specification of the gap between event and "event." That is, I may be involved in an event as trivial as sharpening a pencil or as traumatic as a car crash, but what both events will have in common is that they will be separate from my construction of them as events. I may think about, I may seek to understand, the onetime event of sharpening the pencil or of the auto accident, but those thoughts will always already have drawn away from the uniqueness of the event itself. Wall performs a useful service by pointing out how misguided it is to read Bakhtin's meditation on the dilemma that the necessity of abstraction constitutes for human beings as a wholesale, monologic denunciation of "theoretism." I wish to suggest that in sympathy with Bakhtin's metaphysical (as opposed to pseudoscientific) vitalism, we might usefully see this paradox as a living thing. For the most sustained metaphor Bakhtin employs to figure the problem of relating thought (or in his case, more accurately, discourse) to event is the relation of a living author to his fictional characters. If we can, then, for a moment think of "the problem of the author's relationship [*otnošenie*] to the hero"[2] as a living problem, we would do well to remember Bakhtin's saying that "the life which has no knowledge of the air it breathes is a naive life."

If we sniff the air breathed by the problem of how thought relates to event, it will have the scent of Kant in it. One of the profoundest ways in which Bakhtin relates to Kant (especially to the Marburg version of Kant)—and yes, to Cassirer—is the dedication in each to a philosophy of repair. Each is obsessed with the need to restore a bridge between the opposing shores of absolute event and absolute thought—each is impelled to *connect*—with the paradoxical result in Bakhtin's case that his own thought often seems, precisely, disconnected and fragmentary. Bakhtin, like Kant, never forgets the unavoidability of antinomy in human existence, so connection, as a master category informing all he wrote, might perhaps be better understood as the more complex, indirect linkage we call *relation*.[3]

"Relation" is a central concern to most of the contributors—not surprisingly, since it is at the heart of Bakhtin's whole conception of dialog as well as a major link between him and Kant. The drive to seek linkages is more paradigmatically apparent in Kant, for whom the natural sciences presented the ultimate challenge to any effort to unify sensation and intellect—event as opposed to thought *about* the event. Newtonian laws are important in Kant because, insofar as they are extrapersonal, they raise in the most fundamental way the question of how persons can know them. They are, in Kant's sense, transcendental; yet a particular man—the offspring of Lincolnshire yeomen, born on Christmas Day 1642, a creature inhabiting a unique body that ceased to function eighty-five years later in Kensington—made a connection with, or "discovered," those apparently universal laws bearing the name "Newtonian," thus posing in the most acute form the dilemma Kant addresses in the First Critique: "the possibility of connection at all [*die Möglichkeit einer Verbindung überhaupt*]."[4]

This overwhelming drive to bridge a chasm of difference so great that many other thinkers declare it absolute is arguably what most attracted Bakhtin to Kant. The overwhelming sense of a gap at the heart of existence is announced very early in "Toward a Philosophy of the Act," where Bakhtin is already describing "two worlds [that] confront each other, two worlds that have absolutely no communication with each other and are mutually impervious: the world of culture and the world of life, the only world in which we create, cognize, contemplate, live our lives and die or—the world in which the acts of our activity are objectified and the world in which these acts actually proceed and are actually accomplished once and only once."[5] In a world in which things in themselves are never immediately available to mind, there can be no direct access of the sort connection usually names, only construction of tenuous filiations that bear the general name of relation.

Kant and Bakhtin devise quite different strategies for defending the act of relation's priority to the mere things that relation seeks to link. Of paramount significance here for both is the chapter devoted to schematization that opens the Analytic of Principles in the First Critique. The place of this chapter in Kant's oeuvre is similar to that of the *Timaeus* in Plato's, for just as Plato seeks there to finally explain how it is that ideas and their reflections—for all their disparity—might still exist *together* in the same cosmos, Kant expends the greatest energy here in trying to elucidate the simultaneity of timeless categories and the contingency of embodied experience. In the Deduction, Kant had already argued that "the empirical consciousness, which accompanies various representations, is itself various and disunited and without reference to the identity of the subject. Such a relation takes place, not by my simply accompanying every relation with consciousness, but by my adding one to the other and being conscious of that act of adding, that is, of that synthesis."[6] The question then becomes how the universally valid categories can in fact be combined with the dense particularity of unique experience.

Kant begins the chapter by restating the conditions of cognition (precisely Bakhtin's beginning point in *his* early writings): "In comprehending any object under a concept, the representation of the former must be homogenous [*gleichartig*] with the latter. . . . Thus, for instance, the empirical concept of a plate is homogenous with the pure geometrical concept of a circle, the roundness of which is conceived in the first forming an object of intuition in the latter."[7] Kant concludes that "there must be some third thing homogenous on the one side with the category, and on the other with the phenomenon, to render the application of the former to the latter possible. This intermediate representation must be pure (free from all that is empirical) and yet intelligible on the one side and sensuous on the other. Such a representation is the *transcendental schema*."[8]

Now, there are many ways to specify this theory of schema, but few have been satisfied with Kant's own procedure (avoided here), which is why it has been assigned a special status in Kant scholarship as particularly "controversial" or "mysterious." Robert Pippin has remarked that it is "the most obscure chapter in the *Critique* . . . [which] has been called superfluous, unintelligible, an architectonic anachronism, as well as the most important in the *Critique*, the key to the central argument of the Analytic."[9] The basic problem of Kant's schema is the difficulty encountered by anyone (including Kant himself) who tries to specify the nature of the thirdness[10] which defines that infamous "third thing homogenous on the one side with the category, and on the other with the phenomenon, to render the application of the former to the latter possible." What can render this relation possible?

Bakhtin began his career by accepting the primacy of relation and its corollary that nothing therefore exists in isolation. He then spent his life in pursuit of an answer to the question of absolute identity: If it is not possible, what is the nature of the simultaneity that permits difference while still guaranteeing connectedness? If the answer to so fraught a question can be posed in one word, for Bakhtin it would, of course, be *dialog*. But one of the reasons why the contributors to this special issue are still in dialog with Bakhtin is that dialog by definition (in Bakhtin, at least) is never finished—and nowhere less finished than in trying to understand dialog itself. Which brings me back to the anxiety I noted earlier: it has something, surely, to do with knowing that between ourselves and the world there is no direct connection but only a highly mediated relation. We swim in a sea of Kantian schematization, and yet we do not drown. We *can* negotiate the world with some success; we *can* be in relation to each other meaningfully. Recognition that we live in a world of relations rather than of things does not mean (as some of the more totalitarian postmodernists seem to fear) we are condemned to chaos. That slash in *Bakhtin/"Bakhtin"* (playing to some extent on the bar in Saussure's famous division between a picture of a horse and the word *equus*) marks a discursive space where the two poles are never connected, but always have the potential to be so through the work and play of dialog.

Being on a bridge as shaky as dialog, in Bakhtin's sense of that word, condemns us to be in the middle, a subject position from which we must always look in both directions. For this reason, Janus is a figure frequently invoked by Bakhtin and his interpreters (as Wall reminds us again here). In "Toward a Philosophy of the Act," for instance, we find Bakhtin declaring that "an act of our activity, of our actual experiencing, is like a two-faced Janus. It looks in two opposite directions: it looks at the objective unity of a domain of culture and at the never-repeatable uniqueness of actually lived and experienced life. . . . An act must acquire a single unitary plane to be able to reflect itself in both directions—in its sense or meaning and in its being; it must acquire the unity of two-sided answerability."[11] Thus it turns out that the two-faced figure is actually a trope not for two vectors of being, but for three. Janus, then, is the deity who presides over dialog for many of the same reasons he is the god of paronomasia (the generic term for wordplay, especially punning), hence my insistence that the title of this collection is a pun.

Its significance becomes clearer if we invoke another philologist-trickster and dreamer of relation: perhaps Borges (who is also mentioned in Rachel Falconer's essay) can help us to better understand the complexity of Janus as a metaphor for the thirdness of dialog. At the conclusion (a double ending that is the narrative equivalent of a pun) of "Death and the Compass" (one of Borges's endlessly suggestive detective stories), the detective hero has deduced his way to a crumbling mansion where he will meet his death by solving the crime of his own murder. The mansion's name is Triste-le-Roy, which is suggestive of "triste-le-dieu," with "roy" the monotheistic king of the universe saddened by the complete dominion in this tale of quite another god, whom the hero encounters in the mansion's garden, where "a two-faced Hermes cast a monstrous shadow."[12]

The statue is itself a pun, of course, bringing Hermes and Janus into a striking simultaneity: Hermes, the messenger, must indeed—if he is to serve his mission of translating between the language of the gods and the language of men—look both ways. As Frank Kermode reminds us, "The god Hermes is the patron of thieves, merchants, and travelers; of heralds and what heralds pronounce, their *kerygma*. He also has to do with oracles, including a dubious sort known as *kledon*, which at the moment of its announcement may seem trivial or irrelevant, the secret sense declaring itself only after a long delay, and in circumstances not originally foreseeable. Hermes is cunning, and occasionally violent: a trickster, a robber. So it is not surprising that he is the patron of interpreters."[13] And, as two-faced, he is not to be trusted completely by those in either direction of his double gaze. More important to grasping the utility of a two-headed Hermes as a trope for dialogism is the suggestion that it is precisely through the act of being communicated in opposite directions that messages find their mediated way. For what is hermeneutics if not the construction of relation, which in both Russian and English (*otnnosit/otnošenie*; relation [*relatus/re-ferre*]) has hovering about it the promise of delivery. But only the promise, as John of the Cross knew when he wrote:

> This knowledge by unknowing
> is such a soaring force
> that scholars argue long
> but never leave the ground.
> Their knowledge always fails the source:
> to understand unknowing,
> rising beyond all science.[14]

Notes

1 The obsessive subject of Bakhtin's unfinished early major work on the architectonics of answerability, it is reflected on every page of those works published in English as *Toward a Philosophy of the Act*, ed. Michael Holquist and Vadim Liapunov, trans. Vadim Liapunov (Austin, 1993); and *Art and Answerability: Early Philosophical Essays*, ed. Michael Holquist and Vadim Liapunov, trans. Vadim Liapunov (Austin, 1990).

2 This is, of course, the first section heading of the long essay *Author and Hero in Aesthetic Activity* in *Art and Answerability*. (The subsequent quotation here and in my epigraph is from page 144 of the same essay.)

3 I argued this case at greater length, in connection with Cassirer's eerily similar relation to Kant, in a paper delivered at the Yale conference "New Perspectives on Ernst Cassirer" (4–6 October 1996), which is to be published in a volume devoted to Cassirer and edited by Cyrus Hamlin.

4 Immanuel Kant, *Kritik der reinen Vernunft*, ed. Ingeborg Heidemann (Stuttgart, 1966 [1781]), B129; my translation here and elsewhere unless otherwise indicated.

5 Bakhtin, *Philosophy of the Act*, 2.

6 Immanuel Kant, *Critique of Pure Reason*, trans. F. Max Müller (New York, 1966 [1881]), 78; cf. *Immanuel Kant's Critique of Pure Reason*, trans. Norman Kemp Smith (New York, 1965 [1929]), 153. See also Heidemann, ed., *Kritik*, 212 (B132–36).

7 Müller, trans., *Critique*, 121 (B173).

8 Ibid., 122 (B177); cf. Kemp Smith, trans., *Immanuel Kant's Critique*, 181. See also this passage in Heidemann, ed., *Kritik*: "Nun ist klar, dass es ein Drittes gaben müsse, was einerseits mit der Kategorie, andererseits mit der Erscheinung in Gleichartigkeit stehen muss, und die Anwendung der ersereen auf die letzte möglich macht. Diese vermittlende Vorstellung muss rein (ohne alles Empirische) und doch einerseits *intellektual*, andererseits *sinnlich* sein. Eine solche ist das *tranzendentale Schema*" (214).

9 Robert B. Pippin, *Kant's Theory of Form: An Essay on the Critique of Pure Reason* (New Haven, 1982), 124.

10 This chapter's connection to Bakhtin's lifelong attempt to think thirdness is so patent that I will not belabor it.

11 Bakhtin, *Philosophy of the Act*, 2.

12 Jorge Luis Borges, "Death and the Compass," trans. Anthony Kerrigan, in *Ficciones*, ed. Anthony Kerrigan (New York, 1962), 129–41.

13 Frank Kermode, *The Genesis of Secrecy: On The Interpretation of Narrative* (Cambridge, MA, 1979), 1.

14 "I Came into the Unknown," in *The Poems of Saint John of the Cross*, trans. Willis Barnstone (New York, 1972 [1968]), 59–61; quotation from 61 (Este saber no sabiendo / es de tan alto poder / que los sabios arguyendo / jamás le pueden vencer; / que no llega su saber / a no entender entendiendo, / toda ciencia trascendiendo).

Notes on Contributors

ROBERT F. BARSKY, Associate Professor of English at the University of Western Ontario, is the author of *Constructing a Productive Other: Discourse Theory and the Convention Refugee Hearings* (1994), *Noam Chomsky: A Life of Dissent* (1997), and *Introduction à la théorie littéraire* (1997). He also coedited (with Michael Holquist) a 1991 special issue of *Discours social/Social Discourse*, "Bakhtin and Otherness."

RACHEL FALCONER, Lecturer in English at the University of Sheffield, is the author of *Orpheus Dis(re)membered: Milton and the Myth of the Poet–Hero* (1996) and coeditor of *Face to Face: Bakhtin in Russia and the West* (1997).

MAROUSSIA HAJDUKOWSKI-AHMED, who teaches literature in the French Department and the Women's Studies Program at McMaster University, is also principal investigator and co-chair of the McMaster Research Centre for the Promotion of Women's Health. She has written on Bakhtin and feminist theory, as well as on women writers of Quebec, and is now coediting a book entitled *Voices of Women in Health Promotion.*

KEN HIRSCHKOP, Research Fellow at the University of Manchester, coedited (with David Shepherd) *Bakhtin and Cultural Theory* (1989) and is the author of *Mikhail Bakhtin: An Aesthetic for Democracy* (forthcoming from Oxford University Press).

PETER HITCHCOCK is Professor of Literary and Cultural Studies at Baruch College and the Graduate School and University Center of the City University of New York. His books include *Dialogics of the Oppressed* (1993) and *Oscillate Wildly: Space, Body, and Spirit of Millennial Materialism* (forthcoming from University of Minnesota Press).

MICHAEL HOLQUIST, Chair of the Yale University Comparative Literature Department, has written, edited, and translated numerous Bakhtinian works. The coauthor (with Katerina Clark) of *Mikhail Bakhtin* (1984), the author of *Dialogism: Bakhtin and His World* (1990), and the editor of *Art and Answerability* (1990) and *Toward a Philosophy of the Act* (1993), he is currently writing a book on the history and theory of philology.

VITALII MAKHLIN teaches philosophy at Moscow State Pedagogical University. The author of numerous books and articles on Bakhtin, including *Ia i Drugoi: Istoki filosofii "dialoga" XX veka* (1995), he was one of the principal organizers of the 1995 Seventh International Bakhtin Conference in Moscow.

ANNE MALENA, Assistant Professor of Translation and Francophone Literature at the University of Alberta, is the author of *The Negotiated Self: The Dynamics of Identity in Francophone Caribbean Narrative* (forthcoming from Peter Lange).

NIKOLAI PAN'KOV, Researcher at Moscow State University and Lecturer at Vitebsk State University Belarus, has published widely on Bakhtin and is the editor of the journal *Dialog, Karnaval, Khronotop.*

BRIAN POOLE, who is currently teaching at the Institut für Allgemeine und Vergleichende Literaturwissenschaft, Freie Universität Berlin, is a member of the editorial group for the Russian edition of Bakhtin's Collected Works. His translation of Viktor Duvakin's interviews with Bakhtin is forthcoming from University of Texas Press.

DAVID SHEPHERD is Professor of Russian and Director of the Bakhtin Centre, as well as editor of the Centre's journal, *Dialogism*, at the University of Sheffield. The author of *Beyond Metafiction: Self-Consciousness in Soviet Literature* (1992) and coeditor (with Ken Hirschkop) of *Bakhtin and Cultural Theory* (1989), he has also edited *The Contexts of Bakhtin: Philosophy, Authorship, Aesthetics* (1998).

GALIN TIHANOV, Junior Research Fellow in Russian and German Intellectual History, Merton College, Oxford, holds doctorates from the Universities of Sofia and Oxford. He has written extensively on the history of ideas, literary theory, and comparative literature and is the author of two books on Bulgarian literature (published in 1994 and 1998), as well as a forthcoming book on Lukács and Bakhtin.

ANTHONY WALL, Chair of the Department of French, Italian and Spanish at the University of Calgary, is the author of *Superposer: Essais sur les métalangages littéraires* (1996) and the forthcoming *Denis Diderot and His Bodies that Speak.* In 1997, he convened the Eighth International Bakhtin Conference in Calgary.

The South Atlantic Quarterly

Volume 97

Durham, North Carolina

Contents of Volume 97

No. 1, Winter, pp. 1–226; No. 2, Spring, pp. 227–510; No. 3/4, Summer/Fall, pp. 511–796

STATEMENT OF OWNERSHIP AND MANAGEMENT. *The South Atlantic Quarterly* (ISSN: 00384-2876) is published four times a year in Winter, Spring, Summer, and Fall by Duke University Press. The Office of Publication and the General Business Office are located at 905 W. Main St., 18-B, Durham, NC 27701. The Editor is Fredric Jameson at 115 Art Museum, Duke University, Durham, NC 27708-0676. The owner is Duke University Press, Durham, NC 27708-0660. There are no bondholders, mortgagees, or other security holders.

EXTENT AND NATURE OF CIRCULATION: *Average number of copies of each issue published during the preceding twelve months;* (A) total number of copies printed, 2558; (B.1) sales through dealers and carriers, street vendors and counter sales, 235; (B.2) paid mail subscriptions, 1066; (C) total paid circulation, 1301; (D) samples, complimentary, and other free copies, 89; (E) free distribution outside the mail (carriers or other means), 25; (F) total free distribution (sum of D & E), 114; (G) total distribution (sum of C & F), 1415; (H.1) office use, leftover, unaccounted, spoiled after printing, 1143; (H.2) returns from news agents, 0; (I) total, 2558. *Actual number of copies of a single issue published nearest to filing date:* (A) total number of copies printed, 2883; (B.1) sales through dealers and carriers, street vendors and counter sales, 235; (B.2) paid mail subscriptions, 1051; (C) total paid circulation, 1286; (D) samples, complimentary, and other free copies, 90; (E) free distribution outside the mail (carriers or other means), 25; (F) total free distribution (sum of D & E), 115; (G) total distribution (sum of C & F), 1401; (H.1) office use, leftover, unaccounted, spoiled after printing, 1482; (H.2) returns from news agents, 0; (I) total, 2883.

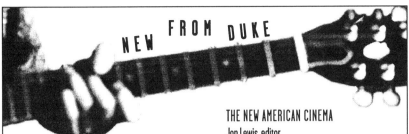

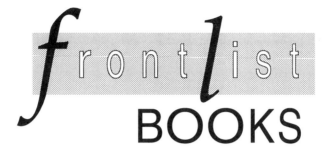

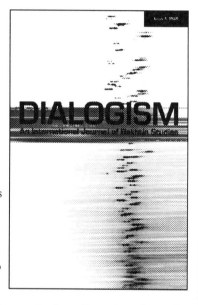